D1192644

GALLIPOLI

EDWARD J. ERICKSON

GALLIPOLI
COMMAND UNDER FIRE

First published in Great Britain in 2015 by Osprey Publishing,
PO Box 883, Oxford, OX1 9PL, UK
PO Box 3985, New York, NY 10185-3985, USA
E-mail: info@ospreypublishing.com
Osprey Publishing is part of the Osprey Group

A CIP catalogue record for this book is available from the British Library
Edward J. Erickson has asserted his right under the Copyright, Designs and Patents Act, 1988, to
be identified as the Author of this Work.

ISBN: 978 1 4728 0669 7
e-book ISBN: 978 1 4728 1341 1
PDF ISBN: 978 1 4728 1340 4

Index by Angela Hall
Cartography by Bounford.com
Typeset in Adobe Garamond Pro, Futura, Gotham and Perpetua
Originated by PDQ Media, Bungay, UK
Printed in China through Everbest Printing Co Ltd
15 16 17 18 19   10 9 8 7 6 5 4 3 2 1

Front cover: A 60-pounder artillery battery in action at Gallipoli, 1915. (IWM, Q 13340)

Osprey Publishing is supporting the Woodland Trust, the UK's leading woodland conservation
charity, by funding the dedication of trees.
www.ospreypublishing.com

CONTENTS

Dedicated to my friend, colleague and comrade-in-arms Professor Gordon Rudd, PhD, Lieutenant Colonel, US Army (Retired) for his encouragement and friendship, and from whom I never stop learning new things.

ACKNOWLEDGEMENTS

In addition to my friend and colleague, Professor Gordon Rudd (to whom this book is dedicated), I would like to acknowledge the many contributions of my friends and colleagues in the production of this book. First and foremost is my editor, Marcus Cowper, without whose advice and interest this book would not have been either written or produced. Thank you, Marcus! I am also indebted to Brigadier Chris Roberts (Australian Army, retired) and Professor Mesut Uyar (Colonel, Turkish Army, retired), who have steadily and faithfully replied to my many questions with solid answers and suggestions. I have reached out successfully to a variety of established international scholars and historians with questions, and for advice, as well, and these include Peter Hart (UK), John Lee (UK), Rhys Crawley (Australia), Graham Clews (Australia) and Klaus Wolf (Germany). I have relied heavily on your brilliant published work and I thank you for your direct and indirect help. At the Marine Corps Command and Staff College in Quantico, Virginia, the active encouragement of Dr. Doug McKenna, the Dean of Academics, and my teaching colleague Colonel Frode Ommundsen (Norwegian Army) have been a constant source of support. At the Marine Corps School of Advanced Studies (SAW), Professor Rudd's colleague Professor Brad Meyer's insights on the nature of command and control were also most helpful. I am also indebted to my students at the Command and Staff College who constantly force me to think critically about what I say and what I write. I would be remiss in not mentioning my copy editor Ruth Sheppard for her critical eye and superb work as well as our wonderful cartographers at Bounford.com. Lastly but most important, thank you Ms Jennifer Collins, my fiancée and partner, for all you do to make my life easier and brighter – day in and day out. I could not have written this book without your love and support.

LIST OF MAPS

LIST OF ILLUSTRATIONS

20. The British logistical buildup on V Beach. (IWM, Q 70378)

21. Slopes of Monash Valley. (AWM, G00942)

22. Infantrymen and Light Horsemen in a trench on Walkers Ridge, Gallipoli. (IWM, HU 53364)

23. British troops and their artillery guns being evacuated from Suvla Bay. (IWM, Q 13637)

24. Distant view from the battleship HMS *Cornwallis* of the evacuation of Suvla Bay. (IWM, Q 13679)

25 A bugler of the Corps Expeditionaire d'Orient. (IWM, Q 13419)

26. Liman von Sanders, Brigadier-General Esat Pasha and Colonel Fahrettin. (David Nicolle)

27. Ottoman staff officers in front of Liman von Sanders' headquarters in the town of Gallipoli. (Colonel Klaus Wolf)

28. German Colonel Hans Kanneniesser standing in front of his clay hut. (David Nicolle)

29. Ottoman infantrymen engaged in training overlooking one of the Gallipoli beaches. (David Nicolle)

30. The Ottoman fort at Canakkale. The 17th-century keep is seen inside the 19th-century coastal defence installation. (David Nicolle)

31. Ottoman soldiers drawing fresh water from a spring. Fresh water was a combat multiplier enjoyed by the Ottoman army. (David Nicolle)

32. The commander of the 125th Infantry Regiment with his staff and regimental Imam. (David Nicolle)

33. A well-camouflaged Ottoman sniper captured by the Australians, Gallipoli (David Nicolle)

34. Ottoman infantry in trench, Gallipoli 1915, the ever-present scrub growing on the peninsula is evident in this photo. (David Nicolle)

35. Ottoman infantry after the Gallipoli campaign 1916. (David Nicolle)

INTRODUCTION

According to historian George H. Cassar, there are more books written about Gallipoli in the English language than on any other campaign in the First World War. If this is true, then why should anyone attempt to add to an already dense field? Moreover, why would an informed reader take on this book? Simply stated, the extant history is incomplete and there are gaps, holes, and niches that still need to be filled in order to achieve a more complete understanding of what happened in that place over a ten-month period in 1915. In particular, the existing history of the campaign focuses on two of the three levels of war – the strategic and the tactical – and does not clearly separate the operational level of war, which connects the two together. *Gallipoli: Command Under Fire* aims at filling the gap, which exists at the operational level of war, in the historiography of the 1915 struggle for the Gallipoli peninsula by examining command and control at field army and corps level.

Conceptually, the operational level of war links the tactical level of war with the strategic level of war. In the 19th and 20th centuries, the operational level of war manifested itself as the planning and execution of a series of major battles or campaigns designed to achieve strategic goals. As a matter of military practice, the operational-level environment is the playing field of army and army group commanders, who employ large-scale units, such as corps, groups and, sometimes, divisions in the conduct of military operations. It is important to note that a campaign is not the same as a battle, which is tactical in scope and usually involves smaller units, such as battalions and regiments or brigades. In effect, the operational level of war describes military campaigns, which are designed to link tactical actions to strategic purposes.

Military operations at the operational level tend to be longer in temporal terms and larger in scope than a single battle, although a single battle may decide a campaign. Commanders at the operational level do not fight battles in the present time; rather, they marshal resources and plan campaigns in the future. They exercise indirect control through subordinate commanders rather than direct control of tactical units. Many military historians consider Napoleon to be the original practitioner of the operational level of war, the hallmarks of which were the waging of large-scale campaigns, employing a number of intermediate commanders (of subordinate armies or army corps), who executed written orders independently. Moreover, at this new level, the term 'battlefield' itself sometimes came to mean an entire country or province. In turn, increasing complexity in the scale of operations and logistics led to the creation of specialized staffs to support extended operations. These innovations in command and control led to a revolution in military affairs characterized by written orders, indirect command by assigning missions (rather than command by personal direction), and reliance on the initiative and capability of subordinate commanders. In this book, the terms in the phrase 'command and control' are used in the context of 'making decisions' and 'influencing the outcome' respectively – in short, command is all about decisions and control is all about execution.

The question that this book seeks to answer is 'to what extent did command and control at the operational level of war affect the outcome of the Gallipoli campaign?' This book is, therefore, a campaign analysis of how operational commanders made decisions; balanced ends, ways and means; and attempted – or in some cases failed – to influence the outcome. It examines institutions, organizations, doctrines, commanders, and events using direct comparison and contrast to expose the interaction of forces as the campaign progressed from planning to execution to conclusion. The thesis of *Gallipoli: Command Under Fire* is that Ottoman command and control was more effective than British command and control, and significantly weighted the conduct and outcome of the campaign in the Ottomans' favour.

The historiography of the Gallipoli campaign – the 'history of the history' – began in 1915 and continues today. It is important for the reader to consider that what we think of as 'history' is a package of facts selected to support a particular narrative. History is not what might be termed 'the truth' and, over time, history itself is evolutionary and itself becomes part of the historiography (or the body of historical literature) of events. Gallipoli has a distinct historiography that is the outcome of an evolving narrative that served a particular agenda, which was contextually important to a particular era. I believe that the 100-year-old historiography of the Gallipoli campaign is in its fourth narrative generation.

Almost immediately after the ending of the Gallipoli campaign in January 1916, a number of participant memoirs appeared in the United Kingdom. These were followed by the publication of the parliamentary Dardanelles Commissions in 1917 and 1919, as the British government struggled to understand and explain why the empire had gone down in defeat to the power that had become known as the 'Sick Man of Europe'. After the armistice in 1918, numerous regimental histories and personal memoirs were published, most notably by the British commander, General Sir Ian Hamilton, who published his two-volume *Gallipoli Diary* in 1920.[1] Sir Julian Corbett's *History of the Great War based on Official Documents, Naval Operations, Volume 2*, covering the Dardanelles naval operations, followed in 1921. C. E. W. Bean published the monumental two-volume Australian official history, *Official History of Australia in the War of 1914–1918: The Story of ANZAC* in 1921 and 1924 respectively. The second volume of Winston Churchill's *The World Crisis*, which covered the entire campaign, appeared in serial form in 1923 and later as a book. C. F. Aspinall-Oglander, himself a participant in the campaign, published the superb British official history *Military Operations, Gallipoli, Volumes 1 and 2*, in 1924 and 1930 respectively, which were based directly on the archival record of the campaign.

These books superbly covered British operations, however, most of the information contained in them about Ottoman operations came from German participant memoirs and sources, such as the German official history, *Der Kampf um die Dardanellen 1915*, written by participant Carl Mühlmann in 1927, the memoirs of General Otto Liman von Sanders, *Five Years in Turkey* in 1928, and Hans Kannengiesser, *The Campaign in Gallipoli* in 1928. The small amount of verifiable information on Ottoman participation came mostly from partial Turkish participant memoirs or from Maurice Larcher's influential *La Guerre Turque Dans La Guerre Mondiale* published in 1926, which cited only 12 per cent of its sources as Ottoman. More diaries and memoirs appeared, notably Compton Mackenzie's *Gallipoli Memories* in 1929. In 1936, Churchill republished an abridged version of *The World Crisis* and C. R. M. F. Crutwell published *A History of the Great War*, both of which sought to make sense of and rationalize the campaign. The Second World War briefly dampened the output of books on Gallipoli but fuelled interest in the study of amphibious operations, which – it may be argued – were the key to Allied victory in the war against Germany and Japan.

This first generation of the Gallipoli history advanced the idea that British success was possible on at least three occasions – 18 March, 25 April and 6 August 1915 – and that the British failed to grasp victory by the slimmest of margins. There were also a number of unifying themes in the first generation of Gallipoli history, which explained British mistakes, thereby making much of the literature an apologia for defeat. The most compelling themes were assertions that the British were unprepared and under-resourced to undertake amphibious operations against a hostile shore, that German commanders were instrumental in training and leading the Ottoman Army, that an accumulation of Churchill's 'terrible ifs' made success unachievable, and that the ox-like Ottoman soldiery were unshakable in their trenches. This early history focused primarily on the strategic and tactical levels of war. At the strategic level, it focused on the debates within the British Cabinet and, particularly, on the decisions that led to the assault on the Dardanelles. At the tactical level, it focused on how the Allies planned and executed combat operations, the gallantry of Allied soldiers, and on the many tactical errors in preparation and execution. Thematically, by the time of the Second World War, the historiography validated the strategic concept itself and advanced the idea that tactical failures, which were out of the control of the British, fatally disabled the campaign. Essentially, the British Gallipoli campaign was seen by Australian, British and German historians as winnable but for the tactical difficulties encountered by the Allies themselves.

A second generation of Gallipoli history began in 1956 with the publication of Australian journalist Alan Moorehead's *Gallipoli*, and Robert Rhodes James's *Gallipoli, The History of a Noble Blunder* in 1965. The histories in this generation exposed few new archival materials and were essentially a re-analysis of the existing historical base. What made them different from previous histories was the analysis of leadership and the apportionment of responsibility for failure. Australian historian John Laffin published *Damn the Dardanelles!* in 1980 and *British Butchers and Bunglers of World War One* in 1988. Professor Peter Liddle added to this by producing a number of experiential works such as *Men of Gallipoli, The Dardanelles and Gallipoli Experience*, which were based on interviews of participants. These works were reflective of the post-Second World War 'lions led by donkeys' school of military historians, who were very critical of First World War generalship.

This second generation of Gallipoli historians questioned the validity of the strategic concept itself and put into question the idea that breaking through the Dardanelles might not have caused regime collapse in the Ottoman Empire. Thus, the Cabinet and its decisions were held accountable for sending the expedition on a specious and under-resourced mission. While these authors challenged the strategic concepts they did not challenge the possibility of tactical success. The second generation of Gallipoli history approached the campaign as winnable but for mistakes in command and control and it began the trend of apportioning blame amongst the British command team. In particular, these historians identified Ian Hamilton's failure to push aggressively Hunter-Weston and Birdwood on 25 April and, again, his failure to push Stopford on 6–9 August 1915. Hamilton was portrayed as a Victorian-era anachronism, the

Mediterranean version of an out-of-touch Western Front chateau general. Moreover, his subordinates were portrayed as inept and casually disconnected second-rate commanders. This was used to explain a basic theme of spectacularly passive and clumsy leadership by Hamilton and his commanders that rationalized why the British failed at Gallipoli. This was especially appealing in the post-Second World War public consciousness when juxtaposed against the spectacularly successful Allied amphibious operations and active leadership displayed in the Second World War. That the campaign itself might have been essentially unwinnable was not considered but rather it was portrayed as a campaign which had gone astray through poor leadership and inept execution.

A third generation of Gallipoli history emerged as younger historians began a new wave of archival and primary source research, which questioned much of the previously received wisdom. In tune with the *Zeitgeist* of the age, these histories stressed the human experience of those participating in war and reflected a growing academic interest in cultural factors in war. Peter Liddle's *Men of Gallipoli, The Dardanelles and the Gallipoli Experience* in 1976 used a massive database of personal interviews of surviving participants. Robin Prior published the landmark *Churchill's 'World Crisis' as History* in 1983, casting doubt on the accuracy of Churchill's version of the events. In 1984, Christopher Pugsley's *Gallipoli: The New Zealand Story* advanced the idea that the campaign was hopelessly muddled. In 1995, Nigel Steel and Peter Hart published *Defeat at Gallipoli* advancing the idea that tactical and logistical problems, combined with poor leadership, disabled the British and, in 1995, Michael Hickey's *Gallipoli* reaffirmed the basic problem of inadequate British leadership. This new analysis remained based largely on English-language sources and confirmed the basic themes of the previous generation of Gallipoli history. These newer histories continued highlighting the combat experiences of soldiers and sailors through the use of testimony and direct quotes, for example Les Carlyon's *Gallipoli* in 2001, Jenny MacLeod's *Reconsidering Gallipoli* in 2004 and Hugh Dolan's *36 Days, The Untold Story of the Gallipoli Landings* in 2010. Importantly, this generation brought to a close a 90-year English-language historiography that was constructed almost entirely using western sources.

This 90-year body of Eurocentric received wisdom had led to a number of generalized beliefs about the Gallipoli campaign that are known today to be incorrect. The most commonly held Western notion about the Ottoman victory was that the Turks stubbornly held on long enough for a series of Allied mistakes to disable the Allied plan. Tactical blame rested on British command failures, lack of artillery and shells, and inexperienced troops and commanders as reasons for failure. At the operational level, it argued that Allied failure was attributed to Ottoman numerical superiority and incompetent execution of the Allied plan. Failure at the strategic level was the result of inadequate resourcing. As supplementary reasons explaining why the Ottomans won, the Western histories basically advanced two ideas. The first was that the Ottomans won because of the generalship of Liman von Sanders and Mustafa Kemal and, second, because their fighting men were incredibly tough and resilient soldiers. The older histories, including the Australian and British official histories, all contained variants of these themes, which are essentially apologia to explain why the Allies lost the campaign. Collectively, the English-language historiography of the campaign treated the Ottoman victory as passive rather than active.

The current fourth generation of Gallipoli history emerged at the turn of the 21st century and is significantly different in that its narrative is inclusive of the Ottoman and Turkish perspective. In essence, the current narration asserts that what the Ottoman Army achieved in superior command and control was instrumental in causing the British defeat. The key to this revisionist view of Gallipoli has been the opening of the Turkish general staff's historical archives to researchers, allowing western historians to reassess the campaigns and battles from the Ottoman perspective.

The Ottoman Fifth Army records reside today in the Turkish general staff's archives in Ankara. The Turkish official histories of the campaign are extensive – the three-volume set on the Gallipoli campaign contains 1,429 pages, and hundreds of colour maps, order of battle diagrams, organizational charts, photographs, and reproduced original documents. Supplementing these resources is the recent publication of numerous memoirs and diaries from Ottoman officers, who held command and staff positions from army level down to battalion level.

The recent work of Edward Erickson, *Ordered To Die, A History of the Ottoman Army in the First World War* (2000), *Ottoman Combat Effectiveness in World War I: A Comparative Study* (2007), and *Gallipoli, The Ottoman Campaign* (2010); Tim Travers, *Gallipoli 1915* (2001); Harvey Broadbent, *Gallipoli, The Fatal Shore* (2005); Robin Prior, *Gallipoli, The End of the Myth* (2009); Peter Hart, *Gallipoli* (2011); and Chris Roberts' superb *The Landing at Anzac, 1915* (2013) have all sought to use the Turkish official histories and military archives more fully to achieve more nuanced understandings of the Ottoman campaign.

With few exceptions, this latest group of contemporary histories continues to feed the public and academic thirst for the human, social and cultural aspects of war. The methodology used to produce such works highlights the individual human experience by quoting the direct testimony of the combatants, both Allied and Ottoman. While this makes a more readable book, this has tended to move the focus of the work downward to the tactical level. Moreover, focusing on people's experiences sometimes obscures an overall understanding of the campaign versus what happened to individuals in the battles. *Gallipoli: Command Under Fire* aims at moving the narrative upwards to the operational level of war using the current inclusive approach.

The methodology used in this book is to make assessments based on comparing and contrasting the decisions and actions of operational-level commanders. In most cases, original sources such as war diaries, operations orders and annexes, and messages are used to examine these issues. The operational commanders were General Sir Ian Hamilton, who commanded the Mediterranean Expeditionary Force, and General Otto Liman von Sanders, who commanded the Ottoman Fifth Army. While other commanders participated, principally Australian, French, German, and New Zealanders, these men commanded at the tactical level. The consequence of this was that, in terms of command and control at the operational level of war, the Gallipoli campaign became a struggle between the British and the Ottoman armies.

The narrative is chronological and links Allied and Ottoman actions as closely as possible in time and space in a narrative format. This work is a campaign history and focuses on the operational level of war primarily at field army and army corps level. Tactics, human interest vignettes, and cultural affairs are only briefly mentioned to support the overall narrative. The framework of *Gallipoli: Command Under Fire* is designed to show how commanders planned their operations, how they executed their plans, and how they adapted when their planning and execution succeeded or failed. The focus is on operational command and control as these factors affected the conduct and course of operations.

I believe that the Gallipoli campaign highlights the art of command as well as the criticality of effective staff work to a far greater extent than other contemporary operations in the early years of the First World War, which makes analysis and argument far more meaningful. The thesis of the book is that the Ottoman Army won the Gallipoli campaign because, at the operational level, its commanders demonstrated a more effective understanding and employment of command and control than its Allied adversaries. This was also true at the tactical level, but it was less important at the lower level simply because the dynamics of trench warfare and battlefield lethality trumped almost everything else. In truth, the Ottomans fielded a very well-led, well-trained, and highly effective army on the Gallipoli peninsula that met the Australians, British and French man-to-man on very even terms.

Relative to its British opponent, the Ottoman Army generated higher levels of effective command and control over the course of the Gallipoli campaign. This was largely the result of superior situational awareness made possible by a more effective reporting system, an institutional and doctrinal climate that encouraged initiative, and a willingness by commanders to influence operations through active supervision and intervention. Their British opponents, consistently over the course of the campaign, made decisions based on inadequate assumptions and misinformation, and then left subordinate commanders to coordinate and execute operations with almost no supervision. In the Second World War, British Field Marshal Sir Bernard Montgomery frequently used the term 'grip' to describe how effective commanders maintained control over operations by a continuous process of oversight and influence.[2] On the Gallipoli peninsula, in the end, it was the lack of grip that doomed the British enterprise to failure.

Chapter One

THE STRATEGIC SETTING

The Gallipoli campaign forms a part of the time-proven British strategic tradition of land power selectively applied from the sea. This is captured by the phrase 'the British Army should be a projectile to be fired by the British Navy', and joint operations between the services had formed a historical bond over several centuries. Traditionally, the small size of the British Army made continental land operations problematic but the mobility of the Royal Navy gave it unmatched strategic reach. This capability gave the British a wide choice of strategic options but these choices were always limited by the capacity of the army to wage war against its larger continental competitors. The British Army had previously engaged in a number of campaigns from the sea, including Flanders, Portugal, and Spain as well as expeditionary campaigns in America and India, but these operations involved smaller forces. In these campaigns, the navy landed the army in undefended locations and neither the army nor the navy had experience in the amphibious assault of defended beaches. Moreover, lack of experience was compounded by a lack of intellectual thought about assault from the sea, which manifested itself in the complete absence of tactics and doctrines about the subject. The possibility of assault from the sea against defended beaches changed dramatically in 1914 as new technologies meant that such tactical challenges as naval gunfire support and landing men on beaches could be overcome.

After mobilization in August 1914, the War Office began to plan fielding a British Army on a historically unheard of continental scale. At the strategic level, the Royal Navy successfully swept the enemy from the sea and pinned its primary adversary, the German High Seas Fleet, into its bases. Meanwhile, the land campaign in France evolved into static trench warfare that offered no quick result even though larger numbers of trained British army divisions were becoming available in 1915/1916. Thus, at the strategic level, the British Empire found itself with surplus strategic capability and capacity. Together these changes encouraged the British War Council to consider strategic options based on large-scale amphibious operations against continental adversaries.

The Ottoman Empire, in contrast, had been disastrously defeated in the First Balkan War of 1912–13, losing a significant portion of its population and core provinces. Its army was shattered and had lost an entire field army as well as the men and equipment of some 20 divisions. In late 1913, a German military mission arrived in Constantinople to assist the Ottomans in rebuilding their army. For the Ottomans 1914 was a year of rebuilding garrisons, re-forming divisions and retraining tactical units. It was also a year of significant restructuring for the army's German-modelled reserve system, which it had used for 40 years. As the Ottoman Army reconstituted its field forces, its general staff rewrote its mobilization and war plans to fit a radically different strategic situation. In the event of war, the pre-war Ottoman Army envisioned a reactive defensive posture at the strategic level but which included offensives at the operational level should opportunities present themselves. Ottoman military capacity, in 1914, can be characterized as reduced from 1912, but as a result of something of a military renaissance, its capability was greater. It may be argued that the Ottoman Army in 1914 was smaller but more powerful than it had been before. At great cost, the Allies misunderstood this about the Ottomans.

Strategic direction in Britain

In 1894, France and Russia signed a secret military alliance as a result of their concerns about an aggressive Germany. Britain remained friendly with Germany until the Kaiser began to build up a large navy in the early 20th century, which drove the British into the arms of Continental powers that it had previously regarded as enemies. In 1904 Britain signed the Entente Cordiale, which was a military understanding with France. It was not an alliance but was designed to support the French by keeping the Germans out of Morocco. In 1907, the British concluded an Anglo-Russian Entente, which lowered tensions between them by dividing Persia into spheres of influence. After 1908, the term Triple Entente was loosely used to describe the military relationships between the three countries. In summary, France and Russia were obligated by a formal alliance to come to the aid of the other in the event of an attack by Germany or Austria-Hungary. Britain had no obligatory alliances with either France or Russia, however, the British military and naval staff had several agreements with their French counterparts that would take immediate effect in the event of war with Germany.

The British and French naval staffs agreed that France, with some Royal Navy assistance, would assume responsibility for the Mediterranean Sea, balancing the Italian and Austro-Hungarian fleets. This would allow the Royal Navy to contain the powerful German High Seas Fleet in its North Sea anchorages and rapidly secure worldwide command of the seas. Moreover, the British and French general staffs agreed that Britain would send an expeditionary force of four infantry divisions and a cavalry division to France in the event of war with Germany. As the years went by, the British Admiralty and the Imperial General Staff developed very detailed plans to ensure that these understandings could be executed seamlessly and rapidly if required. Unlike the continental powers, the British Army had no mobilization plan designed for offensive action at the strategic levels nor were its reserves, known as the Territorial Army, ready to fight on short notice. The Admiralty, on the other hand, was capable of offensive operations immediately as well as rapidly manning its reserve fleet.

Within the British military establishment itself, there were further internal agreements between the War Office and the India Office regarding the potential operational theatres involving the Ottoman Empire. The India Office – which had its own army – took responsibility for the Persian Gulf and Mesopotamia. This allowed the War Office to focus on fielding a British Expeditionary Force (BEF) in France, which soon became the principal planning priority effort of the British Army. When Britain entered the war on 4 August 1914, these external and internal military and naval agreements all fell into place with few problems.

Of the regular British Army, in mid-August 1914, the four-division BEF deployed to France and by mid-September two more divisions had joined it. Two more divisions were in France by November and three more by January 1915. The last regular British division, organized of battalions brought home from India, formed in March 1915. There were 14 Territorial divisions, from which some 23 battalions were sent to reinforce the BEF. In the autumn of 1914, one Territorial division went to Egypt and two went to India, leaving the rest under strength and not ready for combat. Added to this, three weeks after the outbreak of the war, Lord Kitchener organized the flood of volunteers into New Army divisions, the first six of which were known as K1 divisions. Eventually there would be 20 such divisions, organized into four Kitchener New Armies. None of these divisions could be combat ready until the summer of 1915. Additionally, the Indian Army sent a two-division corps to France, an infantry division to Mesopotamia, and a brigade to Egypt. Australia and New Zealand sent a two-division army corps to Egypt. By January 1915, the War Office potentially had a combat-ready force available of three divisions in Egypt, and in addition the Royal Navy had the nine-battalion Royal Navy

Division refitting in England. The 29th Division would become available in March and two Territorial divisions in May–June. In truth, the British Army had almost no excess capacity going into the spring of 1915 and an acute shortage of artillery shells made this even worse.

On the other hand, by January 1915, the Royal Navy's Grand Fleet was concentrated at Scapa Flow and Cromarty and had clamped a tight blockade on Germany. German overseas squadrons had been swept from the seas enabling Churchill, First Lord of the Admiralty, to bring home Admiral Sir John (Jackie) Fisher's fast battlecruisers. Moreover, a dozen new battleships and battlecruisers were coming off the ways to join the first line. In accordance with pre-war agreements, the French navy patrolled the Mediterranean and a small British squadron kept a German battlecruiser inside the Dardanelles. In the spring of 1915, unlike the British Army, the Royal Navy had both surplus capability and surplus capacity.

Britain entered the war in August 1914 with a cabinet system which was ill-suited to strategic direction of modern alliance war. At the strategic level, the British system was one of waging war by committee, of which there were 20 in August. Military and naval policy for the empire was coordinated and implemented by the Committee of Imperial Defence. While this system maintained the defence establishment in peacetime, it was unable to keep up with the competing requirements of alliance warfare, industrial mobilization and strategic direction. By November, this system 'under the stress of war conditions, was beginning to break down'.[1] At the end of that month, in order to move ahead on the pressing matter of war direction, Prime Minister Herbert H. Asquith decided to form the War Council. Initially the War Council consisted of Asquith, Chancellor of the Exchequer David Lloyd George, Foreign Secretary Edward Grey, First Lord of the Admiralty Winston Churchill, First Sea Lord Admiral Sir John (Jackie) Fisher, Secretary for War Field Marshal Sir Hubert H. Kitchener, Chief of the Imperial General Staff General Sir James Wolfe-Murray, Lord Arthur Balfour (former prime minister) and, as War Council Secretary, Maurice Hankey (Secretary to the Committee of Imperial Defence and major in the Royal Marine reserve). In December and January, Secretary for India Robert Crewe-Milnes, Lord Chancellor Richard Haldane, and Admiral Sir Arthur Wilson joined the council. On 10 March 1915, Home Secretary Reginald McKenna and Colonial Secretary Lewis Harcourt also joined. Asquith had wanted to keep the membership of the council to a small number but was unsuccessful in this, and in the end, created a war council that included almost the entire Cabinet plus others.

A great strength of the War Council was that it was made up of unusually well-qualified men, who were Britain's greatest politicians, diplomats, admirals and generals of the age. Set against that great strength, the War Council was composed of highly creative, energetic, and dominant personalities, who were convinced of the rightness of their own thinking and who brought their own agendas into the council meetings. The primary purpose of the War Council was to establish strategic direction for Britain and to balance the ends, ways, and means needed to move along that path. In order to do this, however, the council needed to gain consensus and come to an agreement on these matters, which in the winter of 1914–15 proved particularly difficult. While there was general agreement that the war was likely to last many years there was disagreement on how to win it. There was the knowledge that, as Britain entered 1915, there was surplus naval capacity and a gathering host of newly raised army divisions, but there was disagreement about where to employ these assets. Moreover, these were men of action and, in every member of the War Council, there was the spirit of the offensive.[2]

An influential force in the War Council was its secretary, Maurice Hankey, who, although not a member, acted as a sounding board for ideas of the principals. In the quaint vocabulary of the age, these ideas were often presented as 'schemes', which included amphibious operations in the Baltic Sea, combined operations against Borkum and Zeebrugge, adventures in the Balkans to support Serbia, and amphibious operations in the Mediterranean Sea. Designed to streamline war direction, the War Council made it increasingly complex by blurring the chain of command and lines of responsibility, for example, Lord of the Admiralty Churchill maintained personal correspondence with General Sir John French, commander of the British Expeditionary Force in France. This scattered approach to global strategy frustrated Hankey and just after Christmas 1914, he summarized the crucial issues as he saw them in what was known as the 'Boxing Day Memorandum'.[3] In this memorandum Hankey concisely parsed the three components of Britain's strategic dilemma – the war would be long, the stalemated Western Front could only be broken with new technologies and mass armies, and the naval schemes were unworkable. He concluded, therefore, that the main military effort against Germany was unattainable in the near term with the forces then at hand. Hankey then offered alternatives, which can be summarized as knocking the props out from under Germany, in effect becoming the first real advocate of a group that would become known as the Easterners. Hankey advanced the idea that Germany might be weakened by attacking its allies, the Ottoman Empire or Austria-Hungary, which at the same time offered relief and support to Britain's beleaguered and isolated ally, Russia. In Hankey's words, 'we should endeavour by the means proposed to get assets into our hands wherewith to supplement the tremendous asset of sea-power'.[4]

In strategic terms, this was a peripheral strategy, which would later be termed the indirect approach. To be sure, Hankey was not the true originator of these ideas but he may be seen as a summarizer of concepts.

In the Boxing Day Memorandum, Hankey speculated that a force of three British army corps, in conjunction with the Bulgarians, would be sufficient to occupy the Dardanelles and capture Constantinople. Importantly, Hankey himself believed, based on a personal visit there in 1907, that without Bulgarian or Greek assistance the Dardanelles were unassailable.[5] Nevertheless, the strategy of such an indirect approach had been gathering traction among the members of the War Council and Hankey's summarizations served as a catalyst. The meetings of the War Council in the first two weeks of January 1915 were extremely contentious as they wrestled with the question of where to apply Britain's gathering strength. Kitchener was increasingly convinced that sending a million men to reinforce the BEF was counterproductive and began to swing in favour of peripheral strategic opportunities. This coincided with the thinking of Jackie Fisher and Churchill, who were advancing schemes for amphibious operations in the Baltic Sea, the German Bight and along the Belgian coast. Thus the stage was set for making the decisions that led to the Dardanelles campaign, its failure and, in the end, the fall of the Asquith government.

The first concept for an operational plan for an assault on the Dardanelles came from Vice-Admiral Sackville Carden, commander of the Anglo-French Squadrons, Eastern Mediterranean, on 11 January 1915 in reply to a query from Churchill on 3 January. Churchill had asked whether forcing the Dardanelles was practicable 'by ships alone'.[6] Carden proposed a four-stage operation to reduce the defences of the straits. He was 'careful to point out that the term "defences" included permanent, semi-permanent and field works also guns or howitzers whose positions are not yet known'.[7] Carden's four-stage reduction envisioned the following steps:

A   Reduce the forts at the entrance
B   Clear the defences inside the straits including Kephez Point battery No. 8. During Stages A and B part of the force would be employed in demonstrations of the Bulair lines and coast, and reduce the battery near Gaba Tepe.
C   Reduce the defences at the Chanak Narrows
D   Clear a passage through the minefield 'advancing through Narrows reducing forts above Narrows and final advance to Marmora'.[8]

THE DARDANELLES AND STRAITS

In order to accomplish this Carden requested 12 battleships, three battlecruisers, three light cruisers, 16 destroyers and a flotilla leader, submarines, seaplanes, colliers, ammunition ships, and 12 minesweepers. He did not estimate the time required to complete the breakthrough, citing enemy morale and weather as problematic, but suggested that he might 'do it up in a month about'.[9] Carden's plan was not, at this point, linked to a strategic purpose and he was not asked to plan for anything more than forcing the straits. However, this message planted the seeds of the idea in Churchill's mind that forcing the straits by ships alone was practicable and he asked Fisher and the Admiralty for an opinion on the matter. This generated discussions about what Carden actually required, especially in the way of modern battlecruisers, modern heavy guns and how many French ships Carden was counting on. The next day, Churchill again queried Carden for clarification about whether modern ships were actually necessary, to which Carden replied on 13 January that he needed high-speed ships to deal with the heavily armed battlecruiser *Goeben* in the Sea of Marmara. Churchill kept this correspondence and these estimates to himself.

In the meantime, the War Council debated on strategic policy but, by 9 January 1915, had settled on a general policy, which gave strategic priority to the main theatre in France while rejecting the Zeebrugge scheme, but which left open the decision of where to employ Britain's New Armies as well as the possibility of opening new theatres should France fall into a stalemate. This decision was communicated to General Sir John French, commander of the BEF, who was so troubled by this news that he immediately returned to London.

With General French in attendance, the War Council met at noon on 13 January 1915, and there was an extended discussion over where to focus British strength in the coming months, especially the New Armies and artillery. There was some renewed support for the Zeebrugge operation supporting the BEF's campaign in France as the council swung back in favour of French's plans. Sir Edward Grey then moved the council towards peripheral operations and suggested that the council consider the Adriatic and the Mediterranean theatres. The discussions continued between the tired participants, and the long day seemed to be drawing to a close. Suddenly, Churchill seized on this moment to present his Dardanelles proposal by summarizing Carden's plan and stating that the Admiralty believed the plan was sound. The War Council was immediately re-energized and listened as Churchill unfolded his plan. Everyone except Fisher endorsed the plan which, at this point, was a purely naval attack. Late in the afternoon, Asquith finalized the War Council conclusions along the lines of the 9 January decision and explicitly directed 'the Admiralty should prepare a naval expedition in February to bombard and take the Gallipoli peninsula, with Constantinople as its objective'.[10] According to Maurice Hankey, Churchill sold the council the idea that the fleet's modern guns could destroy the Ottoman defences without coming within range of the defending artillery. Many of the difficulties imagined by Carden were not brought up, nor was a previous study by Admiral Sir Henry Jackson, which indicated that troops needed to be landed to destroy the enemy guns, rather than simply silencing them by fire. Hankey later noted he had no doubt Asquith thought that after the peninsula was isolated its garrison would surrender (thereby rejecting the notion that 'take the Gallipoli peninsula' authorized a land campaign).[11]

The Dardanelles question was sent down to a sub-committee for detailed examination and there were several subsequent War Council meetings that addressed the issue of a coherent alliance strategy for the Balkans. These issues involved drawing Bulgaria and Greece into the war and supporting Serbia by landing troops at Salonika. In the meantime, Churchill turned immediately to the prospect of a naval attack on the Dardanelles by directing the Admiralty to study the requirements. On 15 January, Admiral Sir Henry Jackson submitted 'Remarks on Vice-Admiral Carden's Proposals as to Operations in Dardanelles', which generally concurred with Carden but which was incomplete regarding the last phases of Carden's plan.[12] While Churchill was convinced of the efficacy of the Dardanelles plan Jackie Fisher was not entirely sold on the idea. During the last weeks of January, Fisher began to push strongly for combined operations (the army and the navy) either at Zeebrugge or the Dardanelles rather than a naval-only attack.

The War Council conducted three sessions on 28 January 1915, the first beginning at 11:30am and the third session convening at 6.30pm. The council discussed most of the simmering issues, especially that of how to bring Greece into the war. At day's end several decisions had been made, the coastal operation in France and the Zeebrugge bombardment were cancelled while the naval-only Dardanelles operation was given the go-ahead. Plans to send troops to Serbia via Greece were put on hold but the council leaned heavily in favour of Balkan intervention. It was still unclear exactly how a naval-only attack on the Dardanelles would achieve control of a major city such as Constantinople but, except for Fisher, the council was enthusiastic in its support of this objective. This represented an important shift in British strategic policy, which could previously have been characterized as maintaining the status quo of the separate efforts of the BEF in France and the Grand Fleet in the North Sea, while shifting to an as-yet-to-be determined coordinated effort involving army and navy forces in the Balkan theatre. Fisher was unhappy with this outcome but was co-opted into consensus by funding for new ships. There is no argument among scholars that every member of the War Council saw the immense strategic potential of controlling Constantinople and the straits with the very low opportunity cost of a naval-only attack. It is important to note that, at this point, the War Council understood the idea of coordinated army and navy operations as separate, with the army entering the Balkans in support of Serbia and the navy conducting a single-service assault on the Dardanelles (these were not joint nor could they be necessarily even considered as mutually supporting).

Strategic direction in the Ottoman Empire

Nationalist members of the Committee of Union and Progress (CUP, and in Turkish Ittihat ve Terraki Cemiyeti) conducted a coup d'état on the afternoon of 23 January 1913, which overthrew the Ottoman government in what is called the Raid on the Sublime Porte.[13] The conspirators, including İsmail Enver and Mehmet Talat, forced the prime minister to resign at gunpoint and shot the minister of war to death. By June 1913, the hard-line inner core of the CUP, who were also known as the Young Turks, controlled the Ottoman government.[14] The CUP appointed Sait Halim as the new grand vizier and

Ahmet İzzet Pasha as the new minister of war. Politically, 1913 was the year when the CUP began to construct what would become totalitarian one-party rule over the Ottoman government. The CUP's initial changes in government started in mid-March 1913, with the passing of new laws increasing the powers of the police and the gendarmerie, making them more powerful.[15] This was followed in April by a law that secularized the appeals courts by establishing state control over the *ulema* (a body of religious scholars who interpreted religious law) and religious courts. These laws cumulatively centralized CUP control over the apparatus of government.[16]

German General Otto Liman von Sanders, accompanied by 41 German officers, arrived in Constantinople on 14 December 1913. Under the terms of the contract, Liman von Sanders would not command the Ottoman Army but rather supervised a training mission (known as the German military mission). The officers were distributed as individual advisors to a single infantry division, three regiments, and 11 military training and educational institutions, including the prestigious military academy.[17] One of the most important appointments that Liman von Sanders made was to assign Colonel Friedrich Bronsart von Schellendorf as the assistant chief of staff of the Ottoman Army. Bronsart von Schellendorf was a trained general staff officer and was the author of a doctrinal work titled *The Duties of the General Staff.*

On 3 January 1914, the CUP Cabinet appointed Colonel İsmail Enver to the position of minister of war.[18] Enver was young, charismatic, a long-time member of the CUP's inner circle, and was at the centre of a movement to replace Ahmet İzzet Pasha. Moreover, Enver was brilliant, a graduate of the Ottoman War Academy, a general staff officer and had served in Germany on an exchange tour with the German Army. Once in power, Enver moved immediately to consolidate his grip on the army by forcibly retiring some 1,300 officers on 7 January 1914.[19] Many of these men were elderly, many were undereducated *alayı* (or regimental officers), but others were opponents of the CUP and modernization.[20] On the same day, Enver abolished the Council of Military Affairs, which eliminated a competing source of power within the government.[21] The astonishing rapidity with which Enver carried out what amounted to a bloodless purge clearly demonstrates detailed planning and forethought on his part. Enver's takeover of the Ministry of War completed the ironclad grip that the CUP had on the Ottoman government and the phrase 'Ittihadist Dictatorship' accurately characterizes the Ottoman government for the following five years. Sometimes the Ottoman War Cabinet is described as a triumvirate composed of Enver as Minister of War, Talat as Minister of the Interior and Ahmet Cemal as Minister of the Marine but, in fact, it was Enver and Talat who made the crucial decisions, especially after Cemal went to Syria in early 1915. The grand vizier, Sait Halim, can only be described as a figurehead and CUP puppet.

The appointment of Enver to the critically important Ministry of War portfolio was a key ingredient in the transformation of the Cabinet to a functionally militaristic government. In addition to his portfolio as minister of war, Enver further consolidated his hold over the army by retaining the title of acting commander-in-chief and chief of the general staff as well. Holding these three offices concurrently enabled Enver to establish primacy over strategic direction and policy, to supervise and direct the general staff, and to command the Ottoman Army operationally. It was a staggering consolidation of power in the hands of a single person and no other individual in any country had similar authority.

On 7 April 1914, Colonel Friedrich (Fritz) Bronsart von Schellendorf completed the staff work on the Primary Campaign Plan for the Ottoman Army. This plan was prepared prior to the events of the summer of 1914, and reflected the then-current strategic situation. The Ottoman general staff estimated that the Ottoman Empire would simultaneously oppose both a renewed Balkan coalition of Bulgaria and Greece, and Russia. The mobilization plans subsequently developed supported this intelligence estimate.[22] According to Bronsart von Schellendorf's plan, the Ottomans would field an army of observation on the Greek and Bulgarian frontiers. Although this army was prepared to fight, it would not act provocatively, nor would it engage in offensive operations. In the east against Russia, the Ottomans would attempt to gain the tactical initiative by conducting limited attacks should favourable operational conditions exist in Caucasia.[23] Additional forces from Syria and Mesopotamia were earmarked for transfer to Ottoman Thrace to support this deployment. The principal weaknesses of the plan were perennial shortfalls in artillery and technical units.

The Balkan Wars of 1912–13 had battered the Ottoman economy, crippled its financial system and all but destroyed its army. The defeated Ottomans were in no shape to go to war in 1914. Unlike the 12 complicated mobilization plans of 1912, the war-weary and over-taxed Ottoman general staff had but one mobilization plan in the summer of 1914. Bronsart von Schellendorf approved the plan on 7 June 1914.[24] The plan recognized the supreme strategic importance of the Ottoman Straits and Constantinople and, once again, brought the bulk of the regular army back into European Ottoman Thrace. Under the plan, of 13 regular army corps in the Ottoman Army, five deployed directly to either Thrace or the Marmara region. A further army corps went to Smyrna in western Anatolia. Three army corps deployed against the Russians, and the remaining three went to Mesopotamia, Palestine and Yemen respectively. Even though the weight of the army appeared to threaten Bulgaria, the Ottoman general staff had no plans for cross-border operations or offensive operations oriented towards the west. This mystified the Entente attachés in Constantinople, who had observed the mobilization of 1912 and, moreover, confused reports emanated from the Allied embassies throughout the Balkans. The British thought that the Ottomans were preparing to attack Russia on the Asiatic frontier, while trying to ally themselves with Bulgaria for an attack on Serbia.[25]

Because of their disastrous experiences with the mobilization plan of 1912, the Ottoman general staff realized that their underdeveloped railroads and lines of communications could not support timetable-based deployment schemes. As a result, completion of mobilization schedules became very problematic. As a result, the Ottomans now viewed mobilization as event driven rather than timetable driven. Units were not assumed to arrive at the scheduled times and were only counted in the line when physically reported as being ready. Bronsart von Schellendorf simply had no real idea of exactly when Ottoman units would arrive from their peacetime mobilization stations at their wartime operational positions.

On 28 June 1914, Gavrilo Princip, a member of the secret Black Hand terrorist group, assassinated the Archduke Franz Ferdinand, heir to the Austro-Hungarian throne, and his wife Sophie in Sarajevo. The Ottoman Empire remained outside the ensuing July crisis and spiral towards war, and was not allied with either side. Although the Ottoman Empire had strong diplomatic ties with Great Britain and strong economic ties with France, it can be argued that the Ottoman government was pro-German in 1914. Moreover, within the Ottoman government, a number of notable CUP members could be called Germanophiles, including Enver and Talat, and the army itself was strongly based on the physical and intellectual model of the German military system.

Ottoman foreign policy coalesced on 2 August 1914, when the government signed a secret treaty of alliance with Germany.[26] The treaty did not obligate the Ottoman Empire to enter the war, but it did serve to move the Ottomans closer towards co-operation with the Central Powers. Even so, the Ministry of War declared precautionary mobilization, effective 3 August, setting the empire on a course for war. Importantly, the treaty set the stage for the German battlecruiser *Goeben* and its cruiser consort *Breslau* to find refuge from their British pursuers on 11 August 1914. The arrival of these ships and their aggressive commander, German Vice-Admiral Wilhelm Souchon, directly led the Ottoman Empire into the war on 29 October.

The means for the Ottoman Empire's entry into the war lay with the weak and ineffective command relationship between Vice-Admiral Souchon, commander of the German squadron, and the Ottomans.[27] On 25 October

1914, Enver issued instructions authorizing Souchon to conduct manoeuvres and to attack the Russian fleet 'if a suitable opportunity presented itself'.[28] On 28 October 1914, the Ottoman fleet steamed towards the Russian coast and, at dawn the next day, Vice-Admiral Souchon opened fire on shore batteries at Sevastapol while other Ottoman task forces shelled other Russian cities.[29] On 2 November 1914, Russia declared war and Britain and France, in turn, declared war on the Ottoman Empire as well.

Thus, in the course of a three-month period, the Ottoman Empire drifted from a position of neutrality to that of full-fledged belligerence. With the exception of its partially mobilized armies, the empire was no more prepared to wage modern war than it was when the Archduke was gunned down in Sarajevo. In a case unique among the major powers, the Ottomans had no definite or finely tuned war aims.

Having bound itself to Germany in a secret treaty the Ottoman government then signed a second secret treaty with Bulgaria later that month. These two treaties essentially negated the strategic principles which Bronsart von Schellendorf had formulated in the spring by eliminating Bulgaria as an opponent and potentially adding the Entente powers as enemies of the first rank. Responding to these rapidly changing conditions, Bronsart von Schellendorf adjusted the Primary Campaign Plan on 20 August 1914. The possibility of a direct attack on Constantinople receded with the signing of a treaty of alliance with Bulgaria. However, Ottoman forces continued to concentrate near Constantinople, possibly conducting operations with the Bulgarians against either the Romanians or the Serbs. Although Russia maintained strong forces on the Caucasian Front, the staffs thought that they would not be inclined to attack, since Russia was already heavily engaged against Germany and Austria-Hungary.

On 4 September 1914, Enver ordered Bronsart von Schellendorf to adjust the mobilization and deployment plan to take into account a potentially hostile Greece[30] and, two days later, Enver and Bronsart von Schellendorf altered the strategic priorities of the Ottoman war plan.[31] Using the forces available under the existing concentration plan, Enver ordered the Fourth Army in Syria to plan an attack on the Suez Canal. Similarly, in the absence of a Russian attack, the Third Army was ordered to plan for offensive operations towards Ardahan and Batum in the Caucasus. Ottoman forces in the remaining theatres of Mesopotamia would threaten Afghanistan and India while those in Yemen would attack British-occupied Aden. Unfortunately for Enver and the Ottoman general staff, mobilization of the Ottoman Army dragged out well beyond the time projected, making detailed planning difficult.

Hostilities officially began on 2 November 1914, and by the end of the month, the front had stabilized with the Russians clinging to a salient in Ottoman territory along the Erzurum–Sarakamış axis. In early December 1914, Enver ordered the Third Army to begin planning an offensive. The instructions reaffirmed Enver's intent to conduct a Cannae-like battle of annihilation against the Russians at Sarakamış. The resulting campaign was a catastrophic disaster that resulted in the destruction of two of the three Ottoman army corps involved and the deaths of 30,000 men. While Enver was focused on the Russian Caucasian frontier, Minister of the Marine Cemal Pasha, arrived in Aleppo on 18 November 1914 to take command of the Ottoman Fourth Army, which had been activated in early September. By January 1915, Cemal's Fourth Army concentrated the Ottoman VIII Corps at Gaza for the attack. The Fourth Army managed to conduct a night attack on the Suez Canal on 2 February, which was quickly repulsed.

Thus, the Ottoman Empire entered the summer of 1914 in a reactive strategic posture that centred on defensive operations and without a concentration plan that enabled the massing of its armies at points conforming to its strategic or diplomatic interests. The autumn of 1914 brought a comic opera aspect to Ottoman campaign planning as Ottoman and German staff officers sought to reconcile wildly conflicting ideas about the best path forward for the army's poorly positioned forces. In spite of this, Enver and the Ottoman general staff managed to launch poorly coordinated operational offensives, which served no real strategic purpose other than to tie up Russian and British forces.

The intersection of British and Ottoman strategic policies

Strategic decision-making in Britain was the outcome of a contentious committee-based system in which the members pursued service-centric agendas. This made for slow decision-making which was most often the result of compromise. British decisions taken in the first five months of the war tended towards fulfilling pre-war agreements with the French. On the seas, the Royal Navy successfully pursued the offensive at the strategic, operational and tactical levels. Britain's small land forces, however, conducted strategic, operational and tactical defensive operations, which were essentially reactive. Even the British landings in the Shatt al Arab in Mesopotamia were precautionary to guard the Anglo-Persian oil fields.

In terms of attempting to influence the outcomes of operations, the Admiralty's carefully calculated deployment of battlecruisers to the Falklands enabled the great victory over Admiral Graf Maximilian von Spee's squadron in December 1914. Previously, Churchill also formed an ad hoc infantry division and attempted unsuccessfully to save Antwerp from the German Army. Other than bring divisions to France and Egypt, the War Office made no comparable attempts to influence army operations in France.

Going into February 1915, Britain bound itself to a strategic policy formed by competing interests in the War Council. Reduced to its essentials, in the near term, British strategic policy rested on the successful execution of a low-cost/high-return naval-only assault on the Dardanelles with the goal of knocking Germany's allies out from under her. This was an interim strategic step designed to weaken Germany and, perhaps, strengthen Russia, while Britain readied its New Armies for combat in France. The involvement of land forces for the Dardanelles breakthrough was not seen as critical and then only in a minimal way to assist in destroying permanently the Ottoman coastal forts.

At the strategic level, decision-making in the Ottoman Empire devolved to a single man – Enver Pasha. This unity of command enabled him to make fast and decisive decisions. Enver Pasha made several decisions to conduct operational offensives in the Caucasus and against the Suez Canal. These were under-resourced and failed. However, these decisions indicated purpose and clarity of action. Operationally, once these operations were underway, Enver and the Ottoman staffs made no attempts to influence the outcomes.

Although the Ottoman strategic offensives in the Caucasus and the Sinai had failed spectacularly, the concentration plan brought six army corps and about 20 of the Ottoman Army's best infantry divisions to the Constantinople, Bosporus and Dardanelles theatre. This was an accidental outcome of failed diplomacy and a lack of strategic clarity in the summer and autumn of 1914. It is fair to say that, in February 1915, the triumvirate leading the Ottoman government had no strategic vision or coherent war aims. Moreover, the empire had entered the war with a concentration plan that left its active fronts with less than half of its mobilized army while the army's best units sat idly along the straits. It must be mentioned here that the Ottoman Army used its time well and the idle units trained hard in the months between mobilization and the opening of the Gallipoli campaign.

Effectively, the War Council's planning was one of deliberate choices based on the availability of resources, the stalemate in France and the powerful personalities in the council itself. The outcome of these choices was a campaign aimed at Constantinople by breaking through the Dardanelles, a campaign that proved to be ill conceived and under-resourced. The Ottoman triumvirate, led by Enver making almost unilateral decisions, placed its field armies in positions of near strategic uselessness. However, an accidental outcome of Enver's decisions was the concentration of most of the Ottoman field army within operational reach of the Gallipoli peninsula. As will be seen, at the intersection of these imprecise strategic policies, accidental opportunity favoured the Ottomans while deliberate choice hobbled the British.

Chapter Two

THE OPPOSING CAMPAIGN PLANS

In early 1915, Britain found itself with small land forces mired on the Western Front but with a large surplus naval capacity, which was the result of the successful execution of a global Anglo-French naval policy. To be sure, Kitchener had some 30 infantry divisions in various stages of training but only a small number would be ready for action by the summer. The War Council, encouraged by Churchill, searched for a coherent strategy to employ Britain's large navy in concert with its then-small army in the coming year. The outcome of this was a scheme to force the Dardanelles with ships alone and to compel the Ottoman Empire to quit the war.

The Ottoman Empire, in early 1915, found its two hasty and under-resourced land offensives defeated in the Caucasus and along the Suez Canal. Moreover, the empire's principal armies, containing its best-equipped and most well-trained infantry divisions, were concentrated around Constantinople, the Bosporus and the Dardanelles, in expectation of a war with Bulgaria – which never came. In sum, Ottoman strategy was bankrupt. However, at the operational level, great progress had been made in strengthening the Dardanelles defences for an Allied attack that many felt sure to come.

British plans, decision-making and force planning

Churchill went to France on 31 January to hear Sir John French's views on the diversion of army divisions to the Mediterranean and perhaps to convince him of why this was necessary. General French did not agree and wanted all available reinforcements sent to the BEF. On 9 February news reached the War Council that Bulgaria had contracted a loan with Germany. This was troubling and reopened the discussion about landing troops at Salonika in coordination with the French. While this never happened, over the next several days, Kitchener came to the conclusion that the 29th Infantry Division might be spared for Mediterranean operations. Nearly at the same time Churchill dispatched two Royal Marine battalions from the Royal Naval Division to Mudros harbour on the island of Lemnos for the purpose of furnishing small landing parties to blow up Ottoman guns along the straits. The basic campaign design shifted dramatically when Admiral Sir Henry Jackson wrote a memorandum on 15 February suggesting that the best course of action would be to have a combined navy and army attack and occupy the entire Gallipoli peninsula. The next day, an impromptu meeting of the War Council led to the decision to dispatch the 29th Division to Mudros within nine or ten days, dispatch a force from Egypt if required, and to make these forces available to support the naval attack on the Dardanelles if necessary. This was not a directive for, or a plan to conduct, a combined campaign but it did concentrate major forces for action at the mouth of the Dardanelles. But, at a Cabinet meeting the following day, Churchill asserted that he expected an Ottoman military uprising and revolution when the first fort fell, while Kitchener expected that the army would simply occupy the peninsula rather than have to fight for it.[1]

On 18 February, the French government confirmed that, in addition to providing a naval squadron of battleships, it would provide an infantry division as well. However, as Joffre refused to part with any of his forces in France, on 22 February, the French War Ministry directed the organization of a new division from depots in North Africa and France. The division was titled the 'Corps Expéditionnaire d'Orient' and formally activated on 1 March 1915. At full strength the French planned to assign 18,000 men to it.

Also on 18 February, Churchill ordered two more Royal Marine battalions and five battalions of the Royal Naval Division (RND) to be sent to Lemnos. These forces had no artillery and it was intended that the infantry would be supported by the guns of the fleet. Carden's naval assault began on this day as well. However, the next day, Kitchener countermanded his orders sending the 29th Division to Mudros and instead offered to send part of the Australian and New Zealand Army Corps (ANZAC).[2] Taken altogether, the ANZAC and Churchill's Marines and RND battalions totalled around 50,000 men, which when deployed would all be able to reach Mudros in three days' time. At this point in time, neither the War Council nor the military and naval staffs thought that the troops would be required to fight for the peninsula. At this time the British estimated that the Ottomans had about 40,000 men on the Gallipoli peninsula. Also on 19 February, Churchill minuted Kitchener that he had given instructions for transports sufficient for 10,000 men to be marshalled in Egypt by 27 February. On 20 February Kitchener instructed Lieutenant-General Sir

John Maxwell, in command of British forces in Egypt, to ready the ANZAC for movement by 9 March but also to contact Carden if a smaller force needed to be dispatched sooner.

On 23 February, Maxwell had collected transports sufficient for one brigade. The War Council met again on 24 February and there were contentious discussions between Churchill and Kitchener over the issue of exactly what the land forces would do and whether the 29th Division should be returned to the list of forces allocated to the Mediterranean. Of note, but seemingly ignored at the time, Haldane asked whether there was any truth to the estimate that there were 200,000 Ottoman soldiers positioned in nearby Thrace, which placed any British forces on the peninsula in danger. After much debate, Kitchener declared that if the fleet could not break through the straits alone then it was the army's intention 'to see the business through'.[3] This statement has been seen as a landmark shift in Kitchener's operational thinking about the campaign and the role of the army. He still refused to release the 29th Division. In the meantime, Churchill instructed Carden to use ground forces in small parties to destroy coastal guns. Reports from Maxwell and the French military mission in Cairo alerted Kitchener that the Ottoman defensive preparations were extensive, the Ottoman garrison was commanded by an alert and energetic officer, and that a landing on the peninsula would be hazardous.[4]

The War Council then met again on 26 February in a very contentious debate about the number of troops involved and the work that was expected of them. At this meeting, Hankey stated the obvious – that before the troops could move on to Constantinople they might have to first clear the Gallipoli peninsula.[5] Churchill's repeated insistence that Kitchener release the 29th Division for the operation conflicted with his position that this was a purely naval assault on the straits. Again Kitchener refused to commit the division. ANZAC commander Lieutenant-General Sir William R. Birdwood sailed for Mudros on 24 February and received instructions from Kitchener after the War Council meeting of 26 February. Kitchener explicitly told Birdwood that his force was to limit itself to minor operations involving the destruction of the Ottoman guns and howitzers and not commit to operations against large Ottoman units.[6] Kitchener continued that he expected the enemy to withdraw from the peninsula when the Narrows were forced and told Birdwood to be prepared to hold Bulair with a small force. He then asked Birdwood to send him an appreciation of what Birdwood thought was likely to happen at Constantinople and whether more than 64,000 men would be required.[7] At this time Kitchener was counting on 36,000 men from the ANZAC, 10,000 from the Royal Naval Division and 18,000 men from the French division.

On 28 February Churchill asked Carden to estimate how many days it would take, excluding bad weather, to enter the Sea of Marmara, to which Carden had no solid answer.

British naval campaign planning[8]

The first attack on the outer forts of the Dardanelles was a ten-minute bombardment carried out on 3 November 1914, by an Anglo-French squadron composed of the British battlecruisers *Indomitable* and *Indefatigable* and the French battleships *Vérité* and *Suffren*, from a range of 13,000 yards (11.9km). The British attacked the forts at Sedd el Bahr with eight rounds per turret from both battlecruisers, while the French attacked the forts at Kum Kale in Asia. The object was to observe the effect of ship's guns on forts and, indeed, a magazine at the Sedd el Bahr fort blew up, damaging the fort. The ships had longer-ranging guns than the forts, stayed outside the cannon range of the forts and suffered no damage. However, the attack thoroughly alarmed the Ottomans, who increased the intensity of their defensive preparations.

The British admiral commanding the British East Mediterranean Squadron was 57-year-old Vice-Admiral Sackville Carden, who had been patrolling the entrance to the Dardanelles since 21 September. His squadron also included two cruisers, 12 destroyers and six submarines. Carden had been in charge of the Malta dockyard when Rear Admiral Troubridge was recalled home unexpectedly to explain the escape of the *Goeben*. Following Troubridge's departure the best choice to command the squadron was Rear Admiral Henry Limpus, who was the head of the British naval mission to the Ottoman Empire, effectively Liman von Sanders' naval counterpart. Unfortunately for the Royal Navy, while the Ottoman Empire remained neutral, the Foreign Office deemed it imprudent and ungentlemanly to support Limpus's appointment. Thus, Britain lost the services of the one admiral who had personal knowledge of the Dardanelles defences. Carden, on the other hand, was regarded as second-rate, but was immediately available in September 1914 for what was then a low-priority posting. Carden took a lesson from the 3 November attack, believing that by repeating and prolonging the bombardment it would produce greater results.[9]

Carden's small squadron was gradually increased in size and he was appointed as the commander of the Anglo-French Squadrons, Eastern Mediterranean. The Admiralty began to reinforce him with mostly older pre-dreadnought battleships *Cornwallis*, *Vengeance* and *Triumph*, although the modern battlecruiser *Inflexible* arrived on 24 January 1915 to replace the two battlecruisers returning to Britain for overdue maintenance. As his second-in-command, Carden enjoyed the services of the very experienced and highly regarded Rear Admiral John de Robeck, who was assigned on 22 January with his flagship, *Vengeance*. The French replaced the *Vérité* with the *Bouvet* and they were very fortunate to have the colourful and courageous Admiral Emile-Paul Guépratte commanding the squadron at the Dardanelles. When Carden replied to Churchill's query about forcing the Dardanelles in early January 1915, he had five old pre-dreadnought battleships and two, soon to fall to one, battlecruisers, which was barely enough to keep the Turco-German squadron bottled up in the Sea of Marmara. Carden believed that he could break through the straits in about a month if Churchill met his requirements – 12 battleships and three battlecruisers – which would triple the size of his fleet. Serving as Carden's chief of staff was the brilliant and aggressive Commodore Roger Keyes, who had served as a naval attaché at Constantinople and had often hired a steamer to observe the Dardanelles fortress. Although Carden himself was regarded as second-rank the Admiralty made sure that his principal subordinates were first-class officers.

Carden's squadrons were initially supported from the Royal Navy's distant bases at Alexandria and Malta, but an agreement with the Greeks led to the occupation of Lemnos island in January 1915. Lemnos is 60 miles south-east of the entrance of the Dardanelles and its harbour, Mudros, is one of the finest natural anchorages in the Mediterranean and Aegean Seas. Mudros is 3 miles (5km) across, fully enclosed and with a depth of 30–40 feet (9–12m). It was capable of sheltering hundreds of ships. There was a small sleepy Greek village there with a single pier. All of that began to change on 22 February 1915, when Rear Admiral Rosslyn Wemyss arrived to serve as base commander. Mudros harbour would become Carden's advance base for projecting close-fleet operations against the Dardanelles.

Carden's fleet grew in size as the Admiralty brought in ships from around the globe. The brand-new super-dreadnought battleship *Queen Elizabeth* arrived in February, as did the semi-dreadnoughts *Agamemnon* and *Lord Nelson*, the pre-dreadnoughts *Irresistible*, *Albion* and *Ocean*, and the French *Gaulois* and *Charlemagne*. As the middle of February passed, Carden had his 12 battleships and the Admiralty's promise that the remaining required ships would arrive in time. In addition to these forces, Carden also had 2,000 Royal Marines.

The naval plan itself was a refined elaboration of Carden's message of 11 January to the Admiralty. More accurately it was a campaign plan, involving a series of tactical battles and process-like steps, leading to a strategic objective. According to Churchill the details of the plan were worked out by a Royal Marine captain on Carden's staff named Godfrey, who was also one of the gunnery experts on the *Inflexible*. The finer details of the plan included:[10]

A   Indirect bombardment of the forts at the entrance, reduction completed by direct bombardment at decisive range, torpedo tubes and guns commanding minefield destroyed. Mine fields at entrance cleared.

B   Battleships, preceded by minesweepers, enter straits, working up the straits until Kephez Point battery # 8 can be silenced.

C   Severe bombardment of forts from Gaba Tepe; reduction completed by direct fire at decisive ranges.

D   Battleships, preceded by minesweepers, make their way towards narrows. Forts 22, 23 and 24 bombarded from Gaba Tepe, then direct fire. Sweep the minefields in the Narrows. Fort at Nagara Point reduced by direct fire, battle force proceeds into the Sea of Marmara preceded by minesweepers.

Carden's staff expected that ammunition expenditure would be large. Admiral Jackson at the Admiralty had some ideas about what it would take; by calculating from the 3 November bombardment of Sedd el Bahr that 64 12in. shells had put six enemy heavy guns out of action, his estimate was that it might take ten rounds per gun of the primary armament (10–15in.) on board a ship to put a gun on shore out of action.[11] Jackson then calculated that, based on the number of enemy guns along the straits, it would take at least 2,000 rounds to execute Carden's plan. However, he cautioned that the Admiralty should not attempt the operations without 3,000 rounds of large-calibre ammunition on hand. The Admiralty also noted that the Ottoman guns on 3 November were able to fire heavy shells out to a range of 12,300 yards (11.2km) and calculated from this that British ships ought not to close nearer than 13,000 yards (11.9km) from the Ottoman forts.

In order to accomplish these ends and ways, the Admiralty resourced Carden with the means by sending him almost everything he asked for. Central to the execution of the scheme was a requirement for a ship capable of indirect fire from the Aegean Sea over the Gaba Tepe hills into the Narrows. To do this, the Admiralty staff suggested to Churchill and Fisher that it would be cost-effective and safe to let the new super-dreadnought *Queen Elizabeth* conduct her gunnery calibration exercises against the Dardanelles defences rather than at Gibraltar as scheduled. There were, according to studies conducted by Vice-Admiral Sir Henry Oliver, chief of the Admiralty war staff, other reasons for sending this particular ship, which carried eight of the new and extremely powerful 15in. guns. Oliver was influenced by comparisons that had been made with the German 15in. howitzers, which had demolished the Belgian forts at Liège and Namur in August 1914, with Admiralty studies suggesting that naval guns could be expected to achieve three times more hits on the Ottoman forts than the Germans achieved in

CARDEN'S PLAN TO FORCE THE DARDANELLES

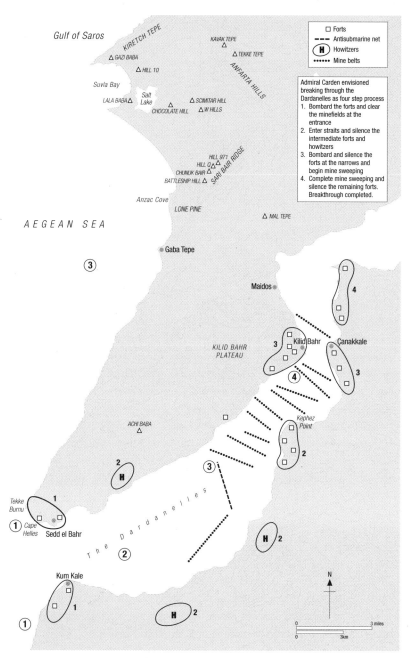

Gulf of Saros

KIRETCH TEPE

△ GAZI BABA

△ HILL 10

KAVAK TEPE
△

△ TEKKE TEPE

ANFARTA HILLS

Suvla Bay

LALA BABA △

Salt
Lake

△ SCIMITAR HILL

CHOCOLATE HILL   △ W HILLS
              △

HILL 971
HILL Q △△
CHUNUK BAIR △
BATTLESHIP HILL △

SARI BAIR RIDGE

Anzac Cove

LONE PINE

△ MAL TEPE

AEGEAN SEA

● Gaba Tepe

③

Maidos ●

4

KILID BAHR
PLATEAU

3   Kilid Bahr ●

Çanakkale ●

3

④

Kephez
Point

ACHI BABA
△

2

③

2
H

3

Tekke
Burnu

1

① Cape
Helles   Sedd el Bahr

The Dardanelles

② H   2

Kum Kale

①   1   2
              H   2

N

□	Forts
---	Antisubmarine net
Ⓗ	Howitzers
•••••	Mine belts

Admiral Carden envisioned
breaking through the
Dardanelles as four step process
1. Bombard the forts and clear
   the minefields at the
   entrance
2. Enter straits and silence the
   intermediate forts and
   howitzers
3. Bombard and silence the
   forts at the narrows and
   begin mine sweeping
4. Complete mine sweeping and
   silence the remaining forts.
   Breakthrough completed.

0   3 miles
0   3km

Belgium. This was based on confidential gunnery tables issued to the fleet; however, the probabilities were conditional on the *Queen Elizabeth* being anchored in clear weather in a stationary position. This was thought possible because the Admiralty data on the gun's ballistics were so precise.

The *Queen Elizabeth* offered more than simply bigger shells, although the 15in. shell weighed 1,920 pounds while the 12in. shell carried by most of the other battleships weighed 850 pounds. More importantly, the 20° elevation and charge of the 15in. guns gave them a 23,734-yard range compared with the 13.5° elevation of the 12in. guns giving them a 16,400-yard range. Furthermore, the heavier 15in. shells were more accurate and ballistically more predictable and the Admiralty calculated that the Ottoman forts could be successfully engaged with shells descending along a trajectory of 15°. The Admiralty also gave specific advice that guns should be fired one at a time, shot-by-shot, rather than the standard Royal Navy salvo firing.[12] However, this was keyed to the requirement that individual rounds could be spotted by an observer and corrections relayed to the ship. This could be done by direct observation by the ship itself or, in principle, by an observer aloft in an aircraft. In theory, therefore, the *Queen Elizabeth* could anchor in the Aegean, fire over Gaba Tepe and destroy forts and guns along the straits. Officially, the essence of the plan boiled down to the destruction of the forts by long-range bombardment followed by minesweeping. There remained vigorous disagreement at the Admiralty about whether 'silenced' meant 'destroyed' and whether troops needed to be landed to guarantee destruction of the enemy guns themselves. Scant attention was paid to the issue of the Ottoman field artillery and howitzers in the hills overlooking the straits.

Carden also asked for fleet minesweepers, which were fast purpose-built naval vessels, but unfortunately for the enterprise, none could be spared from the North Sea. Instead he received 21 contracted North Sea fishing trawlers, with their civilian crews, jury-rigged with cable arrangements as minesweepers. The major problem tactically with these unarmoured (although they did have some iron plating against rifle fire), unarmed, and vulnerable vessels was their top speed of only 5 or 6 knots – they could barely make headway against the southerly flowing current in the Dardanelles which often ran at those speeds. Carden stationed a few junior Royal Navy ratings on each minesweeper to handle the mines and to steady the civilian crew. The powerful Dardanelles current itself, emptying at the mouth of the straits, made it impossible for battleships to moor at anchor for shore bombardment, although that would not become evident until the navy tried to do it.[13] The initial stages of Carden's plan envisioned a 'by ships alone' campaign as no ground troops were available until

23 February, when the two Royal Marines battalions sent from Britain on 6 February were due to arrive in Lemnos harbour.

Ottoman defensive plans[14]

The Dardanelles straits were the most heavily fortified point in the Ottoman Empire and the defensive works there dated back hundreds of years. During the 1880s the Ottoman military, with German advice, started modernizing the straits' fortifications against a naval attack.[15] Until 1912, the defences were composed entirely of coast defence guns, underwater minefields, and searchlights oriented on the straits themselves, which presented a thin string of forts along the water's edge. In the autumn of 1912 the strategic situation changed and, against the threat of a Greek amphibious invasion, the Ottoman general staff ordered a more comprehensive fortification of the entire Gallipoli peninsula itself. The general staff activated an army command on the peninsula to construct and occupy new defensive works guarding the straits' fortifications against an enemy landing in their rear.[16]

During the First Balkan War of 1912–13, the Ottomans orchestrated the basic defensive plans and concepts used subsequently to defend the peninsula in 1915 against the British. Prior to the Balkan Wars the peninsula was a sleepy garrison backwater for the Ottoman Army's 5th Infantry Division and Çanakkale Fortress Command.[17] However, in the Balkan Wars the Ottomans sent a greatly reinforced force to defend the Gallipoli peninsula when the victorious Bulgarian army cut off the peninsula on 12 October 1912. The general staff activated the Çanakkale Straits Forces and Fortification Command and placed the Dardanelles straits and the peninsula under its command.[17] The general staff sent the regular 27th Infantry Division, three reserve infantry divisions, several provisional detachments, a provisional cavalry brigade, and three independent batteries of artillery to the peninsula. The pre-war fortress command of three heavy coastal artillery regiments was absorbed into the new force as well. Altogether for the defence of the peninsula in 1912, the Ottomans had 40,000 men armed with 27,000 rifles, 38 machine guns, and 102 cannons (not counting coastal artillery).[19]

Brigadier-General Fahri Pasha took command of the Çanakkale Straits Forces and Fortification Command and rapidly established the basic defensive plan and layout for the peninsula by establishing four primary defensive groups: one guarding the beaches of the lower peninsula, one guarding the narrow neck of the peninsula (at Bulair), one guarding the Asian beaches, while one remained in immediate reserve. Fahri stationed two of the three reserve infantry divisions in beach defence roles on the peninsula, placed the 27th Division at Bulair and the Menderes Detachment along the Asiatic shore. He kept his third reserve division as a general army reserve at Maidos (modern Eceabat). Thus, by the end of the year, the general configuration of the Ottoman defence was established, which became a template used again in 1915.

The two Ottoman reserve infantry divisions defending the lower peninsula were much weaker than regular infantry divisions and together were approximately the same strength as the Ottoman 9th Infantry Division, which later defended the peninsula in 1915. These two divisions constructed battalion-sized strongpoints on the key terrain features overlooking the beaches. The beaches themselves were covered by company-sized elements and the divisional artilleries were positioned centrally to support the divisional sectors. These units dug trenches and gun pits, developed a road and communications network, and rehearsed counter-attack plans.[20]

Across the straits near the ruins of Troy in Asia, the Menderes Detachment had grown to divisional strength and began similar defensive preparations at Kum Kale and the adjacent coastlines. At Bulair in the peninsula's neck, the 27th Infantry Division faced the Bulgarians and, although defending the peninsula from the north, the 27th Division fulfilled a similar mission in the area as the 7th Infantry Division in 1915.[21] Serving on the Bulair lines as chief of operations was Staff Major Mustafa Kemal (later and more famously known as Atatürk).[22] Fahri established his headquarters at Maidos to command and control both the mobile divisions on the peninsula and in Asia. This command arrangement became formalized as the Provisional Forces Command in December 1912. Although the anticipated amphibious invasion by the Greeks never materialized, there was a pitched battle on the neck of the peninsula during the First Balkan War. In early 1913, Fahri's Gallipoli forces were ordered to conduct a supporting attack in support of an amphibious invasion at Şarkoy.[23] Fahri launched his attack on 8 February and it was a spectacular failure.[24] After the end of the Second Balkan War in 1913, the troops remaining on the peninsula were sent home and it returned to its normal peacetime routines.

After the Balkan Wars, the defence of the Dardanelles returned to the hands of the commander of the Çanakkale Fortress Command. This was a fortress command, which had control over the string of elderly forts and command of a brigade of three heavy artillery regiments. The forts and guns were clustered at the mouth of the Dardanelles and at the Narrows and, in times of peace, were manned at very low levels. This would change in the summer of 1914 and, although the Ottoman Empire would not enter the war until November 1914, the army on the Gallipoli peninsula was active much earlier.[25]

In the spring of 1913, great tension existed between the Ottoman Empire and Greece over the status of the residual Muslim population living in newly Greek-occupied western Thrace. War seemed probable and the Ottoman III Corps was ordered to plan for movement to the peninsula while the Ottoman V Corps was ordered to occupy the famous Çatalca lines. To accommodate this, the reactivation of the defensive plans for the peninsula began in late spring 1914, when Liman von Sanders assigned two officers, General Posseldt as the Inspector of Heavy Artillery and Colonel Erich Weber as Inspector of Fortifications, to the fortress command. On 15 June 1914 Posseldt reorganized the 35 artillery batteries into 22 batteries, in order to centralize training and administration.[26] In July, operations conducted by Greek warships and aircraft near the mouth of the Dardanelles so alarmed the Ottoman general staff[27] that the Ministry of War issued a special limited mobilization order at 11.45am on 31 July 1914 alerting the fortress commander to begin preparations for war and to expect reinforcements.[28] These actions were in no way associated with the July crisis then brewing in central Europe.

The III Corps' chief of staff, German Lieutenant-Colonel Perrinet von Thauvenay, arrived on the night of 8/9 August and began to update the defensive plans the next day. The plans called for the Ottoman III Corps to reinforce the fortress and to provide the mobile forces needed to defend the peninsula.[29] The defensive plans for the peninsula were based on the template from 1913 but with an expanded northern sector that included the magnificent landing beaches at Saros Bay. In early August 1914, the fortress command staff revised their war plans so that three major operational groups defending the straits region aligned with the 1913 template with one group in Asia (unchanged from 1913), one on the peninsula south of Bulair (unchanged from 1913), and one group in the new Saros Bay sector.[30] On 12 August, Enver Pasha alerted the fortress that, although the empire had purchased the *Yavuz Sultan Selim* (ex-SMS *Goeben*) and *Midilli* (ex-SMS *Breslau*), the British might attack through the straits to get at the ships.[31]

Neither the fortress nor III Corps was ready for war in early August 1914. Nevertheless, as a result of the July crisis but separate from their concerns about Greece, the Ottoman general staff decided to conduct national military mobilization as a precautionary measure, even though the empire was not yet at war. At 1.00am on 2 August 1914, the Ottoman general staff sent mobilization orders to the commander of III Corps in Rodosto (modern Tekirdağ).[32] The following day, which was the first numbered day of mobilization (3 August), the Ottoman Army began its preparations for war.[33] Initial strength returns in III Corps of about 15,000 officers and men, or about 30 per cent of required war strength, reflected the low condition of peacetime readiness that the Ottoman Army operated under.[34] Nevertheless, by 21 August, the corps was at full strength with about 13,000 men in each of the 7th, 8th and 9th Infantry Divisions and 2,907 men assigned to the corps troop units. In fact III Corps was the only corps of 13 Ottoman army corps to mobilize within its time requirement of 20 days. On 22 August the regiments and battalions of the corps began to move from home garrisons to staging areas surrounding Rodosto for training and shaking out.

Upon mobilization, the plans called for III Corps to detach the 9th Division to the Çanakkale Fortified Area Command for beach defence and mobile reserve operations. Technically, it still remained under the command of III Corps, but for all intents and purposes, the division fell under the operational control of the fortress commander. On 27 August, the 9th Infantry Division commander began conversations with the commander of the fortress concerning the deployment of his division to the Gallipoli peninsula and by mid-September 1914, the division was moving into observation positions overlooking the peninsula's beaches. This effectively removed the division from III Corps control. After the training regime associated with mobilization the corps began to move into the peninsula. The 7th Division began to deploy there on 29 October and the III Corps headquarters moved from Rodosto to the town of Gallipoli (modern Gelibolu) itself on 4 November. The 8th Division remained in its staging areas outside Rodosto. Thus, when the empire actually entered the war and by the time of the first Royal Navy bombardment (3 November), the Ottomans had three full months of preparation time to position substantial forces for the defence of both the straits (the fortress command) and the peninsula (a mobile army corps of two divisions).

In spite of these preparations, the defence of the Dardanelles remained weak due to the poor condition of the fortifications, the antiquity of many of the cannons, the scarcity of ammunition and supplies, and the lack of good coordination between the fortress command and the corps headquarters. The first Germans to arrive were 160 personnel from the *Goeben* and *Breslau* on 30 August 1914, who were assigned to the forts containing the heavy coastal guns at the Narrows. To rectify the technical deficiencies of the coastal defences, in September the Germans dispatched Vice-Admiral Guido von Usedom, who had expertise in coastal artillery and gunnery, to advise the Turks. Accompanying the admiral were about 500 Germans: coastal defence experts specializing in coastal artillery, communications, military engineering, and underwater mines. None of these men were assigned to the mobile Ottoman III Corps. The

Germans likewise dispatched limited quantities of war material to Turkey through the neutral countries of Romania and Bulgaria.

The Royal Navy's brief bombardment of 3 November 1914 achieved no objective of military value, and indeed, only served notice on the Ottomans regarding the vulnerability of the straits. The attack so thoroughly alarmed the Ottoman general staff that it accelerated the programme of fortification and defensive improvements. However, because of an emerging plan to invade Egypt the general staff decided to detach the 8th Infantry Division from III Corps, alerting it for service on the Sinai front and beginning preparations for its departure in late November 1914. This caused Esat Pasha, the III Corps commander, to dispatch a long report to the First Army outlining the case for more forces to defend the peninsula.[35] As a result the 19th Infantry Division was activated on 1 January 1915 and assigned to III Corps to take the place of the 8th Division.[36]

Defensive planning and training, particularly anti-invasion drills, began in earnest in November 1914, as well as improvements to the seaward defences and construction of additional roads and interior communications. Including the 9th Infantry Division, by mid-February 1915, the fortress command deployed over 34,500 soldiers, armed with 25,000 rifles, eight machine guns and 263 cannon, on the peninsula. Moreover, the mobile III Corps consisting of the fully trained 7th Infantry Division and had 15,000 soldiers in position, armed with 9,448 rifles, eight machine guns and 50 cannon.[37] The unready 19th Infantry Division of III Corps remained off the peninsula in the Rodosto garrison where it was undergoing intensive training under its new commander, the young and aggressive Lieutenant-Colonel Mustafa Kemal.

The ship-killing power of the Çanakkale Fortified Area Command lay in its heavy coastal artillery, which was organized into the 2nd Artillery Brigade and concentrated in 14 permanent forts lining the straits. There were three regiments assigned to the brigade, the 3rd, 4th and 5th Heavy Artillery Regiments.[37] The 2nd Battalion, 4th Heavy Artillery Regiment garrisoned the fortifications on the European side of the Narrows around Maidos and Kilid Bahr. The 1st and 2nd Battalions, 3rd Heavy Artillery Regiment garrisoned the Asiatic narrows forts around Çanakkale. The 5th Heavy Artillery Regiment garrisoned the outer forts at the mouth of the Dardanelles with its 1st Battalion at Sedd el Bahr in Europe and its 2nd Battalion at Kum Kale in Asia. These formations were armed with coastal defence cannons ranging in size from 87mm up to 355mm, however, most of the more powerful heavy ship-killing guns were with 3rd and 4th Heavy Artillery Regiments in the Narrows. Peacetime ammunition supplies were stored in magazines within the forts and the quantities on hand were reported to the fortress commander by type of gun. On mobilization, the brigade's regiments stocked over 8,000 rounds of heavy-calibre ammunition (8–14in.) in magazines adjacent to its guns and maintained several thousand more in its depot facilities.

The 82 fixed coastal guns in the three regiments were, by themselves, insufficient to defend the straits under full wartime conditions against a force such as Britain's Royal Navy and required heavy augmentation, therefore the Ottoman general staff began to deploy additional cannon to the straits from less threatened areas. Throughout August 1914, a variety of cannon arrived at the Çanakkale fortress from the fortresses of Edirne (Adrianople) and Çatalca (Chatalja), as well as from the ships of the Ottoman fleet in Constantinople.[39] The first minefield was laid in the Narrows on 4 August 1914. On 17 August a battery of 75mm ship's guns were sent to the peninsula and on 23 August the first six 120mm howitzers arrived. Alert to the increased dangers posed by the increasingly hostile Entente, the Ottoman general staff ordered further artillery reinforcements to the area from the Bosporus fortress area on 19 September 1914, in the form of the 8th Heavy Artillery Regiment.[40] This regiment was armed with 22 150mm howitzers, rising to a total of 32, and later reinforced by 14 120mm howitzers. It was commanded by Lieutenant-Colonel Mehmet Zekerriya. The regiment began to arrive on 25 September and was assigned kill zones to augment the intermediate defences in an anti-ship role. By 7 November six heavy 210mm mortars were assigned to Zekerriya's regiment as well. So many howitzers arrived that Zekerriya formed a third battalion – the standard in the Ottoman Army at that time was two battalions in artillery regiments. Moreover, as 1915 approached, a variety of smaller field and mountain artillery batteries were also added to the defences.

Additional Ottoman artillery officers and NCOs were assigned from Constantinople to the staff of the fortress commander. On 1 September, German Vice-Admiral Wilhelm Schack, who was a torpedo specialist and previously inspector of coast artillery (1911–13), arrived to assess the defences and render a report to the general staff. His report noted deficiencies in ammunition quantities, the deteriorated condition of the fortifications, and an absence of funds for repair parts and upgrades. He was especially concerned with the torpedo batteries and he judged the fortress unready for combat.[41] Schack's report along with the increasingly complex problems involving integrating the tactical deployment of the incoming mobile artillery battalions with the static heavy artillery regiments caused concern in Constantinople. The Ottoman general staff sent a directive to the fortress on 22 October 1914 to develop a new plan for the defence of the straits.[42] To assist the fortress staff, Enver sent German Vice-Admiral Johannes

Merten as his personal delegate, who with German Lieutenant-Commander Fritz Wossidlo (also referred to as Wasillo) and fortress chief of staff Lieutenant-Colonel Salahattin Adil, formed a planning group to study the problem. On 8 November, the group issued its revised plan, which became the basis for the defence of the straits against enemy ships.[43]

The new plan tactically organized the fortress into four defensive areas, the first or entry area (the outer defences), the second area (the howitzer zone), the third area (the intermediate defences: Kepez–Soganlı), and the fourth area (the inner defences: Çanakkale–Kilid Bahr). The new howitzer zone was a major change to the previous defensive plan and involved the delivery of plunging fire on enemy ships (which had relatively thin horizontal deck armour compared to their vertical side armour). The plan tasked the incoming 8th Heavy Artillery Regiment to provide forces, command and control for the howitzer zone, which was put under the overall command of German artillery specialist Lieutenant-Colonel Wehrle. The creation of the howitzer zone allowed the Turks to integrate effectively the reinforcing artillery with the fortress artillery as well as coordinate procedures for the centralized delivery of fire. Crew training for the men manning the coastal artillery pieces had been ongoing since mobilization but a high percentage of the men were newly conscripted and untrained. To rectify this Merten assigned German non-commissioned officers directly into the Ottoman gun crews.

Additional guns arrived throughout December and January, including more 120mm howitzers; 37mm anti-aircraft guns; and 47mm and 75mm ship's guns. By 18 February 1915, there were a total of 235 cannons operational in the four artillery regiments assigned to defend the Dardanelles.[44] The outer defences were in the hands of 5th Heavy Artillery Regiment, the mobile 8th Heavy Artillery Regiment lay in the howitzer zone, and 3rd and 4th Heavy Artillery Regiments manned the guns assigned to the intermediate and inner defences. So many howitzers arrived that the 8th Heavy Artillery Regiment was again reorganized into four battalions with the 1st and 2nd Battalions composed of three batteries of 150mm howitzers in each battalion and the 3rd and 4th Battalions composed of a mix of 150mm and 120mm howitzers. Ammunition for most of the newly arriving howitzers and field guns was fairly plentiful. The artillery situation report of 26 February 1915 shows 8th Heavy Artillery Regiment was particularly well stocked with 8,229 shells for its howitzers.

Altogether, by the time of the first Allied naval attack in February 1915, the Ottomans had 82 heavy coastal guns operational in fixed positions and some 230 mobile guns and howitzers available for the defence of the Dardanelles, and Mustafa Kemal's infantry division had moved forward to the peninsula to join the 7th and 9th Infantry Divisions earlier that month. Over an eight-month period, with some German advice, trained Ottoman general staff officers developed a comprehensive plan integrating mobile army and fortress units. The plan, mirroring the 1913 template, put small, entrenched infantry units defending the likely invasion beaches and positioned large reserves in protected positions behind the beaches for counter-attacks. As in the 1913 plan, the primary objective was to slow the enemy landings and then launch coordinated counter-attacks to drive the enemy back into the sea. Mobile operations remained the domain of Ottoman officers while the German officers remained focused on the straits defences.[45] However, the new plan significantly altered the straits defensive posture by the inclusion of a howitzer zone between the mouth of the straits and the Narrows.

The intersection of plans

The British and Ottoman plans would intersect on 19 February 1915 and move towards a culminating point on 18 March. Although there was concern in London and amongst some of Carden's staff about the Ottoman field artillery and howitzers, a tactical solution to deal with these systems was conspicuously absent from the British plan. The problem for Carden was that these were highly mobile systems and could not be precisely located or engaged. While Carden's newer ships had heavier deck armour, his pre-dreadnoughts and all smaller ships were vulnerable to high-angle plunging fire. Moreover, his converted former North Sea fishing trawlers were notably vulnerable to any kind of fire, including that from machine guns and pom-poms. While the British were uncertain about the strength and location of the Ottoman 8th Heavy Artillery Regiment, the naval staffs were aware of its existence but failed to account for it with any kind of counter-measures.

The brief bombardment of the Ottoman forts in November 1914 provided British planners with some data and planning assumptions about what it might take to knock out the forts. However, these ideas remained theoretical, as did operations about how to command and control simultaneous operations to defeat the forts and sweep mines. Carden's plan was a work in progress and depended largely on innovation while the operation was ongoing.

The Ottoman plans for the defence of the Dardanelles were simply an extension of previous defensive schemes and operations. As fresh formations flowed into the theatre, they filled in a pre-existing plan that dated to 1912. The assignment of German coast defence specialists improved the tactical proficiency of the gun crews and added depth and experience to the planning teams involved in planning the employment of the howitzers. Unlike the British plan, the Ottoman plan was rehearsed frequently at the operational and tactical levels. By 19 February, Ottoman plans for the defence of the Dardanelles could be characterized as mature and well tested.

The British decision to undertake a naval-only campaign to break through the Dardanelles came at the hands of Winston Churchill, who persuaded his unwilling colleagues to support the scheme. Churchill then acted to provide Admiral Carden with the forces he had requested for the operation. The weight of opinion in the War Council also persuaded Kitchener to support the scheme, to which he committed the ANZAC to follow-on operations at Constantinople. While there was strategic clarity about breaking through the Dardanelles, it was uncertain what would happen after that. In this regard, the strategic goal of the campaign was ambiguous and, in truth, this Dardanelles campaign must be characterized as a campaign of opportunity. The resources that Britain committed to the campaign were limited, with the naval component consisting almost entirely of obsolescent ships that could be spared from the North Sea. The land component consisted of mostly inexperienced troops already present and training in Egypt. The end, ways, and means of this campaign were, therefore, not rationalized in any sense of the word and were not based on any actual professional staff appreciations.

The Ottoman Army's mobilization and concentration plans brought six army corps of the empire's best-trained and best-led divisions to the Bosporus, Constantinople and Dardanelles regions. These deployments anticipated a war against Bulgaria and Greece and not against the Entente powers. However, this turned into a fortunate accident that allowed the Ottoman high command to reinforce the Gallipoli peninsula when increasing threats presented themselves. These reinforcements enabled the Ottoman general staff to maintain a large and combat-ready garrison on the peninsula that always matched or outnumbered the Allied forces that could be brought against it.

At the operational level, Carden decided on a cautious step-by-step reduction of the enemy defences. In his attempts to influence the outcome of his plan, Carden simply refined the original estimate. Tactically, Carden's plans were based on many assumptions about the Ottoman defences and how the defenders would react to an assault. At the operational level, the Ottoman coastal defences along the Dardanelles straits were fixed into a zoned configuration designed to cover the minefields with direct and indirect fire. The Ottoman tactical efforts focused on gunnery and coordination between direct-fire coastal artillery and the groups of mobile howitzers.

Chapter Three

THE NAVAL ASSAULT, 19 FEBRUARY–18 MARCH 1915

The Allied naval campaign began on 19 February 1915 with Vice-Admiral Carden unleashing a deliberate attack on the outer forts. Carden's plan was a step-by-step reduction of the forts to be followed by minesweepers clearing the channels. The Ottoman outer forts were quickly silenced and Royal Marine landing parties were able to blow them up with minimal resistance. However, once inside the entrance of the straits, Carden's fleet encountered the Ottoman howitzer zone. Allied operational tempo slowed to a crawl and Carden attempted to find a tactical solution to the problem. The fleet made several attempts to push through to the Narrows but in each case resistance proved too strong. Intense pressure from Churchill in London created great stress and anxiety for Carden, who was unable to show success despite having the assets he had requested. On 16 March 1915, Carden suffered a nervous collapse and was replaced by Vice-Admiral John de Robeck, who was determined to force the straits. Two days later, de Robeck's attempt failed spectacularly with heavy losses.

The Ottomans were alert and ready for Carden's attacks, although there was great uncertainty about whether the defensive efforts would be successful. In the end, the Ottoman and German gunners proved stalwart and resolute in manning their guns, making Allied naval operations inside the entrance of the Dardanelles all but impossible. The Ottoman victory on 18 March 1915 encouraged the defenders and raised their morale significantly. Moreover, it was tremendously significant because it left John de Robeck convinced that another naval attack would fail.

Ottoman preparations

On 10 December 1913, Brigadier-General Esat Pasha assumed command of III Corps, a subordinate corps of the Ottoman First Army.[1] He had only returned from captivity in Greece on 2 December and was already being hailed in the empire as the Hero of Janina (or Yanya in Turkish). Photos of Esat, who appeared somewhat grandfatherly, belied his active nature and his aggressive command style. Liman von Sanders, who was no great admirer of senior Ottoman officers, described Esat as 'determined and far seeing' and 'knightly and valorous'.[2] Ancedotal, but reflecting his personality, Esat roused himself from bed at 2.45am on 2 August 1914 to read personally the Ottoman Army's mobilization orders.[3]

In late August, III Corps concentrated around Tekirdağ. The 9th Division moved to the Gallipoli peninsula on 9 September 1914, the 7th Division deployed there on 29 October, and Esat's headquarters followed on 4 November.[4] The 9th Division was assigned to the fortress command for the defence of the mouth of the Dardanelles, while III Corps assumed control of Bulair and the Gulf of Saros.

Esat wrote and issued detailed training guidance on 8 November 1914 to his III Corps formations.[5] He specified that units conduct training that included observation techniques, combat and spot reporting procedures, alarm situations, battle drill rehearsals, coordination with the jandarma (Ottoman para-military gendarmerie), and tactical deception measures. On 24 November 1914, the First Army notified III Corps to prepare for an amphibious invasion by the British. This directive stressed the importance of improving the field fortifications in order to delay the enemy landing long enough for powerful counter-attacks to be launched.

III Corps' situational awareness improved as a result of a better understanding of the terrain brought about through the construction of new defensive positions. On 12 August 1914, the 9th Infantry Division's 26th Infantry Regiment at Gallipoli reported its 2nd and 3rd Battalions at war strength. Its 1st Battalion was on detached duty in Basra. By 15 August the regiment had 381 active soldiers, 2,092 reservists, and 199 untrained conscripts assigned to its rolls and on the next day began organizing a new 1st Battalion (sometimes erroneously called the 4th Battalion).[6] Four days later, the regiment was ordered to occupy coastal observation posts and to prepare defensive positions by stationing a company at Sedd el Bahr, a platoon at Gaba Tepe, a company at Ece Limani, and to bivouac the remainder at Maidos.[7] The regiment was augmented with the Bursa Mobile Jandarma Battalion, the divisional mountain howitzer battalion, and a cavalry troop, which were attached directly to the regiment on 13 September. Its commander began combined-arms training with these attachments that week. Later, on 4 October, the regiment developed fire plans from Achi Baba in concert with the 8th Battery, 3rd Mountain Howitzer Battalion and a 105mm howitzer battery.[8]

The division's 27th Infantry Regiment, also stationed in Gallipoli, was partially mobilized several days earlier on 31 July 1914, against a possible Greek amphibious threat. It was assigned an immediate mission to observe and screen the Saros Bay beaches.[9] In an accelerated mobilization, reserves flooded into the barracks and by 1 August, the regiment reported itself at war establishment. On 7 August, the Gallipoli Field Jandarma Battalion, the 2nd Battalion, 9th Field Artillery Regiment, and a cavalry platoon were attached to the 27th Infantry Regiment.[10] On 10 September, Major Mehmet Şefik, the commander of the 3rd Battalion, took command of the regiment.[11] Under Şefik, the regiment concentrated on individual training for its soldiers throughout September and participated in division and army manoeuvres in October. Beginning on 1 November 1914, the regiment participated in special training with a mountain howitzer battalion and a howitzer battery in the reserve area.[12] As the winter progressed, Şefik's frequent orders to his regiments included specific instructions that ensured that the infantry-artillery team jointly coordinated their training.[13] Later, on 15 February 1915, the newly promoted regimental commander, Lieutenant-Colonel Şefik was designated as the Maidos Area commander and his regiment placed in general reserve for III Corps. Şefik immediately began to coordinate and update the artillery fire plans from the centrally located hill mass of Kavak Tepe. The fire plans were developed for the artillery batteries of 3rd Battalion, 9th Artillery Regiment and included targets in the regimental sector (which included the area later known as the Anzac beachhead).[14]

The remaining regiment of the 9th Infantry Division (25th Infantry Regiment) had a similar experience, spending August and September involved in the individual training of soldiers.[15] This regiment was not assigned an immediate tactical mission and remained in training conducting manoeuvres near Erenköy until 17 November when it was moved forward to defend the beaches at Kum Kale. The divisional artillery, 9th Artillery Regiment, was placed in a direct support role to provide fire for the infantry regiments.[16] Supporting arms enjoyed similar experiences.[17] Well-trained artillery batteries from the Polatlı artillery school arrived at Erenköy on 23 July 1914 and were later moved to the peninsula itself.[18]

In addition to the increases in armaments and command arrangements mentioned previously, the fortress command made a number of other preparations for the expected assault. Final coordination was made regarding fire control and lighter guns (37–75mm) were positioned to directly cover the open water inside the mouth of the Dardanelles to prevent minesweeping. On 13 February 1915, a battery of four 37mm anti-aircraft guns arrived from Constantinople to prevent Allied spotting aircraft from hovering over the mouth of the Dardanelles. The fortress command split the battery into two sections and positioned them at the Orhaniye fort in Asia and the Ertuğrul fort at Sedd el Bahr. The observation posts of the 9th Division, along the coastlines, were dug in to resist shellfire and were tied into the reporting network of the fortress. At the same time fields of observation were cleared around the artillery spotting stations on Gaba Tepe and Achi Baba. The torpedo stations and searchlight batteries along the straits were exercised in conjunction with the fortress artillery. Minelayers reinforced the existing belts of underwater mines and laid several new belts.

The Ottoman navy also sent a number of ships to the straits to support the fortress and the army with gunfire support. Initially, a minelayer flotilla and several destroyers conducted operations between 4 and 8 August 1914. On 6 September, the elderly ironclad *Mesudiye* anchored off Nara Point for service as a floating battery. On 13 December 1914, the British submarine B-11 sank the *Mesudiye* in shallow water. Casualties were light and six 150mm and 75mm guns were later salvaged. The navy had some experience in supporting the army with naval gunfire support during the Balkan War on the flanks of the Çatalca lines and brought in more ships. On 18 February 1915, the pre-dreadnought battleships *Torgud Reis* (the former German *Weissenburg* armed with six 280mm and eight 88mm guns) and *Barbaros Hayreddin* (the former German *Kurfürst Friedrich Wilhelm* which was similarly armed) anchored off Maidos and observation stations were established on land for fire control and spotting. The minelayers were very active and by 30 December 1914 had laid nine belts of underwater mines, 323 altogether, across the Narrows.

The British naval assault

Carden launched his first naval attack on 19 February 1915, which was the anniversary of British Admiral Duckworth's fleet's successful rushing of the Dardanelles in 1807. His first objective was the reduction and silencing of the 'outer defences' on the peninsula – the Ertuğrul fort (at Sedd el Bahr, containing two 11in., four 10in. and four 6in. guns), and the Cape Helles fort (with two 9.4in. guns, which comprised 1st Battalion, 5th Heavy Artillery Regiment) and in Asia, the Orhaniye fort (at Kum Kale, containing two 811in., and four 10in. guns, one 8in. and one 6in. gun, which comprised 2nd Battalion, 5th Heavy

Artillery Regiment). The regiment also had a 150mm howitzer battery and an 87mm field artillery battery.

Carden initially sent in three British and three French pre-dreadnoughts. Firing began at 9.51am at a range of 7,700 yards (7km) and continued on the three forts for 45 minutes with no apparent effect. Carden ordered the ships closer and then to anchor themselves to improve gunnery. The Ottoman gunners returned fire sporadically throughout the day. The battlecruiser *Inflexible* joined in at 3.00pm and *Queen Elizabeth* opened fire at 5.00pm. The bombarding fleet stopped firing at 5.20pm and withdrew in order to assess what it had accomplished. There appeared to be small returns for heavy and prolonged firing (139 12in. shells and 760 from secondary armament) with no direct hits on the enemy guns or mountings.[19] Seventy per cent of the guns appeared serviceable, although Carden believed that the magazines had been blown up and Ottoman fire control substantially disrupted. The fleet also learned that anchoring significantly improved accuracy and that direct fire was more effective than indirect fire. Severe weather and low visibility now moved in, effectively halting Carden's operations for the next week.

Operations against the outer defences resumed at 8.00am on 25 February as Carden's fleet approached the straits. In the meantime, the Ottomans had partially restored their defences and General Maxwell in Egypt contacted Carden on 20 February to offer troops. Carden expressed a desire for 10,000 men to occupy the peninsula up to the Soğanlıdere line after he completed the destruction of the outer forts. Churchill learned about this the next day and was not pleased that the operation might exceed his 'naval-only' instructions. On 24 February, the Plymouth and Chatham battalions of Royal Marines under Brigadier-General Charles N. Trotman arrived at Mudros harbour giving Carden 2,000 infantry immediately available for operations. At 10.30pm that evening, Churchill dispatched a telegram to Carden reminding him that the operation on which he was engaged consisted of forcing the Dardanelles without military assistance as Carden himself had described in his 11 January appreciation.[20] Churchill preserved the 'naval-only' character of the operation by further specifying that Carden should only use small parties of troops to destroy guns and torpedo tubes.

Unsatisfied with the results of the previous bombardment, which appeared merely to drive the gunners from their guns, Carden altered his tactics and aimed to destroy the guns. Four battleships, including the newly arrived *Queen Elizabeth*, anchored 12,000 yards (11km) offshore and began deliberate fire on the forts at the entrance. The Ottomans replied and forced several battleships to move back. The *Queen Elizabeth* fired 18 shells into Helles hitting two guns. At

12.45pm Carden sent in two battleships in column to pound the European forts and then repeated this with two French battleships at 2.00pm. By this time, the enemy gunners ceased to reply and Carden concluded that the forts were out of action. To finish the job, Carden ordered two battleships to close within 2,000 yards (1.8km) and plaster the forts with the secondary armament. Simultaneously his minesweepers, covered by three battleships and six destroyers, swept the straits entrance but found no mines. Overall, these were better results than previously achieved because some guns had definitely been destroyed or badly damaged; however, Carden was aware that the Ottomans remained capable of returning fire and ordered operations to continue by landing demolition parties.

At 2.30pm on 26 February, 45 marines landed at Sedd el Bahr to find that only one or two guns were inoperable. Covered by naval gunfire, which drove away a small counter-attack, the marines laid charges and blew up the six largest guns. Another marine party landed at Fort No. 4 and blew up three guns there as well. The lack of resistance encouraged Carden to commence operations inside the entrance. On 26 February, minesweepers moved inside the entrance sweeping the channel followed by three battleships, which began to fire at the rear of the entrance forts. About noon *Albion* and *Majestic* (which had an army howitzer positioned on each of her two turrets) engaged the Dardanos fort and a howitzer battery on the high ground beyond. Howitzer fire began to drop among the British ships and at 4.00pm, *Majestic* received a below the waterline hit causing de Robeck, who was in tactical command, to order a recall. While this was going on inside the entrance, de Robeck noticed unmanned batteries and forts along the entrance and requested permission to land parties to destroy them, which was duly approved. At 2.30pm marines landed simultaneously at Kum Kale and Sedd el Bahr. Ottoman resistance was strong in Asia forcing a withdrawal but three guns were destroyed at Sedd el Bahr.

These successes encouraged Carden, who ordered landing operations to continue in concert with minesweeping. Bad weather on 27 February halted operations although a landing party went ashore and destroyed a battery of 6in. mortars. Due to the weather the fleet did not conduct operations on the next day. Operations resumed on 1 March 1915, when Carden sent four battleships inside the straits to engage Dardanos and the howitzers for a second time. While this was in progress, de Robeck landed marines at Kum Kale, who destroyed the seven remaining guns, as well as six 12-pounders, four Nordenfeldts and a searchlight. While this was a major success the naval operations inside the straits were disappointing and apparently caused no damage. Minesweeping operations in the straits conducted that night were unsuccessful because of Ottoman fire and were abandoned. Carden launched a third attempt against Dardanos on 2 March using three battleships to bombard it most of the day. Belatedly, the fort began to vigorously return fire and by day's end one gun appeared to have been destroyed. Bad weather on 3 March forced Carden to abandon planned operations, although de Robeck was able to land marines at Sedd el Bahr to complete the destruction of the guns located there as well as a 15-pounder battery. Minesweeping continued on the night of 3/4 March with no result. More landing parties were put ashore on 4 March against the Orhaniye fort in Asia but the Ottomans repelled the landings. Although the landing operations by marines had been spectacularly successful with high returns for minimal expenditure, the naval bombardments were disappointing to the staffs. Carden remained concerned about ammunition expenditures: for example, on 3 and 4 March, 121 12in. shells had been fired with no real observable results.

On 5 March, Carden tried new tactics using the magnificent indirect-fire capabilities of the *Queen Elizabeth*. Her targets were the strongest Ottoman forts along the Narrows and she anchored 2 miles to the west of Gaba Tepe in a swept firing position from which she could fire over the peninsula itself. As the *Queen Elizabeth* could not observe the results, three Royal Navy battleships spotted for elevation by steaming in column inside the straits, at right angles to the gun-target line, so that the leading ship could observe the fall of shot before turning away. Seaplanes attempted to perform spotting for direction (left and right lateral corrections) but these either crashed or were ineffective.[21] The *Queen Elizabeth* fired 33 15in. shells against Rumeli Mecidiye and Namazgâh forts, while sustaining 17 inconsequential hits from Ottoman field artillery, which apparently caused little damage to the targeted forts. The indirect bombardment continued on the next day with the *Queen Elizabeth* pulling farther away from shore when the Ottomans brought up 150mm howitzers. This meant that full charges had to be used in order to range the 20,000-yard distance to the target (Fort Çiminlik in Asia), causing concern about tube wear and gun life expectancy. On this day the *Albion* alone spotted the fall of shot because the spotting officers from three different ships had sent contradictory corrections to the *Queen Elizabeth* on the previous day. At the same time, other battleships engaged Dardanos again. Although minesweeping resumed that night, the results of the indirect bombardment were judged to have failed.

De Robeck resumed the attacks against the Narrows on 7 March using two British battleships and several French battleships. Damage was done to some of the inner forts but both British ships were hit numerous times. The following day, de Robeck brought the *Queen Elizabeth* and three battleships inside the straits but poor visibility prevented effective engagement of the forts. This was the last attempt under Carden to do something with heavy ships. Carden's report of 10 March to the Admiralty was conflicted, reporting good progress but stating that concealed howitzer batteries had become as dangerous as the heavy coastal guns.[22] Moreover, Carden noted that demolition parties were essential to render the guns useless. Carden's men experimented with small picket boats sweeping mines on the night of 7/8 March, and again on the following night, but these efforts failed as well. French minesweepers were sent in but they were also unable to make progress against the current and the well-coordinated Ottoman defences. Conventional minesweeping using the civilian trawlers resumed on the night of 10/11 March. Operations using French ships on 11/12 March were unsuccessful and Roger Keyes took command of the minesweeping effort. The French minesweepers made a strong attack on 12/13 March using a different tactic designed to cut the mine cables rather than sweep them to the surface but this did not work either.

The ever-impatient Churchill sent Carden a cable blaming the failed minesweeping on the civilian crew's lack of determination.[23] A frustrated Carden called a meeting with his staff and captains to consider the way ahead. Ideas were kicked around and some officers supported a desperate rush of the Narrows minefields. Carden responded by aggressively pushing a strong assault on 13/14 March using the battleship *Cornwallis* to pound the searchlights while the minesweeping flotilla, heavily augmented by Royal Navy volunteers and reinforced by picket boats and the light cruiser *Amethyst*, drove into the minefields. The assault was a disaster, with two trawlers (of seven) sunk with most of their crew, four trawlers and two picket boats so damaged that they were out of action, and the *Amethyst* badly damaged. By the time the operation was called off, 27 sailors had been killed and 43 were wounded. In spite of these losses, Carden resumed the attacks and the minesweepers returned for the next three nights, but retreated almost immediately when coming under effective and intense Ottoman fire. According to the Ottomans, Carden's minesweeping flotillas swept up a total of 12 mines in three weeks of operations inside the entrance to the straits.

Operational reaffirmation

At the 26 February War Council meeting, Maurice Hankey, who rarely spoke as the secretary, opined that before the Dardanelles could be opened to ships, it might be necessary to clear the Gallipoli peninsula with troops.[24] Churchill, who had already been continually pressing Kitchener to release the 29th Division, again reaffirmed that this had become necessary. Kitchener communicated all this to Maxwell and Birdwood in Egypt identifying the mobile howitzers as potential targets for military operations. Birdwood was also given permission to ask for his entire corps should he think it necessary, which conflicted with his earlier instruction that limited army participation to minor operations. At this time, both Kitchener and Major-General Charles E. Callwell (Director of Military Operations) continued to believe that the Ottoman morale would collapse under the weight of the naval attack, beliefs which were reinforced by Carden's initially positive reports.

The ANZAC General Officer Commanding (GOC) Birdwood went to the Dardanelles in *Swiftsure* on 24 February, spent time at Mudros talking to the naval staffs and was taken up into the straits as far as possible in *Irresistible* with de Robeck. He noted that the forts at the entrance were very visible, unlike the forts inside the straits. Birdwood also noticed that when the *Irresistible* came under fire nobody was able to pinpoint its point of origin. On 3 March he sent a message to Kitchener expressing the view that it would not be possible to restrict the army's involvement to minor operations and he went on to state that he planned to use almost his entire corps to take the tip of the peninsula.[25] He noted that some 40,000 enemy troops occupied the peninsula. Birdwood sent another telegram the following day outlining his ideas about how he would attack the peninsula and, after shifting forces to the Asia shore, attack Bulair. Kitchener sent word back that same day to Birdwood that there was no intention of using the troops thus far concentrated to take the Gallipoli peninsula. When he finally met with Carden on 4 March, Birdwood became convinced that the straits could not be forced by ships alone. On 5 March, Birdwood sent the last of three telegrams to Kitchener stating this belief and adding that the operation must take some considerable time, especially if the weather turned bad.[26]

At the same time that Birdwood was sending these pessimistic assessments to Kitchener, Carden was sending more positive reports to Churchill. On 4 March, Carden reported that, although the operations had been slowed by weather, he expected that it would take 14 days of good weather to break into the Sea of Marmara. An optimistic Churchill replied to Carden with instructions about sinking the enemy fleet, cutting enemy communications and taking the Bosporus from behind. On the same day, Churchill then passed these thoughts along to Kitchener by fixing 20 March as the probable time frame for military operations to start. He reiterated his plea for one good British division to be ready to sail by 15 March and for the French to have their forces ready at Lemnos by the 20th as well. Churchill also noted with pleasure that he had heard Kitchener had chosen General Sir Ian Hamilton as the operational commander in the theatre.

On 6 March, Carden sent a message to Churchill stating the difficulties being encountered with spotting and minesweeping, and also noting that it was absolutely necessary to land and destroy each enemy gun. Subsequently, he continued to ask that ammunition, aircraft and more capable minesweepers be dispatched to rectify these deficiencies. At the Admiralty, Jackson now weighed in with Carden by recommending that the peninsula be occupied before the straits could be considered safe for passage due to the presence of Ottoman artillery. Undeterred, Churchill continued to press Carden for a purely naval rush on the straits. There were multiple views about the way ahead at the War Council meeting on 10 March 1915, at which Kitchener released the 29th Division for operations in the Mediterranean but restricted the use of land forces until the Bosporus was taken and Ottoman fleet destroyed. He also stated that, according to his intelligence, the Allied force available totalled 130,000 men to pit against some 180,000 Ottomans. Kitchener's view was that the assembling army was necessary for landing and defeating the Ottoman Army in the vicinity of Constantinople after the straits had been forced. The following day, Kitchener informed the general staff that he had ordered Hamilton to establish the general headquarters of a Mediterranean Expeditionary Force. On 12 March the Admiralty transferred the Royal Naval Division to Kitchener's command. At the same time Sir Edward Grey and the Foreign Office hoped to bring the Greeks into the campaign actively but by mid-month these efforts had collapsed in the face of Russian obstruction.

Although Churchill had heard Hamilton's name associated with the campaign as early as 4 March, Hamilton himself was not brought into the picture until 12 March, when he was called to Kitchener's office.[27] According to Hamilton, a terse Kitchener outlined the strategic situation in broad terms. He then laid down some instructions indicating that the 29th Division was only temporarily Hamilton's and that it was earmarked for France. Callwell, the Director of Military Operations, joined them and, using a map, took Hamilton through what was known about the Greek amphibious plan to take the peninsula with a force of 150,000 men. When Hamilton asked about his staff, Kitchener brought in James Wolfe-Murray, Chief of the Imperial General Staff and General Archie Murray, who had Major-General Walter P. Braithwaite in tow and introduced Braithwaite as Hamilton's chief of the general staff. Towards the end of the meeting, Hamilton asked for aircraft and pilots, to which Kitchener replied that he had none to offer.

The next day (13 March) Hamilton had a second interview with Kitchener at which he received written instructions outlining Kitchener's expectations for the conduct of the military operation. In summary these were:[28]

1. Large-scale use of land forces was only contemplated in the event that the fleet failed to get through and had exhausted every effort.
2. All British forces must be assembled before undertaking any serious effort.
3. Forcing the straits would not be abandoned and close co-operation between military and naval commanders was required to ensure success.
4. Minor operations to clear or destroy guns might be necessary but with minimal forces and the Gallipoli peninsula was not to be permanently occupied.
5. The key to the peninsula was the Kilid Bahr plateau, which was assumed to be heavily fortified.
6. Establishing an entrenched line at Bulair was permitted but only if it could be supported from both flanks by the fleet and then only with minimal forces.
7. The occupation of the Asian side was 'strongly deprecated'.
8. Until the Bosporus was cleared, the Ottoman fleet destroyed and the Russian corps landed, operations should be undertaken with caution. Once the British, French and Russian forces were in place, combined plans for the defeat or surrender of the Ottoman Army would be effected. Until this happened, street fighting in the city of Constantinople was to be avoided.
9. The army must assist the fleet in cutting Ottoman communications between Europe and Asia.
10. Should the Ottoman Army retire to Asia, the occupation of Constantinople and Thrace should proceed.
11. As British troops might be withdrawn rapidly after the operation, Allied troops should be used as garrisons.

These instructions were an operational reaffirmation of the campaign as Kitchener and Churchill had envisioned it and had agreed to at the 26 February War Council meeting. They also demonstrate that Kitchener remained focused on Constantinople rather than the Dardanelles. However, at the Admiralty on the same day, Jackson sent a minute to the Admiralty chief of staff, Vice-Admiral Sir Henry Oliver, recommending that Carden use the military forces that he had available to occupy and clear the peninsula and from there 'demolish' the Ottoman artillery on the Asian side. Churchill forwarded Jackson's minute to Kitchener and asked for his comment. Kitchener replied immediately stating that unless Ottoman strength on the

WAR COUNCIL CAMPAIGN DESIGN, 13 MARCH 1915

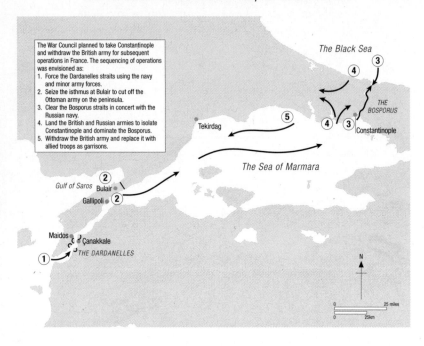

The War Council planned to take Constantinople and withdraw the British army for subsequent operations in France. The sequencing of operations was envisioned as:
1. Force the Dardanelles straits using the navy and minor army forces.
2. Seize the isthmus at Bulair to cut off the Ottoman army on the peninsula.
3. Clear the Bosporus straits in concert with the Russian navy.
4. Land the British and Russian armies to isolate Constantinople and dominate the Bosporus.
5. Withdraw the British army and replace it with allied troops as garrisons.

The Black Sea

THE BOSPORUS

Constantinople

Tekirdag

The Sea of Marmara

Gulf of Saros Bulair

Gallipoli

Maidos Çanakkale

THE DARDANELLES

N

0   25 miles
0   25km

peninsula had been exaggerated and Kilid Bahr less fortified than thought, no large-scale operations should be attempted until the 29th Division arrived. This reply depressed Churchill, who knew that the division would not arrive in theatre until mid-April at the earliest, and who was beginning to sense that the naval-only scheme was unravelling.

'On the afternoon of Friday, 13th March, Sir Ian Hamilton left London by special train with a staff of thirteen officers' bound for Marseilles and the fast cruiser *Phaeton*.[29] On the trip he examined the scant bits of information the general staff had provided him with – the 1912 Ottoman Army handbook, a pre-war report on the Dardanelles defences, and a map. Three intelligence officers had been sent ahead to find out what they could about the enemy defences and would meet Hamilton upon arrival in the theatre. The French general staff was concerned about Hamilton's plans and queried him en route, to which Hamilton provided an evasive and open-ended response. Hamilton characterized his staff as 'bewildered' and, after arriving in Marseilles, Braithwaite showed him the manning chart for his staff with mostly blank spaces where officers' names should have been.[30]

The relief of Vice-Admiral Carden

On 11 March, the Admiralty sent Carden a signal that he should accelerate the tempo of his operations, suggesting that he engage the forts sequentially at decisive ranges, put landing parties ashore to demolish guns, and sweep up the minefields. The message ended with a query as to whether Carden believed that the point requiring decisive action had been reached. It was a thinly disguised, but clear, notice to push ahead rapidly. Carden replied on 14 March in the affirmative but noted that 'in my opinion military operations on a large scale should be commenced immediately in order to insure my communication line'. The Admiralty replied the next day instructing Carden to 'concert any military operations on a large scale which you consider necessary with General Hamilton when he arrives Tuesday night'.[31] The long telegram continued with a detailed step-by-step summary of how the Admiralty expected that Carden would execute a major push into the Narrows and stressed the urgency of the operation. Carden was explicitly instructed not to rush the straits or to commit to decisive military operations without consulting the Admiralty. According to Churchill, these two Admiralty directives were intended to provide Carden with confidence that he had political cover should things go badly and ships were lost. Carden replied at 9.15am, 15 March that he intended to proceed vigorously if he had good visibility.[32]

Confident that action was imminent, Churchill took 'two days' holiday' to tour the front-line trenches in Flanders and it was there, at Sir John French's headquarters on 16 March, that he received a copy of an alarming telegram from Carden to the Admiralty.[33] Carden stated that, on the advice of his medical officer, he was obliged to go on the sick list and he recommended that de Robeck take command of the fleet and its ongoing operations. It is unclear today exactly what was wrong medically with Carden but most historians believe that he suffered some sort of mental and physical collapse. It is clear from the messages between Carden and the Admiralty that he felt pressure to accelerate the assault on the Narrows. It is also clear from the messages, particularly Admiralty 109, 1.40pm, 15 March 1915, which said he would 'be informed later about the ammunition, aeroplanes and minesweepers' that Carden's requests for these assets were being ignored or tabled in London.[34] Carden's dilemma was that the assets he had available were insufficient to the task at hand: principally that his ships needed aircraft for spotting the lateral corrections for indirect fire and he needed faster and more capable purpose-built fleet minesweepers to clear the Narrows. Carden's evasive and ambiguous statements regarding the need for immediate large-scale military operations threw sand in the wheels of the Admiralty's timetable in an unsuccessful attempt to buy more time to resolve his dilemma. Pushed to action and unable to solve the tactical problem, Carden took himself out of command.

With Carden out of the picture, Churchill now had a dilemma of command and continuity of operations involving naval seniority as Rear Admiral de Robeck, the operational second-in-command, was junior to Rear Admiral Wemyss, the actual second-in-command, who commanded the fleet base at Mudros harbour. De Robeck was the man with both knowledge of Carden's plans and experience of command inside the straits while Wemyss was immersed in the detailed administrative planning of fleet support as well as for the imminent arrival of major ground forces. Moreover, Churchill did not have much confidence in de Robeck's abilities. Wemyss spontaneously solved the problem by telegraphing the Admiralty that he was willing to act under de Robeck's orders if that was thought advisable. On 17 March, Churchill approved the temporary promotion of de Robeck to vice-admiral but sent him a personal and secret telegram directly and unequivocally asking whether de Robeck fully supported and would execute Carden's planned assault on the Narrows.[35] De Robeck answered in the affirmative and stated that, weather permitting, operations would begin the next day.

At 3.00pm on 17 March, the *Phaeton* anchored in Tenedos and Hamilton went over to the *Queen Elizabeth* for an initial meeting with de Robeck. Also attending were Wemyss, Keyes and Braithwaite as well as Admiral Guépratte and General Albert d'Amade, who had arrived that same day. De Robeck opened the meeting by explaining his chief difficulty, which he considered to be the enemy's mobile artillery.[36] He confirmed to Hamilton that he intended to attack the following day and that he felt he could force a passage without large-scale military operations. Importantly, de Robeck made Hamilton aware that the Ottomans were feverishly fortifying the peninsula against amphibious assault and, moreover, that Lemnos was unsuitable for the concentration of a large army because of the scarcity of water on the island. These estimates regarding the employment of large-scale forces conformed to Hamilton's understandings and he wired this information to Kitchener that evening. On 18 March, de Robeck wired Churchill, 'Weather fine. Operations about to begin.'[37]

Ottoman reaction

The Ottoman general staff warned the fortress command of the impending attack, which had itself read reports taken from the Athens and Salonika newspapers on 16 February.[38] The initial assault on 19 February barely damaged the outer forts and the Royal Navy ship-to-shore gunnery against point targets

STRAITS DEFENCES, 18 MARCH 1915

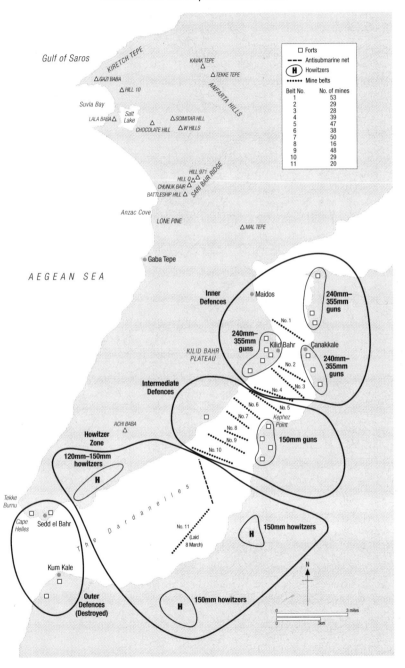

Gulf of Saros

KIRETCH TEPE

KAVAK TEPE
△

△ *TEKKE TEPE*

△ *GAZI BABA*

△ *HILL 10*

ANFARTA HILLS

Suvla Bay

LALA BABA △
Salt Lake
△

△ *SCIMITAR HILL*

CHOCOLATE HILL   △ *W HILLS*

	Forts
– – –	Antisubmarine net
(H)	Howitzers
······	Mine belts

Belt No.	No. of mines
1	53
2	29
3	28
4	39
5	47
6	38
7	50
8	16
9	48
10	29
11	20

HILL 971
HILL Q △ △
CHUNUK BAIR △
BATTLESHIP HILL △

SARI BAIR RIDGE

Anzac Cove
LONE PINE

△ *MAL TEPE*

● Gaba Tepe

A E G E A N   S E A

Inner Defences

● Maidos

□

240mm– 355mm guns

No. 1

240mm– 355mm guns

KILID BAHR PLATEAU

Kilid Bahr
□
□ □
□

Çanakkale
●

No. 2

□

240mm– 355mm guns

No. 3

No. 4

Intermediate Defences

□

No. 5

No. 6

No. 7

Kephez Point

No. 8

150mm guns

No. 9

ACHI BABA
△

Howitzer Zone

No. 10

120mm–150mm howitzers

(H)

Tekke Burnu

□ ● □

Cape Helles Sedd el Bahr

The Dardanelles

No. 11

(Laid 8 March)

(H)

150mm howitzers

Kum Kale
●
□

N
▲

□

Outer Defences (Destroyed)

(H) **150mm howitzers**

0		3 miles
0		3km

69

was notably ineffective.[39] Carden's attacks continued but did not destroy the 5th Heavy Artillery Regiment's guns in the outer forts, however, they did force the crews to abandon them. As a result, the fortress command inactivated the 5th Heavy Artillery Regiment on 25 February and began to reassign most of its men to the 3rd Heavy Artillery Regiment.[40] III Corps commander Esat Pasha ordered Mustafa Kemal to prepare to rotate an infantry battalion into the village of Krithia. The increased intensity of Allied activity, in turn, caused the fortress command to request that the 19th Division be brought down to the peninsula from Rodosto and on 1 March the first battalion of Kemal's division landed at Maidos. At the same time, the 8th Heavy Artillery Regiment began the process of shifting the positions of its batteries of howitzers to prevent their being acquired as targets after firing disclosed their location. This tactic became something of a 'shell game' and continued throughout the campaign.

On 18 February, in addition to its fixed and mobile artillery, the fortress command controlled the 9th Infantry Division for the defence of the Gallipoli peninsula. The division headquarters was co-located in Çanakkale with the headquarters of the fortress command, although the division was deployed on both sides of the straits. Two regiments, the 26th and 27th Infantry Regiments, composed the garrison of the lower peninsula deploying platoons on the beaches while maintaining battalion reserves for counter-attacks. Jandarma units heavily reinforced these regiments and were used for beach observation and defence. The division's remaining regiment lay south of Kum Kale and was a component, with jandarma and depot battalions, of a brigade-sized force designated as the Menderes Detachment. Altogether these deployments put about 8,000 riflemen defending the lower peninsula and about 10,000 riflemen defending the Asian side. Esat Pasha's 7th Infantry Division of 13,000 men guarded the upper peninsula and isthmus of Bulair.

Every day from 2 until 8 March, Carden's fleet shelled the intermediate defences with little result. Carden's attacks were 'utterly lacking in vigor and determination'[41] and the minesweepers made little progress against the current flowing swiftly against them. One of seven minesweepers was sunk by Ottoman gunfire for a gain of three mines exploded. While this left the British unsatisfied, the naval activity was especially worrisome to the commander of the 9th Division, who sent a lengthy message to Cevat Pasha (the fortress commander) expressing concern over the possibility of an enemy landing at Kum Kale.[42] This so worried the Ottomans that the high command notified the 11th Infantry Division to move to the area on 9 March. The arrival of this division was intended to allow the fortress command to pull the 9th Division's regiment out of Kum Kale allowing it to concentrate on the peninsula. On 4 March,

Mustafa Kemal had two infantry regiments and some artillery massed in reserve at the Serafim Farm, which added another 6,000 riflemen to the defence of the lower peninsula. By the end of the first week of March 1915, the entire 19th Infantry Division was in reserve positions just south of Maidos.

During the combat operations that lasted from 19 February until mid-March 1915, the Ottomans fired off about 4,700 artillery shells. However, most of the firing came from the guns of 5th Heavy Artillery Regiment in the forts at the mouth of the Dardanelles and from 8th Heavy Artillery Regiment in the howitzer zone.[43] On 26 February this regiment fired 343 shells. In the action of 4 March the Ottomans fired 292 shells and a further 347 shells on the following day. On 7 March they shot off 714 shells; 51 shells on 9 March; 1,882 shells on 10 March; 28 on 11 March; 41 shells on 12 March; and 974 shells on 13 March.[44] Most of the firing during this period came from the mobile howitzers and from the intermediate defences, while firing from the powerful heavy batteries from the forts at the Narrows occurred only on one day of the battle (10 March).[45]

The naval attack of 18 March

At 11.25am on 18 March 1915, a squadron of the four most powerful British ships went into action by engaging the Narrows forts while older pre-dreadnoughts hammered the intermediate defences. The howitzers of the Ottoman intermediate zone began to return fire from 120mm and 150mm pieces. The howitzer fire was heavy but comfortably inaccurate and ineffective. At 11.55am the guns of the Dardanos and the Baykuş Mecudiye Batteries (150mm guns) began to fire and at noon the Rumeli Mecudiye Battery (240mm guns) joined in. The Allied ships pounded both the howitzer zones and the batteries. By noon many of the intermediate Ottoman forts appeared to have been silenced. Then at 1.20pm the heavy guns of the Anadolu Hamidiye Fort (355mm and 240mm guns) opened fire. Ten minutes later an Allied aircraft appeared over the straits and the European central group (Rumeli Mecidiye, Hamidiye, and Namazgah Forts – all with 240mm guns) began to draw very heavy fire. The Allied naval gunfire cut the underground telephone cables linking the forts to the fortress command centre leaving them isolated in command and control. Enemy fire began to fall effectively on Anadolu Hamidiye and Rumeli Mecidiye causing casualties and temporarily silencing Anadolu Hamidiye.

French battleships closed to within 8,800 yards (8,000m) of the Narrows towards 2.00pm, at which time the Rumeli Mecidiye Fort opened fire. The fort had been hit hard by several direct heavy shells, which killed ten men and wounded 24. The magazines were ablaze and out of the terror and confusion one of the most famous stories in Turkey about the naval attack of 18 March emerged. It involved a heroic corporal named Seyit, who was assigned to the coastal defence fort. The fort's main battery was equipped with four 240mm heavy guns, which fired shells weighing 140–250kg (depending on the type). Corporal Seyit commanded the third gun, which was hit by shellfire at the height of the battle, damaging the auto-loading gear and rendering it technically inoperable. To the amazement of the huddled gunners, the indomitable Seyit lifted one of the rounds onto his back and carried it to the gun. Somehow he loaded the round, aimed the piece and fired the cannon. Popular histories in Turkey assert that Seyit's shell hit HMS *Ocean*, although this has never been confirmed. A famous photo was taken (undoubtedly posed after the battle) of Corporal Seyit carrying a shell on his back and there is a statue of Seyit on the shores of the Dardanelles commemorating this event.

Just after 2.00pm, in the middle of a recall to allow a relief squadron of British ships to move forward, the French pre-dreadnought *Bouvet* suddenly blew up, sinking within minutes. This cheered the Turks, who observed the frantic efforts to rescue the handful of survivors. Howitzer fire renewed, including 210mm fire from the Tenger Havan (heavy mortar) Battery and, although a magazine fire broke out in the Namazgah Fort, the gunners there opened fire about 3.15pm. The Anadolu Hamidiye Fort came back into action five minutes later by firing at *Irresistible*. Shortly thereafter the French *Gaulois* and *Suffren* were both seriously damaged by gunfire. The French squadron was essentially out of action. Undeterred, de Robeck continued to pound the Ottomans, and at 4.00pm sent in his trawlers. Intense fire from the mobile 210mm and 150mm howitzers of the 8th Heavy Artillery Regiment in Wehrle's howitzer zone forced an immediate retreat of the minesweepers. The tide of battle continued to shift against the Allies.

At 4.11pm, the modern battlecruiser *Inflexible* struck a mine and nearly sank. Minutes later the pre-dreadnought *Irresistible* was also mined. At 5.00pm, a discouraged de Robeck called off the operation and a final few rounds were fired at *Irresistible* at 5.30pm from the Rumeli Mecidiye Fort. Although the Turkish guns were now silent, disaster continued to stalk the Royal Navy. At 6.05pm, the pre-dreadnought *Ocean*, after attempting to tow the damaged *Irresistible* out of harm's way, also struck a mine and began to sink. Both battleships were abandoned and sank later that night. The Ottomans held the field and the straits, and their minefields were intact. Moreover de Robeck's fleet had suffered serious losses. Altogether, the Allies lost three old battleships, and suffered two old battleships and a modern battlecruiser seriously damaged.

Against this loss, the Ottomans appeared to have lost a few guns and had a handful of mines exploded. It was small return for a heavy investment.

Most of the Turkish casualties were concentrated in the Rumeli Mecidiye Fort but overall losses were very light, totalling 97 casualties.[46] Four Ottoman officers were killed and one was wounded while 22 soldiers were killed and another 52 wounded.[47] Additionally, three German enlisted men were killed and one German officer and 14 enlisted men were wounded. On 19 March, Cevat Pasha published orders announcing the award of medals for gallantry in action.[48]

The heaviest firing from the large-calibre guns came on 18 March 1915, during de Robeck's climactic attempt to force the Narrows. By this date, the 5th Heavy Artillery Regiment at the entrance of the straits had been eliminated from the Ottoman order of battle due to bombardment and the demolitions of the Royal Marine landing parties. Most of the British accounts of the firing that day characterized the Ottoman firing as particularly heavy, and the Ottoman histories note that 2,250 shells were expended that day. In fact, most of these were the indirect shells from the howitzers and heavy mortars. Altogether on 18 March the 3rd Heavy Artillery Regiment fired 190 shells, the 4th Heavy Artillery Regiment fired 240 shells, and the howitzers and heavy mortars of the 8th Heavy Artillery Regiment fired 1,820 shells. Although 368 more shells were expended than had been fired on 10 March (previously the most intense day of Ottoman artillery firing), comparatively few shells came from the heavy coastal guns in the forts at the Narrows.

Based on his German source (Major Mühlmann), Churchill stated that 'long-range HE' shells alone were effective against armoured ships. Later Moorehead noted that 'armour-piercing' shells (AP) alone had the power to destroy battleships. These statements most likely refer to flat-trajectory heavy ship-killing guns of the type located in the forts at the Narrows. However, it is doubtful whether anybody really knew what types of shells were hitting what targets and exactly what damage was being inflicted by which types of shell. While it may make sense that flat-trajectory HE or AP were the most effective types against battleships, this is by no means certain, since the Ottomans fired a variety of flat-trajectory and high-angle artillery ammunition on 18 March. What is known today is that, of the ammunition available to the heavy guns of 3rd and 4th Heavy Artillery Regiments on 14 August 1914, only 201 rounds of 355/35 and 240/35 calibre were fired on 18 March 1915, and a lesser amount may have been fired on 10 March 1915. None of the remaining heavy guns (in the 210/20–355/22 calibre range) or mortars of these regiments came into action during these engagements. Assuming that the Ottomans fired perhaps 50 rounds from the 35 calibre heavy guns on 10 March, the total expended rounds (regardless of type) in these regiments would have been about 251, leaving a total available inventory of 1,030 shells of all types for these weapons. Since the shorter-ranging heavy coastal guns of lower calibres had not come into action at all on either day, the Ottomans maintained an on-site inventory of at least 4,034 shells of all types for the heavy 210/20–355/22 classes of ordnance. To this must be added 1,106 210/6.4 heavy mortar shells, about 6,000 150/10.8 howitzer shells, and an undetermined number of 120/30 and 120/11.6 howitzer shells. Ammunition for the lighter guns added up to approximately 24,000 shells. While these totals pale in comparison to the astonishing inventories assembled on the Western Front, they are nevertheless significant. Considering that on the heaviest day of firing, 18 March 1915, a total of only 2,250 shells were expended, the Ottomans clearly had enough shells to continue the fight.[49]

Although the Ottoman official history presents an incomplete picture of the total munitions available for the defence of the Dardanelles, it would appear from the data presented that the Ottomans had an adequate supply of ammunition with which to continue the battle. The powerful inner forts on the Narrows that fielded the heaviest guns were the least engaged of the Ottoman forts between 19 February and 18 March 1915. In the immediate aftermath of the 18 March engagement, the Ottomans went to work to redistribute ammunition and to repair damaged guns and guns that had suffered mechanical failure.[50] Moreover, casualties were extremely light and, having observed the sinking or mining of six enemy capital ships, Ottoman morale was sky-high at the end of de Robeck's aborted attack.

Assessments

The most compelling analysis of why the naval attack failed came from the pen of Professor Arthur J. Marder.[51] Marder explained:

> [o]n the technical naval side, the real obstacles were the minefields of the Narrows, against which the minesweeping was utterly inefficient, and their protecting batteries, which the naval guns never silenced. The minefields were the crux of the situation, since the old battleships could evidently be sunk by striking one mine. It could be accomplished only if the minefield batteries could be dominated while the sweeping was going on. But it was not possible for the warships to knock them out. Long-range or indirect fire proved ineffective. To be effective, the ships would have had to close in on the coastal guns and pound away, and this was not possible until the mines were cleared. Thus was the vicious circle complete.'[52]

As Marder noted, the most effective defences of the Dardanelles were the minefields that the Ottomans had begun laying in August 1914. The guns simply provided covering fire to keep them from being swept up by the enemy. Sir Julian Corbett noted the Ottomans had laid nearly 350 mines and calculated the odds that, given this number of unswept mines, only one of 16 Allied battleships could reasonably hope to reach the Sea of Marmara in an attempt to rush the straits.[53] The Turkish histories assert that, in actuality, a total of 402 were laid between 4 August 1914 and 8 March 1915, in 11 lines numbered serially.[54]

Over the past 100 years Western authors have stressed that the Ottomans were unready to defend the straits and the peninsula until April 1915. However, at no time after 17 August 1914 (two and a half months prior to the outbreak of hostilities) were the Dardanelles defences unready to receive an attack. On that date the heavy artillery regiments of the 2nd Artillery Brigade were manned and there were 133 mines laid in the straits. By the outbreak of hostilities, on 3 November 1914, the howitzers of the 8th Heavy Artillery Regiment were in position, as were the 40,000 men of the Ottoman III Corps, and there were a total of 191 mines in the water. On that date, the British had two battlecruisers and two French pre-dreadnoughts and no ground troops other than ships' detachments of marines available for operations.

The ANZAC began arriving in Egypt in mid-December 1914 but it was largely untrained and needed time to organize and train. Its last components arrived at the end of January 1915 and, theoretically, it had about 30,000 incompletely trained men available for operations. However, with the Ottoman Fourth Army offensive aimed at the Suez Canal coming in late January, the ANZAC was locked in place for the defence of Egypt. Whether Kitchener or Maxwell would have released it, at least until mid-February at the earliest, is difficult to determine at best. In any case, by the time of the 19 February naval attack, the Ottoman fortress command and III Corps had 50,000 well-trained men, armed with 34,500 rifles, 16 machine guns, and 313 cannons, on hand for the defence of the straits (as well as 323 mines laid in the Narrows).[55] These units were confident and experienced, and had been exercising their defensive plans for months.

Two thousand Royal Marines arrived at Lemnos on 24 February and, by 18 March, most of the Royal Naval Division was available as well, but these forces had no artillery. However, by that time, the well-trained and well-equipped Ottoman 11th Infantry Division had deployed near Kum Kale to balance the equation. At the end of March, the French division and the British 29th Division arrived in the Mediterranean but they were not loaded or ready for amphibious landings. Balancing these forces, the Ottoman 3rd Infantry Division arrived near Kum Kale on 31 March and a provisional corps-level headquarters activated there as well. Moreover, at the same time, the Ottoman general staff assigned the well-trained 5th Division at Saros Bay to the newly activating Fifth Army. Thus, by 15 April, Hamilton's Mediterranean Expeditionary Force (MEF) comprised 53 infantry battalions (and several cavalry brigades) while Liman von Sanders' Fifth Army comprised 54 infantry battalions (and several jandarma regiments).

Without question the powerful Royal Navy had the potential, with the further marshalling of ships and men, to force the Dardanelles after March 1915.[56] However, this would obviously have entailed greater losses at a period of great danger. Clearly there was no 'open door', nor was there a period of acute vulnerability in the straits' defences, either before or after the Allied naval attacks. There is no substance to the assertion that the British had the potential to force easily the Dardanelles with the forces available to Carden or de Robeck at any time before 18 March or to de Robeck and Hamilton before 25 April 1915.

At the strategic level, the British War Council began the Dardanelles campaign in agreement, but as Carden's attempts to break through failed, opinion in the council began to diverge. Although Churchill remained a staunch advocate of a naval-only campaign against the Dardanelles, Kitchener and the army staff began to waver about whether the campaign would require land forces. This ambiguity trickled down to Carden and, after 12 March, to Hamilton as well. Carden buckled under the pressure leading to a change of command. The War Council then put pressure on the new commander, Admiral de Robeck, to continue with Carden's plan. Operationally, Carden's plans envisioned a sequential and step-by-step reduction of the Ottoman defences.

The Ottoman high command, in opposition, felt no such ambiguity and maintained a strategic focus on the retention of the Dardanelles straits. This enabled them to steadfastly improve and reinforce the defences. Enver also had to maintain strategic balance because Ottoman intelligence indicated that a Russian amphibious descent on the Bosporus would follow an Anglo-French descent on the Dardanelles. The Ottomans were also aided significantly by the fact that Enver Pasha could unilaterally make strategic decisions immediately. This put the Ottomans well inside the Allied decision cycles. Operationally, the Ottoman plans were based on defensive planning that dated to 1912 and which had been refined over time. Of note, the Ottomans abandoned their outer defences almost immediately since they could be attacked at will. This then transferred the Ottoman operational main effort to the inner defences inside the mouth of the Dardanelles, which put the British fleet inside the range fans of Ottoman guns and howitzers.

Tactically, Carden's attacks were tentative and never employed all of his forces in an all-out assault. That said, at each step he took, his staff carefully assessed outcomes, successes and failures, and adjusted the fleet's tactics. When it was apparent that shellfire alone would not destroy the Ottoman forts, Carden turned to landing parties, indicating a willingness to move away from the plan and innovate. Once he had destroyed the outer defences, Carden became more cautious and did not want to risk his fleet inside the straits. The Ottoman tactical response was fairly simple and it revolved around the steadfast manning of lighter coastal guns and the agility of the howitzer batteries to maintain their immunity from Allied naval gunfire.

Chapter Four

ARMS AND MEN: INSTITUTIONS, ORGANIZATIONS AND COMMAND

This chapter orients the reader to the combatant armies as military institutions, with an emphasis on the British and Ottoman forces. For the purposes of this book, the term military institutions includes, but is not limited to, organizations, doctrines and command selection. Today the term has come to include such things as organizational culture and command climate. The Australian and New Zealand Army Corps (ANZAC) is treated as a component of the British Army, for the reason that it was a subordinate element of a larger British force in the campaign itself and because, as a military institution at this point in the war, it mirrored the British Army in almost every significant way. The focus of the chapter is at corps and field army level, reflecting the kinds of manoeuvre units employed at the operational level of war in 1915.

The British Army

As the dominant European naval power, Great Britain's army had remained small in comparison to those of its continental rivals. Unlike the navy, which bore the title Royal, the British Army came into being with the Act of Union in 1707 with the amalgamation of English and Scottish regiments into a single army and was the junior service. The army was primarily expeditionary and conducted land campaigns of limited scale and duration, although at times – such as the peninsular campaigns in the Napoleonic Wars – the army might remain engaged for an extended period. Importantly, the British Army was a professional force composed of long-service volunteers and remained so until the First World War. This tradition, as well as financial constraints, kept the army to a very small size and it remained based on a system of local regiments. However, the army's poor performance in the Crimean War led to the Cardwell reforms of the 1870s, which fundamentally changed the British Army as an institution by localizing and linking regiments to counties, standardizing regimental organizational structure, eliminating the purchase of commissions, and shortening enlistment options to create a reserve force. The Childers reforms in 1881 then established a system of regimentally linked regular and militia battalions, creating what amounted to a sizeable but decentralized reserve force. In the 19th century, for operations overseas, the British Army formed ad hoc combat divisions with no fixed or standardized organizational basis, moreover, it had no formally organized military staffs, such as the German and French armies were developing. Likewise the combat experiences of the British Army were related to the policing of the empire and remained largely colonial and expeditionary. The Boer War – when half a million men were sent to South Africa between 1899 and 1901 – changed everything for the British Army.

The Boer War was a conventional war between small units for a brief period before it devolved into a counter-guerrilla conflict on a scale previously unthinkable for Britain. Many of the early encounters were disasters for the army and the counter-guerrilla campaign that followed was enormously costly in resources and time. Like the Crimean War, the Boer War exposed many defects in the British military system, which were embarrassing and costly to the empire. The War Office convened a commission of inquiry to determine what had gone wrong and recommend changes. In early 1904, the committee, led by Lord Esher, released the *Report of the War Office (Reconstitution) Committee*, which was popularly known as the Esher Report. The report recommended significant changes in military policy, including the establishment of an army council (modelled on the board of admiralty), the establishment of a general staff, and the reorganization of the War Office. In turn, the Esher Report drove further reforms aimed at modernizing the army and making it more efficient. Known as the Haldane reforms, it was these early 20th-century reforms that had the most important impact on the British Army at Gallipoli.

Sir Richard Haldane served as the Secretary of State for War 1906–12, and his legacy was to provide Britain with a deployable and expandable army in 1914. There were two drivers of change that Haldane reacted to – first there was the Esher Report and, second, there were increasing tensions with Germany as well as a growing friendly relationship with France. In 1904, Great Britain and France signed the Entente Cordiale formalizing colonial claims and ending a 500-year history of animosity between these countries. Informal talks between the military staffs of both countries began shortly thereafter. The First Moroccan Crisis of 1905–06 between Germany and France increased tensions visibly and alarmed many in the British government. The Admiralty was already gravely concerned about German naval expansion and was poised to undertake a programme of building the new dreadnought battleships. Haldane took it upon himself to prepare the British Army for continental war and to move towards standardization.

Haldane's first major step in 1907 was to create a formal expeditionary force composed of six standardized infantry divisions and a cavalry division (in its earliest form known as the Striking Force). He followed this by pushing the Territorial and Reserve Forces Act of 1907 through parliament, which established a reserve of 14 Territorial infantry divisions and 14 Territorial cavalry brigades. Over the next two years, army training regulations were rewritten to include the lessons of the Boer War and a university- and public schools-based Officers' Training Corps was established. In 1909, Haldane replaced the ineffective general staff, which had been established in 1904, with the Imperial General Staff. This organization did not have the overarching authority or expertise of its German and French counterparts and, rather than directing military operations, the Chief of the Imperial General Staff (CIGS) became the military advisor to the Cabinet and his staff responsible for administrative rather than operational matters. Although not formally allied with France, British officers began informal staff talks with their French counterparts, which by 1911 had matured into a promise to send the expeditionary force to France in the event of a German invasion.

After the Crimean War, a part of the Royal Military College evolved into the Staff College at Camberley in 1857. Initially the Staff College was not popular in the British officer corps, but after the Franco-Prussian War of 1870–71, it gained credibility and an increasing number of capable men chose to attend. Selection was by examination or by recommendation. The Staff College course was two years in length and not much priority was given to examinations. Unlike its German and Ottoman counterparts, however, the British Staff College never gained prestige or a dominating role in defence matters. Moreover, in comparison to Germany, the British staff course was weak on staff procedures and tactics. Camberley graduates were noted as having 'passed staff college' (psc) and in 1914 there were only 447 psc in the entire British Army.[1] The main dilemma, of course, was the fact that few of the students or faculty had previous staff experiences and few of the graduates went to high-level staff assignments after completing the course. Although Britain had a general staff after 1909, it did not have a general staff corps of Staff College graduates to assign to such an organization. The Esher Report had recommended the creation of such a *corps d'élite* but this idea conflicted with the somewhat casual attitude towards professionalism that characterized pre-war British officers.

As an institution, the British Army by 1914 was something of a work in progress. It was moving out of a century of small wars and colonial experiences and into an era of continental obligations. It was unique among the European powers in that it was composed of volunteers, which severely limited its expansion in wartime. Its general staff had been in existence for ten years and there were an alarmingly low number of available Staff College graduates. Moreover, there were internal institutional politics that periodically affected the high command, which revolved around cliques (commonly referred to as rings or gangs) of officers and their protégés. In 1914, the men running the British Army were characterized by their association with Field Marshal Lord Roberts and their records of participation in the Boer War. The British Army was, generally, apolitical but of concern in the summer of 1914 was the recent Curragh Mutiny, staged by conservative army officers, who refused to implement reforms in Ireland.

Unlike its continental counterparts, the British Army had no field armies organized during peacetime. After 1907, there were, however, plans for an expeditionary force to deploy to France in the event of a German attack on that country. The General Headquarters (GHQ) of the expeditionary force existed only on paper and activated only for several army manoeuvres before the war. As a result, the British Army had almost no experience in the conduct of large-scale operations. The BEF in France and the Egyptian Expeditionary Force (EEF) were formed in August 1914 and became the controlling army-level headquarters for the deployed British forces. Kitchener established a third GHQ for the Mediterranean Expeditionary Force (MEF) on 11 March 1915 with the assignment of General Sir Ian Hamilton as Commander-in-Chief (CinC) and Major-General W. P. Braithwaite as Chief of the General Staff (CGS). In 1915 British expeditionary force staffs were led by a CGS but the composition of the staff varied greatly according to the size and mission of the force.

Hamilton and several officers left London two days later before the staffs could be assembled. Over the next month, officers from the UK and Egypt joined the MEF staff in the Mediterranean. As constituted, the MEF staff comprised a general staff officer 1 (Operations) (GSO1), who functioned as the chief of plans and operations. Administration was handled by a deputy adjutant general (DAG) and logistics by a deputy quarter master general (DQMG). There were special staff officers for artillery, engineers, signals and supply and transport, who all worked for the CGS as well.

As a result of the Esher Report's recommendations, the British Army inactivated six army corps districts, which were largely paper formations anyway, and replaced them with administrative districts. In terms of operational-level formations, the British Army in 1914 had only seven regular division and one corps headquarters organized and staffed for war service. This was a result of financial penury rather than a statement of the army's approach to modern war. These formations were I Corps at Aldershot and six numbered infantry divisions. There were 85 infantry battalions remaining or enough to man a further seven infantry divisions, but these were scattered throughout Britain's worldwide empire. The I Corps commander was also 'double hatted' as the commander of the Aldershot Training Command and spent much of his time supervising routine training activities rather than preparing plans for war. With the exception of two divisions concentrated near Aldershot, the other four organized infantry divisions were scattered in garrisons throughout the British Isles. There was a second corps headquarters on Salisbury Plain (II Corps) but its staff existed on paper and it was only activated periodically for exercises. Moreover, II Corps' subordinate infantry divisions were spread out in the Southern Command and its corps support units were nonexistent. This situation made gaining individual or collective experience in the conduct of operational staff procedures almost impossible.

Three British army corps served in Hamilton's MEF but none of corps units or the corps staffs were in existence before the war.[2] The Australian and New Zealand Army Corps (ANZAC) was activated in late November 1914 in India under Lieutenant-General Sir William Birdwood, who with eight officers left Bombay on 12 December en route to Egypt. There the remainder of the 70-officer and 500-man staff came together over the next few months. After the campaign began, the MEF activated a second corps on 24 May 1915, which was known initially as the British Army Corps. This headquarters became VIII Corps on 1 June 1915, with Lieutenant-General A. G. Hunter-Weston as its first commander. Later in the campaign, the British IX Corps formed in Britain on 17 June 1915 with Lieutenant-General The Honourable Sir Frederick Stopford as its commander. Within the corps headquarters itself, a brigadier-general, general staff (BGGS) supervised a GSO1 and a combined DA (deputy adjutant) and QMG (quarter master general) officer, effectively separating responsibility for operations and intelligence from administration and logistics. The headquarters staff also had specialized senior artillery, engineer, signals and medical staff officers.

British army infantry divisions in 1914 were organized differently from their European counterparts, which generally had two brigades of two regiments, totalling 12 infantry battalions. British divisions also had 12 battalions but they were organized into three brigades of four battalions, each commanded by a brigadier-general. A British division also had 76 artillery pieces, 24 machine guns and small numbers of engineers, cavalry and logistics units for a total assigned strength of about 18,300 officers and men. This was, of course, the on-paper authorization of a British division but this did not reflect the composition, training or the combat effectiveness of individual divisions. British infantry divisions were commanded by major-generals, who were predominantly in their mid-50s.

By 1915, four distinct groups of British infantry divisions had emerged as a result of mobilization.[3] The first group comprised the regular army divisions composed of trained professionals led by career officers. The second group was the Territorial divisions, which were composed of civilian part-time soldiers of varying training and experience. Many of the commanders of battalions and higher formations were regulars. The third group was the divisions of Kitchener's New Armies composed of eager volunteers. The New Army divisions were characterized by masses of untrained but willing and patriotic civilians, who were trained and led mostly by retired officers and non-commissioned officers. A fourth group comprised the colonial infantry divisions of the white Commonwealth nations, which were a blend of a few regulars, former militia, and part-time compulsory trainees, with a larger mass of volunteers. The Indian Army, which did not provide infantry divisions for the Gallipoli campaign, represented yet a fifth type of infantry division. Additionally, the Royal Navy created a Royal Naval Division composed of a Royal Marine brigade and two brigades of naval reservists and civilian volunteers, which was an anomaly in the force structure. With the exception of the Indian Army, which provided a brigade, all of these types of divisions saw action in the Gallipoli campaign.

While there are a number of definitions about what the term 'doctrine' means in a military sense, this book will use the concept that doctrine is an institutionalized, and agreed upon, general framework for thought and action. The heart of British doctrine in 1914 was *Field Service Regulations (1909) Part 1 (Operations)* (FSR I), which was a very prescriptive tactical manual concerned with matters at the division level and below.[4] By design, the regulations 'enshrined the philosophy of decentralisation at the tactical level within units'.[5] There was almost nothing in the regulations that was helpful – such as campaign planning, for example – for a commander at corps level or above. Such operational principles as it contained were largely found in Chapter VII, titled 'The Battle', which provides a glimpse into how the officers of the British Army thought about war. This chapter established a view of war that was profoundly

Jominian in that it recommended commanders seek the decisive battle through the concentration of forces at the decisive point (usually a weak point in the enemy position). Of note, commanders were instructed to gain the initiative by superiority of fire, manoeuvre their forces and then launch the decisive blow. While manoeuvre figured in the British concept of operations, FSR I was a firepower-based system. Additionally, Chapter VII contained instructions for fighting encounter battles and for deploying an advance guard, both of which would manifest themselves on 25 April.

If FSR I contained very little instruction about the operational level of command, it contained nothing at all about the conduct of amphibious operations. FSR I contained general principles for movement by sea and clearly established that the navy was in command of such operations. However, on the matter of assault from the sea it was silent. Moreover, FSR I did not contain any recommendations about the conduct of alliance warfare nor did it contain any guidance on combined operations (known as joint operations today). It is also important to note that Chapter VI of FSR I was titled 'Information', illustrating the absence in 1914 of what is now known as intelligence, which is a staff product resulting from the collection and analysis of information.

There are a number of academic positions today about the art of command in the British Army in 1914. One historian asserted that it rested on a system of umpiring within which commanders exercised a 'hands off' decentralized method of control.[6] In such a system, subordinates operated independently from an understanding of the commander's intent and with little interference from above. Another historian asserted that corps-level commanders were caught in a paradox of regimental tendencies that were in conflict with Staff College training, creating a 'hybrid' complex.[7] Other opinions point to the existence of a protégé system of advancement and its associated loyalties and liabilities. I subscribe to the theory that the British Army system of command is best described as one of 'restrictive control,' which is based on the centralization of decision-making. It is characterized by 'rigidity, conformity and a reliance on exact orders'.[8]

The above four methods of command were the result of a philosophy of combat that embraced structure. This philosophy stressed obedience, detailed planning and adherence to the plan, and the application of standard solutions. In essence, this philosophy of combat relies on Jominian theory that combat is controllable and that detailed calculations reduce risk and assure success. In any case, the British Army also valued highly individual initiative, independence and courage, which did not formally or informally translate into useful institutional values. There is scholarly agreement about the British Army's ethos, which was profoundly offensive. As a system of command, it is fair to say that the British Army was tactically adept but, at higher levels, unsupported by meaningful doctrine and hindered by a lack of direct experience in leading large units in operational settings. Its organizational tendency tended to be reactive rather than proactive in solving tactical problems.

Many officers in the British Army in the early 20th century were active readers who consumed a large and easily accessible literature that dealt with reform, the impact of emerging technologies, and what future wars might look like. Combined with the robust literature of military history then available in Britain, this supplemented, but did not make up for the absence of doctrine and experience. Of note, General Hamilton exemplified many of the traits valued by the British Army and, subsequently, became something of a data point in the literature about the British Army's art of command during the First World War. He was widely read, tactically experienced and courageous, and had even written about the future of war, but none of this particularly equipped him for army-level command.

British strategic and operational commanders

General Sir Herbert Horatio Kitchener was born in 1850 and was commissioned into the Royal Engineers. He went on to make a name for himself in Britain's small wars, including command in the Sudan Campaign and in the Second Anglo-Boer War. Kitchener never attended the Staff College and was not a member of any of the late 19th-century rings, upon which promotion seemed to depend in the British Army. He appeared disinterested in most things not exclusively tactical or directly related to his work at hand and has been characterized as distant and remote. He rose to high command because he could get things done. On the eve of the First World War Kitchener was Britain's senior and most well-known soldier. In the summer of 1914 he was serving as the Sirdar of Egypt but was home on leave and pressed to serve as Asquith's Secretary of State of War. In this position Kitchener was not technically commander-in-chief of Britain's army, but functionally that was the relationship he had with General Sir Ian Hamilton. Both Hamilton and Birdwood had been part of Kitchener's favoured inner circle during the Second Anglo-Boer War. Importantly, Kitchener's pronouncements had great weight in the strategic calculus of when and where to apply British land power in the first two years of the war. However, he was often shackled by the committee system, which compelled British decision-makers to seek consensus rather than rapid and decisive action.

General Sir Ian Standish Monteith Hamilton was born in 1853 and was commissioned into an infantry regiment. He served in India and was later badly wounded at Majuba Hill in the First Anglo-Boer War, losing the use of his left hand. He recovered and went on to campaign extensively in India and Africa. In the Second Anglo-Boer War he fought frequently and successfully and became a favourite of Kitchener's. From 1904 to 1905, Hamilton was an observer with the Japanese army in Manchuria during the Russo-Japanese War. There he saw the realities of modern war in some of the largest conventional battles of the early 20th century. When he returned, Hamilton published *A Staff Officer's Scrap-Book during the Russo–Japanese War* about his experiences and observations. He spoke four languages and read widely. He wrote poetry, a risqué novel, and a book about future war titled *The Fighting of the Future*. Although he was not a Staff College graduate he was considered extremely able and as having an up-to-date understanding of modern war. The German general staff published a short biography of Hamilton in 1914 describing him as the single most experienced soldier alive anywhere in the world at the time. In the summer of 1914, Hamilton was serving as General Officer Commanding Mediterranean and Inspector-General of Overseas Forces.

Lieutenant-General Sir William R. Birdwood was born in 1865 and was commissioned into an Indian Army lancer regiment. He served in a mounted brigade and then on Kitchener's staff during the Second Anglo-Boer War and commanded a brigade on the North-West Frontier in 1908. Birdwood was not a Staff College graduate and he was known for his unusual habits – he was a teetotaller, non-smoker and he exercised daily. In the summer of 1914 he was a major-general serving as Secretary of the Indian Army Department.

Major-General Sir Aylmer Hunter-Weston was born in 1864 and was commissioned into the Royal Engineers. He had extensive tactical experiences in India and Africa and was wounded in action there. He attended the British Staff College in 1898–99, where he was the Master of the Staff College Hounds. During the Second Anglo-Boer War, Hunter-Weston served in the field as a column commander and on Kitchener's staff. In the summer of 1914, he was commanding the 11th Infantry Brigade at Colchester and went to France with the BEF's 4th Division. He fought at the battles of Le Cateau and the Aisne, becoming known for supervising command from a motorbike. Hunter-Weston was promoted to major-general to take command of the 29th Division in March 1915.

Lieutenant-General Sir Frederick Stopford was born in 1854 and commissioned into the Grenadier Guards. He participated in several campaigns in Africa as an aide-de-camp and held a number of adjutant posts in the

Guards Brigade. In the Second Anglo-Boer War, Stopford served as secretary to commanding generals. In the first decade of the new century he remained in London commanding the Guards and the London district. He had almost no personal experience of leading men in combat and he was not a Staff College graduate. Nearing retirement in the summer of 1914, he held a ceremonial posting as the Lieutenant of the Tower of London.

With the exception of Hunter-Weston, none of the senior British commanders were Staff College graduates. None had experience in the planning or conduct of operational-level operations involving corps-sized or higher formations. Hunter-Weston had commanded a brigade on the Western Front, but otherwise, none of these men had experience in modern high-intensity conventional combat. They were willing to overlook failure by subordinates and they demonstrated unlimited optimism in their ultimate success despite all evidence to the contrary. They were committed to the principle that the man on the spot made the best decisions and they were unwilling to interfere with the actions of their subordinates. Often when incomplete information arrived, or when it failed to arrive entirely, they attempted to push forward anyway.

The Ottoman Army

The Ottoman Army's origins preceded the establishment of the empire and, in many ways the army was the first of Europe's modern armies. Going into the 20th century, the Ottoman Army, as an institution, was largely the product of the Hamidian reforms dating from the early 1880s, which were themselves a response to the disastrous defeat of the Russo-Turkish War of 1877. These reforms began when the sultan asked Germany to establish a military reform mission in the Ottoman Empire, resulting in the dispatch of Colonel Kaehler and four officers to Constantinople in April 1882.

The German military reform mission implemented changes in the curriculum of the Ottoman War Academy, the most important of which was the German system of training based on practical application of military subjects. However, Kaehler was unsuccessful in implementing a modern reserve system. He was joined in June 1883 by Major Colmar von der Goltz, who would remain in the empire for the next 25 years and who would have a long-lasting impact on the Ottoman Army. After Kaehler's death, von der Goltz took over and immediately changed the curriculum to a more rigorous German standard and established competitive entrance examinations. This led to establishment of a general staff corps based on the German model and, in turn, led to the Ottoman Army implementing German doctrines and training models at the tactical and operational levels. In this system, the army selected its crème for a War Academy education and from that small pool of graduates, the army chose its general staff officers. Moreover, the Ottomans began to send increasing numbers of upwardly mobile young Ottoman general staff officers to Germany for training tours.

By 1914, the Ottoman general staff corps had been in existence for several generations and had produced a large number of highly qualified general staff officers. These men were the Ottoman equivalents of British officers, who were 'psc'. There were, however, important differences in that the Ottoman general staff corps was a genuine *corps d'élite* composed of carefully selected officers, who were educated in a rigorous three-year curriculum duplicating that of the German War Academy. The curriculum stressed the operations of higher-level formations, as well as foreign languages and international law, and culminated in German-style staff rides in its final year. Graduates were rank ordered in an order of merit list, which determined both assignment precedence and seniority. Graduates were advanced three years in grade and designated general staff officers. The army transferred their files to a specialized staff section for career management and the officers themselves were carefully and deliberately rotated between staff and command assignments at increasingly higher levels. With an annual output of over 100 officers, in 1914, there were about 4,000 general staff officers on active duty (a number greatly exceeding its British counterpart of trained staff college graduates of 447 in 1914).

Although Kaehler failed to establish a continental-style reserve system, von der Goltz pushed through such a programme in November 1886. These reforms established numbered field armies, as well as two-year mandatory conscription for Muslim citizens, and a system of permanent first- and second-line reserve regiments and divisions. Von der Goltz also standardized uniforms and expanded the army's formal schools system. In peacetime the numbered field armies functioned as army inspectorates, which took responsibility for the training and manning of the reserve units. In the early 20th century there were about 40 active and 40 reserve infantry divisions in the Ottoman Army. However, in the catastrophic defeats in the Balkan Wars of 1912–13, the Ottoman reserve system failed the test of mobilization and proved unready to meet the demands of modern war. This was largely a failure of financial resources rather than a systemic problem within the reserve system itself. This led the army's chief of staff, Ahmet İzzet Pasha, to undertake unprecedented reforms in the reserve system in December 1913 by eliminating the entire structure of organized reserve infantry regiments and divisions. At a stroke, İzzet Pasha eliminated the standing reserve force thus destroying the Ottoman Army's immediate ability to expand its number of divisions in the event of war.

İzzet Pasha's *New Organisation of Active Forces according to Army, Independent Corps, and Infantry Division Areas of December 1913* stabilized the active army at 36 infantry divisions. Moreover, the reorganization altered the structure of the basic infantry division itself by establishing it as a reduced-strength cadre formation of approximately 40 per cent of its authorized wartime strength. This dovetailed into İzzet Pasha's new reserve concept wherein reservists assembled at regimental depots and then as individuals were assigned to fill the infantry divisions to full wartime strength. After 1913, mobilization planning undertook to fill the 36 infantry divisions to full strength rather than to field complete reserve divisions (or even complete reserve regiments). Other than a few cavalry divisions in eastern Anatolia, the Ottoman Army had no counterpart to a European model of reserve armies.

The Ottoman Army was a multi-ethnic, multi-linguistic army made up of the many national groups living inside the empire. The composition of Ottoman army regiments varied widely according to where they were raised and garrisoned, with units in Mesopotamia, Syria and Palestine being predominately Arabs. After the winter of 1914–15, its combat forces were almost entirely Muslim, with its Christian conscripts relegated to labour battalions and service units. Ottoman conscripts were generally illiterate and men who could read and write were often made into corporals. University and professional men were commissioned as reserve officers, while the regular officer corps was composed of the graduates of the Ottoman Military Academy. Unlike the British Army, the Ottomans had no established professional non-commissioned officer corps and relied on junior officers to train its soldiers. This produced an army of very uneven capacity and, as a result of the Balkan War defeats, observers in 1914 characterized the Ottoman Army as tactically clumsy, poorly led and unmotivated, and even afraid of coming to grips with the enemy. In truth, Ottoman soldiers often proved reliable, immune to hardship, and capable of extremely rapid mobile operations. The strength of the army, therefore, tended to exist in individual general staff officers at the top of the institution and in individual soldiers at the bottom.

Since the late 1820s, the Ottoman military was organized on an archaic dual-command system of a general staff and a headquarters of the commander-in-chief, neither one of which was fully empowered to execute wartime duties. In the spring of 1908, the grand vizier convinced the Cabinet to update the Ottoman command system, the first step of which was to empower the Ministry of War to supervise organizational, logistical and acquisition planning for the army and at the same time eliminate the headquarters of the commander-in-chief. In this way, the general staff then assumed primacy for war planning and the conduct of operations, and in 1909, was reorganized as well. Under its chief of staff, the Ottoman general staff established four divisions; the First Division handled training and operations, the Second Division handled intelligence, the Third Division handled organization, security and mobilization, while the Fourth Division handled mapping. Subsequent changes in 1911 created three additional divisions handling logistics, budget, and a special division to manage the assignments of the corps of general staff officers. Like its British counterpart in 1914, the Ottoman general staff was an evolving and growing organization.

The Ottoman military employed numbered armies from the 1880s, which in peacetime operated as a German-modelled inspectorate system. For example, the First Army Inspectorate mobilized as the Ottoman First Army. In 1911, the numbered army staffs were reorganized to mirror the staff organization of the general staff. Each army headquarters was authorized a trained general staff officer as the army chief of staff supervising four staff divisions; operations, intelligence, quartermaster, and personnel and administration. The First Division (operations) was considered as the first among equals and often drew a general staff officer as its incumbent. There were signals, military police and other support units assigned as well. Ottoman staff functions mirrored those headquarters above and were replicated by those headquarters at lower levels. The Ottoman Fifth Army, which fought at Gallipoli, was not a pre-war formation and its headquarters activated on 27 March 1915. However, its commander, chief of staff, and most of the principal staff officers all had previous experience in field army headquarters.

Until 1911, the Ottoman Army had no formally organized army corps headquarters and the numbered field armies directly commanded divisions. In that year, Ahmet İzett Pasha established 13 army corps, of which 12 were assigned to field armies. Ottoman army corps headquarters were authorized 92 officers and 365 junior reserve officers and men. At its full strength of three infantry divisions and associated corps artillery regiment, an Ottoman army corps was authorized 41,000 men and 6,700 animals. These headquarters were in the process of activation when the First Balkan War broke out in the autumn of 1912. Although a small number of Ottoman general staff officers had served on exchanges with German army corps staff, the army had no institutional experience or tradition of corps-level command. Unready or not, the Balkan Wars forced the practical application of command and operations at army corps level on the Ottoman Army. By 1914, Ottoman army corps headquarters were fully functional and commanded and staffed by experienced men.

The Fifth Army had two corps headquarters assigned to its rolls on 25 April 1915. The most important of these corps was III Corps, which had been in existence since its constitution in 1911. III Corps was led by Brigadier-General Esat Pasha, who had been in command for 16 months. Both Esat and his chief of staff, Lieutenant-Colonel Fahrettin, were Ottoman general staff officers. The second Fifth Army corps was XV Corps, which was activated on 1 April 1915 as a provisional headquarters, under the command of German Colonel Erich Weber. As the campaign progressed after the Allied landings, the Fifth Army received the following corps as reinforcements: I, II, V, VI, XIV, XVI and XVII Corps, of which the first four were pre-war headquarters.

One of the most exciting military organizational innovations of the early 20th century was the establishment of the triangular infantry division by the Ottoman Army in July 1910. This concept was the shared innovation of Ahmet İzzet and von der Goltz, who had returned to advise the Ottomans on army modernization. The new Ottoman infantry division discarded the European continental model of two brigades of two regiments each and replaced it with a division composed of three infantry regiments supported by an artillery regiment of three battalions. Altogether the new Ottoman infantry division contained about 13,000 men supported by 36 artillery pieces and 12 machine guns. This triangular regimental architecture mirrored the triangular divisional organization at corps level above and the triangular battalion arrangement below the regiment. It proved ideally suited to the rotational requirements of trench warfare that evolved in the First World War. Like the corps headquarters, each division had a chief of staff and numbered staff divisions mirroring the higher staffs. Although authorized major-generals as commanding officers, colonels and lieutenant-colonels commanded Ottoman army divisions, with average ages ranging from late 30s to mid-40s. Like the Ottoman corps headquarters, the triangular divisional architecture was untested at the beginning of the Balkan War and the army experienced difficulty in employing the new organization. The test of combat validated the concept and, by 1915, Ottoman divisional organizations proved resilient and capable of the cross-attachment of regiments and battalions.

Four of the five Ottoman infantry divisions that initially fought in the Gallipoli campaign were organized as pre-war active divisions but they may be differentiated into two forms of organizations. The first were those divisions that retained all three of their pre-war organic infantry regiments, including the 5th, 7th, and 9th Infantry Divisions. These divisions were mobilized in early August and were continuously trained. The other form of division was characterized by the division headquarters being assigned new regiments. This was caused by the Ottoman Army's expansion mechanism, which reassigned regiments from existing divisions to new divisions. This was an unintended consequence of İzzet Pasha's 1913 reorganization of the reserve. The 3rd Infantry Division's original regiments, the 7th, 8th, and 9th Infantry, were reassigned as the nucleus of newly raised divisions and the 3rd Division, in turn, received the 31st, 32nd, and 39th Infantry Regiments. Similarly, Mustafa Kemal's 19th Infantry Division, activated on 1 January 1915, lost its 58th and 59th Regiments in February; these were then replaced by the 72nd and 77th Infantry Regiments from Syria.

As a result of the continuous presence and influence of the German military reform mission, Ottoman Army doctrines and regulations were mirror images of their German counterparts. For example, the *Felddienst Ordnung, 1908* and the *Exerzier-Reglement für die Infanterie, 1906* were translated and published as *Hidemati Seferiye Nizamnamesi* and *Piyade Taliminamesi* respectively. Platoon- and company-level tactical regulations such as *Beifrage zur Taktischen Ausbildung unser Offiziere, 1904* was published as *Takımın ve Bölügün Muharebe Talımı*. Ottoman officers routinely translated other materials into Ottoman Turkish, for example, Mustafa Kemal translated Karl Litzmann's instructions for the conduct of company combat as well as other German books. These doctrinal works, like their British counterparts, stressed the importance of the offensive by means of securing fire superiority followed by an infantry assault.

Beginning in 1869, Helmuth von Moltke (the Elder) published his seminal doctrinal work, the title of which translates as *Instructions for Higher Units*, which in 1885 became the basis for modern army- and corps-level operations. These instructions specifically addressed the conduct of war at the operational level of war by stating principles involved in campaign planning to achieve strategic objectives. Like the tactical regulations these products were based on offensive principles and allowed for the implementation of decentralized command. The Ottoman Army however, did not choose to translate and implement this level of doctrinal instructions for its forces since army corps headquarters did not exist in the Ottoman Army until 1911; there was no real point in doing so. Moreover, many Ottoman general staff officers were fluent in German and the third year of the War Academy curriculum covered these operations anyway. It seems reasonable to suggest that it was relatively unnecessary to translate German instructions for Ottoman commanders at corps level and above, however, it was necessary to translate German tactical manuals for the remainder of the officer corps, who were neither Staff College trained nor fluent in foreign languages.

Command in the German Army of 1914 is often as 'directive command' within which, command is described as decentralized.[9] Commanders at all levels are assigned tasks and are resourced to fulfil them, but are not instructed how to accomplish the mission, nor are they over-supervised during its execution. The German system of command was known as *Aufstragtaktik* or 'mission orders'. The Ottoman Army mirrored its German model and also employed such a system of decentralized command, both doctrinally and practically. The evolution of the *Aufstragtaktik* system has been attributed to Helmuth von Moltke and was the result of a profoundly Clausewitzian philosophy of combat that saw combat as inherently chaotic and unpredictable. This philosophy of combat demanded flexibility and initiative because it required commanders to exercise adaptability to circumstances and rapidity of action.

Within two months of replacing Ahmet İzzet Pasha as minister of war in January 1914, Colonel Enver Pasha had involuntarily retired almost 1,300 ageing officers who he felt were obstructions to modernization or who were opponents of the Young Turks.[10] This cleared the way for Enver to issue specific instructions for retraining the army in line with correcting the deficiencies outlined by Major Asım six months earlier.

Enver released General Orders Number 1 on 14 March 1914, which contained detailed guidance for the conduct of army troop and unit training at the tactical level.[11] The first section of the order dealt with the imperative to exercise direct leadership from the front. Section two dealt with tactical instructions for moving from march columns rapidly into combat formations, offensive operations and immediate counter-attacks, defensive operations including rapid entrenching, integration of machine guns, and the development of effective artillery fire support. These measures were to be integrated immediately into the training of the army and demonstrated an institutional willingness to address problems in a meaningful way.[12] Significantly, General Orders Number 1 showcased a newly found awareness by the Ottoman Army of the importance of firepower by stressing the imperative of quickly establishing combined-arms fire superiority over the enemy.

On 24 May 1914, the Ottoman general staff published general orders that contained comprehensive instructions for the writing and formatting of war diaries.[13] The orders also contained a list of the units required to maintain war diaries. The format was standardized into seven sections covering organization and signals; orders, reports, and operations; missions; logistics; personnel and animals; special trials and experiments; and special instructions. The war diaries were classified as secret documents, and were opened and closed for operations or at the end of each calendar quarter. Completed war diaries were sent quarterly to the Ottoman general staff.[14] At the same time, the formats of written battle reports and situation reports were standardized in the Ottoman Army's

Instructions for Field Service (*Hidemati-ı Seferiye Talimnamesine*).[15] Spot reports also followed a specified format but could be either oral or written. This movement towards standardization of reporting, combined with the recent combat experience of the officer corps who demanded information from their subordinates, enhanced situation awareness in the Ottoman Army in comparison with the British Army.

In summary, operational doctrines for field army and corps units in the Ottoman Army were a combination of German methods that were merged with the Ottoman Army's lessons learned from the Balkan Wars. This created levels of effectiveness that were higher than those of their enemies. At the tactical level, organizationally and doctrinally, the Ottoman Army fielded a state-of-the-art divisional architecture that was supported by a broad base of practical experience based on what did and what did not work on the modern battlefield. A uniform, 'bottom up' information reporting system, combined with coherent command and control transmitted down the chain of command, connected these two levels of war in the Ottoman Army. The cumulative effect of these factors was the creation of an army that arguably possessed greater combat effectiveness than its opponents in 1915.

Ottoman strategic and operational commanders

İsmail Enver Pasha was born in 1881 and, because of his brilliant performance, went almost directly to the Ottoman War Academy after commissioning, where he came first in his class. In addition to being a trained general staff officer, he was an influential member of the CUP and an ardent advocate of modernization. In 1909 he served a tour as an attaché in Germany and was known to admire the German military system. Enver had a tremendous positive impact on the rebuilding of the Ottoman Army in 1914. He held concurrently the portfolios of minister of war, acting commander-in-chief, and chief of the general staff. As the acting commander-in-chief, he was entitled to issue direct orders in the sultan's name to the army. In this capacity, Enver exercised almost total authority over the strategic direction of the Ottoman Empire's war. During the Gallipoli campaign, Enver was in a position to affect the commitment of resources and priorities to the defence of the Dardanelles. His decisions, unlike those of Kitchener, were not subject to the tyranny of a committee system and were immediate and direct.

General Otto Liman von Sanders was born in Pomerania in 1855 and he was commissioned in 1874 into the cavalry. He earned a place in the Prussian War Academy and held the standard posts on the German general staff.

Liman von Sanders had never visited the Ottoman Empire, although he knew the Minister of War, Ahmet İzzet Pasha, very well from regimental duty in Cassel and from when İzzet had been assigned to him, while he was on the general staff, for instruction in staff duties. He had earned a title and combined it with his own name and the name of his late Scottish wife. In the summer of 1913 he was one of the senior division commanders in the Prussian army and held command of the 22nd Infantry Division in Cassel. Until the First World War Liman von Sanders had no combat experience. He was somewhat prickly and did not particularly care for most of the Ottoman officer corps.

Brigadier-General Esat (later Bülkat) Pasha was born in 1862 in Ioania, Greece. Esat attended the Military Academy in 1884 and then served as a regimental officer.[16] In 1887, he was selected to attend the Ottoman War Academy, and graduated with the class of 1890. He spoke three languages and he was sent to the Prussian War Academy, from which he graduated in 1894. Esat had typical general staff assignments and fought in the Greek War as a regimental commander. He commanded a brigade and he was the chief of staff of the Ottoman Third Army. Esat briefly commanded the 5th Infantry Division and then the 23rd Infantry Division in the Balkans. On 26 September 1912, at the beginning of the First Balkan War, Esat was assigned as the commander of the Provisional Yanya (Ioania) Corps. The Yanya Corps and its fortress were the linchpin in the Ottoman defences of western Macedonia and Albania. The fortress was modern and self-sufficient with a corps-sized garrison of several infantry divisions, which swelled to six infantry divisions as reinforcements arrived. Over the course of the war, Esat conducted a skilful defence as the Greek Army of Epirus besieged the city. Of note, Esat's performance in corps-level command steadily grew better as the siege progressed. His command was characterized by an ability to form quickly ad hoc groups of divisional size to hold key terrain features. These provisional groupings were assigned to senior officers and were tailored to the specific tactical mission. Esat was able to fend off numerically superior attacks and he also grew in his understanding of the modern battlefield.[17] He assumed command of III Corps on 10 December 1913.[18]

Colonel Erich Paul Weber held command of the Fifth Army's XV Corps on 25 April 1915. He was born in 1860. He was a Prussian general staff officer and he had arrived in the Ottoman Empire in 1913. Prior to his assignment as a corps commander, he had been the Ottoman Army's Inspector of Engineers and Pioneers. Weber would move up to command the Southern Group in May 1915 on Cape Helles replacing Lieutenant-Colonel Eduard von Sodenstern (who briefly commanded the group).

Mustafa Kemal (later Atatürk) was born in Salonika in 1881 and graduated from the Ottoman War Academy in 1905. As a young general staff officer he was assigned to the Ottoman Third Army headquarters, then in Salonika (in what is now Greece). At that time, Salonika was a hotbed of revolutionary nationalist activity and Kemal became associated with the Young Turk movement. He marched on the capital with the Action Army in 1909 and served as a regimental commander in 1911 of the 38th Infantry Regiment. After a brief tour on the general staff, Kemal was sent to Libya on 1 January 1912 to organize tribal resistance to the Italian invasion. He returned in November 1912 and was assigned to the Gallipoli Army as its chief of operations. After the Balkan War, political differences with Enver forced him to take an assignment in Bulgaria as the military attaché in Sofia and then to Belgrade as an attaché. Kemal returned on 20 January 1915 to take command of the 19th Division. He took command of the Anafarta Group in August 1915. His career went on to span the War of Independence and he became the first president of the modern republic of Turkey.

Mehmet Vehip (later Kaçı, 1877–1940) was Esat Pasha's younger brother; and he had graduated from the War Academy. In the early 1900s he served as chief of staff of the Diyarbakır Infantry Division and as commander of the Ezincan Military School. By 1909 he was a member of the Otoman general staff corps and moving up rapidly. In the Balkan Wars he served with Esat in the Yanya Corps as chief of staff during the siege. In 1914, Vehip was in command of the 22nd Infantry Division in the Hijaz, which at that time was engaged in counter-insurgency operations. He returned in the spring of 1915 to command the Ottoman Second Army. After service on the Gallipoli peninsula, he returned to re-form the Second Army in the autumn of 1915. Later in the war, he commanded the Ottoman Third Army and the Caucasian Army Group. Vehip was regarded as a capable and professional officer, who performed well in both command and staff assignments. After his retirement he travelled to Ethiopia to advise Haile Selassie's troops against the Italians in 1936.

The Fifth Army chief of staff was Staff Lieutenant-Colonel Kazım (later Kazım İnanç), who was born in 1880. He remained in this position for the duration of the campaign. Lieutenant-Colonel Kazım was ideally suited for this critical staff appointment under Liman von Sanders partly because he spoke fluent German.[19] More importantly, Kazım graduated from the Ottoman War Academy in 1902 and was appointed to the elite general staff officer corps. He served immediately thereafter in the general staff's operations directorate. This was followed by two command tours in infantry battalions. On 20 March 1911, Kazım was sent to Germany for a one-year training tour with the German Army.

When he returned he served as a corps chief of operations, a field army chief of logistics in the Balkan Wars and as the general staff chief of intelligence. When war broke out he was serving as the First Army chief of operations but moved up to chief of staff on 12 February 1915.

The operational-level commanders of the Ottoman Fifth Army were all War Academy graduates and members of the general staff corps. Because both the German and Ottoman War Academies used the German curriculum, this ensured uniformity of education and thinking. German and Ottoman commanders shared a common outlook towards doctrine and the planning and execution of combat operations. The Ottoman operational commanders had deep tactical and operational experience in combat and in peacetime settings. They had extensive practical experiences as staff officers on strategic and operational level general staffs. Moreover, all senior Ottoman commanders at Gallipoli had recent experience in the waging of modern conventional war during the Balkan Wars of 1912–13. In addition, all had experience in the pervasive counter-insurgency campaigns waged by the Ottoman Empire during the period from 1890–1912.

The French Army

The French Army in 1914 was more like its Ottoman and German opponents than its British partner. It was a continental mass-conscripted force led by professionals with its soldiers serving for three years and then transferring into an organized reserve. Its tradition of military dominance went back to the age of Louis XIV and it stood proudly on the memory of the age of Napoleon. Although France had lost the Franco-Prussian War of 1870–71 and the provinces of Alsace-Lorraine in 1871, the army as an institution chose to view this as the product of flawed political leadership rather than as a paradigm shift in the military balance in Europe. That said, the devastating losses in 1871 served to energize a comprehensive rebuilding of the French military machine. Beginning in 1872, France established a Superior Council of War that included the president of the republic and senior generals. This was followed, two years later, by the enlargement and expansion of the general staff along the lines of its successful German adversary. By the early 1880s, the French Army established a genuine chief-of-staff system which mirrored the German system pioneered by von Moltke and which was supported by a professionally trained corps of general staff officers.

The political situation vis-á-vis Germany after 1871 favoured the financing and rebuilding of a large army, which itself had broad popularity among the citizens of France. However, the French Army was heavily politicized and there were periodic power shifts between Catholic and socialist officer constituencies. Anti-Semitism ran high in France and the Dreyfus Affair brought this into sharp focus. The resulting scandals brought a wave of anti-militarism in France as the army became increasingly unpopular and by 1905 its combat effectiveness had dropped.[20] Despite political shifts in France over the next decade, the general staff slowly rebuilt both the prestige and the strength of the army back up to high levels. By 1914, the French Metropolitan army was well equipped, well trained, and possessed high morale. Like Germany, France also had a large suite of organized reserve divisions and corps that could mobilize within a very short time. This was not, however, the army that France sent to Gallipoli.

France had a two-tier military system, which evolved as a consequence of the acquisition of a second colonial empire in the 19th century. By 1900, it became French military policy to establish a colonial army that differed significantly in composition and training from its continental forces. The French colonial army was composed of indigenous peoples, locally recruited into regiments, which were commanded by professional long-service French officers and NCOs. The colonial army was trained, equipped and employed for counter-insurgency warfare and for the enforcement of French rule in Africa and Asia. It was widely and deeply experienced in the small colonial wars of the ages and it provided opportunities for the French officer corps to gain combat experience in a non-European tactical environment. The French colonial army was not equipped to fight a European opponent and was underequipped with machine guns and artillery. Moreover, its experience lay in expeditionary campaigning rather than in mobilization and concentration of large-scale forces.

Before 1870, France did not have standing field army headquarters or organized army corps headquarters and this lack of organizational and command experience hurt its military performance during the Franco-Prussian War. In 1871, the first permanent peacetime corps headquarters were established but, after the collapse of the Second Empire and the departure of Napoleon III, the French government and people were reluctant to encourage a climate fostering military autonomy. As a result, there was resistance to the idea of establishing a field army in peacetime. In 1888, skeleton structures were activated but it was well into the 1890s before standing field army-level headquarters were established in France. The entente with Russia in 1892 accelerated the coordination of war plans and, by the early 1900s, staffs at all levels were deeply engaged in war planning as well as in conducting massive military exercises in the autumn. By 1914, corps-level staff work reached high levels of proficiency and there was a generation of French officers who were well trained at the operational level of war.

In 1914, the French Army conformed to the European standard and French army corps were organized with two infantry divisions and a supporting corps artillery regiment. Each infantry division was composed of two brigades of two regiments, for a total of 12 infantry battalions. The division also had an artillery regiment of some 54 field guns. Altogether, French infantry divisions comprised around 16,000 officers and men. During the Gallipoli campaign the French organized the Corps Expéditionnaire d'Orient (CEO) on 22 February 1915 under Major-General Albert d'Amade. Lieutenant-Colonel Descoins was assigned as his chief of staff. Initially the CEO was composed of a single army division that was activated by assembling miscellaneous independent regiments from North Africa as the French high command was opposed to taking troops from the Western Front for use in peripheral operations. The CEO's First Division, commanded by Major-General Joseph Masnou, was composed of one Metropolitan infantry regiment, two mixed Colonial infantry regiments and a mixed Zouave and Foreign Legion regiment. A similar CEO Second Division, under Major-General Maurice Bailloud, was organized and sent to the peninsula in early May 1915.

French doctrine famously favoured *l'offensive à outrance* (the all-out offensive), which was seen by French theoreticians and leaders as the way to solve the tactical problem. Like its British, German and Ottoman counterparts, French doctrine stressed gaining fire superiority and then assaulting the enemy with the rifle and bayonet. If anything, it relied more than the others on a Clausewitzian concentration of force at the decisive point regardless of cost. Enthusiasm for this waned as anti-militarism spread in France in the early 20th century and the lessons on firepower from the Russo-Japanese War of 1904–05 were absorbed. However, the doctrine was revived at lower levels by a handful of aggressive and nationalistic colonels and, in 1911, chief of staff Joseph Joffre ordered the application of these ideas to higher levels. In October 1913, the French Army published new regulations concerning the employment of large units (corps, army and army group), which was followed in December by new regulations for the employment of smaller units (regiment, brigade and division). Both of these regulations rested on the doctrinal principle that only offensive operations could lead to decisive results and that attacks should be launched as soon and as violently as possible in order to maintain the morale and fighting spirit of the army. Importantly, the new regulations de-emphasised preliminary bombardments by the artillery to soften the enemy before an attack and pushed the artillery into a supporting role. New infantry regulations, published in April 1914, asserted that the supreme weapon remained the bayonet. Historians of this period have come to call these unifying doctrines the 'cult of the bayonet'.

THE DARDANELLES AND APPROACHES, 1915

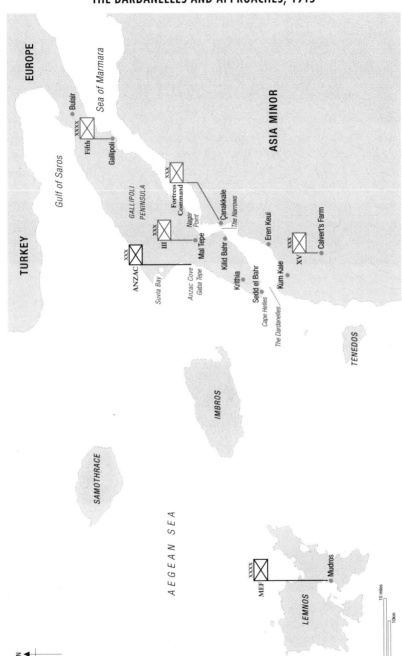

Institutional, organizational and tactical conclusions

Although the British and French did not realize it in the spring of 1915, their armies faced an adversary that possessed high degrees of institutional combat effectiveness. The British expected to encounter an army that was 'ill-commanded and ill-officered'.[21] Instead they encountered officers at company, battalion, regiment, division and corps level who were aggressive and skilled in the conduct of war. Specifically, as a group, what could the Ottoman command team do that the British, and the French to a greater extent, could not? They could pass reliable reports up and down the chain to provide a clear picture of unfolding events. They could plan, coordinate, and execute artillery fire support. They could act without direction, but within the commander's overall intent. They led from the front and personally made on-the-spot decisions. They could cross-attach companies, battalions, and regiments with ease. They could concentrate and move.

The organizational architecture of the Ottoman Army lent itself to the effective ability to cross-attach regiments and battalions. The original triangular architecture of Ottoman infantry divisions, dating from 1910 and refined in the Balkan Wars, proved highly flexible and allowed the Ottomans to concentrate forces effectively. It was possible for the Ottomans to take a regiment or battalion from one division and attach it to another division with no real loss of combat effectiveness. Artillery, jandarma, engineers, and cavalry enjoyed a similar capability. This capability enabled the Ottomans to tailor their forces by assigning units to a particular commander, unlike the British who tried to do this with infantry brigades within a divisional context. Making this all the more powerful, Ottoman commanders were much younger than their Anglo-French counterparts at every level above battalion. Allied corps commanders, for example, were men of 55–62 yeaars old, while Ottoman corps and group commanders ranged from 36–52 years old.

Similarily, the Ottoman Army at Gallipoli was tactically effective in its effective use of specific techniques to secure objectives. This capability stemmed mainly from the Army's firepower-based doctrines and from its multi-dimensional combined-arms training programmes. In terms of training, the Ottoman Army laid down detailed training guidance in the spring of 1913 based on its experience in the Balkan Wars. This guidance was relevant to modern war. During the mobilization and in the months prior to the battle, the army continued to adhere to this guidance. The men were hardened by long marches. Artillery, engineers, machine-gunners, and cavalry worked with their infantry counterparts to iron out how to achieve mutual support'. Commanders held terrain walks and fire-planning exercises. Detailed rehearsals were conducted. All of this was based on the experience of the Balkan Wars. Combined-arms training was encouraged and was executed at all levels. This was reinforced by the experience of the commanders, who were combat veterans of those wars and who understood the dynamics of modern firepower. Time after time, relatively small groups of Ottoman soldiers were able to seize fire superiority and devastate their enemies with effective machine-gun and artillery fire.

By way of contrast, the British Army was trapped inside antiquated doctrines that stressed the individuality of the separate combat arms. Moreover, the training cycles of the ANZAC and the 29th Infantry Division did not include any combined-arms training or exercises. The strength of the British Army was its magnificent infantry, especially the regulars, who were too few in numbers. The Ottomans themselves felt that the British were unsuccessful because of 'the use of too small forces at different attacking points' and 'the poor quality of English commissioned officers'.[22] Moreover, the Otomans 'all agreed that these officers were brave but inexperienced, and did not seem to know how to command or lead their soldiers into battle'.[23] Later, the British parliamentary Dardanelles Commissions would agree with and reinforce these conclusions.

As the following chapters will reveal, in overall terms, the Ottoman Army, which was often outnumbered and always outgunned at Gallipoli, was not outfought by its Anglo-French enemy. As the campaign progressed, the Ottomans proved resilient and formidable opponents. The Ottoman Army was well trained, adhered to standardized and well-understood doctrines, and possessed an appreciation of the reality of modern war. Its commanders were, likewise, experienced and well trained, and they led from the front. In combination, these institutional, organizational and leadership capabilities provided the Ottoman Army with high levels of military effectiveness relative to their adversaries.

Chapter Five

THE AMPHIBIOUS ASSAULT, 19 MARCH–30 APRIL 1915

The failure of Carden's plan to force the straits by ships alone led to a short interlude during which de Robeck, heavily influenced by the generals, decided against continuing the operation. Although the strategic objectives remained unchanged, de Robeck's decision led to a fundamental change in the design of the campaign itself. In turn, his decision, made in isolation without consultation with or approval from his superiors, imposed a larger commitment in time and resources on the War Council in London. In effect, de Robeck's unilateral decision irrevocably and fundamentally put Hamilton's army on a collision course with its Ottoman opponent.

The outcome of de Robeck's decision was a plan to conduct a joint and combined land campaign, supported by the navy, designed to seize the Kilid Bahr plateau. Unfortunately for the British, by altering the end state to a geographically centred land objective, the new plan required substantially more means, in the way of land forces, as well as unproven and non-doctrinal methods, which included an amphibious assault on contested shores. Moreover, massing the necessary forces and the complexity of the tactical planning pushed the launch of the new operation into mid-April at the earliest. This delay gave the now alerted and very worried Ottomans significant time to reinforce the peninsula and activate a field army headquarters for its defence.

Operational planning on both sides produced comprehensive and detailed campaign plans, although the Ottoman plan was a refined version of a plan that dated back to 1912, while the British plan was written in about a month. On 25 April 1915, these plans intersected as the Anglo-French landing unfolded into the first week of combat.

Changes to the British campaign design

De Robeck's after-action report of 18 March 1915 outlined the disastrous day his fleet had endured but made no mention of any success.[1] A second message to the Admiralty added that, with the exception of ships lost or damaged, his squadrons were ready for immediate action. However, he also noted that 'the plan of attack [meaning Carden's plan] must be reconsidered and means found to deal with floating mines'.[2] Churchill and the War Council met at 11.00am, 19 March, approved the reinforcement of de Robeck's fleet with four battleships, and encouraged him to continue the assault. An Admiralty message to this effect went to de Robeck and also asked for his assessment of damage done to the enemy forts. De Robeck replied on 20 March that he was reorganizing his minesweeping fleet by outfitting destroyers, torpedo boats and picket boats in order to conduct faster and more thorough operations in daylight. He hoped to be in a position to renew operations in three or four days' time. He then added that floating mines seemed to have been the cause of his defeat and finally added his assessment that the fleet had silenced the forts at the Narrows and the batteries guarding the minefields had been put to flight.

While de Robeck was deciding these matters, Hamilton had also made up his mind, two days previously, to move his administrative and logistical base from Lemnos, where there were no facilities, back to Egypt. His staff was also receiving detailed appraisals about the Ottoman Army and the peninsula's defences from Colonel C. H. M. Doughty-Wylie and Captain W. H. Deedes, both of whom had spent substantial time in the Ottoman Empire, and who had arrived at Lemnos on 18 March. In a 20 March message to de Robeck, Hamilton proposed to move the land forces to Alexandria and Port Said, leaving de Robeck with 4,000 Australians at Lemnos and 2,000 marines on ships at Tenedos. De Robeck replied that evening that a delay would be appropriate for political reasons, at least until the attack was resumed in a few days' time, indicating that up until 21 March he was committed to continuing the naval assault.

While these exchanges were happening, Hamilton sent Kitchener his assessment that he no longer believed that the straits could be forced by ships alone and that his troops would be required in full strength. Kitchener replied immediately that if large-scale military operations were required to clear the peninsula then these must be undertaken and carried through. On 21 March Hamilton discussed the situation with Wemyss and d'Amade, and separately with Birdwood, all of whom supported his notion that large-scale military operations were necessary. On 22 March, de Robeck invited Hamilton to attend a meeting at 10.00am on the *Queen Elizabeth*, which also included Wemyss, Birdwood, Braithwaite and Captain Pollen. According to Hamilton's diary, de Robeck sat down without discussion and summarily told the group that he could not get through the straits without the help of troops.[3] De Robeck later asserted that he was prepared to continue the naval attack, but changed his mind when Hamilton offered the co-operation of his army. However, Wemyss later wrote that he and de Robeck had come to this conclusion earlier on 19 March.[4] It is unclear exactly when de Robeck abandoned the idea of a 'naval-only' operation, but his pronouncement fitted into Hamilton's beliefs and his predisposition to commit his army to a large-scale military operation. Weather and timing also played a role in the outcome of this meeting – the new minesweepers would not be ready for action until 4 April and Hamilton said he could not land men until 14 April, although Birdwood pressed for an immediate landing with all available troops.

De Robeck sent the Admiralty a telegram on 23 March attempting to explain what he had agreed with Hamilton, which Churchill read with consternation.[5] De Robeck began by saying that the army would not be in a position to undertake operations before 14 April and continued into an explanation that, even if the fleet broke through into the Sea of Marmara, all the coastal guns must be destroyed or the straits would close up behind the fleet. He ended by stating that a decisive joint effort could not be mounted until mid-April. An alarmed Churchill convened an immediate meeting of his staff and proposed a reply to de Robeck essentially restating the Carden plan and directing him to resume the attack with all dispatch. Churchill highlighted his belief that the enemy was short of ammunition and had a limited supply of mines. To his dismay, Fisher, Wilson and Jackson (who had always disliked it) turned against the 'naval-only' operation and supported de Robeck and Hamilton's joint campaign proposal. Under extreme institutional pressure from his subordinates, Churchill gave in and abandoned his position. A defeated Churchill composed a long telegram to de Robeck that finally went out on the evening of 24 March, which affirmed that the army should seize the Kilid Bahr plateau at the earliest opportunity. However, Churchill then outlined all of the reasons why de Robeck ought to resume the naval attack in the meantime, reminding de Robeck again about the enemy's ammunition shortages and pointing out that German submarines might arrive soon making naval operations difficult. However, it was now too late to alter de Robeck's mind as he had concluded irrevocably that, without significant help from the army, his fleet could not break through the straits.

Conceptually, there was nothing planned beyond the idea that a joint operation would be undertaken, and there had been no balancing of ends, ways and means. As early as 16 March, Hankey had submitted a list of pointed questions to Asquith explicitly questioning the extent of preparations for military action. Believing that the 'naval fiasco' of 18 March was the result of inadequate staff work, Hankey sent a note to Asquith on 19 March recommending that a joint planning committee be set up.[6] The next day, Hankey produced a detailed memorandum for Asquith outlining the possible courses of action and the corresponding associated risks involved in landing at various locations on the peninsula.[7] He pointed out the obvious that there had been no staff analysis for the use of the troops and that the operations were proceeding on the basis that 'so many troops are available and they ought to be enough'.[8] Again, he pleaded for the establishment of a planning staff and noted that a fortnight invested in planning might save months in carrying out the operation. On 24 March, Hamilton and his staff sailed for Port Said aboard the *Franconia*. He sailed knowing that Kitchener was unhappy with delaying the operation until mid-April, and to counter this, prodded Kitchener with his own words regarding the assembly of forces to ensure the full weight was thrown in. In fact, it was Kitchener's own reversal to send the 29th Division that now delayed the operation, which Hamilton also pointed out in a back-handed manner. Further messages between Churchill and de Robeck between 25 and 27 March failed to encourage the fleet commander to action.

Campaign planning now passed to Hamilton and the general staff officers of the general headquarters of the Mediterranean Expeditionary Force (MEF). In coordination with the naval staff, Hamilton's staff began to move the forces to staging bases in Egypt – the Royal Naval Division, less the marines, and the French division were sent to Alexandria, and the 29th Division, then en route from England, was directed to stop and reconfigure their loading at Malta. Hamilton requested 20–30 armoured lighters capable of landing 400–500 men to be sent out to him (these never arrived). On 29 March, Hamilton decided to bring the 29th Division directly into Alexandria and diverted the Royal Naval Division to Port Said. Hamilton and his staff arrived in Alexandria at 3.00pm on 26 March and went straightaway to Cairo to confer with Maxwell.[9] Major-General Alymer Hunter-Weston, GOC 29th Division, along with the first ship containing his men arrived on 27 March. D'Amade and five transports of the French division arrived the next day at Alexandria and, on this day, the general staff forwarded instructions to the ANZAC regarding disposition of troops in transports and landing of transport and ammunition. The staff spent 29 March coordinating with the Malta dockyard regarding the construction of a trestle pier, developing instructions about how to man and manage the lighters which were available, and the cross-loading of transports for the Royal Naval Division. Until 1 April the focus of Hamilton's staff was on the administrative details of staging the incoming land forces in Egypt and the tactical details involving movement and loading.

Thus, in the period 18–31 March 1915, the entire British campaign design changed from a 'naval-only' design to a concept involving a joint and combined operation. The strategic objectives had not changed nor had the idea of landing the MEF near Constantinople, however, the first phase of the British campaign plan changed substantially. The Carden plan, and by assumption of command, de Robeck's plan as well, was centred on controlling temporarily a limited amount of land along the straits in order to accomplish the clearing of the minefields in the Narrows. Tactically, Carden's naval plan was built around the idea of silencing of the coastal forts and rendering the Ottoman Army's mobile artillery ineffective for at least long enough for the mines to be cleared so that the battle fleet could move into the the Sea of Marmara and destroy the Ottoman navy. Both Carden and de Robeck envisioned a follow-on operation to move the land forces to the vicinity of Constantinople. De Robeck, singularly and unilaterally, discarded the 'naval-only' scheme on 22 March, although he was reinforced in this decision by Hamilton's belief that the straits could not be forced by ships alone. Hamilton, for his part, chose to interpret liberally Kitchener's instructions of 13 March that large-scale land forces could be employed if the fleet failed, but not before all British forces were assembled in theatre. In spite of Churchill's desire to attack immediately, these decisions framed the redesign of the operational campaign. The principal factor in complying with Kitchener's instructions lay not with where to employ the available land forces, but in where to assemble and ready them to be employed en masse. Unfortunately for the British planners, the MEF could not be supported or staged at Lemnos or Tenedos. This dynamic drove Hamilton's decision to stage the bulk of his army in Egypt, which in turn, led to the start of operations being fixed for mid-April. A frustrated Churchill could only watch as his schemes disintegrated because of decisions made by operational commanders in theatre.

British operational planning

The MEF's Administrative and Quartermaster staff arrived on 1 April and Hamilton sent word to de Robeck that he proposed to return and rejoin the fleet commander on 7 April in order to write final orders for the operation. With his MEF staff united in Egypt Hamilton undertook the design of his campaign, which was evolving based on input from Kitchener and from his own assessments of the situation. Kitchener had pointed out on 13 March that the Kilid Bahr plateau was the key to the peninsula, a view that was also held by de Robeck and Birdwood. As a result of this, Hamilton went to

Alexandria with the idea that he would employ the MEF on the lower peninsula. As he had personally seen the beaches there, he had some ideas on landing sites for the navy. On 2 April, the MEF staff received the results of the navy's beach reconnaissance which asked Hamilton to switch several of the possible landing sites. The navy also asked Hamilton to send some staff officers to Mudros to assist in the co-operation of planning. Kitchener sent more advice to Hamilton on 3 April suggesting that Cape Helles and Morto Bay offered the best landing sites and recommending that a feint landing be conducted north and south of Gaba Tepe.[10] Kitchener also noted that he presumed that Hamilton would attack the Kilid Bahr plateau in force and occupy it in preparation for destroying the forts at the Narrows. He concluded the message noting that he could not provide enough artillery ammunition for the MEF to destroy barbed-wire obstacles.

The war diary of the MEF general headquarters first mentions a 'plan of operations' at 12.20pm on 4 April and it is clear that Hamilton had something definite in mind at this point.[11] Hamilton ordered Birdwood to move the ANZAC to port for embarkation on 4 April to be followed by 29th Division on 6 April. Delayed for a day by bad weather, Hamilton and the general staff sailed on the *Arcadian* at 6.15am on 8 April for Lemnos carrying a signal company and a printing section with them.[12] Hamilton arrived there at 6.00am on 10 April and at 9.30am went to the *Queen Elizabeth* to brief de Robeck. At 8.00pm that day Hamilton sent a message to Kitchener confirming that the MEF would conduct landings as he had suggested.[13] However, Hamilton told Kitchener that he felt the Gaba Tepe feint might develop into a 'real landing' and that the fleet would simultaneously bombard and demonstrate off the Bulair lines. Tactically, Hamilton made the point that he intended to 'keep the enemy occupied everywhere' which, in turn, would fix the large number of Ottoman reserves that were poised for counter-attacks. Hamilton also mentioned that his main anxiety was landing under fire followed by the rapidity with which he could seize a covering position. As before, the British commander mentioned that weather was, in the final analysis, the ruling factor.

Hamilton's plan included the term 'covering position', which does not appear anywhere in the *Field Service Regulations (1909) Part 1 (Operations)* (FSR I). These regulations contain a section on movements by sea that include general administrative principles for the embarkation and debarkation of troops, animals and equipment, but contain no information or suggestions for an amphibious landing. Moreover, the *Manual of Combined Naval and Military Operations, 1913* prescribed the administrative functions of command and control in landing operations on an unoccupied coast (mostly involving the establishment of beach masters and landing parties), but likewise included nothing in the way of amphibious tactics or how to manage such operations. It is important to consider that no military or naval establishment in the world in 1915 had formal doctrinal concepts for amphibious warfare; Hamilton and the MEF staff were innovating as they designed the campaign plan. In essence, in a period of about two weeks without doctrines or field service regulations, Hamilton had reduced the tactical dilemma to the essentials of amphibious operations, which were getting a foothold ashore under fire from an enemy-held beach, establishing a covering position or defensive perimeter, and then attacking out of it to seize an operational objective. Furthermore, as an operational design, in two weeks, he had decided on a complex campaign plan that sought to achieve operational surprise through the conduct of feints and diversions which, at tactical level, aimed at fixing the enemy's reserves in order to land and seize the objective.

The morning of 11 April found de Robeck in agreement with Hamilton's plan including the addition of the Bulair demonstration and bombardment. Hunter-Weston and his staff arrived at Lemnos, Birdwood that evening, and the ANZAC staff the following morning. Hamilton issued his Force Order No. 1 on 13 April, which outlined in some detail the first phase of his operational design for the campaign.[14] He stated that the object of the expedition was 'to assist the fleet to force the Dardanelles by capturing the Kilid Bahr plateau, and dominating the forts at the Narrows'. Hamilton's general plan envisioned the 29th Division landing at Cape Helles and the ANZAC landing on the long beach north of Gaba Tepe, while a portion of the French division landed at Kum Kale and the Royal Naval Division conducted a feint landing and demonstration at Saros Bay (including a bombardment of Bulair). In modern doctrinal terminology, Hamilton planned a joint and combined campaign, that is to say, a multi-service and multinational effort. Operationally, Hamilton was trading mass and a heavily weighted main effort in an attempt to achieve operational surprise. Some of this was due to the nature of the beaches, which were tiny and widely scattered, forcing him 'to separate his forces and the effect of momentum, which cannot be produced by cohesion, must be reproduced by the simultaneous nature of the movement'.[15] Hamilton's assumption was that the enemy commander-in-chief would be deluged with 'SOS' messages from five or six places spread over a 100-mile-long area, making it difficult to concentrate reinforcements appropriately.[16] This, Hamilton reasoned, gave the MEF a planning window of opportunity of about 48 hours to execute the operation.[17] Organizationally, Hamilton directed Birdwood and Hunter-Weston to task organize their units tactically into a covering force and a main body. This corresponded to Hamilton's concept of a

HAMILTON'S PLAN TO SEIZE KILID BAHR

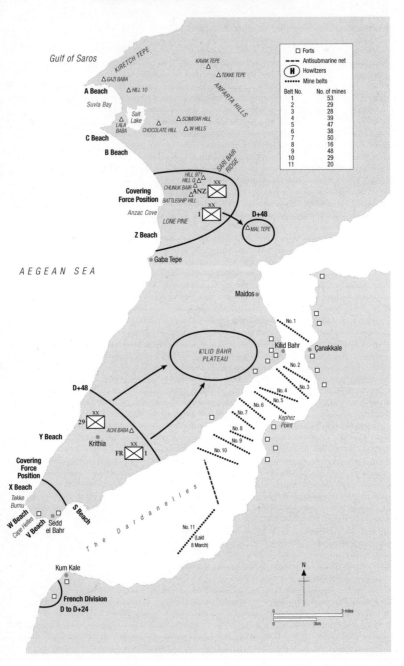

Gulf of Saros

KIRETCH TEPE

△ GAZI BABA

A Beach

Suvla Bay

KAVAK TEPE △

△ TEKKE TEPE

△ HILL 10

ANFARTA HILLS

△
LALA
BABA

Salt
Lake

△ SCIMITAR HILL

△ W HILLS

△
CHOCOLATE HILL

C Beach

B Beach

□	Forts
– – –	Antisubmarine net
Ⓗ	Howitzers
••••	Mine belts

Belt No.	No. of mines
1	53
2	29
3	28
4	39
5	47
6	38
7	50
8	16
9	48
10	29
11	20

HILL 971 △
HILL Q △△
CHUNUK BAIR △
△ ANZ
BATTLESHIP HILL

SARI BAIR
RIDGE

**Covering
Force Position**

Anzac Cove

LONE PINE

1

XX

XX

D+48

△ MAL TEPE

Z Beach

● Gaba Tepe

A E G E A N   S E A

Maidos ●

No. 1

□

□

□

□

Kilid Bahr ●

Çanakkale

D+48

*KILID BAHR
PLATEAU*

□

□

□

No. 2

□

□

□

□

No. 4

No. 3

29

XX

△ ACHI BABA △

□

No. 5

No. 6

*Kephez
Point*

Y Beach

Krithia ●

FR

XX

1

No. 7

No. 8

□

No. 9

□

**Covering
Force
Position**

No. 10

X Beach

*Tekke
Burnu*

□

W Beach

Cape Helles

V Beach

Sedd
el Bahr

S Beach

T h e   D a r d a n e l l e s

No. 11

(Laid
8 March)

Kum Kale

□

N

□

**French Division
D to D+24**

0		3 miles
0		3km

covering position from which the main attack would be launched. This was innovative thinking at its best and indicates that Hamilton considered the problem of amphibious assault against a hostile shore as something akin to a movement to contact. The closest doctrinal concept in 1915 for the covering force idea was found in Chapter V (Protection) of the 1909 FSR, which prescribed an advance guard to precede the main body during a movement to contact. The advance guard's mission was to protect the advance, fix the enemy and then to secure a position from which the main body might launch an assault. Hamilton's covering forces were to fight their way ashore into a beachhead that was large enough to support the massing of the main body inside it. Hamilton also planned to disembark the main bodies directly after their respective covering forces had landed building a further assumption that the covering forces would enjoy some measure of success sufficient to assure space for the main bodies to unload.

Hamilton's instructions to Birdwood specified a covering force of about a brigade (roughly 4,000 men in three stages) landing on a single, wide beach, with the objective of securing what would become known as First Ridge.[18] This left a main body of four infantry brigades. The objective of the main body was to seize the ridge between Sari Bair and Mal Tepe for the purpose of threatening or perhaps cutting the enemy's north–south communications and ability to reinforce the lower peninsula. Hamilton's instructions for the 29th Division were more explicit, specifying landing on five tiny and widely separated beaches at the tip of the peninsula and employing five infantry battalions as covering forces, leaving Hunter-Weston with a main body of seven battalions.[19] The objective for 29th Division's covering force was the Achi Baba hill and a line across the peninsula at that place. A particularly vexing tactical problem for Hunter-Weston was that the covering force beaches were not contiguous and the link-ups between them somehow had to occur simultaneously from expanding beachheads. The objective of his main body was the seizure of the Kilid Bahr plateau itself. Although the 29th Division was smaller than the two-division ANZAC it was Hamilton's principal effort. Like Kitchener and Churchill, this reflected the confidence Hamilton had in the capacity and capability of British regulars versus incompletely trained Australians, marines and naval personnel, and the French.

Hamilton's plan committed his entire force to active operations of some kind, leaving him with no operational reserve and little capacity to influence the outcome once the troops started to land; although initially he planned to hold a single battalion in tactical reserve (the Plymouth Battalion, RMLI) in transports at his own disposal and prepared to land on Y Beach if circumstances permitted. Detailed coordination with de Robeck's staff continued simultaneously with MEF staff planning involving complex plans for transporting, landing and supporting a force of 75,000 men, 16,400 animals and 3,100 vehicles on hostile shores.[20] As the next week passed, Hamilton and his subordinate commanders began to make changes to the plan at the tactical level, the most notable of which was the use of the collier *River Clyde* to increase the number of men who could be landed at Sedd el Bahr. This was in response to the concerns voiced by Hunter-Weston, whose initial enthusiasm had begun to wane after personal reconnaissances by ship during which he observed the enemy preparations and fortifications overlooking his landing beaches. Commander E. Unwin, RN commanding HMS *Hussar* proposed that the collier *River Clyde*, which could carry 2,000 men (or an additional two battalions of infantry), could be modified with armour plate and sandbags, a battery of machine guns, and doors cut into the hull, and then run aground on the beach after which gangways would be lowered to enable the swift mass debarkation of infantry. While this added significant strength to the covering force on one beach it removed men from Hunter-Weston's main body. Hamilton made another change by directing Hunter-Weston to make a landing at Y Beach with an infantry battalion and, furthermore, he committed the Plymouth Battalion to the endeavour as well. These changes effectively gave the 29th Division's covering force seven and a half battalions and left only five and a half battalions in Hunter-Weston's main body, while at the same time removing an immediate reserve from Hamilton's personal control.

On 16 April, the naval staffs sent directions for 'Observation Officers' Fires' to the army staffs containing instructions about how to coordinate naval gunfire and, on the same day, Hamilton sanctioned landing of the King's Own Scottish Borderers under the cliff west of Krithia (Y Beach) attaching the Plymouth Battalion to the 29th Division to accommodate this. He also requested more information on the beaches themselves from de Robeck. Hamilton sent final instructions to d'Amade on 18 April, inviting him to effect a landing at Kum Kale with the object of 'engaging the attention of the Turks'.[21] Hamilton clearly stated that this was a diversion, although the occupation of space in Asia denied the enemy artillery locations from which to shell Allied transports in Morto Bay. He also instructed the French commander to be prepared to pull out quickly and reposition his force at Cape Helles to participate in the general advance. On 20 April, Hamilton issued his final instructions for the covering forces to Birdwood and Hunter-Weston.

De Robeck and Hamilton fixed 23 April as the date for the landings at a meeting on the *Queen Elizabeth* on 19 April. Hamilton received an intelligence report from Kitchener later in the day that described the recent fighting at Basra and gave warning that the Ottoman Army might be tougher than previously thought.[22] The message read: 'The Turkish troops were well disciplined, well trained and brave. Their machine guns had been well-concealed, and were used with great effect and their trenches were admirably situated ... they had to be turned out ... with the bayonet'. Kitchener continued with the note that the Turks retired 16 miles during the night and continued retirement the following day. Hamilton reprinted this and distributed it to his commanders. Hamilton now possessed detailed tactical information about the overall combat effectiveness of the Ottoman Army, he had aerial observation of the enemy positions and a fairly comprehensive idea of the Ottoman order of battle, and he had the opinions of Doughty-Wylie and Deeds as well as the observations and anxieties of Hunter-Weston. In the immediate days before the landing he had contentious conversations with Birdwood and Hunter-Weston, who vigorously advocated for a night landing and a dawn landing respectively. The naval staff issued instructions for its beach masters and beach parties, as well as plans for controlling the Dardanelles after the fleet had passed through. An enthusiastic MEF intelligence staff published an instruction about encouraging the surrender of Ottoman soldiers using phrases from the Turkish language, such as 'throw down your rifles!' and 'surrender!'

Hamilton had decided to position himself with de Robeck on the *Queen Elizabeth* and on 21 April he chose a handful of staff officers who would accompany him to the overcrowded flagship for the landings. That afternoon Hamilton issued supplementary instructions to d'Amade outlining his final additions to the tactical plan.[23] He directed the French to 'come up in line with the 29th Division preparatory to a general advance on the Kilid Bahr plateau'. Hamilton expected that he would have to interrupt the debarkation of the 29th Division's transport and animals so that the French could deploy into the crowded Cape Helles beachhead. In order to control these events, Hamilton suggested that d'Amade position himself on the French flagship and ensure the presence of 'English signallers'. Whether Hamilton's inclusion of the French directly in the main effort on Kilid Bahr was a reaction to a more dismal intelligence picture of the enemy or to the fact that Hunter-Weston had less than half of his division available as his main body is unclear today. The War Office estimated that the MEF would suffer 5,000 casualties and, belatedly, the MEF staff wrote instructions titled 'Suggested action in the event of the 29th Division or the Australians failing to establish themselves ashore'.[24] The exact date of the operation's start lay in de Robeck's hands and was entirely a function of weather. Originally planned for 23 April, at 10.00am on 21 April, de Robeck delayed the operation until 24 April and then delayed it again the next day for another 24 hours until 25 April.

Hamilton's campaign plan was daring and innovative and it broke new ground as an operational and tactical method. However, the plan rested on a number of planning assumptions that had to prove valid in order for success to be achieved. The principal of these assumptions were that naval gunfire would effectively replace the army's field artillery; that the covering forces would secure their objectives rapidly; that the enemy commanders would hesitate to commit reserves for a period of 48 hours; and that British regulars could overcome fierce resistance by virtue of their professionalism. Moreover, the British commanders and staffs assumed and expected that Ottoman resistance would be heavy initially but then would decline and collapse. There was no master timeline written by the MEF staff but it was expected that the ANZAC would reach Sari Bair and what came to be known as Third Ridge in the first 24 hours while the 29th Division would reach Achi Baba during the same time period. Within the next 24 hours, the ANZAC would secure Mal Tepe, effectively isolating the enemy garrison on the Kilid Bahr plateau while the 29th Division consolidated on Achi Baba. Sometime shortly thereafter the 29th Division would shift to the left flank as the French came up to take up the right flank on the Achi Baba line, after which both divisions would attack to seize the Kilid Bahr plateau. From there Hamilton's artillery would dominate the Narrows and, in a short time, reduce the Ottoman forts to rubble, enabling minesweeping to begin. It was not inconceivable that the fleet might pass the Narrows about a week after the initial landings.

What is often ignored in assessments of the Gallipoli amphibious operation is that in a period of about 30 days, starting on 22 March (de Robeck's decision not to pursue a 'naval-only' operation) and ending on 21 April (the day de Robeck and Hamilton expected the joint and combined operation to begin), Hamilton and de Robeck's staffs put together an entire, well-coordinated campaign plan to conduct a five-division amphibious operation on a hostile shore. It is fair to say that the navy and Birdwood had done some preliminary work but, on the whole, this was a plan written from scratch. The fact that Hamilton's A & Q staff did not arrive from Britain until 1 April, and Hamilton and his staff were in Alexandria until 8 April, makes this achievement even more noteworthy. That Hamilton could conceptualize, what was at the time, such an unorthodox operation and impart it to his staff so that it actually came off is even more remarkable. Nothing like this had ever before been attempted nor were there any doctrines, training or similar experiences available from which to draw conclusions. After the Second World War, historians and the public were so familiar with successful assault landings that it became easy to forget how difficult these operations were and fashionable to characterize Hamilton's landings as badly planned and poorly executed. That the officers and men involved in the Gallipoli landings achieved such successes as they did was a monumental achievement undertaken in almost impossible circumstances.

It may be useful to consider that until March 1915 the British Army itself had not conducted any large-scale offensive operations in the war, although it had landed the BEF in France, the EEF in Egypt, and advanced a single division in Mesopotamia. In fact, Sir John French's BEF conducted Britain's first large-scale offensive operation of the war at about the same time as Hamilton's Gallipoli landings. It may therefore, be useful to compare and contrast the BEF's earliest offensive operation in France – a four-division attack on 10 March 1915 at Neuve Chapelle – which it had been planning and preparing since mid-January. The operational commander, General Sir Douglas Haig, began serious planning on 12 February, and he had significant general staff resources at his disposal as well as artillery totalling 90 guns and 60 howitzers to support the 72,000-man attack on an attack frontage of about 8,000 yards (7.3km) from positions that they had occupied for months. Moreover, French's artillerymen had stockpiled artillery ammunition for months – it was the Neuve Chapelle offensive that had drained most of Britain's artillery shell production, forcing Kitchener to deny Hamilton's requests for ammunition. Neuve Chapelle may be compared with Hamilton's operation, which employed a 75,000-man force, supported by several hundred naval guns, launched from distant staging areas in Egypt and Lemnos against points 62 miles apart. Haig's attack collapsed in three days, while after three days Hamilton was just getting started.

Ottoman operational planning

The British landings at Kum Kale on 4 March alerted the Ottoman general staff to the vulnerability of the Asiatic shore. Consequently on 9 March the well-trained 11th Infantry Division, stationed at Balıkesir on the southern coast of the Sea of Marmara, was alerted for deployment to the straits.[25] Five days later the division began to move to Ezine (south-east of Kum Kale) and, by coincidence, it closed on the town as the naval battle raged on 18 March. The arrival of the new division did not alter the seaward defence at Kum Kale, which continued to be an ad hoc assortment of the 9th Division's 25th Infantry Regiment, the 64th Regiment, which was newly arrived from the 3rd Division, and several jandarma battalions. For the moment, the 11th Division lay in reserve.

Thus by the naval attack of 18 March, the Ottoman defence was solidified into a sort of bi-zonal defensive deployment: the middle peninsula and isthmus

OTTOMAN DEFENCES, 26 MARCH 1915

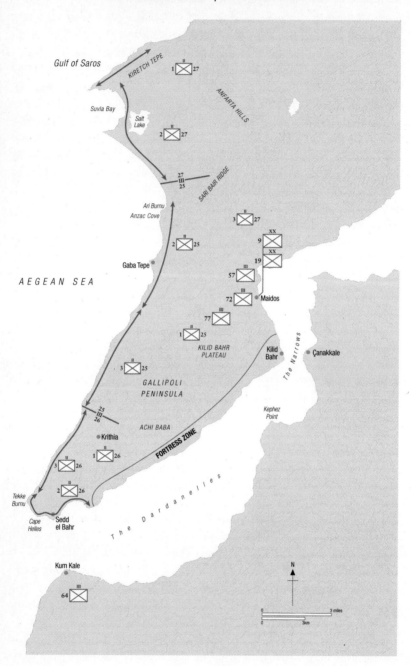

Gulf of Saros

KIRETCH TEPE

1 | 27

ANFARTA HILLS

Suvla Bay

Salt Lake

2 | 27

27 ||| 25

Ari Burnu
Anzac Cove

SARI BAIR RIDGE

3 | 27

9 XX

2 | 25

19 XX

Gaba Tepe

57 |||

AEGEAN SEA

72 ||| Maidos

77 |||

1 | 25

KILID BAHR PLATEAU

Kilid Bahr

The Narrows

Çanakkale

3 | 25

GALLIPOLI PENINSULA

Kephez Point

25 ||| 26

ACHI BABA

FORTRESS ZONE

Krithia

1 | 26

3 | 26

2 | 26

Tekke Burnu

The Dardanelles

Cape Helles

Sedd el Bahr

Kum Kale

64 |||

N

0   3 miles
0   3km

of Bulair were held by III Corps under Esat with the 7th and 19th Divisions, while the fortress command, under Cevat, was responsible for the straits defences, the 9th Division in the lower peninsula and Asia, as well as the Menderes Detachment at Kum Kale. The arriving 11th Division also fell under Cevat's command. Contrary to some western histories, which assert that the straits were split up the middle, their defences were always unitary under the fortress commander (until the activation of the Fifth Army). The principal weakness of the defensive arrangements at this time was the failure to concentrate the 9th Division, which had two regiments in Europe and one regiment in Asia.

An urgent message to Enver from Cevat Pasha, the fortress commander, two days after the naval attack on 18 March requested the release of the 11th and 19th Divisions from reserve for tactical use at Gaba Tepe and Kum Kale respectively in order to concentrate the 9th Division on the southern end of the Gallipoli peninsula.[26] Subsequently, Enver approved the movements of the 9th and 11th Divisions but retained Kemal's 19th Division near Maidos.[27] By 31 March the entire 9th Division was concentrated in the lower peninsula together with two jandarma battalions. The Ottoman general staff also notified Cevat that Hamilton had brought 40,000 French and 50,000 Australians to Mudros harbour. These messages highlight, not only the concerns of the Ottoman general staff about an Allied invasion immediately after the attack of 18 March, but indicate that the Ottoman intelligence services were focused on the MEF. A now thoroughly worried, but highly energized Enver Pasha decided to reorganize his forces at the Dardanelles. On 24 March 1915, Enver asked General Otto Liman von Sanders, who was then in command of the First Army, to take command of a proposed Ottoman Fifth Army. Liman von Sanders, who had previously turned down command of the Ottoman Third Army in the Caucasus, accepted the assignment. The next day, Enver sent orders to the Ottoman general staff outlining the new command arrangements that would transfer all mobile units from the fortress command and III Corps to the newly activating army.[28] The new German commander himself arrived on the peninsula on 26 March accompanied by two German captains as aides-de-camp (Prigge and Mühlman) and his chief of staff, Ottoman Lieutenant-Colonel Kazım.

Enver published the formal activation orders on the same day that Liman von Sanders arrived, assigning the new Fifth Army the following units: Esat Pasha's III Corps (7th, 9th and 19th Infantry Divisions), Faik Pasha's II Corps (4th and 5th Infantry Divisions), a provisional corps to be activated under German Colonel Erich Weber (3rd and 11th Infantry Divisions), and an independent cavalry brigade.[29] But almost immediately thereafter II Corps and the 4th Division were deleted from the Fifth Army order of battle while

5th Division was retained as an independent division. The map on page 118 shows the deployment of the 9th Division on 26 March 1915.

The new Fifth Army commander established his headquarters in the town of Gallipoli and spent his first week in command inspecting the area of operations. Like the British, Liman von Sanders concluded that the Kilid Bahr plateau was the most important piece of key terrain in his area of operations and that enemy landings at Cape Helles and Gaba Tepe were the most dangerous enemy course of action.[30] He also judged that enemy landings in Saros Bay were potentially extremely dangerous since that would allow the British to cut off the peninsula. The Fifth Army general staff began to arrive with the assignment of Captain Mümtaz as chief of operations and Major H. Hüsnü as chief of administration, both of whom were graduates of the War Academy and trained general staff officers.

The remainder of 3rd Division left Constantinople by ship and arrived at Erenköy on 31 March. As a result of Liman von Sanders'observations, the 5th Division remained at Saros Bay, while the 3rd Division proceeded to the Asian side and the area around Calvert's Farm, where Colonel Weber had set up his newly established provisional corps headquarters on 1 April 1915.[31] Colonel Weber, in turn, deployed the 3rd Division to take over the Kum Kale beach defences and sent the 11th Division to take over the 9th Division's positions at Besika Bay on 5 April 1915.[32] The tactical arrangements mirrored those of the 9th Division on the peninsula with company-level defences on the beaches backed up by strong battalion- and regimental-level reserves. Over the next two weeks, minor changes were made to the tactical disposition of the combat forces and the Fifth Army staff concentrated on improving the logistical lines of communications. In particular, three rations depots and one munitions depot were moved closer to the corps headquarters and the 20-metre and 40-metre pontoons from III Corps' bridge trains were sent to the newly activated XV Corps.[33]

Over the next several days the Ottoman high command sent several machine-gun companies, four jandarma battalions and an artillery battalion to reinforce Fifth Army. On 7 April, the Fifth Army issued Liman von Sanders' defensive operations order for the impending campaign.[34] It contained no surprises and formally assigned the subordinate corps and divisions defensive missions in their sectors of responsibility. Colonel Weber's provisional corps was formally activated as the Ottoman Army's XV Corps. Liman von Sanders ordered Mustafa Kemal's 19th Division to move from Maidos to Bigalı and assigned it the mission of Fifth Army general reserve with instructions to be prepared to return to Maidos for deployment to Asia if required. There were

OTTOMAN DEFENCES, 25 APRIL 1915

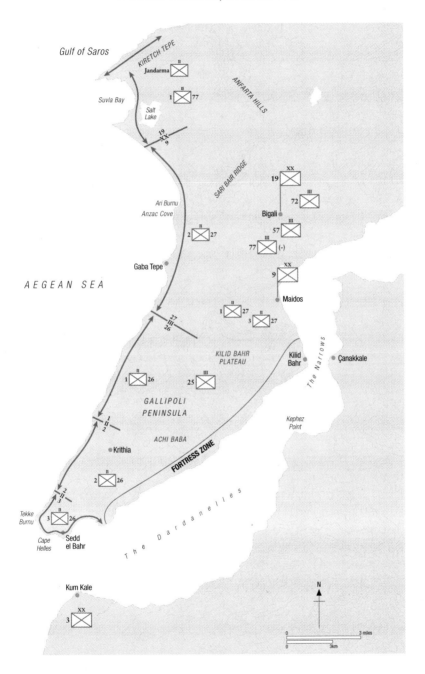

Gulf of Saros

KIRETCH TEPE

Jandarma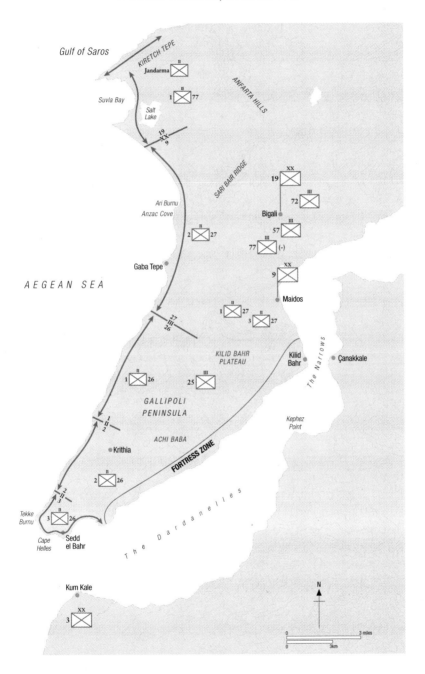

Suvla Bay

1 [ ] 77

Salt
Lake

ANFARTA HILLS

19
XX
9

SARI BAIR RIDGE

Ari Burnu
Anzac Cove

Bigali

19 [ ] XX

72 [ ] III

2 [ ] 27

57 [ ] III

77 [ ] (-) III

Gaba Tepe

9 [ ] XX

Maidos

AEGEAN SEA

1 [ ] 27

3 [ ] 27

*KILID BAHR
PLATEAU*

Kilid
Bahr

The Narrows

Çanakkale

1 [ ] 26

25 [ ] III

*GALLIPOLI
PENINSULA*

1
2

ACHI BABA

Krithia

FORTRESS ZONE

Kephez
Point

2 [ ] 26

The Dardanelles

2
3

Tekke
Burnu

3 [ ] 26

Cape
Helles

Sedd
el Bahr

Kum Kale

N

3 [ ] XX

0   3 miles
0   3km

121

tactical instructions dealing with artillery coordination, battle drills, day and night marches and manoeuvres, and reporting procedures. However, these instructions simply restated previous Ottoman Army standardized procedures that had already been implemented by the Ottoman corps and division commanders themselves. Importantly, Liman von Sanders' orders placed less emphasis on defence at the water's edge and explicitly noted that the tactical battle would be won or lost through the launching of decisive concentrated counter-attacks within the first 48 hours.[35]

The Ottoman Army's dispositions were criticized heavily by General Otto Liman von Sanders in his memoirs and the perception that defences were poorly sited and improperly prepared has persisted to this day. He was particularly critical of the number of reserves available for counter-attacks.[36] Liman von Sanders asserted that '[t]he positions of five existing divisions up to March 26 had to be altered completely. They were posted on different principles and distributed along the entire coast ... there were no reserves to check a strong and energetic advance'.[37] However, the Ottoman defences were quite robust prior to the arrival of Liman von Sanders on 26 March 1915 and included substantial numbers of well-positioned reserves.[38] In fact, the Ottoman deployment on that day included 12 infantry battalions in immediate reserve. Although Liman von Sanders shifted the 19th Infantry Division north from Maidos to Bigalı, he would actually add only a single battalion to the total tactical reserves available on 25 April.[39] Moreover, the concentration of the 3rd, 9th and 11th Divisions was already in motion before he arrived. Based on this evidence, the impact of Liman von Sanders on the pre-battle deployment of the Ottoman Fifth Army appears minimal.

Comparison of planning and operational efforts

Broadly speaking, the MEF and Fifth Army's planning efforts were completed in about a month by improvised staffs. Hamilton had some advantage by using the work that Birdwood and his ANZAC staff had put into thinking about amphibious landings and that de Robeck's staff had done on landing army units and supporting them with naval gunfire support. Similarly, Liman von Sanders took over an operational area for which an accumulated two-year planning effort had taken place, and refined it. In both cases, the army-level commanders were new to the theatre and had to create their own staffs from newly arriving personnel.

The opposing campaign plans both recognized the Kilid Bahr plateau as the key terrain feature along the straits, the possession of which would determine the outcome of the campaign. The Fifth Army plan aimed to retain the plateau while the MEF plan aimed to seize it. Both plans recognized the importance of the first 48 hours as a critical time frame for determining success. The MEF intended to be in a position to seize the Kilid Bahr plateau by the end of that period while the Fifth Army intended to have contained the beachheads and be in a position to launch large-scale counter-attacks. The MEF aimed at fixing the Ottoman reserves using deception and diversions for the first 48 hours and, reciprocally, the Fifth Army intended to work out where the British main effort was and release substantial reserves in the same period.

At the operational level, Hamilton depended on manoeuvre from the sea to confuse the enemy in order to achieve surprise as to the actual location of his main effort. At the tactical level, Hamilton depended on the individual superiority of the British and Allied soldiers under his command to defeat the Ottoman Army decisively. This was especially true of his choice of British regulars and professional French soldiers for his decisive attack on the Kilid Bahr plateau. He also relied on a massive amount of naval gunfire to make up for the MEF's inability to get its artillery ashore quickly, as well as for its overall shortages of artillery ammunition. Liman von Sanders intended to shift his forces at the operational level for large-scale counter-attacks to push the British back into the sea. For its part at the tactical level, the Ottoman Army depended on combined-arms tactics and rapid decision-making by subordinates to make up for numerical inferiority at the points of encounter.

The landings, 25 April 1915

Hunter-Weston intended that his entire covering force of seven and a half battalions would be ashore by 7.00am, 25 April.[40] Field artillery would land after that, followed by the five main body battalions, of which two battalions from the 87th Brigade would land at W Beach and form the divisional reserve. Brigadier-General H. E. Napier, with two battalions of his 88th Brigade, was scheduled to land at V Beach as the major element of the main body and push on to Achi Baba. The opening naval bombardment at Cape Helles began at 5.00am and shortly thereafter the men of the covering forces landed. Hunter-Weston's main effort would be made at X, W and V Beaches, with supporting landing made on both flanks – at Y Beach to the north-east of X Beach and at S Beach to the east across Morto Bay from V Beach.

Brigadier-General S. W. Hare was named in the GHQ orders as the covering force commander; however, he was also the commander of the 86th Brigade. Hare's 86th Brigade – composed of four battalions and reinforced by half of a fifth – was split and landed at W and V Beaches. Hare himself planned to land

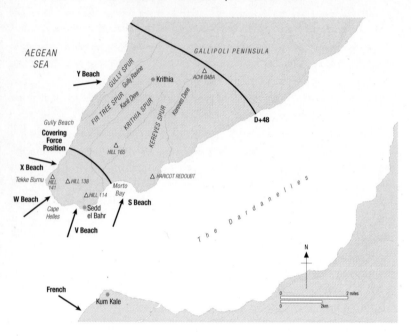

CAPE HELLES LANDINGS, 25 APRIL 1915

AEGEAN SEA

GALLIPOLI PENINSULA

Y Beach

GULLY SPUR

Gully Ravine

• Krithia

△ ACHI BABA

FIR TREE SPUR

Kanli Dere

KRITHIA SPUR

KEREVES SPUR

Kereves Dere

Gully Beach

Covering Force Position

D+48

△ HILL 165

X Beach

Tekke Burnu

△ HILL 141

△ HILL 138

△ HARICOT REDOUBT

Morto Bay

△ HILL 114

W Beach

Cape Helles

• Sedd el Bahr

S Beach

V Beach

The Dardanelles

N

French

Kum Kale

0 ___ 2 miles
0 ___ 2km

at W Beach and take command of the united forces of his brigade, which he expected would link up shortly after landing. The landing at W Beach was famously stopped at the waterline by the well-disciplined Ottomans and the 1st Battalion, the Lancashire Fusiliers famously won 'six VCs [Victoria Crosses] before breakfast' trying to fight their way ashore. Nevertheless, by 7.15am the battalion had established a small foothold on the beach but Hare, who had come ashore and was courageously leading his men forward, was seriously wounded. Progress at W Beach then ground to a halt.

Things were even worse on V Beach as the tows carrying the 1st Battalion, the Royal Dublin Fusiliers, and the *River Clyde*, carrying two battalions of Munster Fusiliers and Hampshires, approached shore later than planned in the face of fully alert Ottoman defenders. The converted and heavily loaded collier did not reach the beach, grounding out in shallow water, and the tows were mostly destroyed on the beach. The attack was stopped cold and the men were slaughtered as they tried, unsuccessfully, to gain a foothold. Despite a number of heroic attempts to get ashore, the battalions at V Beach were held there throughout the entire day and suffered heavy casualties. At X Beach, Brigadier-General W. R. Marshall landed with two battalions of his 87th Brigade on a beach that was lightly defended by the enemy. By 11.00am, Marshall's men had pushed some 800 yards (730m) inland and held the crest of the high ground overlooking the beach. But there they were held up by a determined defence.

Aboard the *Euryalus*, Hunter-Weston had encouraging reports from Y, X and S Beaches by 7.30am but had heard nothing from W and V Beaches. He assumed that those landings had also been successful and ordered the landing of the main body at 8.30am. This sent Napier and the 88th Brigade staff into V Beach at about 9.30am, where Napier and his brigade-major were both killed trying to lead men ashore. At 10.21am Hunter-Weston signalled to Hamilton that it was not advisable to send more men to V Beach. Over on W Beach the main body battalions added to the weight of the covering force already there and allowed forward progress towards Hill 138 to resume.

The landing at Y Beach was unopposed and inordinately successful allowing the 1st Battalion, King's Own Scottish Borderers, under Lieutenant-Colonel A. S. Koe and the Plymouth Battalion of the Royal Marine Light Infantry under Lieutenant-Colonel G. E. Matthews to push almost into the village of Krithia. Matthews, as the senior man, was in command of the force and was ordered to push inland and then link up to the south-west with the 87th Brigade at X Beach. He had no orders that were discretionary and, throughout the day, received no orders to the contrary. Matthews' failure to use independent initiative and take Krithia is regarded as the great missed opportunity of the landings.[41] In Matthew's defence, he followed his orders, moreover, he had no artillery and the marine battalion was packed full of newly recruited and untrained men. Enemy counter-attacks later in the day convinced him to assume a defensive posture. The S Beach landing by three companies of the 2nd Battalion, South Wales Borderers was also successful but it lacked the strength to do anything more than secure a perimeter on the headlands around the small beach.

Hamilton and five staff officers boarded the *Queen Elizabeth* at 1.00pm on 24 April, while the remainder of the GHQ remained aboard the *Arcadian*. In the absence of combined amphibious doctrines, co-locating himself next to de Robeck seemed the logical place to command. Hamilton occupied the tiny cramped conning tower with de Robeck and could only observe outside through narrow slits in the armour.[42] There was no room inside for Hamilton's staff, who occupied spaces scattered around the ship. Hamilton's subordinate commanders were located on four different ships supervising their respective landings and he had communications with them via the navy's wireless. Two of Hamilton's staff officers were detailed to accompany the landings and to report what they observed – Lieutenant-Colonel Williams to V Beach and Captain Bolton to W Beach. De Robeck's flagship arrived off Cape Helles at 5.20am the next morning and

Hamilton's communications began to break down almost immediately. This was partly a result of the concussion of the *Queen Elizabeth*'s guns firing as well as the general unreliability of radios in 1915. It was also a function of the lack of standardization inherent in the British reporting system, which provided commanders information when they asked for it but incompletely required subordinates to report on their own initiative. By mid-morning, Hamilton had only a very sketchy understanding of the unfolding landings and much of that was due to personal observation from the flagship, which cruised up and down the coast.

The MEF War Diary for 25 April comprises nine pages of incoming reports and several things are immediately apparent from reading it.[43] The sequence is not written chronologically, for example, the second page stops halfway down at midnight and is followed by an entry for 7.00am. A subsequent data entry stops at 5.12pm and then restarts at 4.30pm. This indicates the maintenance of multiple diaries, which were consolidated as the day went by. Moreover, the MEF staff maintained the intelligence diary on the *Arcadian*. It is also apparent that Hamilton received information from four primary sources. The bulk of the reports on 25 April came from de Robeck's ships, which were supporting the landings, and which reported what they were observing on land. The most prolific individual source of information was army Captain Harry Bolton at W Beach; sometimes Vice-Admiral Wemyss – who was on *Euryalus* with Hunter-Weston – offered bits of information that came from aircraft and balloons. Hunter-Weston reported intermittently and the least frequent source of information was Birdwood. Overall, the MEF War Diary gives an impression of chaos and uncertainty as the day of the landings passed. With the exception of the very junior Captain Bolton, who seemed to have a number of creative ideas about advancing the tactical situation, none of Hamilton's subordinates asked for anything other than naval gunfire support and casualty evacuation.

Hamilton has been criticized by almost every historian for his seemingly casual performance on 25 April and, in particular, for his inability to control the battle or to alter the plan in order to reinforce success. It is, therefore, important to understand what Hamilton knew and when he knew it. The MEF War Diary records the following significant information that Hamilton probably would have known about given his scattered staff:[44]

5.10am – Landings in progress
5.35am – Birdwood reported 4,000 men ashore
6.42am – Visual report – Australian Brigade making good progress
7.00am – Visual report – Covering forces on Skyline of X and W (in fact, this was in error as W was held on the beach)

– *Goliath* reported an easy landing at Y Beach at 6.40am

7.35am – *Grampus* reported covering force ashore at W Beach

8.30am – Visual report from *Queen Elizabeth* – no progress at *River Clyde*, V Beach enfiladed by pom-poms and rifle fire

    – Hunter-Weston wired for a hospital ship

    – Request for fire support on Sedd el Bahr.

9.21am – Progress made at W Beach, query from Hamilton to 29th Division regarding 'whether they would have to get some more men ashore on Y Beach if trawlers available'

    – *River Clyde* failing, further requests from V Beach for naval gunfire support

10.00am – Bolton reported W Beach taken at 6 am

10.35am – Bolton asked if V Beach can support W Beach by moving on Hill 138

10.45am – Reply from Hunter-Weston and Wemyss – they think it is inadvisable to land more men on Y Beach as this will delay debarkation of the main body

10.55am – *River Clyde* failed. All boats and crews destroyed. Troops pinned on beach

11.30am – Hunter-Weston reported he had decided that troops bound for V Beach should go to W Beach instead

11.35am – *River Clyde* reported inadvisable to send more men to V Beach

    – Bolton reported no progress at W Beach as nothing has landed since early morning. And the Lancs had advanced only to edge of Hill 138

12 noon – Wemyss reported troops on W Beach had taken Hill 114. No progress at V Beach because of snipers

1.30pm – d'Amade reported all is well at Kum Kale landing

2.00pm – first comprehensive report arrived from Hunter-Weston – No change at V Beach. S and Y Beach landings are successful. W Beach attacking towards Hill 138

2.30pm – Bolton at W Beach reported Royal Fusiliers forced to retire because of counter-attacks and have established an 800-yard perimeter around X Beach. Bolton asked if troops on Y Beach can push to their right to draw enemy

3.10pm – Bolton reported X and W Beaches are linked up. Attack on Hill 138 progressing but held up by wire making further progress impossible

4.30pm – ANZAC reports 13,000 infantry and one mountain battery ashore. Hard fighting

5.12pm – Report from Hunter-Weston – organizing attack from W Beach towards V Beach. Heavy casualties, one brigadier killed and two brigadiers wounded

5.51pm – Troops on de Totts's are isolated (S Beach) and exposed to heavy fire

5.55pm – Hunter-Weston reported the assault working towards Hill 138 will go after dark

7.00pm – Hunter-Weston reported – Worcesters captured Hill 114 (this was an error – not Hill 114 but knoll to east of Hill 138). Pushing from V Beach. Y Beach counter-attacked. All troops ashore except from *River Clyde*. Will advance against Achi Baba tomorrow.

– *Agamemnon* reported French troops landed between Kum Kale and Achilles Tomb

Nightfall – semi-circle around X Beach. Same at W Beach. Many casualties at V Beach. Enemy still holds Hill 138.

8.45pm – Message from Birdwood – he had personally been ashore – situation found not very satisfactory. Difficult country. 2,000 casualties. Heavy shrapnel and rifle fire. ANZAC facing nine battalions plus machine guns.

9.00pm – Hunter-Weston came on board the flagship and personally reported to Hamilton.

12 midnight – Brigadier-General Carruthers came on board *Queen Elizabeth* and reported ANZAC situation serious. Hamilton decided to hold position gained at Anzac throughout the night.

What can be said of British command and control on 25 April? At the operational level, Hamilton had no actual decisions to make on that day. Likewise, he was unable to influence the outcome as the day progressed. Some historians have criticized Hamilton heavily for not overriding Hunter-Weston at 10.45am and insisting that more men be landed at Y Beach. This 'what if' is based on the idea that taking Krithia seemed possible on the morning of 25 April; however, seizing Krithia seems improbable because the Ottomans had a reserve infantry company marching there at 7.00am. Moreover, Hamilton's plan explicitly ordered the battalions from Y Beach to attack southward towards X Beach and not north-east towards Krithia. Presumably the trawlers, which Hamilton said were available to do this, were the four that had previously towed the covering force onto S Beach, however, it is not clear where these ships were nor how they would connect with one of Hunter-Weston's main body battalions.

In fairness to Hamilton, he recognized the opportunity at Y Beach on the morning of 25 April, queried Hunter-Weston but then received a reply that made tactical sense thereby ending the matter. One historian noted that Hamilton intervened by ordering 29th Division forces from V Beach be landed instead at W Beach, however, the MEF War Diary states that

Hamilton was informed of this change at 11.30am – indicating that Hunter-Weston made the decision.[45] In fact, Hamilton's landing plan left him with no operational reserve immediately available for exploitation or reinforcement. Moreover, he was never in possession of real-time information about the tactical situation unfolding ashore. Inadequate communications and inefficient reporting systems combined with Hamilton's personal location inside the *Queen Elizabeth*'s armoured conning tower left him isolated from his staff and from effective command of his forces. In truth, the only decision Hamilton made on 25 April was to order the ANZAC at midnight to stay and dig in.

At the tactical level, Hunter-Weston's principal decision on 25 April revolved around shifting main body forces from V Beach to W Beach. Some historians attribute the decision not to reinforce Y Beach to Hunter-Weston and a recent historian asserted that Hunter-Weston was institutionally and intellectually focused on V Beach where the fighting was heaviest and the landing in danger of failing, blinding him to the tactical opportunity at Y Beach. The official history noted that the failure to exploit Y Beach was a lost 'golden opportunity'. But it is important to keep in mind that the decision was the combined result of Hunter-Weston's discussion with Wemyss and that, from a naval perspective, trying to adapt spontaneously by landing men previously destined for other beaches at Y Beach would have delayed debarkation of Hunter-Weston's main body. In fact, at 9.30am, Hunter-Weston had already shifted the 1st Battalion, the Essex Regiment to land at W Beach and 1st Battalion, the Border Regiment had landed at X Beach. At the same time, Hunter-Weston's three remaining main body battalions were then inbound to X and W Beaches for a noon landing. Whether he could have disengaged one of those battalions and shifted them north to Y Beach is extremely problematic. Finally, Hunter-Weston had not clearly established overall command at Y Beach and adding more troops further compounded the real problem there. It is clear that by landing all five of his main body battalions at X and W Beaches, Hunter-Weston was in control and focused on success rather than failure. In fact, the problem at Y Beach was never the amount of men there, instead it was the basic mission itself which oriented the force towards W Beach.

Hunter-Weston spent 25 April on the cruiser *Euryalus* mostly off W Beach, in part, because that ship was assigned responsibility for the debarkation of 18 tows. During the day few accurate messages made their way to Hunter-Weston. Apparently none of the messages sent by the two battalion commanders (Matthews and Koe) from Y Beach arrived on the *Euryalus* at all. Moreover, it was impossible for Hunter-Weston to make a meaningful contribution by going ashore himself on 25 April because the beachheads were tiny and not interconnected. Whether his personal presence could have restored initiative to the stalled attacks is problematic to evaluate.

At Z Beach, the landings were slightly offset at a small cove to the north of the intended site but the covering force got ashore anyway. The ANZAC commanders, like Hamilton and Hunter-Weston, placed themselves on warships – Birdwood on HMS *Queen*, while the 1st Australian Division commander, Major-General Bridges and his staff were aboard HMS *Prince of Wales*. Both the corps and division commanders were out of real-time communications with the covering force. Unfortunately, this left Sinclair-MacLagan in control of the landing and enabled him to divert the corps' main effort from the covering force's geographical objective to fighting a battle with the Ottoman Army.[46]

At Z Beach (see map opposite), the ANZAC landings were badly misplaced at a small cove to the north of the intended site but the covering force got ashore anyway. The Australians started to land at about 4.45am, 25 April, and rapidly scaled the rugged heights advancing to what became known as Second Ridge. Within the hour they were in contact with Ottoman forces, meeting resistance. The covering force was commanded by the 3rd Australian Brigade brigadier, Colonel Ewan Sinclair-MacLagan. Uncertain, he halted. It was obvious to Sinclair-MacLagan that his brigade had landed in the wrong spot but he did not move to the front to observe personally the situation. Sinclair-MacLagan had been against the operation from the start and Ottoman resistance enabled him to shift to the defensive on Second Ridge. Moreover, heavy fires from Gaba Tepe convinced Sinclair-MacLagan that his right flank was exposed. At 5.30am the first battalions of the main body, Colonel James McCay's 2nd Australian Brigade, started to land on the beach.[47] According to Birdwood's plan the mission of McCay's brigade was to move on the left and take the Sari Bair Ridge. As the first battalion landed, Sinclair-MacLagan sent it to the right and subsequently persuaded McCay to abandon his orders and take his entire brigade to the right of the 3rd Australian Brigade. This decision put the ANZAC into a defensive posture for six hours on Second Ridge.

Sinclair-MacLagan's decision to shift the divisional force that was supposed to move through his thin covering force and take on the corps' principal objective – Sari Bair Ridge and Hill 971 – ruined the execution of Birdwood's plan. Although three more brigades were inbound, none were tasked in Birdwood's plan to move on Hill 971. Bridges landed at 7.20am, went to the top of Second Ridge to observe the battle, and then returned to the beach. Like

ANZAC LANDINGS, 25 APRIL 1915

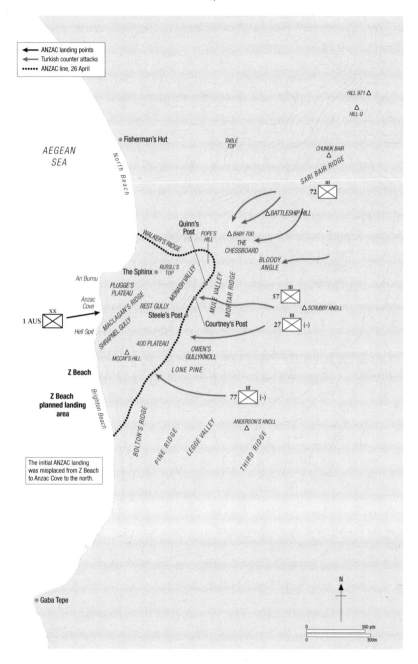

ANZAC landing points
Turkish counter attacks
ANZAC line, 26 April

AEGEAN SEA

Fisherman's Hut

North Beach

HILL 971 △

△ HILL Q

TABLE TOP

CHUNUK BAIR △

SARI BAIR RIDGE

72 III

△ BATTLESHIP HILL

Quinn's Post

POPE'S HILL

WALKER'S RIDGE

△ BABY 700

THE CHESSBOARD

BLOODY ANGLE

The Sphinx

RUSSELL'S TOP

Ari Burnu

PLUGGE'S PLATEAU

MONASH VALLEY

MULE VALLEY

MORTAR RIDGE

57 III

Anzac Cove

MACLAGAN'S RIDGE

REST GULLY

Steele's Post

△ SCRUBBY KNOLL

27 III (-)

Hell Spit

SHRAPNEL GULLY

Courtney's Post

1 AUS XX

400 PLATEAU

△ MCCAY'S HILL

OWEN'S GULLYKNOLL

LONE PINE

Z Beach

Z Beach planned landing area

Brighton Beach

BOLTON'S RIDGE

77 III (-)

ANDERSON'S KNOLL △

PINE RIDGE

LEGGE VALLEY

THIRD RIDGE

The initial ANZAC landing was misplaced from Z Beach to Anzac Cove to the north.

Gaba Tepe

N

0   300 yds
0   300m

131

Sinclair-MacLagan, Bridges judged that the corps' right flank needed more forces. As the battalions of his 1st Australian Brigade came onto the beach over the next several hours, Bridges dispersed them in company packets to reinforce Sinclair-MacLagan. According to historian Chris Roberts, command and control of the division was badly fragmented.[48] About 8.00am, Brigadier-General 'Hooky' Walker, the corps chief of staff landed with the intent of keeping Birdwood informed, however, when the New Zealand Brigade commander failed to arrive later in the morning, Walker took command of the brigade, thereby taking himself out of the corps to division chain of command.

The Australian and New Zealand Division began to land at 10.00am and the ANZAC had a second opportunity to remedy the collapsed plan. The division chief of staff landed to discuss the situation with Bridges, the outcome of which was a decision to deploy the New Zealand Brigade to the left of the 3rd Australian Brigade. Part of this brigade came ashore and by 2.30pm had its advanced battalion on Baby 700. Birdwood and Godley came ashore at 3.00pm to discuss the situation with Bridges but nobody went up the hill to look for himself. Birdwood returned to his ship leaving Bridges in tactical command of where to deploy Godley's remaining brigade as it landed. An Ottoman counter-attack retook Baby 700 at about 4.30pm, so worrying Godley that he sent his remaining New Zealanders there to reinforce the line; as darkness fell he sent his 4th Australian Brigade there as well. Bridges and Godley were so demoralized by the failed plan and the onslaught of Ottoman attacks that they asked Birdwood to come ashore.[49] He did so at 8.00pm and, in the ensuing conference, both division commanders urged Birdwood to evacuate the corps. Walker was also in attendance and urged Birdwood not to evacuate. Birdwood returned to his ship and passed the decision up to Hamilton by sending Brigadier-General Carruthers to the *Queen Elizabeth*.

Two decisions stand out at Anzac on 25 April. The first was that Sinclair-MacLagan fatally disrupted the 1st Australian Division's plan by sending McCay's brigade away from the division's main objective. The second important decision was Bridges' commitment to a defensive battle that ultimately drew in both of Godley's brigades. Birdwood made no decisions at all and, moreover, lost control by allowing his subordinates to influence the battle by supporting their own needs rather than to press on towards the corps' objectives. Like Hunter-Weston, Birdwood seemed to be predisposed towards ensuring that his entire force debarked rather than to paying close attention to the securing of the initial covering position. As a result, by the end of the day the fragmented and dispersed ANZAC lay on the Second Ridge rather than on Sari Bair, Hill 971 and Third Ridge as planned.

Ottoman command and control on 25 April

Liman von Sanders spent the night at his army headquarters in Gallipoli. Beginning about 3.00am on 25 April 1915, a constant stream of combat reports from the 9th Division began to flow into III Corps headquarters, which indicated that landings were imminent, and these reports passed to the Fifth Army headquarters at 5.00am. By 6.00am, reports from the 9th Division clarified the scope of the Anzac and Cape Helles landings.[50] Liman von Sanders and his adjutants went out to the high ground at Bulair to observe the reported landings. Judging that the ANZAC landings were the main effort, Esat rode out by automobile at 8.00am from his headquarters in Gallipoli to Bulair to brief Liman von Sanders, who was observing the activity in Saros Bay.[51] Esat came with maps and overlays to make a case for shifting reinforcements south. After briefing Liman von Sanders Esat requested the immediate release of his 7th Division, which was refused by Liman von Sanders; however, the Fifth Army commander agreed to give priority of effort to the Anzac landings.[52] This meant that the reinforcement flow would be directed to Kemal rather than Halil Sami at Cape Helles. Liman von Sanders then asked Esat to return and take personal command of the battles raging on the southern part of the peninsula, while he remained at Bulair to judge for himself whether the British were conducting a feint there.[53] Before departing Esat wrote a hasty order to his 7th Division ordering them to remain in place, but informing them that his headquarters was moving to Maidos. He also warned them to be prepared to move south quickly if ordered.[54]

At noon on 25 April Liman von Sanders ordered XV Corps to send an infantry regiment to Maidos to reinforce Esat.[55] Colonel Weber responded that the French had landed at Kum Kale entirely occupying his 3rd Division. He continued by insisting that landings were expected in 11th Division's sector as well and he maintained he was unable to send troops. The Fifth Army staff then sent an urgent message ordering Weber to send a regiment from 3rd Division immediately and ordering Weber to reinforce 3rd Division by shifting 11th Division units northward. These messages were transmitted through the telephone exchange of the fortress command and, unfortunately, Weber's reply was misrouted and arrived late (at 5.00pm).[56]

Thus as evening fell no reinforcements had been sent to III Corps. An infuriated Liman von Sanders sent a third message demanding that Weber's nearest regiment be dispatched immediately and that Weber must send a second regiment as well. In order to accomplish this rapidly, three Ottoman general staff officers went to work via telephone. They were Staff Captain Nihat, XV Corps chief of operations, fortress chief of staff Lieutenant-Colonel Selahattin

Adil and III Corps chief of staff Colonel Fahrettin. Nihat put the 64th Regiment on the road at 8.15pm to the town of Çanakkale where Selahattin Adil had ships waiting at the piers. The regiment arrived at Kilye pier in Maidos at noon on 26 April where Fahrettin had guides waiting to bring the regiment to its staging area behind the Anzac beachhead. Shortly thereafter Nihat dispatched the 33rd Infantry Regiment in train, which duly arrived on the peninsula shortly after noon as well.

The reports of III Corps' and XV Corps' commanders and staffs were consolidated by the Fifth Army under the direction of the chief of staff, Lieutenant-Colonel Kazım. The speed of transmission of information to Enver in Constantinople was quite rapid with the Ottoman general staff often having possession of information within two hours of an event. Messages were ciphered and assigned a log number and a priority. High-priority messages were carefully managed to ensure positive control. The time it was sent and the time the general staff acknowledged receipt were logged, as well as the time that the acknowledgement was passed to the commander or duty officer.[57] The bulk of the message traffic between the Fifth Army and Constantinople was sent by telegram over the civilian wires of the Administration des Telegraphes de L'Empire Ottoman. Additionally, the Çanakkale fortress maintained wireless communications with the ships of the navy anchored at Istiniye and in the Golden Horn and it was possible to pass information rapidly via this means as well.[58]

At the army corps level, Esat Pasha returned to III Corps headquarters at Gallipoli and proceeded to Mal Tepe, a hill nearer the Anzac front, where he re-established his headquarters at 2.00pm.[59] There at Mal Tepe in the late afternoon, Esat made his most important decision by changing the divisional boundaries and sectors to accommodate the improvised mixing of the 9th Division and the 19th Division at Anzac. By appointing Kemal as the 'Ari Burnu (Anzac) Front Commander' and attaching the 27th Infantry Regiment to the 19th Division, Esat effectively transferred the coastline sector of 2nd Battalion, 27th Infantry Regiment to Kemal. This formalized the ad hoc command structure and unified the Ari Burnu front under a single commander, Mustafa Kemal, while freeing Halil Sami to focus on the Cape Helles landings.

Colonel Weber in XV Corps began to receive a similar stream of reports at about the same time as III Corps. Weber had three potential coastal landing areas of tactical concern (from north to south): the village of Yenikoy, Little Besika Bay, and Big Besika Bay. The 3rd Division held the coast to a point south of Yenikoy from which the 11th Division held the coast to a line parallel with the inland town of Ezine. Kum Kale itself was, apparently, not thought to be as likely a location for a major landing as the larger bays to the south. After learning that Lieutenant-Colonel August Nicolai alerted his own 3rd Division in the early hours of 25 April 1915, Colonel Weber put the adjacent 11th Division on alert at 6.00am with orders to put two thirds of the soldiers into their defensive trenches. Soon after, concentrations of Allied ships in Besika Bay made it seem that landings were imminent there. However, as the French landings were delayed it remained unclear to XV Corps where the Allies might actually land. After the French finally landed at Kum Kale, Weber waited for the larger landing he expected to be launched on one of the three principal beaches to the south. Finally at 3.35pm he sent the 126th and 127th Infantry Regiments forward to positions overlooking both Little and Big Besika Bays. These regiments would remain there, held in place by the French naval demonstrations. Meanwhile, Lieutenant-Colonel Nicolai's regiments went into action at Kum Kale and stabilized the situation there by mid-afternoon.

At division level and below a number of tactical decisions stand out which contributed to the decisive Ottoman success on 25 April 1915. It must be noted that much of the Fifth Army enjoyed success largely due to its comprehensive defensive campaign plans that slowed the enemy long enough for counter-attacks to be readied and launched. However, it is important to remember that Ottoman and German tactical commanders, on their own initiative, made decisions that concentrated forces and firepower creating significant combat power at the points of battle. The most important decisions were made by the 9th Division commander, Halil Sami, and the 19th Division commander, Mustafa Kemal; while Lieutenant-Colonel Nicolai, commanding the 3rd Division at Kum Kale, simply cordoned off the French.

The first Ottoman commander in a position to influence the outcome of the landings was Halil Sami, whose division sector included both Anzac and Cape Helles. At 5.55am on 25 April Halil ordered his 27th Infantry Regiment, which had already been readied for movement by its commander, to execute a counter-attack on the Anzac landings.[60] At about the same time, Mustafa Kemal alerted his best regiment for movement to the landing sites and at 7.00am, he had the 57th Regiment marching towards the Third Ridge under his personal command. There were now two Ottoman regiments from different divisions moving to attack the ANZAC, a fact recognized by Halil Sami, who issued immediate orders to the 27th Infantry Regiment at 8.25am.[61] Unhampered by command prerogatives, Halil Sami ordered his regimental commander, Lieutenant-Colonel Şefik, to coordinate his operations with Kemal. The regiments arrived on the high ground overlooking the advancing Australians and by 11.30am, Kemal and Şefik had agreed to a coordinated counter-attack supported by artillery.[62] The result of these attacks and Sinclair-MacLagen's shift to the defensive was that the Australian advance stalled and the division and the other brigade commanders went into a defensive posture. By releasing tactical control of his 27th Infantry Regiment to Mustafa Kemal, Colonel Halil Sami had effectively and informally cross-attached what might be termed a regimental combat team to the 19th Division, which ensured that the senior man on the spot (Kemal) enjoyed unity of command.

Meanwhile, at Esat Pasha's III Corps field headquarters on Mal Tepe it was apparent that all immediate reserves were committed to containing the Allied landings and it was necessary to revise the command arrangements to reflect the realities of the battle on the ground. From a purely technical perspective, Mustafa Kemal was fighting in Halil Sami's sector. Reacting swiftly to reorganize his corps, Esat designated Kemal as the Ari Burnu Front Commander and attached the 27th Infantry Regiment to his new command.[63] In effect, this transferred the coastline sector of the 2nd Battalion, 27th Infantry Regiment (stretching from a point south of Gaba Tepe to a point north of Fisherman's Hut) from Halil Sami's 9th Division to Kemal's 19th Division. This also formalized the co-operative working arrangement that Halil Sami and Kemal had evolved earlier in the day. Esat Pasha now had Mustafa Kemal focused on the ANZAC at Ari Burnu and Halil Sami focused on the British 29th Division at Cape Helles. As Kemal's remaining two regiments arrived later in the day, he was able to deploy them on the flanks of his continuing counter-attacks.

At Cape Helles, the 1st and 3rd Battalions of 26th Infantry Regiment held the beaches long enough for the regimental commander to deploy his remaining battalion to block Y Beach while reinforcing X and W Beaches. While this was happening, Halil Sami remained focused on the Anzac landing, which he regarded as the major threat to his sector and failed to release his remaining reserve regiment for action. It was not until 2.15pm that Halil Sami ordered the 3rd Battalion, 25th Infantry Regiment forward for a counter-attack on Y Beach.[64] This left the 9th Division with two infantry battalions remaining in reserve and, despite requests to III Corps for help, no inbound reinforcements. Reluctant to commit his remaining battalions, Halil Sami delayed until 6.30pm before ordering the 25th Infantry Regiment to reinforce the desperate struggles at X, W and V Beaches.[65] In the meantime, the 26th Infantry Regiment lost control of the heights overlooking W and V Beaches, allowing Hunter-Weston to consolidate his beachhead.

Command and control in comparison

At the operational level, Hamilton and Liman von Sanders made very few decisions on 25 April. In Hamilton's case, this happened because he was essentially isolated by an ineffective reporting system, and his poor choice of personal command location. Moreover, he had left the MEF with no reserves and no alternative plans to shift his unengaged forces (the Royal Naval Division and a French brigade). In combination, Hamilton had no decisions to make and he was unable to control the landings or to influence the battles themselves. Similarly, Liman von Sanders was poorly positioned because he was predisposed to believe that Hamilton would land at Bulair or Saros Bay and went there in order to command what he believed would be the decisive encounter. As the day progressed, he ordered the transfer of two regiments from XV Corps to reinforce III Corps but kept the 5th and 7th Divisions in position until the following day. The XV Corps regiments that Liman von Sanders transferred from Asia did not enter the fight until midday on 27 April.

At corps level, Esat's actions at this stage of the battle reflected an understanding of modern command and control that was unusual for its time. Within a span of 12 hours, Esat had identified what he believed was the enemy's main effort, approved the execution of very successful decentralized counter-attacks, briefed the Fifth Army commander and requested reinforcements, restructured his divisional sectors in the heat of battle, and moved to the critical point where he could personally control III Corps' main effort.

Birdwood, like Hamilton, was poorly positioned and out of touch with the situation on shore. As early as 6.00am on 25 April Birdwood had lost control of his battle when a brigade commander redirected a main body brigade away from the ANZAC's principal geographic objective. This was compounded when his divisional commanders failed to rectify this mistake as subsequent waves of brigades arrived. Birdwood's sole trip ashore resulted in inconclusive guidance for his subordinates. The opportunity existed for Birdwood to rectify the mistakes but by losing control of the battle, he was unable to influence its outcome. As he had failed his subordinates, as evening fell, Birdwood failed Hamilton by passing on the question of evacuation. Further illustrating Birdwood's incomprehension of what had happened, several days later Birdwood recommended Sinclair-MacLagan – 'who organised and commanded with utmost dash my covering force' – for promotion.[66]

Ottoman division, regiment and battalion commanders were uniquely active on 25 April and went beyond the simple exercise of the responsive defensive plans. They did not wait for orders and acted on their own initiative when in possession of information. Kemal and Şefik are the best exemplars of this but Halil Sami kept his head admirably as well. This speaks to the German system of command and the operating climate that existed within the Ottoman Army as well as to a reporting system that pushed information upwards. In essence, Ottoman commanders were able to make decisions and control operations because of superior personal and institutional awareness. Bridges and Godley deferred to brigade commanders and were notably deficient in personal and institutional situational awareness. Hunter-Weston, on board a battleship, was reduced to being a casual observer, whose principal decision was not to reinforce Y Beach and whose only contribution to the battle was to divert one main body battalion from V Beach to W Beach.

On 25 April, with the exception of Birdwood and Bridges, British commanders had few opportunities to make decisions that could affect operations. They were clearly not in control of the battles and unable to affect the outcomes in their favour. Bridges' and Godley's decisions and actions led to dispersion and loss of the initiative. Reciprocally, the decisions and actions of their Ottoman counterparts led to concentration and gaining the initiative over the ANZAC. The wisdom of Hunter-Weston's decision not to reinforce Y Beach is contested by historians but was probably the right one. His actions led to the concentration of effort at X and W Beaches, which ultimately led to the 29th Division successfully getting off the beaches.

Tactical consolidation

Hamilton awoke at 4.00am on 26 April to a situation that was unchanged from the previous evening. He did read a message from Hunter-Weston outlining a plan to relieve V Beach from W Beach. At 6.25am Hunter-Weston requested that Hamilton land a French regiment and artillery at W Beach to assist in this effort.[67] A number of messages crossed paths between Hamilton and Hunter-Weston confirming that the French would land at W Beach but that isolated Y Beach was in jeopardy. As the day progressed, Hunter-Weston's brigades pushed forward and by 3.00pm the 29th Division held a contiguous line connecting X, W, V and S Beaches. Hamilton expected that Hunter-Weston would renew the offensive the next day and take Achi Baba. As the *Queen Elizabeth* passed Y Beach at 4.30pm, Hamilton noticed that his battalions had gone, leaving only petrol tins in view. That night the French Metropolitan Brigade and the troops from Y Beach landed and joined the 29th Division in its compressed beachhead. Hunter-Weston planned to renew the offensive towards Achi Baba at noon on 27 April when the French brigade was projected to be ready to attack.

At Anzac, Birdwood's corps spent the day under artillery and sniper fire. Command and control continued to devolve as brigade commanders straightened their lines and tried to sort out the mixed-up units. Shrapnel fire continued to plague the Australians and the ANZAC War Diary for 26 April reflects no guidance from the corps commander or his staff.[68] There was no relief that day for the beleaguered Ottoman III Corps as Kemal and Halil Sami consolidated their lines and attempted to hold the enemy in position until reinforcements arrived. Thus the first vital 48 hours passed with neither the ANZAC nor the 29th Division in possession of the covering positions assigned to them by Hamilton. Moreover, neither force was psychologically or operationally positioned to resume offensive operations.

On the positive ledger for the Allies, messages arrived indicating that Cox's 29th Indian Brigade was loading at Port Said to reinforce the ANZAC. The full strength of the French division was also becoming available. At Kum Kale, the French landing – which was originally not envisioned to remain on shore for more than 24 hours – had stretched into several days and had inflicted severe casualties on the Ottoman XV Corps. Nevertheless, in accordance with Hamilton's plan, the French diversionary force evacuated Kum Kale on the night of 26/27 April and prepared to deploy onto the peninsula.

At 1.50am on 26 April 1915, the Fifth Army headquarters sent a ciphered telegram to Enver Pasha at the Ministry of War outlining Liman von Sanders' plans for the next few days.[69] The Fifth Army reported that the 19th Division was conducting night attacks and that XV Corps (in Asia) was in contact with the enemy and holding the line successfully. The telegram noted that no landing had occurred at Saros Bay and that Liman von Sanders intended to send reinforcing units (two divisional equivalents) from XV Corps and 7th Division to the 9th and 19th Division sectors. The message ended with a notation that the Fifth Army had telegraph communications with both fighting fronts, and wireless communications with the straits fortress command and with the battlecruiser *Yavuz* (ex-*Goeben*). The first reinforcing units (the 33rd Regiment and 64th Regiment) were alerted for movement concurrently with the dispatch of the telegram.

The ciphered message to Enver Pasha in the early hours of 26 April reflected Liman von Sanders' most important contribution to the decisive defeat inflicted on Hamilton's landing force. The Fifth Army commander had spent the day personally observing and evaluating the diversionary Allied operations at Saros Bay and was not deceived by the manoeuvre. With three divisions in contact with the enemy, Liman von Sanders committed his remaining two divisions to the fights at Anzac and Cape Helles. In doing so, he stripped away the defenders from the Bulair isthmus and from the French front (itself a diversion) at Kum Kale in Asia. This bold decision indicates an unusually high degree of situational awareness at army level (by 1915 standards) and reflected the capability of subordinate Ottoman units to transmit accurate and timely information. This decision enabled Liman von Sanders to mass his forces inside the British decision cycle. Early in the morning of 26 April (5.10am), the 19th Division's chief of staff, Staff Major Izzettin, was already coordinating with III Corps concerning the reorganization of forces.[70]

A delay in the arrival of the French battalions forced Hunter-Weston to postpone his advance on Achi Baba for another 24 hours. He did shift the incoming French as well as the Royal Naval Division's Drake Battalion into his right sector, relieving the tired men from V and S Beaches. Hunter-Weston launched a minor ground-gaining attack that afternoon to straighten his lines and position his combined force for the attack. He also formally assigned lieutenant-colonels to replace the killed and wounded colonels who had commanded his brigades. The 29th Division staff issued his attack order that afternoon, which put the 87th Brigade, 88th Brigade and the French 175th Regiment on line, and held the 86th Brigade in divisional reserve. The objective was Hill 472, which was to the north of Krithia; for this attack Hunter-Weston had some 17 battalions (the 29th Division and five French battalions) available. Notably, this attack still left the Achi Baba hill mass (the original division covering position) in Ottoman hands.

Likewise, the Ottomans received reinforcements on 27 April amounting to roughly an entire infantry division. The 9th Division received a seasoned full-strength infantry regiment, a jandarma battalion, and some artillery. This brought Halil Sami's division back up to its authorized strength of nine infantry battalions. Mustafa Kemal also received two fresh and well-trained regiments, bringing his total of infantry battalions up to an astonishing 16. The ever-aggressive Kemal used both fresh regiments to launch coordinated night attacks on the ANZAC left and centre positions, and Halil Sami also used his fresh regiment in a night attack on the 29th Division, but neither succeeded.

Halil Sami received three fresh infantry battalions early in the morning on 28 April and these were filtering into the front-line trenches by 7.00am. To accommodate these forces, Halil Sami tactically reorganized his division into two battle groups, called 'wings' by the Ottomans, each under the command of a single regimental commander.[71] His artillery commander also centralized the artillery battalions and batteries into two groups to support the infantry. Although, the 9th Division's arrangements were incomplete at 8.00am they were still sufficient to turn back Hunter-Weston.

Hamilton's first MEF offensive, 27–28 April 1915

The Anglo-French combined attack began at 8.00am and Hunter-Weston positioned himself on Hill 138 in overall command of the combined force. He assigned Brigadier-General Marshall and a temporary staff to command the two-brigade advance of the 29th Division, which led to considerable confusion about who received which reports.[72] Initially, the division made considerable progress but by noon the attack had all but collapsed. In the middle of the battle Hamilton chose to make his first trip ashore and visited Hunter-Weston, who occupied a dugout on Hill 138. Hamilton then tried to visit d'Amade but was informed that d'Amade had left to visit him on the *Queen Elizabeth*. Meanwhile, while the battle raged, Marshall committed the reserve brigade but it made no further progress and the attacks ground to a halt. Overall the combined attack gained little ground at considerable cost. Hunter-Weston's reports to the MEF indicated that the attacks failed because of ammunition shortages and slowness by the French.[73] This battle came to be known as the first battle of Krithia.

Along the ANZAC perimeter, Kemal received another regiment on 28 April and, like Halil Sami, he also began to reorganize his expanded command into wings. In response to Birdwood's requests, Hamilton diverted the Royal Naval Division's Marine Brigade to the ANZAC and it arrived during this period. At the same time, Hamilton sent the remaining uncommitted brigade of the Royal Naval Division to Cape Helles to reinforce Hunter-Weston. In doing so, he fragmented the Royal Naval Division as an organizational entity.

Allied command and reorganization

The tone of Hamilton's cables to Kitchener was generally upbeat but Kitchener began to wonder about the operation when the covering positions were not occupied within the first 48 hours. Kitchener reaffirmed to Hamilton that he could request another division from Egypt but Hamilton merely hinted that he might need it. Things came to a head in London on 27 April when Kitchener received an alarming cable from French Admiral Guépratte bluntly suggesting that reinforcements for the MEF were urgently required or the campaign risked failure.[74] Kitchener immediately ordered Maxwell in Egypt to send the 42nd East Lancashire Division to the peninsula. Maxwell also prepared a large draft of replacements for the ANZAC and another for the 29th Division, which he dispatched on 30 April and 1 May respectively. Maxwell also suggested that he be authorized to dispatch two dismounted cavalry brigades to the MEF.

Guépratte's cable also energized the French government to commit more heavily to the endeavour by sending a second division. On 30 April, the high command alerted the 156th Division, commanded by General Bailloud, for service at the Dardanelles.[75] Designated as the 2nd Division of the Corps Expéditionnaire d'Orient, the division was ordered to embark at Marseilles on

2 May. The Minister of War also decided to recall d'Amade and replace him with 48-year-old General Henri Gouraud, who sailed for the peninsula with his chief of staff on 14 May.[76]

This accumulation of forces arriving in early May would give Hamilton a two-division corps at Anzac and two-division French corps at Cape Helles. In addition, it provided him with three independent British infantry divisions – the 29th, the 42nd and the Royal Naval Divisions – as well as an independent brigade. It is not clear from the MEF War Diaries or from Hamilton's memoirs how Hamilton intended to command effectively these units. The obvious solution was to have formed a British army corps headquarters, but Hamilton retained overall command of the three divisions until the end of May. However, after the failure of his fragmented main effort at Cape Helles on 6–8 May, Hamilton appears to have decided that a British army corps needed to be formed in order to unify British tactical command.

At 10.00am, 30 April, Hamilton left the *Queen Elizabeth* and joined his staff on the *Arcadian*. There were a number of issues affecting Hamilton's relationships with his subordinates. According to Hamilton's diary there were a number of 'knotty points to settle between Hunter-Weston and d'Amade' and Hamilton appeared frustrated at his inability to physically meet the French commander, who always seemed to be absent when Hamilton visited.[77] This resulted in a 'rather chilly' meeting between them on 2 May. Previously Hamilton and d'Amade had to reconcile the dispatch of messages so that the 'communiques issued in England and France might not clash'.[78] Hamilton also had lingering second thoughts about the 'what ifs' at Y Beach and asked Hunter-Weston several times about who had ordered the withdrawal of forces from there on 27 April. To which Hunter-Weston explicitly denied having done so. In spite of these tensions, Hamilton retained confidence in Hunter-Weston and decided to place the incoming 29th Indian Brigade as well as the 2nd Australian Brigade, Royal Naval Division and two RN battalions under the command of the 29th Division. Hamilton's staff informed General Paris that 'the Gen. Commdg. regrets temporarily breaking up his division, but it wd. best serve general interests'.[79]

Most of these issues came about because Hamilton intended that the MEF would achieve its principal objective within the first week of operations. There were no alternate or fallback plans to allow for an extended land campaign. When the first 48 hours passed and his forces were not even close to the planned covering positions Hamilton maintained high levels of optimism and his cables exuded confidence. This is difficult to understand because he understood the importance of beating the Ottoman commander's decision cycle – which by that time, would have worked out where the main effort was, and would have been able to shift forces to the threatened sector. It is even more difficult to comprehend Hamilton's failure to ask directly and immediately for reinforcements, which were readily available in Egypt. It is easy to criticize Hamilton for his failure to influence the battles and for failing to find an adaptive approach towards altering his campaign plan; however, much of the blame can be attributed to the absence of the type of situational awareness enjoyed by the Ottomans.

Strategic, operational and tactical conclusions

At the end of the first week of combat on the Gallipoli peninsula, the Ottoman Fifth Army held the British and French to two small beachheads. The literature of the campaign is rich with commentary explaining why this happened, most of which deal with tactical issues. At the strategic level, the question of balancing ends, ways and means must be addressed. In looking at the operational level, however, the plans themselves must come under scrutiny as well as command and control capabilities of the opposing forces.

At the strategic level, indecision in London led to an on-again, off-again approach to the expedition, which signalled to the Ottomans that an invasion was coming. However, the actual decision to shift the British effort from a naval campaign to a land campaign was made by de Robeck, who unilaterally halted the ongoing naval campaign. The War Council did not agree with this but failed to order him to continue the assault on the Dardanelles. As the Allies drifted into an unwanted and unplanned land campaign, the War Council made no efforts to reassess the ends, ways, and means that might be required to execute successfully such an endeavour. Although Kitchener made some suggestions regarding the campaign plan, he sent no new forces to the MEF. The end result was that Hamilton led a patchwork army of divisions of varying capabilities and capacities.

In opposition, strategic direction in Constantinople proceeded with the utmost clarity. In the 37 days between 18 March and 25 April, Enver Pasha activated the Fifth Army headquarters, a corps headquarters and deployed two first-class infantry divisions, a cavalry brigade, four jandarma battalions, an artillery battalion and several machine-gun companies to the new army. Thus, by the day of the landings, the Ottomans had significantly increased the quantity of forces on the peninsula, consolidated unity of command, and deployed forces that were qualitatively equal or superior to their British opponents.

At the operational level, Hamilton recognized that he could never achieve surprise and he hoped that he could overcome this by an overly complex plan that would cause Liman von Sanders to delay releasing his reserves. This led to a loss of mass and simplicity as Hamilton's forces were spread over large areas. His plan depended on a number of assumptions that proved disastrously flawed. Hamilton made no provisions for an operational reserve and, furthermore, placed himself on the *Queen Elizabeth* where he could not influence the outcome anyway. Notably, Hamilton and his commanders and staffs were more concerned with administration and logistics in their planning than they were with the conduct of combat operations. The MEF lost the initiative within hours of the initial landing on 25 April.

The Ottoman operational plan dated back to 1912 and although Liman von Sanders tinkered with it, he did not fundamentally change its precepts or its design. Notably, the plan was rehearsed continuously, especially regarding the release of the operational reserve (the 19th Division), and Ottoman commanders had confidence in its workability. Unlike Hamilton's plan, the Ottoman plan was flexible.

At the tactical level, British commanders failed to control their forces effectively. At corps level, Birdwood exercised no control over his unfolding operation whatsoever. At division level, all three British division commanders left operations in the hands of their brigadiers and chose to stand by when things were going badly wrong. This was especially true in the two ANZAC divisions. Ineffective reporting left British division, corps and MEF commanders without accurate or timely information. No tactical objectives set for the first day were taken and subsequent operations failed to take the intermediate objectives in the following days.

The Fifth Army performed magnificently at the tactical level. Ottoman corps, division, regimental and battalion commanders exercised individual initiative and, with numerically inferior forces, held the British to small beachheads. At Anzac Mustafa Kemal's brilliant attacks paralysed the ANZAC commanders and put them on the defensive by midday. This loss of the initiative left the ANZAC trapped in broken ground for months and it hardly moved from its initial positions. Ottoman reporting was extremely effective which gave Ottoman commanders superior situational awareness. This allowed them to mass reserves well inside the 48-hour planning window that Hamilton had counted on. Finally, the Ottoman Army demonstrated the capability to control operations by massing well-trained, resolute and well-led soldiers.

Winston S. Churchill, First Lord of the Admiralty, 1911–15.

General Sir Herbert Horatio Kitchener, Secretary of State for War, 1914–16.

Admiral Sir John Arbuthnot (Jackie) Fisher, First Sea Lord, 1904–10, 1914–15.

Vice-Admiral Sackville Carden, Commander, Anglo-French Squadrons, Eastern Mediterranean, 1914–16 March 1915.

Left to Right: Commodore Roger Keyes, Chief of Staff to Vice-Admiral de Robeck; Vice-Admiral John de Robeck, Commander of the Naval Forces in the Dardanelles (16 March 1915–18); General Sir Ian Hamilton, Commander in Chief of the Mediterranean Expeditionary Force (17 March–16 October 1915); Major-General Sir Walter Braithewaite, Chief of the General Staff, Mediterranean Expeditionary Force (17 March–16 October 1915).

General Sir Charles Monro, Commander-in-Chief, Mediterranean Expeditionary Force, 16 October 1915–1916.

Lieutenant-General Sir William R. Birdwood, General Officer Commanding, Australian and New Zealand Army Corps, December 1914 to January 1916.

Lieutenant-General Sir Frederick Stopford, General Officer Commanding, IX Corps, 16 June–15 August 1915.

Major-General Sir Aylmer Hunter-Weston, General Officer Commanding, 29th Division and VIII Corps, February–17 July 1915.

Major-General Sir Henry de Lisle, General Officer Commanding, 29th Division, and IX Corps, 24 May 1915–16.

Général de Division Albert d'Amade, Commanding General, Corps Expéditionnaire d'Orient, 22 February 1915, 22 February–15 May 1915.

İsmail Enver Pasha, Minister of War, Acting Commander-in-Chief and Chief of the General Staff, 1914–18.

General Otto Liman von Sanders, Commanding General, Ottoman Fifth Army, 26 March 1915–28 February 1918.

Brigadier-General Esat Pasha, Commanding General, III Corps and Northern Group, Autumn 1913–16.

Brigadier-General Vehip Pasha, Commanding General, Ottoman Second Army and Southern Group, 9 July-9 October 1915.

Colonel Mustafa Kemal, Commanding General, 19th Division, Ari Burnu Front and Anafarta Group, 1 January–10 December 1915.

Above: Steam pinnace towing landing boats. The pinnace released the boats close to shore and they were then rowed to shore.

Below: British troops on V Beach after the Cape Helles landings.

Above: Royal Naval Division training at Lemnos.

Below: The British logistical build-up on V Beach.

Main: Slopes of Monash Valley, The rugged terrain of the ANZAC perimeter is apparent as soldiers cling to the steep.

Inset Right: Infantrymen and Light Horsemen in a trench on Walkers Ridge, Gallipoli. The Light Horseman smoking in the background and the Private in the foreground were father and son, thought to be Ernest Sidney Cavalier (No. 581, 22nd Battalion, 6th Brigade) and Ronald Ernest Cavalier (No. 854, 4th Battery, 1st Division) respectively.

British troops and their artillery guns being evacuated from Suvla Bay on rafts in daylight, December 1915.

Distant view from the battleship HMS *Cornwallis* of stores burning on the beach after the evacuation of Suvla Bay, December 1915.

Above: A bugler of the Corps Expeditionaire d'Orient sounding a call at sunset on a French transport ship.

Below: Liman von Sanders (centre) observing machine-gun drill. Brigadier-General Esat Pasha is to his left and III Corps chief of staff Colonel Fahrettin is to his right.

Above: Ottoman staff officers in front of Liman von Sanders' headquarters.

Below: German Colonel Hans Kanneniesser standing in front of his clay hut.

Above: Ottoman infantrymen engaged in training overlooking one of the Gallipoli beaches.

Below: The Ottoman fort at Canakkale. The 17th-century keep is seen inside the 19th-century coastal defence installation.

Above: Ottoman soldiers drawing fresh water from a spring. Fresh water was a combat multiplier enjoyed by the Ottoman army.

Below: The commander of the 125th Infantry Regiment with his staff and regimental Imam.

Above: A well-camouflaged Ottoman sniper captured by the Australians, Gallipoli.

Below: Ottoman infantry in a trench, Gallipoli 1915, the ever-present scrub growing on the peninsula is evident in this photo.

Ottoman infantry after the Gallipoli campaign 1915.

A main Ottoman communications trench in the 16th Infantry Division sector.

Ottoman wounded unloading from ferries in Constantinople.

Officers of the Ottoman 57th Infantry Regiment gather for tea, Gallipoli front 1915.

Ottoman battalion intelligence officers celebrate a formal meal behind the lines.

Chapter Six

THE OTTOMAN COUNTER-OFFENSIVES, 1 MAY–5 AUGUST 1915

The first week of fighting on the Gallipoli peninsula ended with two widely separated and precariously small Allied beachheads on the peninsula. Hamilton's MEF had lost the operational initiative and the Ottomans sought to gain it. Both Enver Pasha and Lord Kitchener were unhappy with this result and both pushed the operational commanders to action. Both leaders would work to send reinforcements to the peninsula in attempts to find an early victory. As the number of divisions committed to the campaign increased, both the Ottomans and the British reorganized their operational forces in order to control them more effectively. Unsuccessful tactical offensives led to the imposition of an inconclusive stalemate.

At the strategic level, Enver provided absolute strategic clarity and was unwavering in his determination to support the campaign. Kitchener and the War Council, on the other hand, vacillated and only reluctantly decided to support the endeavour well past the point when earlier resolution might have been decisive. At the operational level, British commanders gave up control of reserves to subordinates and were unable to focus combat power effectively, while their Ottoman opponents easily and routinely massed forces quantitatively and qualitatively. The effective formation of groups at the tactical level also gave the Ottomans unity of command at Cape Helles, a capability that gave them an edge in battle.

Ottoman operational reorganization, late April 1915

At the end of April 1915, the Ottoman III Corps found itself fighting on two separate fronts – Anzac and Cape Helles – and commanding regiments that cumulatively totalled over seven infantry divisions. At Anzac, Mustafa Kemal, a lieutenant-colonel, was commanding a corps equivalent of troops with his tiny divisional headquarters. A similar situation existed at Cape Helles and, moreover, Esat was forced to divide his attentions between two separate fronts. On 28 April, the 15th Division was inbound as a reinforcement and the time had arrived for the Fifth Army to reorganize its forces to fit the ongoing campaign. On the night of 28/29 April, Liman von Sanders sent orders activating a Southern Group to control the forces at Cape Helles, however, the group remained under III Corps command.[1] In the absence of an available headquarters, he ordered the commander of the 5th Division, German Colonel Eduard von Sodernstern, to assume command of both the 7th Division and 9th Division, effective at 9.00am the next morning. Accordingly von Sodernstern established his new headquarters and, while learning about the situation from Hali Sami, was joined by Captain Carl Mühlmann and Colonel Hans Kannengiesser, who had been sent to assist by Liman von Sanders. None of the Germans spoke Turkish so an Ottoman reserve officer (who was an Arab) was assigned as a translator. This was the entire staff of the Southern Group – three Germans and an Ottoman reservist.[2] Nevertheless, von Sodernstern was quick to act issuing his first orders at 3.00pm, which divided the Southern Zone into right and left sectors, under Colonels Halil Sami and Remzi respectively.

The 7th Division was in sector by midday 29 April 1915. Also on this day, the inbound 15th Division was afloat and the Ottoman general staff ordered the 16th Division to the peninsula as well. All of these reinforcements were destined for the Southern Group and Liman von Sanders ordered von Sodernstern to prepare an offensive operation.[3] Meanwhile, Enver was pressuring Fifth Army to attack the invaders and Liman von Sanders, in turn, pressed Esat and von Sodernstern for action.

On the afternoon of 30 April, von Sodernstern received orders from Fifth Army ordering him to conduct a night attack on 1/2 May using units from all three divisions in his sector. Altogether the Southern Group placed 18 and a half battalions supported by three machine-gun companies and ten artillery batteries against a combined Anglo-French force of 30 battalions, supported by 30 machine-gun companies and 23 artillery batteries (not counting the powerful guns of the Allied fleet).[4] The Southern Group launched its attack at 10.00pm but the attack immediately failed. Losses were heavy in the confusion of the night attack as the Ottomans reached the British trenches. Von Sodernstern tried to bring reinforcements from Krithia but these did not reach the British trenches until past 3.00am, by which time the Ottoman assault had ground to a halt. Nevertheless, the fresh troops threw themselves forward but were stopped by British counter-attacks. In the darkness Ottoman companies and platoons became hopelessly intermixed and lieutenants often found themselves in command of company-sized groups.[5]

By 3.00am von Sodernstern received reports from both divisions that his offensive had failed with heavy casualties, which were especially severe among the junior officers. The modern Turkish official history suggests two reasons for the failure of the 1/2 May night attack.[6] First, the Southern Group staff consisted of only three people, who were simply unable to process the reports in time so as to be able to reinforce the attack. Von Sodernstern had parts of the 15th Division standing by for just such a contingency. Second, the central tactical telephone exchange, which was located in Krithia, broke down limiting effective communications.[7] Encouraged by their defensive success, the British and French launched a major counter-attack across the entire front at 10.00am, 2 May, which failed completely within an hour. However, it did serve to delay Ottoman attempts to untangle the intermixed units and re-establish effective command and control.[8] Balancing the Ottoman losses, the 16th Division arrived on the peninsula, as did a German machine-gun detachment.

The 5th Division closed on the reserve staging areas and the Southern Group began to plan for another night attack. As a result of the previous success against the French, and also because the 9th Division had been in continuous action since 25 April, von Sodernstern decided to launch the main effort in his left sector.[9] The relative proximity of the French trenches compared to the deeper no man's land on the British front was an additional factor but the 9th Division was ordered to conduct a support attack anyway. His orders surprised the division commanders, who were trying to reconstitute their battalions. Throughout 3 May, the Southern Group staff (three officers) feverishly put together a plan. Staff Captain Nihat worked the telephones with East's chief of staff to shift additional artillery shells south to support the attack.[10] Meanwhile, the 15th Division commander and chief of staff spent most of the day at the Southern Group headquarters trying to get a grip on the situation. Von Sodernstern's final attack order was not released until 7.00pm because it had to be translated from German into Ottoman Turkish.[11] He organized an eight-battalion assault supported by five artillery batteries to attack at 11.00pm. His plan involved the 15th Division attacking in columns. Von Sodernstern clearly expected success because he held two battalions of the 56th Infantry Regiment in reserve and warned its commander to be ready to conduct 'pursuit operations'.[12] Finally, he notified his divisional commanders that he intended to shift his headquarters forward from the vicinity of Achi Baba to the 7th Division command post at 7.00am, 4 May to better control the battle.

The French held their lines with 12 battalions supported by 33 artillery pieces and a dozen heavy machine-gun companies. The attack began quietly at 11.00pm but immediate French fire turned the Ottoman assault into a huge uncontrollable mass, which broke into the French trenches. By 12.30am the Turks had penetrated almost to the Morto Bay beaches, however, von Sodernstern's telephone lines were again destroyed by enemy fire and he was unable to release his reserves.[13] As dawn approached von Sodernstern, apparently unaware of the success gained by the 15th Division, gave the order to retreat.[14] The Southern Group had lost over 10,000 men in a four-day period.

Ottoman operational reorganization, 5 May 1915

On 5 May 1915, Liman von Sanders issued orders revising the tactical groups commanding the various zones of the battle area. He designated the Asian shore as the Anatolian Group, the Cape Helles area continued as the Southern Group, the Anzac area was designated as the Northern Group, and the vulnerable northern Aegean beaches were designated as the Saros Group. Group commanders assumed full tactical authority over all forces in their sectors regardless of unit affiliation or organization. The III Corps staff became the nucleus of the new Northern Group and Esat Pasha took over the direct control of the fighting at Anzac from Mustafa Kemal. The III Corps formations fighting at Cape Helles were detached from his command at the same time. Mustafa Kemal returned to his role as a division commander.

Recognizing the limitations of the absence of a proper staff, Liman von Sanders replaced von Sodernstern and appointed Colonel Weber and Weber's XV Corps staff as the nucleus of the Southern Group's new headquarters staff. Coming from the relatively quiet Asian shore, the XV Corps staff was shocked by the confusion and bloodletting that had characterized the Cape Helles battles of early May.[15] Indeed, it took two more days to sort out the survivors and to reorganize them back into their organic units. In the same way that Esat took over from Mustafa Kemal, Weber took over from von Sodernstern and, importantly, Weber brought with him a corps-level staff of 15 officers and 164 soldiers (as well as 91 animals) with which to more effectively plan operations.[16]

In the middle of the reorganization, Liman von Sanders received an unexpected cable from Enver Pasha proclaiming the battles on the peninsula of supreme military and political importance to the empire and, moreover, promising reinforcements to continue the attacks.[17] Liman von Sanders would continue to receive such surprises because the Ottomans had bypassed him (and the Germans) by establishing direct communications between Enver and his classmate, Lieutenant-Colonel Kazım, the Fifth Army chief of staff, who independently sent reports to the general staff.[18] Kazım believed that the attacks should continue without pause so that the British and French would be unable to dig deep and comprehensive trench lines. The Allies for their part were under similar pressure from London to break through what they believed were weakened Ottoman divisions holding hastily constructed fieldworks. Fortunately for the Turks it was Ian Hamilton who decided to attack first.

British tactical reorganization and the second MEF offensive, 5–8 May 1915

After Hunter-Weston's failure to seize Krithia, Hamilton set about planning a second attempt to seize the Achi Baba covering position using the incoming reinforcements from Egypt. Although the Ottomans launched major night attacks, these were repulsed by the front-line forces and did not impose a major disruption on the MEF's offensive planning. Hamilton decided on 2 May to renew the MEF's main effort at Cape Helles.[19] He had a number of reasons for continuing the main effort there, not the least of which was the fact that the Kilid Bahr plateau remained the main objective of the land campaign. Moreover, the ANZAC remained mired in very bad terrain without tactical space for its artillery while the 29th Division and the French had got their guns and ammunition ashore. Hamilton met with Birdwood on 3 May ordering him to send two brigades and his remaining 20 unlanded field artillery pieces to Cape Helles. Hamilton was also under pressure from Kitchener, who cabled him on 4 May, stating that he hoped to see a push on Achi Baba the next day.[20]

However, the reduced strength of the 29th Division – Hamilton's main offensive instrument – made an attack tactically very difficult. In fact, losses were so heavy in Hunter-Weston's 86th Brigade, which had made the landing at V Beach, that Hamilton decided to dissolve the brigade entirely. Balancing this loss, Hamilton had a number of options for the employment of the incoming brigades from Egypt, of which two arrived in time for the assault on Achi Baba. In Force Order No. 5, published on 4 May 1915, Hamilton ordered another attack on Achi Baba at 11.00am on 6 May.[21] The order also contained instructions for a major reorganization of the British forces on Cape Helles. Hamilton attached the incoming 29th Indian Brigade and 125th Brigade, from the 42nd Infantry Divsion, to the 29th Division. He dissolved the 86th Brigade and attached its shattered battalions to the 87th and 88th Brigades. This gave Hunter-Weston four full-strength brigades, two of which were fresh. Having widely dispersed the Royal Naval Division, Hamilton now created an ad hoc

Composite Division, under General Paris, which was composed of a two-battalion composite naval brigade as well as Bridges' 2nd Australian Brigade and Godley's New Zealand Brigade, which were both coming from Anzac to Cape Helles.[22] Finally, as d'Amade's French had taken a pounding from the Southern Group's night attacks, Hamilton attached the Royal Naval Division's 2nd Naval Brigade to Masnou's 1st Division. All the available artillery, including five batteries of ANZAC guns, were placed under the GOC 29th Divisional artillery.

Hamilton's concept for the operation employed the heavily weighted and reconstituted 29th Division in the main attack with the French division keeping abreast. Unlike his plan for the landings of 25 April, Hamilton decided to maintain an operational reserve and assigned the newly constituted Composite Division as the MEF general reserve. The first objectives were Krithia village for the British, and Kereves Dere for the French with the final objective being the summit of the Achi Baba hill mass and lateral ridge. However, at 10.10am, on 6 May the MEF informed General Paris that the GOC 29th Division had 'been given the power to issue orders to him for employment of the General Reserve'.[23] By assigning this authority to Hunter-Weston, Hamilton once again gave up any ability he had to influence the outcome of what became known as the second battle of Krithia.

The ANZAC artillery landed on 4 May, while Birdwood's two infantry brigades landed on the morning of 6 May and moved into reserve positions. Hunter-Weston issued his operations order for his division on 5 May and he envisioned a three-phase operation.[24] In Phase I, the 87th and 88th Brigades, with the Indians in divisional reserve, and supported by artillery fire, would advance about a mile and entrench. In Phase II, the advancing 88th Brigade would pivot right seizing Krithia and all brigades were to establish an entrenched line 1.5 miles to the north of the village. During both phases, Hunter-Weston ordered Brigadier-General Marshall, commanding the 87th Brigade, to assume 'general control' of all three brigades.[25] In Phase III, on order, the 87th Brigade and the Indian Brigade would advance and take Achi Baba. The Allied artillery, like its Ottoman opponent, was semi-centralized into four groups and preparatory howitzer fire on the enemy trenches was scheduled to begin at 10.30am.

The combined attack on Achi Baba began on time with Allied brigades putting about 75 per cent of their combat power on the line with the remainder in reserve. The attack made very little progress as Ottoman machine guns and artillery shrapnel bursts held the attack. By evening the attack frittered away and stopped, having gained about 400 yards (360m). The official history attributes the failure to an overall shortage of artillery ammunition but it does not appear that reserves were employed effectively or at all. After coming ashore in mid-afternoon to confer with Hunter-Weston and d'Amade, Hamilton ordered the advance to continue the next day at 10.30am.[26] In the meantime, the fresh 127th Brigade landed and was attached to the Composite Division. Hamilton then took the New Zealand Brigade from the Composite Division and gave it to the 29th Division giving Hunter-Weston another brigade.

Hamilton's attack renewed with a preliminary bombardment at 9.45am after which the infantry went forward but by 1.00pm the attacks had stalled along the entire front. Hunter-Weston attempted to re-energize the attack by ordering brigades forward under a brief artillery bombardment. Again the failed attack ended by nightfall with hardly any gain of ground. According to the British official history, casualties were light. Hamilton ordered the attack to continue on 8 May and Hamilton himself intended to establish a command post on Hill 114. The attack orders did not reach the brigades until about 9.00am on 8 May. A short bombardment began at 10.15am after which the infantry advanced but achieved almost no forward movement. The attacks really began in earnest about 5.00pm with the 29th Division and the French pushing very hard but again these failed.

Hamilton's second Allied assault intended to seize the Achi Baba heights was a combined Anglo-French general attack using about 25,000 troops, of which three brigades were fresh. Hunter-Weston, in more-or-less overall command, used a two-day period to plan the initial attack and committed many tactical errors including inadequate personal reconnaissance, ineffective control (passing *de facto* command to Marshall), incomplete orders that reached the troops too late, and most importantly, employing spent soldiers who were in a state of total exhaustion. For his part, Hamilton once again failed to maintain a grip on the operation by abrogating tactical command to Hunter-Weston. He also allowed his staff to undertake the temporary combining of brigades into ad hoc divisions. Moreover, at MEF and divisional command level, an ineffective reporting system did not enable situational awareness leading to an inexcusable failure to commit divisional and MEF reserves to influence the outcome of the battle. The three-day offensive was a daily series of dismally unoriginal direct frontal attacks, which consumed 6,500 Allied casualties but gained almost no ground. Of note, on 10 May, Hamilton's Brigadier-General, Royal Engineers, produced 'Notes on Landing,' which was critical of the procedures from the *Manual for Combined Operations*. However, none of the notes reflected tactical lessons; the notes were purely administrative and logistical in nature.

From the Ottoman perspective, the Allied attacks pre-empted premature Ottoman attacks and actually allowed the Southern Group to continue its reconstitution efforts. Although the British thought there were about 20,000

Turks on hand, modern Turkish histories assert that there were about half that (10,000) available, supported by 24 machine guns and 40 artillery pieces. Weber's German chief of staff, Major von Thauvenay, was sufficiently alarmed by the Allied attacks that he persuaded Weber, as well as notifying Admiral von Usedom, to order the Southern Group to retreat to the Soğanlıdere line behind Achi Baba. However, Liman von Sanders immediately ordered the Southern Group to stand fast. Von Thauvenay was thereafter relieved of his duties, but he remained in his position as chief of staff until the week of 8–12 June when he was replaced by Lieutenant-Colonel Salahattin Adil.[27]

On 9 May, the MEF went over to the defensive and Hamilton again shuffled his brigades by returning the 125th Brigade and 127th Brigade from the Composite Division to the 42nd Division. In return the 2nd Naval Brigade rejoined the Composite Division. Finally, Hamilton moved the now re-formed 42nd Division into reserve. On 11 May, Hamilton consolidated the Cape Helles position for what he termed 'siege warfare' and two days later, reallocated the defensive frontages there.[28] It is at this point that Hamilton gave up trying to regain the operational initiative. The 126th Brigade arrived enabling Hamilton to pull the shattered 29th Division into reserve and on 12 May, the MEF's left sector was held by the 29th Indian Brigade and the 42nd Division. Oddly, Hamilton seemed content to let Hunter-Weston continue as a sort of quasi-corps commander. On 14 May, the Royal Marine Brigade and the 1st Naval Brigade from Anzac transferred to Cape Helles joining the Composite Division.

The 1st Light Horse Brigade and the New Zealand Mounted Rifles Brigade landed at Anzac between 10 and 12 May and, on 16 May, Hamilton returned the 2nd Australian Brigade from Cape Helles to Anzac as well. On 14 May Birdwood was lightly wounded and the next day, the Australian division commander, Major-General Bridges, died after being wounded while walking the trench lines. Finally, Hamilton returned the New Zealand Brigade to the ANZAC on 19/20 May as well. These movements thus consolidated all of the ANZAC's infantry brigades under their parent divisions.[29]

Despite the failures to take Achi Baba, Hamilton remained convinced that with additional forces he might regain the initiative and, on 10 May, asked Kitchener for two additional divisions. Kitchener put the 52nd Division on notice for deployment to the Mediterranean that day. The War Council met on 14 May and considered three options regarding the expedition to the Dardanelles, which were: 1) abandon the enterprise, 2) send strong reinforcements, or 3) keep the existing units up to strength and send one fresh infantry division (the 52nd).[30] The meeting was contentious (Churchill called it 'sulphurous') and the council reached no decision.[31] Nevertheless, Kitchener took the initiative and cabled

Hamilton to develop an appreciation of what was required to finish the task and to base his estimate on the assumption that adequate forces were available. A subsequent message from Kitchener confirmed, however, that only one reinforcing division would be sent out and that Hamilton must manage with the forces at hand.

Hamilton and Hunter-Weston blamed the failure to take Achi Baba on several things, the principal of which were too few artillery pieces and too little ammunition, particularly, high-explosive shells. Hamilton's messages to Kitchener repeatedly asked for more of each and confirmed his belief that more firepower was the key to overcoming the Ottoman trenches. Their second assessment of the failures led the British commanders to believe that the offensive had been undertaken in too much haste. In fact, the three assaults of Krithia were, in modern terminology, hasty attacks – in that they were quickly planned, incompletely resourced, and unrehearsed by the troops involved. After taking a defensive posture on 11 May, Hamilton turned to the idea of a deliberate offensive at Cape Helles and two days later imposed rigid artillery ammunition expenditure constraints designed to stockpile shells.

Hamilton remained fixed on Achi Baba as the key to the Kilid Bahr plateau and he supported Hunter-Weston, who wanted another direct, although deliberate, assault on the heights. Both commanders remained focused on mass, of both men and firepower, as the determinate for success. Birdwood, however, chaffing at his defensive role, offered an early operational solution based on manoeuvre and surprise. On 13 May, Birdwood sent a very innovative appreciation to Hamilton suggesting that with more men (Birdwood asked for the Indian Brigade) the ANZAC could sweep around to the left through the village of Buyuk Anafarta and seize the lightly held Koca Chemen Tepe (Hill 971).[32] From those commanding heights, the ANZAC would sweep down Gun Ridge and take Mal Tepe, cutting off the peninsula. Hamilton's marginalia illuminate his fixation on his original plan and on Achi Baba. He thought that the ANZAC was doing a fine job fixing the enemy and that the Indian Brigade was more usefully employed at Cape Helles. However, Hamilton's most compelling sidenote was the comment 'Why left? Right is the way we want him to go vide instructions'.[33] Due to Hamilton's closed mind, Birdwood received a negative reply informing him that the commanding general understood the ANZAC's dissatisfaction with a holding-force mission but that it was important for the overall effort. This did not stop Birdwood from bringing back the idea on 16 May, outlining how he would take Hill 971 and, acknowledging Hamilton's query about going to the right, offered to put in any division the MEF might give him on his right flank.[34] Hamilton again replied in the negative but asked for a formal appreciation of these ideas.

The night attack of 18/19 May 1915

On 13 May, Enver notified Fifth Army that powerful reinforcements were on the way, which included the 2nd and 12th Infantry Divisions.[35] The 2nd Division was one of the army's premier divisions from I Corps in the capital. It was well trained and consisted of its original organic infantry regiments. It was commanded by Lieutenant-Colonel Hasan Askeri, brother to the famous guerrilla commander Süleyman Askeri.[36] The 12th Division was similarly well trained and, moreover, Enver promised to send artillery and also to accelerate the flow of replacement soldiers to the Fifth Army corps to fill the depleted ranks to authorized strength. With this information Esat presented Liman von Sanders with an offensive concept, which was based on the idea that the Allies' main effort at Cape Helles created an opportunity to attack a weakened Anzac perimeter.[37] He also noted that he had two fresh regiments from the 16th Division on hand as well as additional 210mm and 120mm artillery and he requested one of the incoming divisions. The 2nd Division began arriving from Constantinople on 11 May and received telephonic orders to move into its staging area at Sarafim Farm two days later. Because of the threat of Allied aerial observation the division marched at night. On 14 May, it received orders committing it to the Northern Group. A second telephonic order, at 11.15am on 17 May, sent the division and regimental commanders to Esat's headquarters on Mal Tepe where the III Corps staff had been intensively planning an attack on Anzac.[38]

The mood and morale in the Northern Group was very optimistic as evidenced by a report from Colonel Mustafa Kemal, which highlighted the positive effect that shelling three torpedo boats and six transports and forcing them to withdraw had on those watching from the Ottoman positions.[39] Kemal was also well pleased with the available artillery, the presence of the 2nd Division, and with troop morale. In reply, German Major Raymond carried secret and special orders to Kemal alerting him to the fact that the Northern Group would attack within the next 24 hours. The formal offensive authorization from Fifth Army arrived at the group headquarters at 1.50pm, 17 May and specified the attack time as 3.30am, 19 May 1915.[40] The orders specified that the entire 2nd Division would march from Sarafim Farm at 7.30pm on 18 May, leaving packs and baggage behind. Esat was tasked to provide the incoming 2nd Division soldiers with a hot meal as they arrived in their tactical assembly areas. The 2nd Division infantry and artillery regimental commanders were directed to meet at 5.00pm that day to recon the routes and assembly areas and to rehearse the movement with their battalion commanders on the morning of 18 May. The attack was to be carried out by two wings, and all attacking units were to be in their final positions by 2.00am on 19 May. In turn Esat moved his group headquarters to Kemalyeri (Scrubby Knoll) that day and sent his subordinates their warning orders on the afternoon of 18 May.

The operations order for the night attack of 18/19 May 1915 was released at 8.00pm, finalizing what the subordinate commanders already knew: Kemal's 19th Division would attack the north, the 5th Division the centre, the 2nd Division the Kanlısırt area (Lone Pine), and the 16th Division the south.[41] In addition the Gaba Tepe detachment was to throw a battalion in to support the left flank of the 16th Division. When the assault waves entered the Anzac trenches the Ottoman artillery was to begin shelling the beaches and reserve areas to prevent Australian reserves from reinforcing the front lines. Esat intended to launch a massive simultaneous human wave of 42,000 infantrymen at 3.30am on a scale hitherto unseen on the peninsula.[42] Esat reckoned that he would pay a heavy price in blood – 30 per cent of the men committed – but that in six and a half hours, the Anzac beachhead would be eliminated.

In turn the subordinate division commanders issued their own orders organizing their attacks. Unfortunately for the Ottomans, British RNAS aerial reconnaissance had picked up on the large masses of Turks unloading at Akbaş pier moving towards Anzac and the Australians had, likewise, noticed a lull in the ordinarily heavy daily fire on 18 May. Accordingly, both ANZAC divisions were warned at 5.00pm to expect an assault. As darkness fell the 12,500 Australians holding the perimeter were shelled heavily and at 3.00am, 19 May, they stood to arms in their trenches and readied themselves for an assault.

Esat's divisions came out of their trenches at 3.30am. Kemal's experienced men took the fewest casualties and were able to seize parts of the Australians' first line of trenches largely due to the favourable dead ground that masked their attack.[43] The soldiers of Hasan Askeri's 2nd Division fared the worst and were mown down like wheat in the open ground by Australian machine-gun and rifle fire. His commanders, trapped in no man's land, tried to lead small groups of the hardy Turkish soldiers forward but to no avail and at 5.10am he sent a message to Esat reporting failure.[44] The 16th Division apparently achieved some small degree of surprise but by 5.00am were stopped as well. Such success as the Northern Group achieved lay in only a handful of company-sized elements sitting in the Australian trenches.

As the reports of failure poured into the group's new Kemalyeri headquarters, which was located just a kilometre behind the 2nd Division's trenches, Esat decided to continue with daylight attacks.[45] The 19th Division committed its reserves and renewed the fight but the attack finally stalled at 9.30am. The 5th Division renewed its bloody attacks until 10.00am before quitting. The shattered 2nd Division was hopelessly mired with its battalions intermixed around the few surviving cadres of leaders and was unable to renew the offensive. The 16th Division attempted to renew the attack but called it off at 10.00am as well. A discouraged Esat telephoned Fifth Army at 11.20am to report the failure of the offensive after seven hours of combat.[46] He praised the heroism of his soldiers and blamed the singularly heavy Australian machine-gun and rifle fire for the defeat. He noted that casualties were high, amounting to 50 per cent in some units, but that he had yet to receive the strength returns from his divisions. Liman von Sanders then ordered the 2nd Division pulled out of the line for duty as the Fifth Army reserve. Losses were extremely heavy among the 2nd and 5th Divisions. Final casualties were about 3,500 killed and over 6,000 wounded.[47]

Esat's Northern Group's offensive failed primarily because it depended on the element of complete surprise rather than a preliminary bombardment closely tied in time to the assault waves. Instead, the Australians were ready and waiting. Even so, the sheer scale of the attack – some 30,000 men in the initial wave – should have led to some larger degree of success and it is a tribute to the resolute bravery and fire discipline of the Australian infantry and machine-gunners that it failed so utterly. Famously, a temporary ceasefire was arranged so that the surviving wounded trapped in no man's land might be recovered and the dead might be buried – within days of the attack the rotting corpses were causing acute hygiene problems in the Australian trenches. Negotiations to arrange the 'Anzac armistice' dragged on but finally on 24 May from 7.30am to 4.30pm a mutually satisfactory ceasefire was conducted during which around 3,000 dead Ottoman soldiers were buried on the spot.[48]

Subsequent modern Turkish analysis points to inadequate supplies of artillery ammunition which forced Esat to forego a conventional artillery preparation, the massing of the 2nd Division which exposed the operation to aerial observation, and the attempts to relieve units on the front after dark as contributing factors to the failure. With the complete failure of the 19 May attack, Liman von Sanders ordered the aggressive Esat to suspend offensive operations as it was now clear that the Australians were more than capable of holding their own against almost any number of Turks who could reasonably be ranged against them. Operations at Anzac now entered a period of relative quiet. Elsewhere on the peninsula the Ottoman 12th Division began unloading on 16 May and moved into positions in the Southern Group. Alert to the possibility of a renewed Allied landing in Asia, the Ottoman general staff put I Corps and the 1st Division on movement orders south. Liman von Sanders assigned these units to the Kum Kale area and attached the 3rd Division to I Corps on 28 May 1915. In order to rationalize the operational area, Enver assigned Staff Colonel Feyzi's XVI Corps to the Saros Bay area.

Hamilton's third MEF offensive, 4–6 June 1915

On 17 May, Hamilton dissolved the Composite Division and re-formed Paris's Royal Naval Division, which formally rejoined the MEF Order of Battle as a tactical unit.[49] With this adjustment completed, all MEF infantry divisions were composed of their original organic brigades with the exception of the 86th Brigade, which had been dissolved and replaced by the 29th Indian Brigade in the 29th Division. There were now three British infantry divisions on Cape Helles alongside the French army corps of two infantry divisions. The French corps was commanded by General Gouraud who relieved d'Amade on 15 May, and who had Colonel Girodon as his chief of staff.[50] British tactical coordination on Cape Helles was achieved by Hamilton delegating *de facto* authority to Hunter-Weston, and Hamilton was quite satisfied with his subordinate's performance. However, as Hamilton's mind crystallized towards a deliberate offensive there arose the requirement for a corps-level command to coordinate the detailed vertical and horizontal planning which accompanies and defines deliberate operations. As such, Hamilton requested and received War Office approval to activate an army corps to be commanded by Hunter-Weston.

On 24 May, Hamilton issued Force Order 16, which placed the 42nd Division and the Royal Naval Division, for tactical purposes, under the command of temporary Lieutenant-General Hunter-Weston 'until the formation of the army corps to which he has been appointed'.[51] Lieutenant-Colonel H. E. Street of the 29th Division was appointed corps chief of staff. On the same day Hamilton cabled the War Office asking for a new commander, who was junior to Hunter-Weston, to command the 29th Division. He also asked for an army corps headquarters and a corps-level signals company. Two days later, Hamilton queried Kitchener about the availability of qualified primary staff officers for the corps headquarters. On 29 May, Hamilton received word that three 'psc' officers (two captains and a major) would be sent from Egypt.[52]

Hamilton decided to fight a general action on 31 May and he, Hunter-Weston and Gouraud agreed to a plan of attack that day. Hunter-Weston issued VIII Corps Order No. 1 on 1 June, which contained tactical instructions for offensive operations and warning orders to his divisions alerting them for future offensive operations.[53]

It is hard to categorize Hamilton's third MEF offensive as anything other than a limited tactical offensive because the objectives for the force were merely the Ottoman trench lines themselves. Hamilton's instructions continued 'if, on the attainment of these objectives, a further advance is found practicable, the enemy must be driven back as far as possible'.[54] There was no mention of Krithia or Achi Baba as objectives to be gained. Hamilton ordered his corps commanders to pay particular attention to artillery support and he stressed the importance of mastering the details. Although the two-corps MEF attacked along the entire front, the depth to be achieved was envisioned as only 650–800 yards (600–750m). Once again, Hamilton delegated control to the corps commanders by ordering them to coordinate their operations rather than under MEF staff supervision.

Hunter-Weston's VIII Corps Order No. 3 described a 4 June combined attack with the French and was highly detailed.[55] Of note was a corps staff product called a 'Table of Objectives', which was a matrix cross-referencing divisions and brigades with their associated first and second objectives. Hunter-Weston retained command of the corps reserve but then he gave command of the reserve to Brigadier-General W. R. Marshall, of the 87th Brigade. In addition to his own brigade, Marshall had two brigades from the Royal Naval Division and three other infantry battalions, making a total of 13 infantry battalions under Marshall's command. Once again, the command arrangements for the reserve were awkward and overly complex. VIII Corps' artillery was grouped to support the attacks and Gouraud lent the British six batteries of French 75s to further support the attack. Two battleships, a cruiser and two destroyers also lent fire support via wireless messages.

There was no actual corps scheme of manoeuvre nor did Hunter-Weston identify a main effort. Hunter-Weston ordered each of his three infantry divisions to attack with a single reinforced brigade, and on the far left flank, Cox's reinforced Indian Brigade attacked as well. Surprise was forfeited as well with a phased three-and-a-half-hour bombardment, after which the first infantry wave was to assault the first objective at noon and, 15 minutes later, the second and heavier infantry wave was to pass through the first wave and assault the second objective. After seizing the second objective, the second wave and reserves would begin to consolidate against counter-attacks. At this point, a decision would be made whether to press forward or not. The British commanders believed that careful planning and elaborately worked out details would overcome the enemy and the principles of war. Gouraud's plan was similar, with the 1st Division attacking on the right and the 2nd Division on the left over a 1,000-yard front. One regiment remained in corps reserve in each division. Across the trenches the Southern Group was in fair shape as June began with the 9th Division holding the right and the 12th Division holding the left. In reserve Weber had the 15th Division north of Soğanlıdere, four battalions from the 7th Division, and 25 batteries of artillery. Importantly, the Southern Group developed and rehearsed counter-attack plans.[56] Against them Hamilton massed about 22,000 French and 24,000 British infantry with another 7,000 British infantry in reserve.

The bombardments began, as scheduled, at 8.00am on 4 June. A pause scheduled for 11.20am occurred in an attempt to fool the Ottomans into manning their trenches but artillery firing resumed ten minutes later.[57] Because of the intensity of the artillery preparation observers thought that the Ottoman front-line trenches were obliterated. At noon the first wave went over the top and immediately faced intense machine-gun and rifle fire. Along most of the front initial progress gained the enemy trenches but immediate and effective counter-attacks and heavy casualties forced most back into their own trenches. By 1.30pm the Indians, the French and the Royal Naval Division were back in the own lines, but the brigades of the 29th and 42nd Divisions had gained their first objectives. Unfortunately for the Allies, 'the broad principle of using reserves to exploit success rather than to redeem failure had not yet been established'[58] and Hunter-Weston and Gouraud committed their reserves in support of the failed attacks on the flanks. By 5.15pm all but the 127th Brigade were back in their own trenches with casualties amounting to around 6,500 men. Observing these setbacks was the new commander of the 29th Division, Major-General H. de B. de Lisle, who had arrived from France that evening.

The British official history asserts that the battle was lost because Hunter-Weston used his reserves to attack the Ottoman lines which were still held by the Turks, in effect, reinforcing failure while the successful brigades were left unsupported and vulnerable to Ottoman counter-attacks. Moreover, the author, Aspinall-Oglander, speculated that a victory was possible because the Turks appeared disorganized and 'all would have been lost' with a continuing British attack.[59] However, as none of the Southern Group reserves were actually committed and were in good positions as night fell on 5 June, it is hard to imagine a different outcome. In fact, at 7.30pm Liman von Sanders sent a message to Enver reporting a successful defence and indicating that Weber intended to counter-attack because the enemy was tired and weakened.[60]

On 5 June the Southern Group concentrated its reserves for a 9th Division counter-attack using a large formation of two columns. Weber sent reinforcing battalions from the 2nd and 12th Divisions and altogether there were 11 infantry battalions (five in the right and six in the left column) for the assault. Supporting the 9th Division, the adjacent 12th Division organized a reserve group on its right flank to put pressure on the enemy trenches.[61] The attacking troops began moving forward at about 1.00am on 6 June and went over the top as scheduled at 3.30am. Reports filtered back at 6.00am and 6.45am indicating that the right column had seized the first line of enemy trenches and the left column was similarly successful and had taken five enemy machine guns. There had been heavy fighting inside the British lines for over one and a half hours. Throughout the fight the Ottoman artillery attempted to suppress the Allied guns but with no success. The Ottoman attacks ground to a halt as the British counter-attacked to stabilize the line. Colonel Weber noted in his after-action report that fighting continued for the remainder of the day but these resulted in no changes to the general situation. Third Krithia ended with heavy losses on both sides. Liman von Sanders asserted the Southern Group suffered 9,000 casualties while Colonel Weber reported 6,000 casualties of whom 'at least one third died'.[62] In any case, because of the losses on both sides heavy fighting at Cape Helles subsided until late in the month.

Ottoman reorganization, mid-June 1915

Alert to the stalemated situation on the peninsula, the Ottoman general staff ordered the II Corps headquarters (commanded by Brigadier Faik Pasha), the 6th Infantry Division and three Jandarma battalions south. The 6th Division joined XVI Corps on coastal defence duty on the narrow peninsula neck at Saros Bay, while the II Corps headquarters and the 6th Division's 18th Infantry Regiment continued onward to Cape Helles and Anzac. By this time in the campaign the Ottoman divisional orders of battle were hopelessly confused, with many regiments cross-attached from their original organic parent formations. None the less the Ottoman divisions continued to maintain their combat effectiveness by easily adapting to the situation.[63] On 7 June 1915 Liman von Sanders began to feel nervous about the Kum Kale shore and informed the Asia Group commander (also I Corps commander) Mehmet Ali to review the defensive arrangements of his formations. On that day he also issued orders, which relieved and replaced several division commanders, including the 9th Division's Halil Sami, who was sent to Constantinople after 44 continuous and intense days of combat.[64] Colonel Kannengiesser replaced him in command of the division. Von Sodernstern was also formally replaced in 5th Division by Lieutenant-Colonel Hasan Basri. Of note, a small but prescient change was made in the Northern Group by assigning a Bavarian major named Wilhelm Willmer to command an ad hoc detachment, the Anafarta Detachment, to watch Suvla Bay.

On 8 June the Fifth Army staff conducted a conference for the group chiefs of staff at which the Southern Group chief of operations, Staff Captain Mehmet Nihat, presented a 48-page paper about the recent battles at Cape Helles. It was apparently at this conference that a fatigued Lieutenant-Colonel von Thauvenay presented the tactical situation in the Southern Group as 'hopeless' and pleaded for fresh reinforcements,[65] an act that led to his relief as group chief of staff that very day. The concerns surfaced at the conference generated dialogue about taking advantage of the current operational lull in combat to conduct relief in place operations moving the Southern Group divisions in contact to the rear and replacing them with fresh units. The Fifth Army staff concurred and ordered the group to go ahead with this concept. The Southern Group acted swiftly by issuing orders the following evening (perhaps leading to the conclusion that Mehmet Nihat anticipated this and had already devised such a plan).[66] Colonel Weber ordered the 9th and 12th Divisions to pull back on the night of 11/12 June, while at the same time the 11th, 7th, and 2nd Divisions would relieve them in the lines from right to left respectively. While putting fresh men in the trenches, this also put three divisional headquarters forward to relieve the strain on senior commanders as well. Conducted under conditions of great secrecy for fear that the Allies would discover and take advantage of the dangerous manoeuvre, the relief in place went off successfully.

Liman von Sanders remained concerned about the depleted condition of his divisions and began to press the Ottoman general staff for reinforcements and replacements. Enver rebuffed his requests but within days wired Liman von Sanders that the political situation allowed him to send assistance to Fifth Army. Between 13 and 16 June the Fifth Army and the general staff traded messages about exactly what was required on the peninsula, but Enver did not commit any actual forces. Finally, on 17 June, Liman von Sanders sent off a message to Enver requesting authority to move II Corps, 4th and 6th Divisions south to Cape Helles,[67] prompting Enver to reply immediately that he did not want these units committed to combat piecemeal.[68] However, Enver also promised to dispatch the Second Army headquarters from the capital area and the 8th Infantry Division, then entrained near Smyrna (modern Izmir) en route from Palestine, to reinforce Fifth Army. Once these formations were in situ at Saros Bay, Liman von Sanders would be free to move his divisions south. On 19 June, the general staff put 5,000 replacements into the pipeline to Fifth Army to bring its depleted formations up to strength. Of course this number was insufficient to replace casualties of the magnitude suffered by Fifth Army and Liman von Sanders asked for more. He also requested that Enver direct Major-General Cevat Pasha, the straits fortress commander, to release artillery and ammunition to the Fifth Army. Liman von Sanders based this on the assumption that the straits were unlikely to be attacked; Enver concurred, and on 21 June Cevat released three batteries of 150mm howitzers and one battery of 105mm guns to the Fifth Army.

Reorientation of British strategic priorities

On 7 June a new Dardanelles Committee convened to consider the strategic dilemma that had been left unresolved on 14 May.[69] Once again Churchill aggressively dominated the discussion and advanced a very persuasive argument based on the situation in France. Churchill argued that neither the Germans nor the Allies had the resources to break through the trenches in the near term and asserted that any British effort there would result in losses disproportionate to the effort expended. Furthermore, he argued that the Dardanelles continued to offer breathtaking strategic opportunities for directly supporting the faltering Russians and building alliances in the Balkans. He continued by recommending that Hamilton be provided with any and all resources that he required to prevail on the peninsula. Churchill ended his argument by stating that the limited British artillery ammunition stocks could be more efficiently used in a smaller-scale offensive against the Ottomans rather than against the Germans. Kitchener, whose opinion had taken an about-turn in early June, now vigorously supported Churchill's line of reasoning. The committee ended its deliberations with a decision to send out three additional divisions.[70] These were additional to the 52nd Division, the first element of which – the 155th Brigade – had landed on 6/7 June. Churchill also pointed out that a gain of 8 miles against the Ottomans essentially won the campaign while a similar gain in France was insignificant. This was a significant shift in British strategic priorities, which previously regarded the Dardanelles as a 'sideshow' but which now elevated Hamilton's campaign to the empire's strategic main effort.

Hamilton's re-energized MEF staff began working on a new plan on 8 June in reaction to the news that three fresh divisions would arrive by mid-July. Four courses of action were considered – new landings at Bulair, or landings in Asia, another effort at Cape Helles to reach the Kilid Bahr plateau, or a major attack from Anzac on Mal Tepe.[71] There was opposition to new landings from the naval staff because of the now very real threat of German submarines. Hunter-Weston remained convinced that with fresh divisions and an abundance of howitzers and shells he could take the plateau, but the MEF staff did not believe he could get much past Achi Baba. As such there was great interest among the MEF staff in Birdwood's recommendations involving Chunuk Bair, a hill on the Sari Bair Ridge which was the left flank covering force objective. By mid-June, Hamilton had settled on Birdwood's schemes and told him to expect the 52nd Division and the three new divisions. On 14 June Gouraud weighed in in support of the idea of a main effort from Anzac as well.[72] Between mid-June and early July, Kitchener committed two more additional divisions, more howitzers, and extra ammunition to the enterprise and notified Hamilton to this effect on 5 July 1915. Counting the 52nd Division, whose 156th Brigade landed on 12–14 June, Kitchener now committed six divisions and a corps headquarters to support Britain's revised strategic priorities.

The three new divisions were to be sent out organized as an army corps and Hamilton traded cables with Kitchener in search of an aggressive commander. On 9 June, Kitchener proposed Lieutenant-General Sir Bryan Mahon, then underemployed as the commander of the 10th Division, while Hamilton wanted either Lieutenant-General Sir Julian Byng or Lieutenant-General Sir Henry Rawlinson from the BEF in France.[73] However, Sir John French would not release either man. Seniority also came into play as Mahon was a senior lieutenant-general and, in the end, Kitchener and Hamilton settled on Lieutenant-General Sir Frederick Stopford. He was senior to Mahon, charming, courteous and keenly interested in his profession but Stopford had never commanded troops in war. He was also 61 years old and his health was far from good.

In the meantime, Hamilton supported the recommendations of Hunter-Weston and Gouraud that smaller limited attacks, which were very carefully planned and fully supported, could make gains locally on Cape Helles. This recognized the inadvisability of poorly resourced frontal attacks as well as limited the potential losses of VIII Corps and the French corps. This was important because the replacement drafts from Britain and France were failing to keep up with losses and failed to maintain battalions at full strength. Moreover, the British replacement drafts reaching the peninsula were laden with men of lower efficiency and training.[74] Kitchener also had cabled Hamilton to conserve the energies of the expeditionary force until reinforcements enabled it to strike a decisive blow.

MEF independent divisional attacks

After the front-wide attacks of early June at Cape Helles failed, Hamilton authorized Hunter-Weston and Gouraud to conduct smaller divisional-scale attacks to seize locally favourable objectives. By this time, the Ottoman Southern Group had 42 infantry battalions on hand, but these were considerably weakened from weeks of combat. Strength returns from the Southern Group chief of staff, Lieutenant-Colonel Hüseyin Selahattin, on 20 May showed 26,022 men present for duty out of an authorized strength of over 42,000 with losses reported as 16,178.[75] He also noted that the 'old divisions' were notably reduced compared to the newly arrived divisions.

The French launched the first of these smaller attacks on 21 June at Kereves Dere, which the Turks call the battle of 83 Rakımlıtepe (Hill 83). The attack was planned with two regiments assaulting at 6.00am after a 45-minute artillery preparation. The French objectives included the hill and two Ottoman redoubts known as the Haricot and the Quadrilateral. Ammunition was plentiful and the French left no details to chance. The objectives were held by the 2nd Division, which had been in position since 13 June.[76] The French assault broke into the right flank Ottoman trenches but failed on the left. The fighting was bitter and the division committed its reserve battalion. By 7.30am two Ottoman corps reserve regiments were moving forward as well and at 10.25am Colonel Weber put the 34th Infantry Regiment from the 12th Division lying in reserve near Achi Baba on the road south. However, none of these reserves were needed as the 6th Infantry Regiment was able to hold the French by themselves and most of the French were pushed back by mid-afternoon. The Ottoman division noted that substantial reserves were in place to prevent further attacks.[77] By 1.00am, 22 June, Hill 83 was firmly in Ottoman hands and they counter-attacked at 2.00am.

The next day, the French renewed their assault at 2.15pm against the right flank of the 1st Infantry Regiment, which took very heavy casualties. A comprehensive situation report from the commander of the 34th Regiment, Major Yümnü, noted that the French attack was particularly fierce and well supported by hand grenades and artillery fire.[78] The battle frittered away into the night of 22/23 June and a half-hearted French attack on the Quadrilateral failed the next day. Minor fighting continued until 25 June before the French quit. The battle ended with the French in possession of some of the forward Ottoman trenches on Hill 83 (Kereves Spur) and in a somewhat better tactical position. The 2nd Ottoman Division was so weakened by the battle that Weber decided to pull it to the rear replacing it in the line with the fresh 12th Division.

Hunter-Weston launched his divisional attack on his left flank along an axis of attack defined by Gully Ravine or Zığındere. The Ottoman 11th Division opposed the British attack, which lay entirely within this division's defensive sector and the key village of Krithia lay just 1,800 yards (1,500m) behind the Ottoman forward positions. According to the Turkish histories the Fifth Army believed the tactical and morale situation to be well in hand. Hunter-Weston assigned the assault to the 29th Division, which was now under the command of Major-General de Lisle, reinforced with the Indian and the 156th Brigades. The British were extremely well prepared and had very up-to-date maps based on recent aerial observation. They had 77 British and French artillery pieces, including 21 howitzers, and had a cruiser and two destroyers available for naval gunfire support as well. Because the previous failures at Krithia were thought to be related to the insufficient weight of the artillery bombardment, de Lisle was authorized to expend a third of the ammunition stocks at Cape Helles. The attacks were deliberately planned with meticulous attention to details and pitted the 87th, 88th and Indian Brigades against Gully Ravine and the 156th Brigade against Fir Tree Spur.

Harassing fire began about 2.00am on 28 June 1915 and the main bombardment commenced at 9.00am. Ottoman situation reports went to the division headquarters at 9.20am, 9.55am, and 11.00am, the last reporting a major ground attack on the lines that started at 10.45am.[79] Because the Ottoman positions were incompletely wired in, the British seized the forward trenches within minutes. As noon approached, Indian troops had advanced over 1,100 yards (1km) on VIII Corps' left flank nearing what they called the Nullah; in response to this the Ottoman 127th Infantry Regiment moved forward to blocking positions behind the 33rd Regiment.[80] At the same time (noon), Colonel Weber released the Southern Group's immediate reserve, two battalions of the just-arrived 16th Infantry Regiment from the 6th Infantry Division, which was located only 1 kilometre east of the 11th Division headquarters, to the 11th Division.[81] These forces immediately conducted a violent counter-attack on the Indian Brigade that raged for about three hours.[82]

Message traffic on the night of 28/29 July between Liman von Sanders and Enver resulted in orders to Colonel Weber to counter-attack using the incoming II Corps formations. Weber began to plan accordingly and early on 29 July he appointed the II Corps commander, Brigadier-General Faik, as right wing commander. Colonel Weber placed the 7th and 11th Divisions directly under Faik's command.[83] He also ordered the 12th Division to prepare to launch small raiding parties to support Faik's assault. For his part, Liman von Sanders ordered Esat's Northern Group to return five battalions of the 9th Division, which was reconstituting itself behind Kum Tepe, to Weber's control.

Faik spent the afternoon positioning his artillery near the Triyandafildçiftliği (Triyandafil Farm), moving his incoming units into position and finalizing his orders. Faik issued his corps attack order at 6.00pm.[84] At 7.30pm the artillery preparation would begin and 30 minutes later, from right to left the 124th Infantry Regiment, 16th Infantry Regiment, 33rd Infantry Regiment and 126th Infantry Regiment would assault. In addition to the divisional artillery batteries, two 150mm howitzer batteries lent their fire and the incoming 1st Division was ordered to man the third defensive line by 8.30pm. The previously prepared raids by the 7th and 12th Divisions were ordered forward to confuse the enemy as well. Faik's attack went off as scheduled but quickly bogged down in the face of heavy machine-gun and artillery fire. By midnight, some portions of the British first line of trenches had been taken but the attack had made little progress beyond that. A follow-up attack was hastily organized in the dark and launched prematurely. Unsurprisingly it was 'scattered rather than concentrated' and failed under intensive machine-gun fire.[85]

Faik was undeterred by these reverses and began to plan for further attacks using the relatively fresh 1st Division. However, because of the disorganized state of II Corps, only a minor attack was attempted on the night on 1 July, with no results. That night messages from Liman von Sanders poured into Faik's headquarters encouraging him to wipe out the British salient on the Turks' right flank. Faik created a regimental-sized assault force and directed the commander to load the men up heavily with hand grenades. The 2 July attack began badly with little of the artillery support that had been planned and the advance stalled causing the commander to commit his reserve. The officers manoeuvred the assault into the trenches, but pushing the enemy back was 'like pushing mud'.[86] The attacks continued well past dawn on 3 July but by 10.30am it was clearly apparent that the 1st Division was incapable of further attacks.

Fortunately for the Turks, the Fifth Army commander had secretly set units in motion to reinforce the Southern Group. Previously on 1 July Liman von Sanders ordered the Asia Group commander, Brigadier-General Mehmet Ali, to deploy to the peninsula with his I Corps staff and the fresh 3rd Division. By 12.30am on 3 July the corps headquarters and the advance parties of the 3rd Division were arriving on the peninsula. Accompanying Mehmet Ali was his corps chief of staff, German Major Eggert, and Staff Captain Tevfik. In addition to these forces the Fifth Army had accelerated the flow of the 5th Division inbound from the north as well. Early in the afternoon of 3 July Liman von Sanders arrived at the Southern Group's headquarters at Salimbeyçiftliği to confer with Colonel Weber. Mehmet Ali and his staff had arrived there earlier in the day and, after a brief nap, were working with Weber's staff. The outcome of this meeting was a massive change in the operational posture of the group and a revised offensive plan to attack the next day. Orders began to go out immediately at 2.40pm to the 4th Division (then in reserve) to relieve the 12th Division (then in the line) beginning at 9.00pm that night. In addition, the 4th Division was ordered to shift six 47mm naval guns and 1,800 shells west to support the offensive. By late afternoon, Mehmet Ali began to issue orders directly to the commanders of the 3rd and 5th Divisions to plan for an attack.

The extra day of planning enabled Mehmet Ali to construct a plan launching six battalions of the 3rd Division to the west of Gully Ravine and four battalions of the 5th Division to the east. He held two battalions of the 5th Division in immediate reserve just south of Triyandafıldçiftliği. While in comparison to earlier Ottoman attacks, the infantry force seemed smaller than past practice, the artillery plan was significantly more complex. The Ottoman artillery was organized into a right wing group and left wing group.[87] This centralization of artillery assets mirrored the successful artillery command arrangements used in the battles of Çatalca in the Balkan Wars.[88] The artillery was organized into two components, a light group composed of field artillery batteries, and a separate heavy group of 105mm, 150mm and 210mm howitzers. The light group was assigned detailed fire plans designed to suppress the fire from the British trenches while the heavy group was assigned a counter-battery mission to suppress the British artillery. This was the most well-coordinated artillery plan employed by the Turks on the peninsula, reflecting an understanding of the weaknesses of earlier failures. Altogether, Mehmet Ali planned to throw almost 14,000 fresh troops into the attack. Confidence levels were running so high that Liman von Sanders personally invited the Austro-Hungarian military attaché, General Pomiankowski, accompanied by Fifth Army chief of staff, Lieutenant-Colonel Kazım, to view the attack from Weber's headquarters on 5 July 1915. Liman von Sanders hoped to persuade Pomiankowski to press his government to attack Romania and restore direct communications with Constantinople.[89]

Over the night of 4/5 July, the assaulting battalions moved into attack positions in the forward trenches of the 1st Division, which was then holding the line. The attack began with 30 minutes of demonstration fire in the 7th Division's sector and then at 3.30am the light artillery group opened fire on the British trenches. Ammunition shortages limited the preparation fire to 15 minutes, at which time firing stopped while the Ottoman infantry went forward. The artillery, now reinforced by the heavy group, shifted to the south to pound the British artillery positions and the men went forward with fixed bayonets at 3.45am. According to the British official history the Ottoman artillery bombardments caused little damage to either the British trenches or to the British artillery. The Turks broke into the first line of British trenches but at terrible cost. Platoons were 'cut in half' and then 'cut into quarters'.[90] Reports indicated that the British forward trenches had been taken but casualties were severe and heavy fire kept the men pinned (sheltered) in the enemy's trenches.[91] These reports were quickly passed up the chain of command to Mehmet Ali, who was working out of the Southern Group headquarters. In order to continue the attack, he passed orders to his reserve to move forward.

British machine-gun and artillery fire was fierce and at 6.50am they began to counter-attack with ready reserves. They began to take back their trenches from the Turks, information which was quickly passed back from the 3rd Division by its German commander, Lieutenant-Colonel Nicolai. Now worried that the attack might fail, Mehmet Ali directed his reserves to reinforce the 3rd Division. At 8.20am, Lieutenant-Colonel Nicolai was able to report that the

CAPE HELLES FRONT, MID-JULY 1915

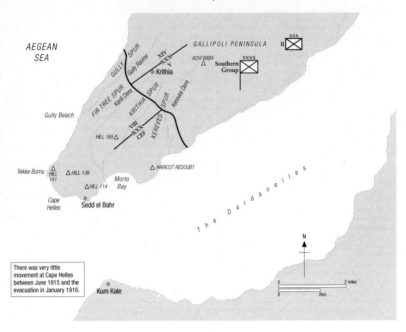

two reinforcing battalions had entered the fight. Meanwhile, on the left, the Turks had penetrated 550 yards (500m) into the enemy lines but were also being counter-attacked. By 11.45am the survivors of the assaults were streaming back through the Ottoman lines. As darkness fell, Liman von Sanders left the Southern Group headquarters and returned to his own headquarters at Yalova. Casualties from Mehmet Ali's attack were heavy.[92] When these losses are combined with the casualties from the other divisions for the entire period, Ottoman losses for Gully Ravine approached 16,000 men.

Ottoman operational reorganization, July 1915

On the evening of Tuesday 6 July 1915, Fifth Army sent orders to the Southern Group informing Colonel Weber that the Ottoman general staff had ordered the I Corps headquarters and the 3rd Division to return to the Asian side of the straits. This movement was the precursor of a major reorganization of the Southern Group designed to inject fresh commanders and forces into the battle area. In truth both Enver and Liman von Sanders were very unhappy with the tactical situation in the Southern Group. According to a later report written by the group operations officer, Staff Captain Nihat, regarding the attacks of 29/30 June, Faik's II Corps operations were characterized by an exceptionally slow tempo.[93] Nihat also asserted that Colonel Weber was preparing plans to withdraw to the Soğanlıdere line and that preparations for pulling back 35 artillery batteries were also in place. He continued that he understood from a telephone conversation with Fifth Army chief of staff, Lieutenant-Colonel Kazım, that Liman von Sanders wanted to set matters right in the Southern Group (Kazım, it must be remembered, was in constant contact with his academy classmate, Enver Pasha). After Mehmet Ali's failure, Nihat continued, there was a consensus that Weber, although a good soldier, was tired and dispirited having been engaged in combat continuously since 6 May. There was clearly a crisis of confidence at the end of the first week of July 1915 in the ability of Colonel Weber to continue in command.

Both Fifth Army and the Ottoman general staff were aware of the increasing strength of the Allies at Cape Helles, which indicated that the fight for Achi Baba and the plateau overlooking the straits was the Allied main effort. Ottoman intelligence reports confirmed an accurate appraisal of the increases in Allied strength at Cape Helles that included the landing of the Royal Naval Division, the Indian Brigade, the 52nd Division, and dismounted Australian cavalry.[94] Intelligence regarding the composition of the second French division was also very accurate and comprehensive.[95] As a result Ottoman reinforcements went to Colonel Weber to oppose Hunter-Weston at Cape Helles rather than to Esat Pasha to oppose Birdwood at Anzac. At the same time, the staffs were aware of the heavy losses suffered by the Southern Group.[96] These factors coalesced around the gathering opinion that a change was needed at the tip of the peninsula. On 6 July 1915, Enver sent Liman von Sanders a telegram informing him that Vehip Pasha, the commander of the Ottoman Second Army, would take command of the Southern Group.[97] Accompanying Vehip were some of the Second Army staff officers, who would combine with the Southern Group staff to form a new group headquarters. Moreover, the Ottoman XIV Corps (8th and 10th Infantry Divisions) and V Corps (13th and 14th Divisions) were put on orders to deploy to the Southern Group as well. This was to become effective on 9 July after which Colonel Weber would return to Germany.

It is evident from the redeployment of Mehmet Ali's I Corps back to the Kum Kale operational area in Asia that the Ottomans were also concerned about their weak flanks, which were now rather exposed as the forces previously stationed there were drawn into the battles on the peninsula. In fact, internal Fifth Army messages in early July indicated an appreciation of the danger to both Asia and Saros Bay.[98] On 4 July, Colonel Fevzi was notified that the exhausted 12th Division would be sent to his Saros Group (XVI Corps) for reconstitution and coastal defence duty. Liman von Sanders also planned to redeploy the 5th Division to Esat's Northern Group as well.[99] Taken together, these changes rebalanced the operational posture of the Fifth Army by reinforcing the wings (Asia and Saros Bay), while at the same time cleaning up the messy and overlapping command arrangements in the Southern Group. In his memoirs, Liman von Sanders, related that by 16 July rumours of an impending Allied landing were rife and that on 22 July he received word from the chief of the German general staff that landings could be expected in Asia or Saros Bay.[100] In light of the actual Allied landings at Suvla Bay in early August 1915, it seems evident that Enver and Liman von Sanders exercised prescient and prudent strategic and operational direction.

The Ottoman 8th Division and XIV Corps, which was commanded by German Colonel Bruno Trommer, began to arrive in the operational area on 8 and 11 July respectively. Brigadier-General Mehmet Vehip arrived at Fifth Army headquarters on 8 July and the next morning, accompanied by Staff Colonel Nihat, went to Southern Group headquarters. Vehip issued his first orders in command at 5.30pm, 9 July, by sending warm greetings to his troops, who numbered about 45,000. That day the first battalions of the 14th Division began to arrive as well while the V Corps headquarters reached the rail terminus at Uzunköprü. On 11 July, Vehip issued his operational plan and map overlays, which organized the defensive area into the First Area (on the right flank) and the Second Area (on the left flank).[101] Trommer's XIV Corps was assigned the First Area and disposed the 1st and 11th Divisions in line from the right. Brigadier-General Fevzi's V Corps headquarters had not arrived but the Second Area disposed the 7th and 4th Divisions in line from the right and was backstopped by the 6th Division in group reserve. Vehip noted that, for the moment, the Second Area divisions would remain under Southern Group Command. Vehip alerted his group on 11 July with orders giving them three days to finalize their defensive preparations as increased British artillery fire indicated that an enemy offensive was in the making.

The action of Achi Baba Nullah or Second Kereves Dere, 12–13 July

General Gouraud was seriously wounded visiting a hospital near V Beach on 30 June. General Bailloud, commander of the 1st Division, assumed command of the CEO and continued the offensive spirit of Gouraud by recommending another combined attack at meetings with Hamilton and Hunter-Weston.[102] The 157th Brigade reached Cape Helles on 3 July thus completing the 52nd Division's order of battle. Hamilton had hoped to keep the 52nd Division intact for his August offensive but when Kitchener notified him that the MEF would receive a fifth new division, he decided to keep the pressure on the enemy.[103] As a result, Hamilton authorized another limited multinational attack aimed at seizing the Ottoman trenches along the Anglo-French seam using the two fresh brigades of the 52nd Division and both French divisions. Hamilton hoped to launch the attack on 7 July but problems with the French artillery delayed the attack until 12 July. Finally, the 38th Brigade from the 13th Division arrived at Cape Helles on 7 July followed by the division commander, Major-General F. C. Shaw, and some of his staff on 12 July.

In order to position the 52nd Division for the attack, the MEF withdrew the Royal Naval Division from the line and filled it, from left to right, with the 157th and 155th Brigades. One of Hunter-Weston's enduring 'lessons learned' was that even the smallest attack against the strongly dug-in and well-disciplined Ottomans must be heavily supported by artillery bombardments.[104] His attacks in May were conducted over wide attack frontages supported by weak and unconcentrated artillery, but increasingly in June, VIII Corps turned to narrower attack frontages heavily supported by artillery. The corps staff concluded that there was a shortage of artillery relative to the trench footage to be assaulted, which led to the idea that all available artillery should be used to support one single brigade. This conceptualization by the VIII Corps staff produced a uniquely awkward plan, causing the attack to be split in time using two brigades attacking abreast – but nine hours apart – each supported sequentially by all of the VIII Corps artillery. That this was thought likely to succeed relied on an intelligence appreciation that Ottoman morale was very low and likely to collapse. Even the Ottoman trenches were described by Aspinall-Oglander as 'haphazard', 'irregular' and 'confusing'.[105] Such Allied thinking is difficult to comprehend after the reverses of April and May.

Hunter-Weston then turned tactical planning over to Major-General G. G. A. Egerton, who led the untested staff of the 52nd Division, and who ordered a direct frontal attack in four waves.[106] The 155th Brigade would launch its attack at 7.35am simultaneously with four battalions each from the two French divisions. All available British artillery and half of the French artillery were tasked to support the 155th Brigade. In addition, but only to be used in emergencies, Egerton had his 156th Brigade, which was still recovering from its failed assault of 28 June. Egerton's second attack, using the 157th Brigade, was scheduled for 4.50pm and Hunter-Weston retained the final decision as to its execution. The MEF made a great effort to ensure that the 52nd Division had the most updated maps and information about the Ottoman trench system, which were identified on British maps with identifications such as Trench E11 and E12. Planning proceeded but, extremely concerned with operational security, the VIII Corps staff directed that maps and hand-drawn sketches were not to be carried forward from the British trenches. This caused consternation among the assault leaders, who were told to memorize the spatial characteristics and distances to their objectives. Making things worse, updated accurate trench diagrams of the enemy positions were only made available on 10 July, but these failed to find their way down the British chain of command to the men who needed them. In fact, even the updated British trench diagrams were terribly inaccurate regarding Trench E11, which was the 157th Brigade's objective.

Naval gunfire and aerial bombing began at 4.30am on 12 July and the artillery preparation started 30 minutes later, which was scheduled to drop some 60,000 shells on the Ottomans over a three-hour period. The Allied infantry went over the top at 7.35am into fierce machine-gun fire, which caused very heavy casualties. The 155th Brigade stormed the first lines of enemy trenches, however, most of its battalion and company commanders were killed or wounded. As a result, Egerton's reporting system broke down immediately, causing a loss of situational awareness at brigade and division headquarters respectively. Staff officers sent forward to find out what was happening never returned and effective command and control in the 13th Division collapsed. Nevertheless, based on inaccurate reports and sensing disaster, Egerton sent one of his two reserve battalions into the fight at 11.30am and sent the remaining battalion forward at 1.00pm. He followed this by telephoning the VIII Corps headquarters urgently expressing that Hunter-Weston not cancel the afternoon attack.

On the Ottoman side, in the 7th Division sector, the 20th Infantry Regiment reported at 8.55am that they had 'blown apart' the attacking enemy units and had retaken the trenches lost in the initial assault. In the adjacent 4th Division sector, the French had done somewhat better and the situation there was regarded as 'dangerous'. As a result the Ottoman division commander committed his reserve to stabilize the situation. At about 4.00pm Ottoman artillery units began to pound the exposed Allied infantry.

Such confusion reigned that by midday, Hunter-Weston was unsure as to whether he should continue with the scheduled second attack. However, after the French agreed to launch a supporting attack, he decided to continue with the planned attack by the 157th Brigade. Egerton was notified and he sent his senior staff officer forward to tell the battered 155th Brigade to use this opportunity to push on to its objectives. Hunter-Weston then moved the Royal

Marine Brigade, under Brigadier-General Trotman, forward as a local reserve for Egerton, but with strict guidance that it was not to be employed without VIII Corps' approval.

The 157th Brigade attack went in as scheduled at 4.50pm with 'great dash'.[107] However, based on inaccurate trench maps and incomplete intelligence and in the face of fierce resistance it foundered almost immediately. In particular, the E12 trench was found to be only a shallow scratch, incapable of providing the assault troops with adequate cover and leaving them vulnerable to enemy fire. Hunter-Weston ordered Trotman to send several companies of marines forward. As night approached, the Allied attacks were all but finished and, finding himself with almost no information about what had happened, Hunter-Weston ordered Trotman to occupy the now empty 52nd Division trenches with the Royal Marine Brigade. As dawn broke on 13 July, Hunter-Weston found himself with no more situational awareness than he had had at midnight. He became anxious as the morning passed without any reassurance from Egerton and became disturbed as troubling reports came in about the chaotic situation on the front. However, he sent encouraging reports about the assault upward to Hamilton who, at 1.30pm, 'wanted to congratulate the 52nd Division but wants to know whether they really deserve it'.[108]

At 11.00am, after conferring with the French, Hunter-Weston asked for permission to renew the attacks, which was approved by Hamilton. Hurrying back to his command post, Hunter-Weston informed Trotman that he was to attack with his brigade at 4.30pm. This fresh attack by three worn-down battalions launched, and by 8.00pm the Royal Marines had reached the E12 trench but were themselves pushed back with heavy casualties.

At 5.30pm, Hunter-Weston recalled Egerton to the VIII Corps headquarters and relieved him of command.[109] He then placed Major-General Shaw, the 13th Division commander – who had just arrived on the peninsula – in command of the 52nd Division. Shaw, now in executive command, had no knowledge of the situation on a front containing the mixed units of the 52nd Division with Trotman's Marine Brigade, who it must be said was also filling in as the temporary commander of the Royal Naval Division. That night, Shaw sent one of his own staff officers and the GSO1 from Egerton's staff forward to examine the situation. Their report the next morning (14 July) confirmed a very tenuous hold on the forward lines, after which the shattered 155th Brigade was withdrawn and replaced by units of the Royal Naval Division.[110] The last British offensive at Cape Helles ended badly with heavy casualties. The official history asserted that the efforts were worth it because the Ottomans sustained more casualties than the Allies, but in truth, by 20 July, with the exception of the 13th Division, no British or French units on Cape Helles were capable of offensive action.

The Allied attack caught the Southern Group in the middle of reorganization and the Ottoman divisions in contact were still directly under Vehip's command. As the battle developed Vehip left the fighting to his subordinate division commanders, whose reports indicated that the situation was in hand. This was a sound decision and left Vehip free to manage the reinforcement flow. At 9.15am, he ordered the acceleration of two regiments of the incoming 6th Division into a staging area in the left flank rear of the 4th Division (near Domuz Dere).[111] The deployment was conducted with stealth and the incoming regiments were ordered to camouflage themselves immediately upon arrival in their staging areas. The first companies began to arrive at Domuz Dere soon after 1.00pm. Sometime that afternoon, Fevzi Pasha and the V Corps staff arrived at Vehip's Salimbeyçiftliği headquarters and prepared to take control of the tactical battle. As night fell on 12/13 July 1915, Vehip and Fevzi coordinated the battle handover of the left sector of the front. Group orders were issued that night formally transferring the Second Area to V Corps' control and also assigning the 4th, 6th and 7th Divisions to Fevzi's command.[112] Vehip's staff also coordinated artillery support with the First Area and began to plan for a night counter-attack using Fevzi's troops.[113] Fighting was dulsatory and he made preparations with his division commanders for a night attack.[114] However, as the day progressed it was apparent that the Allied will to continue the battle was finished and they withdrew from most of the Ottoman trenches that they retained. The necessity for a counter-attack evaporated and Vehip cancelled the operation entirely, thus bringing the battle to an end by nightfall on 13 July.

Fifth Army operations, 14 July–6 August 1915

Esat's Northern Group conducted divisional attacks on 29 June and 12 July with small results. Minor fighting then continued around the ANZAC perimeter throughout July, characterized by trench raids and mining operations. Neither Esat nor Birdwood had either the capability or the desire to renew the heavy fighting that had previously depleted their strength. Esat chafed at the lack of reinforcements and replacements, which were mostly being sent to the Southern Group.

Enver Pasha dispatched a telegram to Liman von Sanders on the night of 15/16 July expressing the idea that although Fifth Army had been sent new divisions, the difficulty of executing successful offensives grew with each passing moment.[115] He directed that the new divisions be integrated quickly with the experienced divisions in order to learn the tactical conditions more rapidly. This would assist them in preparing for new offensive operations. For his part, Liman von Sanders was more concerned with the physical and psychological reconstitution of his army. The following day, Enver fired off another alarming telegram to Liman von Sanders asserting that he knew conclusively from intelligence sources that the British were about to execute an amphibious landing in Saros Bay.[116] He demanded an update on the status of Fifth Army units in that area and directed that all replacement soldiers then going to Fifth Army be sent to the divisions guarding the Saros Bay region. Moreover, he indicated that he considered an adequate garrison for the area to be two full army corps and he wanted the Ottoman XVII Corps to be sent there. A follow-up message on 18 July from Enver asserted that he now knew that the British intended to strike at Bulair. In spite of these two messages, Liman von Sanders did not think the narrow neck of Bulair was a viable landing site and personally thought that the invasion might come either in Saros Bay or nearer the middle of the peninsula. Nevertheless, he put the troops at Bulair and Saros Bay on high alert and ordered them to rehearse their plans thoroughly and as secretly as possible. On 25 July, the Asia Group began to send Fifth Army messages warning that the commander believed a landing was imminent there as well and that he was coordinating with the German artillery commander, Colonel Wehrle, for heavy artillery support against ships. Following up on this news, Liman von Sanders coordinated with Admiral von Usedom in the straits fortresses to conduct exercises to determine how fast the ferry and road system could support the reinforcement of the Asian side of the straits.[117] Adding to the array of opinions, Esat Pasha sent messages to Fifth Army that he believed an enemy attack was building oriented on the Çonkbayırı-Kocaçimen plateau (Sari Bair Ridge) while his brother, Vehip, agreed with Enver.[118] On 28 July 1915, Enver Pasha came to the peninsula for briefings and to see the situation for himself. As July ended there were clearly a variety of conflicting opinions about where the actual blow would fall.

Strategic, operational and tactical conclusions

At the strategic level, Enver was initially slow to reinforce the peninsula, largely because the Ottoman high command was concerned about the possibility of a Russian amphibious landing near the Bosporus. As this threat receded in June Enver was able to shift several army corps and their divisions south to join the struggle on the peninsula. In order to do this Enver effectively managed the strategic build-up of forces in the straits region by using it as a strategic reserve.

In this regard he was materially assisted by its proximity to the Dardanelles and by excellent land and sea lines of communications.

Likewise, the British War Council, energized by Kitchener and Churchill, recognized that the means in the hands of Sir Ian Hamilton were inadequate to accomplish the task at hand, and determined to reinforce the MEF. This involved a significant shift in Britain's strategic thinking, which was brought on by the recognition that six divisions could not shift the strategic balance in France, but might be used to a greater strategic effect at the Dardanelles. This shift in British thinking came too late to alter the operational equation on the Gallipoli peninsula mainly because the time-space relationship penalized British deployments from the United Kingdom to the northern Aegean Sea. Moreover, effective Ottoman intelligence always alerted the Ottoman high command of impending Allied massing of forces.

At the operational level, Hamilton lost the initiative as his forces became enmeshed and fixed in his two beachheads. At MEF level, there was no operational manoeuvre during this period. Because of this he was unable to mass forces at the operational level or to re-establish an operational reserve. He remained fixed on the seizure of Achi Baba and stripped forces from the ANZAC in an attempt to take it using direct frontal attacks. It may be said that there was clarity in Hamilton's operational objective but this was achieved by reducing the ANZAC to a holding force. In some ways, the MEF organizational architecture compromised the effective use of the three British infantry divisions at Cape Helles, a fact that was finally corrected with the establishment of VIII Corps on 5 June. However, even when this was achieved, the MEF never coordinated Anglo-French operations at Cape Helles, preferring instead to let the corps commanders coordinate operations. Finally, in the absence of an operational-level offensive, Hamilton satisfied himself with localized divisional attacks which failed to gain ground and merely frittered away manpower and artillery ammunition.

The Ottoman Fifth Army formed effective operational-level combat groups to coordinate the efforts of subordinate army corps. Liman von Sanders seized the initiative at operational level through the conduct of massive night attacks that forced the Allies into a reactive posture. The Fifth Army successfully massed forces, first at Anzac, and then shifted the army's main effort to Cape Helles. The Fifth Army enjoyed the service of a number of effective Ottoman and German corps and division commanders, but Liman von Sanders was not reluctant to relieve ineffective commanders who faltered when the situation seemed impossible.

At the tactical level both armies misread the tactical lessons when the fighting reduced to continuous trench warfare. Both sides believed that tactical failures reflected too high a priority on hasty attacks and moved towards deliberate attacks, which were better planned and more fully supported. Although the shortage of artillery ammunition came to dominate British tactical planning, both armies attributed the failure of their attacks to an acute shortage of artillery ammunition and sought ways to overcome this deficiency – the Fifth Army through centralization and the MEF through reducing its attack frontages and launching sequential attacks supported by all available artillery. Both sides retained the tactical initiative at Cape Helles, which shifted there continuously during these months, because they saw the Achi Baba heights as the key terrain feature in this phase of the campaign.

Hamilton created an ad hoc composite infantry division as an expedient means of focusing combat power at Cape Helles. In doing so, he reduced other divisions to ineffectiveness and left senior commanders with little to do. He allowed his principal subordinate commanders to hand over direct control of the tactical battles to brigadiers in a process known as 'executive command'. This ruptured effective control of battles particularly because the reporting system failed to provide information that enabled the tactical commander to employ reserves effectively. Additionally, 'executive commanders' were frequently overloaded with too many units and too many responsibilities.

Tactical performance in the Fifth Army remained superior to that of its Allied opponents. The Ottomans were able to mass defensively and offensively for large-scale attacks. The fact that their attacks failed spectacularly spoke more to 1915 battlefield dynamics than anything else. Ottoman corps and division commanders routinely were able to cross-attach regiments effectively throughout this period. Finally, superb reporting systems in the Ottoman Army enabled Fifth Army commanders at all levels to make decisions and execute them in a timely and effective manner. The result of this was that Fifth Army commanders were able to influence positively and successfully the outcomes of battles to a greater extent than Allied commanders.

Chapter Seven

THE ANZAC BREAKOUT, 6–28 AUGUST 1915

The operational and tactical stalemates at Cape Helles and Anzac could not be broken with the troops at hand. The Ottomans had almost emptied their deep Thracian force pool of well-trained divisions and had all but given up trying to drive the invaders back into the sea. Strategically, in the summer of 1915, the Ottoman high command began to look to Germany and Bulgaria as a way out of the deadlock. This would come by way of crushing Serbia and by re-opening the land lines of communications with Germany and Austria-Hungary. Enver was confident that this would unleash a flood of artillery ammunition and, perhaps, even actual reinforcements, such as heavy artillery batteries, and he was certain that the battered Fifth Army could hold on until winter.

In Britain, the War Council came to the conclusion that the mass of Kitchener's New Armies would not be ready for action until 1916 and, moreover, artillery and shell production would not support them even if they became ready to deploy and fight overseas. This realization forced the council to the redefinition of strategic priorities as it felt that the small number of divisions actually available in the summer of 1915 might be used to greater effect against the Ottomans at the Dardanelles. In turn this led to the resolution to provide Hamilton with fresh reinforcements with which to renew the offensive and regain the initiative. This fitted neatly into a scheme that Birdwood had suggested to break out of the Anzac perimeter by seizing the entire Sari Bair Ridge, including Chunuk Bair and Hill 971. Hamilton's revised campaign plan shifted the MEF's main effort from Cape Helles and Achi Baba to Anzac and Mal Tepe, although the campaign's operational objective – the Kilid Bahr plateau, remained unchanged. Kitchener put a fresh army corps – IX Corps commanded by Lieutenant-General Sir Frederick Stopford – on orders for the Mediterranean and the stage was set for the ANZAC breakout and a second supporting amphibious operation.

British planning for the August offensive

Hamilton warmed to Birdwood and his chief of staff Lieutenant-Colonel Andrew Skeen's ideas for seizing Chunuk Bair in mid-June and began actively thinking about its implementation.[1] Birdwood's appreciation for how many troops would be required varied over the course of a month but he finally settled on a total of six brigades with which to execute the surprise night *coup de main*.[2] In the end Birdwood's requirement devolved to the spatial characteristics of the tiny Anzac beachhead, which did not accommodate the massing of large numbers of men. Hamilton's dilemma then became one of where to employ the six new incoming divisions with the most effect, which cumulatively totalled 18 brigades plus their divisional artillery. The main effort of Hamilton's original plan was on Cape Helles but Hunter-Weston's repeated failures to take Achi Baba made this appear problematic. But after conversations with de Robeck, whose fleet expected new anti-submarine nets and purpose-built armoured flat-bottomed landing lighters, Hamilton began to lean towards another amphibious landing. The military and naval staffs revisited the landing options, including Asia and Saros Bay and by 27 June, Hamilton decided to include a large landing immediately south of Suvla Bay in support of Birdwood's scheme.[3]

The means at Hamilton's disposal were the fresh assets coming out from Britain, and counting the 52nd Division, the MEF would have four divisions and a corps headquarters available for offensive operations at the beginning of August. The MEF's operational objective (the campaign 'end') – the Kilid Bahr plateau – remained the same but Hamilton's revised intermediate objective would be the capture of a position astride the peninsula from Gaba Tepe to Kilia Bay, including Mal Tepe. This would result in either the Fifth Army abandoning the Kilid Bahr plateau or being forced to defend it from two, opposite directions. The way that the MEF would conduct the August offensive was to designate Birdwood's ANZAC as the main effort and then subordinate all other actions to supporting it. Altogether this was a significant alteration to the original operational design of the campaign.

Birdwood was asked directly by Hamilton to provide his ideas about how the ANZAC main effort might unfold and what support would be required. On 1 July, Birdwood sent Hamilton his revised concept, which he reframed as a phased operation.[4] Birdwood now believed, in the first phase, the ANZAC should conduct a turning movement to seize not only Chunuk Bair, but also Hill 971, Battleship Hill and the entire Sari Bair Ridge. Simultaneously with this, the 1st Australian Division would launch a diversion at Lone Pine to secure the right flank while an amphibious attack secured the Chocolate and W Hills on the left. Birdwood also recommended that, if three incoming divisions were made available for a landing, they push on to seize the Kavak Tepe and Tekke Tepe range. In the second phase the remaining incoming divisions would push onward to the Dardanelles themselves. This idea fed the predisposition of the MEF staff to conduct a large landing at Suvla Bay. Subsequently, Hamilton then decided to land two divisions under a separate commander at Suvla to take the Chocolate and W Hills, relieving Birdwood of that task and he informed the ANZAC on 2 July of his decision. He also told Birdwood to expect the 13th Division, a brigade of the 10th Division, the 29th Indian Brigade and additional artillery as reinforcements for the offensive. Since somebody else was securing the Chocolate and W Hills, Birdwood's requirement fell to five brigades, which Hamilton agreed to provide. Hamilton gave Birdwood a free hand in planning the operation, subject only to Hamilton's final approval. Finally, after discussions, Hamilton and Birdwood decided that the operation would begin when the moon would rise two hours past midnight on 6/7 August.

In support of the ANZAC main effort, Hamilton decided to launch diversionary attacks using Hunter-Weston's VIII Corps at Cape Helles in an attempt to convince Liman von Sanders that the MEF remained focused on Achi Baba. Hamilton also decided to assign the amphibious landing at Suvla Bay to Stopford's incoming IX Corps. Additionally, Hamilton retained Stopford's 53rd Division, which would be concentrated at Imbros by 6 August, as the MEF general reserve.

With the operational details fleshed out with Hamilton, Birdwood and Skeen began to work on the ANZAC breakout plan itself. What emerged, after consultations with his divisional commanders, was an extremely complex and high-risk plan. Birdwood envisioned the turning movement on Chunuk Bair and Hill 971 erupting out of the left flank of Godley's New Zealand and Australian Division, which he designated as the corps' main effort. There were a number of options for command and control, including designating a separate major subordinate commander for the turning movement, but Birdwood decided that Godley would command the entire main effort. This meant that, in addition to supervising the assault, Godley was responsible for a supporting attack at the Nek and for securing the existing trench lines as well as securing both flanks of the assault. To accomplish all of these tasks, Birdwood assigned two brigades of the 13th Division and the 29th Indian Brigade to Godley's New

HAMILTON'S PLAN FOR THE ANZAC BREAK-OUT

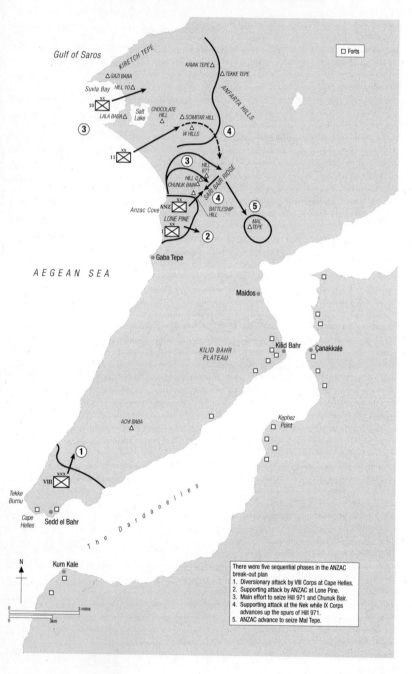

There were five sequential phases in the ANZAC break-out plan
1. Diversionary attack by VIII Corps at Cape Helles.
2. Supporting attack by ANZAC at Lone Pine.
3. Main effort to seize Hill 971 and Chunuk Bair.
4. Supporting attack at the Nek while IX Corps advances up the spurs of Hill 971.
5. ANZAC advance to seize Mal Tepe.

Zealand and Australian Division, which already comprised two infantry brigades and three dismounted mouted rifle brigades.[5]

Extensive but surreptitious reconnaissance of the ANZAC left (or northern) flank by Godley's New Zealanders and Australians had been ongoing since the landings. The terrain was rugged in the extreme and neither side held the line with continuous trenches, preferring an outpost line of small posts. Unlike the remainder of the ANZAC front, which was strongly held by both sides, there were tactical opportunities present on the flanks of the Sari Bair Ridge and, over the previous months, a number of small reconnaissance parties had penetrated the porous enemy front up the steep valleys almost to the top of the ridge. The reports of this were so encouraging that in June Birdwood and Skeen had expanded their original concept to include the seizure of Hill 971 as well as Chunuk Bair, which created two objectives that needed to be taken simultaneously. Since Hill 971 was, by far, the most difficult climb, Birdwood thought to assign this assault to Cox's Indian Brigade, which contained three battalions of Gurkhas, who were known to be 'hill men', capable of making the arduous climb.[6] However, as time passed, Hamilton refused to release the Indian Brigade from Cape Helles until immediately before the attack, causing Birdwood to wonder whether it might be better to reassign the mission to his 10th Division battalions, which were already present. In the end, Birdwood reinforced the Hill 971 column by adding Brigadier-General J. Monash's 4th Australian Brigade to the effort.

As planned the ANZAC assault would be composed of two main assault columns and two flanking covering force columns.[7] To prevent the assault force from being held up, the covering force would move out as darkness fell and secure the outpost line. Additionally, the left covering force, commanded by Brigadier-General J. H. Du B. Travers and composed of two battalions of the 40th Brigade, was ordered to extend northward and connect with the arriving IX Corps. The right covering force, commanded by Brigadier-General A. R. Russell and composed mostly of dismounted New Zealand cavalry, maintained contact with the division and was ordered to push the Ottomans off their outpost line on the high ground. The left assaulting column, commanded by Brigadier Cox, but composed of two brigades and a mountain artillery battery, numbered over 5,000 men. The column led with the Australian brigade, which after working its way up the Aghyl Dere by 1.00am, would push out two battalions to the left to occupy the Abdul Rahman Spur while the Indians pushed out two battalions to take Hill Q. At 2.00am the re-formed column would then dispatch the remaining two Australian and two Indian battalions to seize Hill 971, which would be in British hands by 3.00am. The overly optimistic

time-distance calculations allowed three and a half hours to travel 3 miles up
very steep and difficult terrain in nearly total darkness and the route to be taken
was un-scouted. The right assaulting column, commanded by Brigadier-General
F. E. Johnson, was composed of the New Zealand Infantry Brigade with an
Indian mountain battery and two battalions of the 13th Division. This force
would split, climbing up two valleys – Sazli Dere and Chailak Dere – and would
rendezvous between 1.00am and 2.00am on the saddle between Table Top and
Rhododendron Spur. From there the column would advance 1,000 yards
(900m) to Chunuk Bair, which was reported unoccupied by the enemy. Like
the left column, the right column's route was un-scouted and was extremely
difficult and confusing in the darkness.

This was not a simple plan and Godley attempted to put himself in a
position to control it as it unfolded by establishing his battle headquarters at
No. 2 Post.[8] Although each assaulting column had its own reserves, Godley kept
six New Army battalions in division reserve for the support of his assaulting
columns.

But there was even more to the complex ANZAC breakout plan: strong
enemy counter-attacks were expected on Chunuk Bair and Godley planned for
a reserve column of New Army troops to follow the assaulting columns in order
to defeat the enemy and then launch the second phase of the offensive to break
the Ottoman grip on the high ground. In this phase, Johnson's force would
assault down the ridge and attack Baby 700 from the rear while the 3rd Light
Horse Brigade attacked it simultaneously across the Nek at 4.30am on 7 August.
Finally, because any attack on the north-eastern flank of the Anzac beachhead
involved the seizure of the 400 Plateau, Birdwood ordered the 1st Australian
Division to conduct a diversionary attack at Lone Pine. There were differences
of opinion regarding the start time of the Lone Pine diversionary attack;
Birdwood wanted a midnight attack, but the final plan settled on late afternoon
assault on 6 August. In the worst case this would simply be a feint to deceive the
Ottomans but, in the best case, it would result in the seizure of key terrain.

The success of the ANZAC breakout plan depended on the seizure of
Chunuk Bair and Baby 700, which were the key terrain features in the Ottoman
defensive scheme. If these objectives could not be taken the ANZAC was going
nowhere. To achieve these objectives, Birdwood decided to attempt an
unrehearsed night assault over un-scouted ground to a precise tactical timetable.
He then delegated command to an overworked division commander who
further delegated command to brigade level. Moreover, neither the corps nor
the division operations orders reveal command and control mechanisms
necessary to influence the battle if things did not go as expected. As he had done

SUVLA BAY LANDINGS, 6 AUGUST 1915

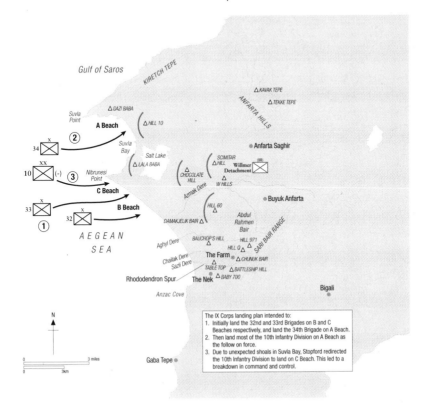

Gulf of Saros

KIRETCH TEPE

△ KAVAK TEPE

△ TEKKE TEPE

ANFARTA HILLS

△ GAZI BABA

Suvla
Point

A Beach

△ HILL 10

● Anfarta Saghir

Suvla
Bay

Salt Lake

△ LALA BABA

SCIMITAR
△ HILL

Willmer
Detachment

34 [X]

②

x

10 [X] (-) ③

Nibrunesi
Point

△
CHOCOLATE
HILL

△
W HILLS

● Buyuk Anfarta

C Beach

33 [X]

B Beach

32 [X]

①

Azmak Dere

△
HILL 60

DAMAKJELIK BAIR △

Abdul
Rahmen
Bair

SARI BAIR RANGE

AEGEAN
SEA

Aghyl Dere

BAUCHOP'S HILL
△

HILL 971
△

HILL Q △

Chailak Dere
Sazli Dere

The Farm
△

△ CHUNUK BAIR

Rhododendron Spur

TABLE TOP

△ BATTLESHIP HILL

The Nek

△ BABY 700

Bigali
●

Anzac Cove

N
↑

0 ⊢⊢⊢⊢⊢⊣ 3 miles
0 ⊢⊢⊢⊣ 3km

Gaba Tepe ●

The IX Corps landing plan intended to:
1. Initially land the 32nd and 33rd Brigades on B and C
   Beaches respectively, and land the 34th Brigade on A Beach.
2. Then land most of the 10th Infantry Division on A Beach as
   the follow on force.
3. Due to unexpected shoals in Suvla Bay, Stopford redirected
   the 10th Infantry Division to land on C Beach. This led to a
   breakdown in command and control.

on 25 April, once again Birdwood decided essentially to put his corps on automatic pilot. In combat, there is a difference between a risk and a gamble. In both cases a commander calculates the odds – but a risk may be militated by actions taken to influence the outcome should things go wrong. A gamble throws the dice with no ability to influence the outcome. In this case, Birdwood went beyond risk and took a huge gamble.

According to Hamilton's diary for 11 July, 'Stopford and his Staff turned up from Mudros. Stopford in very good form'.[9] The staff of the newly formed IX Corps had embarked at Avonmouth for the Dardanelles on 20 June, just four days after forming at the Tower of London. Kitchener assigned Stopford four divisions – the New Army 10th and 11th and the Territorial Army 53rd and 54th – for the newly established corps. Stopford carried a personal message to Hamilton from Kitchener, asserting that Kitchener was certain that success

185

could only be gained by achieving surprise. After discussions revolving around the absolute necessity for Stopford not to divulge Hamilton's plans, Hamilton sent Stopford to find Aspinall-Oglander for detailed briefings on the MEF. Unexpectedly, however, as the infant planning process began, Hamilton notified Kitchener that VIII Corps commander Hunter-Weston had 'broken down and may have to be invalided home'.[10] On 17 July, Hamilton sent Stopford to Cape Helles temporarily to relieve Hunter-Weston, who was 'worn out' and medically unfit.[11] Hamilton felt this was an opportunity to give Stopford 'a rare chance of learning how to do it and how not to do it'.[12] Stopford was told to take with him one staff officer who was junior to Brigadier-General Street, while the IX Corps staff remained on Imbros.[13] On 22 June, Hamilton visited Stopford at the VIII Corps command post to give him written instructions on the role IX Corps would play in the forthcoming offensive.

As previously described, the MEF plan assigned the ANZAC as the main effort and relegated IX Corps to a supporting role. At the operational level Hamilton identified the MEF objectives as the capture of Hill 305 and 'the capture and retention of Suvla Bay as a base of operations for the northern army'.[14] Tactically, Hamilton ordered Stopford to capture the two horns of the bay, the Chocolate and W Hills, and to secure a footing on Tekke Tepe Ridge. Hamilton stressed the importance of securing Chocolate and W Hills by a *coup de main* before daylight. The orders state 'it is hoped that a division will be sufficient for the attainment of these objectives'.[15] Hamilton also 'hoped that the remainder of the force will be available for an advance on Biyuk Anafarta with the general object of moving up the spurs ... to assist General Birdwood'. Hamilton assigned Stopford his 11th Division and the 10th Division less the 29th Brigade. He further noted that 4,000 men could be landed initially and that three full brigades could be ashore by daybreak. Of note, Hamilton explicitly ordered Stopford not to divulge the plan below division commanders and a tiny number of selected corps and division staff officers. Later in the afternoon Stopford expressed confidence in the plan to Aspinall-Oglander, who had remained on the peninsula to go over the details with him. The next day, Stopford summoned his senior staff officer, Brigadier-General H. L. Reed, to come over to the peninsula to talk over the plan.

On 24 July the medical staff sent Hunter-Weston back to Britain to recuperate and Major-General W. Douglas was appointed as the temporary commander of VIII Corps. This released Stopford from learning the ropes in VIII Corps and he rejoined his own headquarters on Imbros on 26 July. Three days later, Hamilton sent Stopford his 'Final Instruction from GHQ' for the Suvla Bay operation, which characterized his 22 July guidance as 'a rough outline of the task ...

allotted'.[16] Hamilton reaffirmed Stopford's primary objective as the securing of a base of operations and restated the importance of Chocolate and W Hills. Moreover, Hamilton refined IX Corps' secondary purpose and ordered Stopford to 'give such direct assistance as in your power to the GOC ANZAC in his attack on Hill 305 by an advance on Biyuk Anafarta with the object of moving up the eastern spurs of that hill'. Hamilton's guidance, therefore, after seizing the beachhead, oriented IX Corps towards the south-east and the Sari Bair Ridge. Stopford and his staff now took over detailed planning and, in the words of Aspinall-Oglander, 'the breath of indecision began to blur the outlines of Sir Ian Hamilton's scheme'.[17] The first whiff of this indecision came in a letter from Stopford to Hamilton on 31 July, expressing Stopford's conviction that Tekke Tepe Ridge must be taken, as well as Kiretch Ridge. Furthermore, Stopford expressed the fear that these operations would absorb all of his forces leaving none to assist Birdwood. While this conformed closely to Hamilton's scheme it contained major reinterpretations of IX Corps' mission but the MEF sent nothing in reply correcting Stopford's interpretation of the operational design.

Stopford's IX Corps landing order, Operations Order No. 1, issued at 11.00am, 3 August, reveals a dilution of Hamilton's intent. Stopford and his staff's assessment of Hamilton's guidance led them to the conclusion that in order to achieve the corps' primary objective 'the security of Suvla Bay will not be insured until he is in a position to deny the enemy the heights which connect Anafarta Sagir and Ejelmer Bay' or what was called the Tekke Tepe Ridge.[18] While this might seem like a small change, this served to orient the IX Corps operation directly east from Suvla Bay rather than to the south-east. Aspinall-Oglander noted a 'lack of precision' in the MEF orders was 'reflected and magnified' in the IX Corps plan.[19] Tactically, it led IX Corps to land more troops inside the bay itself on A Beach rather than on B and C Beaches to the south. Although the phrases 'covering force' and 'covering positions' were not used in the August orders, Stopford tasked Major-General F. Hammersley's 11th Division to land at all three beaches and secure positions about 1,000 yards (900m) inland. Moreover, Stopford gave control of the two infantry brigades of the 10th Division to Hammersley for the landing, thus elevating Hammersley to command of the entire corps. These two brigades were to be brought in through A Beach for the purpose of securing Kiretch Ridge (on the far right flank). The operational and tactical design of IX Corps' and 11th Division's published orders stop at that point. What would happen once the initial positions were reached was not explained at all and Stopford's orders simply noted 'subsequent action by the whole force will be governed by a correct appreciation of the situation'.[20]

Hamilton had allowed Stopford the latitude to plan his operations, subject to Hamilton's approval. In the time between Stopford's letter of 31 July and the publication of the IX Corps plan on 3 August and again between then and the landings on 6 August, Hamilton and his staff failed to change any part of Stopford's orders. This led to a significant misunderstanding as to what IX Corps was supposed to achieve on landing. Moreover, the IX Corps plan did not adhere to a specific and precise timetable, as did the ANZAC plan, and simply urged commanders to move as rapidly as practicable. Other than ordering operational and tactical start times, Hamilton and his MEF staff did not attempt to coordinate corps operations as they unfolded in real time. Birdwood was operating on a tightly directed timetable and Stopford was not. It was the job of the MEF staff to coordinate these adjacent operations. Finally and once again, a British corps commander handed over control of corps-level assets to a subordinate division commander.

With Hunter-Weston invalided home, Major-General Douglas assumed temporary command of VIII Corps but, because he was unfamiliar with the overall situation, the senior staff officer of the corps, Brigadier-General H. E. Street, acted as the *de facto* commander during this period.[21] Street had been Hunter-Weston's right-hand man since the landings and saw the tactical problems through the same lens as his chief. As a result, Street believed that the continual shortage of high-explosive shells was a crucial determinate in the corps planning process. Tasked by the MEF to conduct a diversionary attack on 6/7 August, Street and the corps' planners fell back on the artillery-centric concepts used during the 12 July Achi Baba Nullah battle. The corps' objective was to flatten out an elbow in the Ottoman trenches which could be attacked from the west and from the south. Owing to shortage of artillery and shells, all the corps artillery would support a late afternoon attack from the west by a 29th Division brigade on the northern half of the objective and then, the next morning, all of the artillery would support an attack from the south by a brigade of the 42nd Division on the southern half of the objective. Like Achi Baba Nullah, these attacks were sequential rather than simultaneous but had the advantage of heavier than normal fire support. It was expected that 'by dividing the operation into two halves the weight of the artillery available would enable both parts of the objective to be taken with comparatively little trouble'.[22]

At the operational level, the MEF plan designated the ANZAC as the main effort and reinforced Birdwood with five additional brigades. At the same time, the MEF relieved the ANZAC of the burden of securing its northern flank by assigning IX Corps that mission as well as establishing a secure base of operations at Suvla Bay. Meanwhile the tired VIII Corps would attempt to fix Ottoman attention and reserves at Cape Helles. However, once again, Hamilton demonstrated an inability to mass at the operational level by allowing a force of over 12 divisions to concentrate a mere three brigades as the MEF main effort. Moreover, Hamilton again displayed an inability to plan control measures that would enable coordination between Birdwood's timetable and event-driven attacks and the 'as practicable' advance of Stopford's IX Corps. Finally, Hamilton again fragmented the organizational integrity of divisions by assigning parts of IX Corps to Birdwood and, at the tactical level, he allowed Birdwood to fragment his units while overloading a division commander. In the end, Hamilton's violations of the principles of war – unity of command, mass, economy of force, simplicity – could only be compensated for by surprise, manoeuvre and his unbridled faith in the superior combat effectiveness of his soldiers.

Ottoman planning

By early August there were a number of indications that the Allies intended to attempt a naval attack to force the straits as well as conducting a second large amphibious operation. On 4 August Liman von Sanders alerted Faik's II Corps (4th and 8th Divisons) to be ready to deploy to the Asian side. To the north of Willmer's detachment, the Fifth Army formed a cavalry screening force called the Tayfur Detachment to screen the coast up to the Bulair lines. On the north-western shoulder of the ANZAC perimeter Mustafa Kemal expressed concern over the weakness of the Willmer Group, which lay to the immediate rear of his sector. Kemal later claimed to have accurately predicted that the assault would come by way of Sari Bair and Suvla Bay.[23] However, this did not square with the III Corps staff's appraisal and, apparently fooled by the ANZAC deception measures, Esat sent a revised secret appreciation of the situation to Liman von Sanders on 5 August that identified enemy activity aimed at the area between Gaba Tepe and Lone Pine. Moreover, he outlined the positions of the battalions that he had set in place to prevent any breakthrough in this area. After discussions with Liman von Sanders, Esat also moved Kannengiesser's 9th Division to an area along the coast between Gaba Tepe and Krithia.

By early August Vehip had solidified the defence of the Southern Group using three operational corps commands. Trommer's XIV Corps held the right flank with the 1st and 10th Divisions while Fevzi's V Corps held the left flank with the 13th and 14th Divisions. Each division in line put two regiments forward and held one in reserve. Supporting them was Major Rıfat's artillery group. Behind Achi Baba and along the Soğanlıdere line lay Faik's II Corps with the 4th Division to the north of Soğanlıdere and the 8th Division on the western shore. It was a well-balanced posture characterized by defence in depth and reserve capability (almost half of Vehip's combat power was in reserve).

MEF diversionary operations

Hamilton's second operational offensive began with British artillery at Cape Helles firing at 2.20pm on 6 August; the Ottoman artillery group returned fire immediately and effectively.[24] At 3.50pm the 88th Brigade attacked the strongly held lines of the 10th Division across 300 yards (270m) of no man's land. The British attack was an immediate and massive failure (with 2,000 casualties out of 3,000 men involved). Ottoman reports to Fifth Army at 4.30pm noted that the 10th and 13th Divisions had been attacked but that the enemy failed to gain a foothold.[25] De Lisle, the 29th Division commander, played with the idea of sending in his reserve 86th Brigade but wisely decided against it. As scheduled, at 9.40am, 7 August, the British 42nd Division launched a similar attack employing the 125th and 127th Brigades, which resulted in a similar bloody repulse with the exception of a vineyard seized in the 13th Division's sector. A supporting French attack on the 14th Division began at 10.00am that day and met with the same result. According to the Turkish histories the French attack was supported more effectively with machine-gun and artillery fire, which allowed them to get into the Ottoman trenches with bayonets and hand grenades. Nevertheless, with great difficulty, the French were forced back by Ottoman counter-attacks as well. Vehip's evening report that night outlined the defensive success and mentioned that the 14th Division had captured 38 men.[26] The Ottoman XIV and V Corps were so successful that on neither day did Vehip have to commit his general reserve (II Corps) to the fight.

Operations at Anzac began with a brigade-sized diversionary attack at Lone Pine on the evening of 6 August 1915, which, if successful, would be followed by the remainder of the 1st Australian Division seizing Gun Ridge and Scrubby Knoll.[27] While this was a diversion it was also a serious attack designed to take and hold ground in order to relieve pressure on the main axis of advance.[28] Esat's Northern Group deployed the 16th and 19th Divisions northward from Gaba Tepe. The right flank of Mustafa Kemal's 19th Division was flanked by a single battalion of the 14th Infantry Regiment holding a series of strongpoints in the broken terrain (rather than a continuous trench) along the slopes of Sari Bair Ridge. Esat held the 5th Division in close reserve just behind his artillery belt. Despite efforts at secrecy the Turks had noticed increased activity on the ANZAC piers as early as 5.30am, 6 August, which caused them to increase their artillery firing into the Australian beachhead. However, Esat and Liman von Sanders remained focused on the beaches south of Gaba Tepe, where they had positioned the 9th Division earlier.[29]

Artillery and naval gunfire began to fall on the Ottoman lines starting at 3.00pm, 6 August and at 4.30pm the bombardment focused on the lines of the 16th Division. The division commander, Colonel Rüştü, had the 125th Infantry Regiment in the line on what the ANZAC called Johnston's Jolly and the 47th Infantry Regiment on what was known as Lone Pine.[30] The Turks had occupied their trenches for some time and had covered much of the front line with logs and earth as protection against artillery fire. The Australian trenches, which protruded towards the Turks in a bulge called the Pimple, were less than 100 metres from the Northern Group lines. At 5.30pm the 1st Australian Brigade came out of their trenches and raced into the Ottoman lines. There, a bitter hand-to-hand fight using bayonets and hand grenades quickly developed as the Australians struggled to dislodge the Turks from their underground positions. Casualties on both sides were unusually heavy but within 30 minutes the Australians held the first line of enemy trenches.

Learning of the enemy's success, Northern Group commander Esat's reaction was immediate and predictable. At 6.00pm, he ordered Colonel Kannengiesser's 9th Division to move three infantry regiments with artillery into positions behind Gaba Tepe and the 15th Infantry Regiment (5th Division) to march as quickly as possible to Lone Pine. As the tactical situation stabilized near 7.00pm, Esat decided to go over to the offensive and launch a counter-attack. Colonel Rüştü was able to organize a regiment and three reinforcing battalions quickly and launched a powerful counter-attack after dark at 11.00pm.[31] Again fighting was exceptionally violent but the Turks were only able to recover the 47th Regiment's second line of trenches.[32] Undeterred by this failure, Rüştü wanted to continue the attacks and requested additional reinforcements from the adjacent regiments on his left flank.[33]

Liman von Sanders' report to Enver on the morning of 7 August noted that the extreme violence of the ANZAC assault had pushed back the line at Lone Pine some 330 yards (300 m).[34] Esat was displeased with the night's failure and telephoned Rüştü from his Kemalyeri headquarters at 5.45am to insist that the forward line of trenches be retaken. Moreover, Esat promised that the adjacent 19th Division would render assistance.[35] Rüştü replied that there was not enough strength left to conduct further attacks. Events soon made Esat's demands largely irrelevant as the battles to the north gained momentum. Nevertheless Esat sent him a battalion from Gaba Tepe, which Colonel Rüştü launched in an attack on the afternoon of 8 August. Again the fighting was fierce and hand to hand with bayonet and hand grenades. Parts of the Ottoman first line of trenches in the centre were retaken but violent Australian counter-attacks retook the line soon after. That night Esat sent more reinforcements and Rüştü attacked with these fresh troops at 5.00am, 8 August, retaking part of their line on the right. Hard fighting continued relentlessly all day, all night, and into 10 August. Finally Esat ordered a halt to the attacks and, in the end, the Australians held on to most of their initial gains made on 6 August.

From the British perspective the battle at Lone Pine served its purpose, which was to divert Esat and to draw in his available reserves. In fact, the Northern Group committed three entire regiments and a battalion to the fight at Lone Pine – a force that exceeded the strength of an entire Ottoman army division.[36] However, as Aspinall-Oglander also rightly pointed out, when Esat put Kannengiesser's regiments on the move towards Lone Pine he unintentionally created a powerful and immediately available force, which was diverted to Chunuk Bair in time to narrowly divert disaster.

Early in the evening of 6 August, Liman von Sanders began to receive reports from Suvla Bay and the ANZAC perimeter alerting him to Hamilton's attacks. He prompted his chief of staff, Lieutenant-Colonel Kazım, to order the Southern Group – which according to Vehip's reports appeared to have things well in hand at Cape Helles – to send two regiments from the 4th Division to reinforce the Northern Group. By 10.45pm the Southern Group alerted the 4th Division commander, who soon put the regiments on the road to the north. This left Vehip with one regiment in reserve to cover the Soğanlıdere line and on 7 August, he was ordered to put an 8th Division regiment on the road north as well.[37] Further instructions from Liman von Sanders followed later that day pointing out that as II Corps commander Faik was not urgently needed at Cape Helles that he be sent north to join four regiments coming south from Saros Bay.[38] It is clear from this exchange of messages that the Allied attacks at Cape Helles on 6/7 August 1915 did not fix Ottoman reserves in place nor fool either Vehip or Liman von Sanders into believing them to be a major effort. Indeed, the rapidity of the Fifth Army reaction indicates a well-developed sense of situational awareness that enabled a coherent tactical response.

These were not the only reinforcements that Liman von Sanders deployed to the centre of mass of the peninsula. The Fifth Army sent warning orders to the Saros Group on the night of 6 August to be prepared to send XVI Corps south. In the meantime, at 1.45am, 7 August, XVI Corps was ordered to send a regiment to Anafarta but the regiment did not make it onto the road until 5.00am.[39] Then at 6.30am Liman von Sanders ordered Ahmet Fevzi (Saros Group commander and XVI Corps commander) to bring two 7th Division regiments with an artillery battalion as well as the 12th Division to Anafarta in order to conduct counter-attacks on the morning of 8 August. These forces were on the road shortly thereafter and a forced all-night march brought them nearly to Büyük Anafarta on the morning of 8 August. The 6th Division and the Independent Cavalry Brigade remained at Saros Bay to cover the beaches. Ahmet Fevzi himself reached the Fifth Army headquarters at 2.00pm, 7 August where Liman von Sanders briefed him on his plan to conduct a counter-attack from the vicinity of Kücük Anafarta.

Realizing that Liman von Sanders was facing a crisis situation, the Ottoman general staff sent warning orders to Field Marshal Colmar von der Goltz and the headquarters of the Ottoman First Army, then in Constantinople, to prepare to deploy to Saros Bay. In Asia Mehmet Ali was also ordered to dispatch forces across the straits as well. It is clear from the scope of these movements that Liman von Sanders was certain by midnight on 6/7 August that Hamilton's main effort lay to the north of Anzac rather than at Cape Helles, Saros Bay or Asia.

The battle for Sari Bair, 6–8 August 1915

The British called the ridge line on the north face of the ANZAC perimeter Sari Bair and along its length nested three hills. The hills grew higher from south to north and were called Battleship Hill (Düz Tepe), Chunuk Bair (Conkbayırı) which was 286.5 yards (262m) high, and Koca Chemen Tepe (Kocaçimen Tepe) which was 331 yards (303m) high. Hamilton's main effort was an assault that was intended to seize the two highest hills on Sari Bair, which would open the way to seizing the straits. The southern two thirds of the ANZAC perimeter were mostly continuous trenches but due to the broken terrain the northern third was composed of fortified posts and unconnected pieces of trenches. The Ottomans opposed this with a similar defensive layout and, as a result, there were only a few isolated Ottoman outposts on the ravine-laced slopes of Sari Bair held by small detachments of men. Here the Ottomans and the ANZAC depended on the extremely broken terrain as defence against a large-scale assault. Hamilton's plan capitalized on this weakness and he planned a surprise assault using columns to penetrate between the Ottoman posts and scale the heights during the hours of darkness.

Major-General Godley's attack began soon after dark on 6 August with the left and right covering forces clearing the Ottoman outpost lines to create secure flank protection for the main assaults.[40] At 10.45pm the left assaulting column began to make its way up to the summit of Hill 971 (Koca Chemen Tepe) while the right assaulting column began its climb to take Chunuk Bair and then wheel south-west to capture Battleship Hill. Both columns were to achieve these results by an hour before dawn on 7 August. Then shortly after dawn, as the Australian Light Horse attacked the Nek (a thin ribbon of land leading to Baby 700) friendly troops coming down from Battleship Hill would hit Baby 700 simultaneously from the rear. The left assaulting column immediately became lost and had to backtrack putting it well behind schedule. Control broke down all along the single column of men stretching miles up a gorge. At 2.30am, Monash attempted to deploy his battalions and, as dawn broke at 4.30am, they found themselves spread out only along the lower spurs of the ridge. The right column made better progress, with a battalion reaching the Table Top but at dawn it was also about 1,300 yards (1.2km) from the summit of Chunuk Bair. As a result of this failure, the right assaulting column was not in a position to attack the rear of Baby 700 as scheduled.

One of the most controversial events of the campaign was the dawn attack on the Nek by the Australian 3rd Light Horse Brigade under Brigadier-General F. G. Hughes.[41] The Nek was a narrow causeway 25–40 yards (23m) wide linking Baby 700 and Russell's Top. Six hundred men of two regiments would attack at 4.30am, after a brief artillery bombardment, in four waves of 150 men. Although no man's land was only 60 yards (50m) wide there was no cover or concealment whatsoever. Supporting attacks were also conducted from Pope's and Quinn's Posts. The Light Horse attack went off as scheduled, however, the enemy was not simultaneously assaulted from their rear as expected because the assaulting columns never made it to their objectives. Additionally, the artillery bombardment ended ten minutes early leading to alert defenders manning their trenches. The assault was a disaster with massive casualties. Why it was not called off initially or in mid-stream remains a controversy today. However, it is certain that Godley at No. 2 Post had no idea what had happened on the ridge above him and was thus unwilling to call off the attack, which was an integral part of the complex plan to seize Sari Bair Ridge.[42]

Most of the English-language historiography asserts that the Koca Chemen Tepe (Hill 971) and the Chunuk Bair hill masses were virtually undefended on 6 August, an idea which is based on the memoirs of Colonel Kannengiesser. In fact the Ottomans had considerable combat power there well before the ANZAC assault. The first report of the attack flashed up the Ottoman chain of command at 1.30am, 7 August, from the 19th Division. This report identified a raiding column (*avcı kolu*) of approximately two companies in strength going up Chailak Dere and another raiding column going up Aghyl Dere.[43] The report estimated an overall attacking strength of two regiments and noted that firing had been heard in the lines of the adjacent battalion. Unknown to the ANZAC intelligence staff, the Ottomans had positioned a regiment in reserve on the north-western slopes of Hill 971, which deployed a battalion in the outpost line along what the Allies called Table Top and Bauchop's Hill and its remaining two battalions on Abdul Rahman Spur. Additionally, the 1st Battalion, 32nd Infantry Regiment of Major Willmer's Group was positioned nearby (halfway between Hill 971 and the village of Büyük Anafarta).

As his skirmishers delayed the assault columns in the early hours of 7 August, the 14th Regiment's commander, Lieutenant-Colonel Ali Rıfat, deployed a battalion and two companies to the forward slopes of Abdul Rahman Spur blocking the 4th Australian Brigade, while the remaining two companies went south to block the 29th Indian Brigade.[44] At the same time, the 72nd Infantry Regiment's commander, Major Mehmet Münir, extended his lines northward to block the New Zealand Brigade. Thus, by dawn a coherent Ottoman tactical response emerged to Hamilton's main effort. Kannengiesser, the commander of the incoming 9th Division arrived at Esat's Northern Group headquarters at 4.40am where he was briefed and ordered to take command and form a detachment on Hill 971. Esat also ordered him to move his 64th Regiment and 25th Infantry Regiment, then on the march, to the area near Hill Q for counter-attacks. While Kannengiesser was at the Northern Group headquarters, a situation report arrived from Mustafa Kemal that men had repulsed an attack at 4.30am and inflicted heavy casualties on the enemy.[45] This was, of course, the disastrous Australian Light Horse attack on the Nek. Kannengiesser arrived at Hill Q about 6.30am, August 7, with the advanced elements of his 64th Regiment where he found some of the survivors of the 14th Regiment eager to counter-attack and other men eager to retreat.[46] He quickly ordered the 64th Regiment into the line and the 14th Regiment to conduct a counter-attack, and his arriving 25th Infantry Regiment to occupy Chunuk Bair. Willmer's 1st Battalion, 32nd Regiment had also moved forward to a position immediately behind the 14th Regiment.

By 6.00am Godley understood that his attacks had failed and he decided to reinforce Cox's left assaulting column with Brigadier-General Cayley's 39th Brigade in order to continue the attack.[47] Cayley met with Cox at 7.00am and received orders to assault Chunuk Bair in co-operation with the Indians. Cayley then returned to his brigade and attempted to move it uphill into position, however, even in broad daylight his battalions became lost, backtracked and, at 4.00pm, Cayley only had half a battalion in place. On the right, Godley received word at 8.00am that Johnson's column had halted short of its objective and that Johnson did not consider it prudent to push on. Godley ordered an immediate assault.

At 8.00am, Kannengiesser briefed the tactical situation as he knew it to his chief of staff, the 25th Infantry Regiment commander, and the 2nd Artillery Regiment commander. The ANZAC attacks on the high ground intensified about 9.00am as Johnson's New Zealanders attacked the 14th Regiment and heavy naval gunfire began to pound the Ottomans on Chunuk Bair. The Indians also joined in the attack and only the direct fire of a quick-firing mountain battery, which had arrived with Kannengiesser, saved the position.[48] Recognizing the danger, Kannengiesser sent in the men of his 25th Infantry Regiment to reinforce the battered 1st Battalion, 14th Regiment, which seemed about to collapse. But then, at this critical moment, Colonel Kannengiesser was seriously wounded in the chest and evacuated.

The commander of the 4th Infantry Division, Lieutenant-Colonel Cemil, arrived after an all-night march and saw Esat at 4.30am, who ordered him to bring on his men as fast as possible. At 6.30am, Cemil assembled his division command group at Kemalyeri, where they were continuously updated on the unfolding battle. Northern Group messages reveal that Esat received accurate and timely information from Kannengiesser and Mustafa Kemal that enabled him to react to the rapidly changing situation.[49] One of Cemil's regiments was ordered to Kuru Dere and another to Battleship Hill.[50] About noon, the Northern Group staff telephoned Cemil and told him that Kannengiesser had been wounded and that he and the 10th Infantry Regiment should go immediately to Conkbayrıyı where he would receive written orders. At 1.10pm, Cemil arrived at the 9th Division command post to find that Esat had assigned him to command what was styled the Aghyl Dere Detachment, which was to be composed of the 14th Regiment with two batteries of artillery, Kannengiesser's 25th Infantry Regiment and 64th Regiment, and his own 10th Regimentt and 11th Regiment.[51] His mission was to take up where the badly wounded Kannengiesser had left off and defend the Sari Bair heights. As he had done previously, Esat Pasha created an ad hoc battle group under a single commander tasked to deal with a particular tactical and geographic situation. At 3.30pm, Cemil reported that the enemy attacks had apparently been stopped along a line well below the summits and that the troops were digging trenches.[52] He also noted that he was preparing to deliver a night counter-attack. At 7.00pm news arrived that Willmer's group was successfully holding a new enemy landing at Suvla Bay.[53] Now alerted to the threat to his north Cemil cancelled the night bayonet attack and directed the 64th Regiment to concentrate on fortifications and creating immediate reserves.

By 4.00pm on 7 August Godley recognized his assault had failed but he calculated that with rest his battalions were well positioned to renew the assault the next morning. Moreover, Birdwood had moved the 38th Brigade from corps reserve to No. 3 Post to replace the 39th Brigade which had been committed. Godley drafted orders that evening for a general assault by Cox on Hill 971 and Hill Q and by Johnson on Chunuk Bair. Cox now had 13 battalions under his command but they were widely scattered and he had little idea where they all were.[54] Nevertheless, he organized them loosely into four assault columns, fragmenting brigades, orienting them on both objectives. Cayley was left with no battalions and nothing to do. Johnson, with six battalions in a more compressed position, intended to assault his single objective with three battalions abreast.

On the night of 7/8 August, Colonel Ahmet Fevzi, commander of the Saros Group, who had come down to Anafarta, telephoned Cemil and informed him that 'tomorrow the 7th and 12th Infantry Divisions would attack the enemy from Anafarta'.[55] He continued with instructions that Cemil would take command of the incoming 33rd Regiment and the 11th Artillery Regiment and simultaneously attack from the vicinity of Dağ Çeşme. This was a surprise to Cemil who had not yet been informed that Liman von Sanders was placing the Sari Bair position under Colonel Ahmet Fevzi effective at 9.00am, 8 August.[56] In the early hours of 8 August Cemil moved two battalions into reserve positions behind the front lines and then put fresh battalions from the 11th Artillery Regiment into the line between Kemal's 19th Division and the remnants of the 1st Battalion, 14th Regiment. Thus by dawn a substantial defence was established on Chunuk Bair.

As dawn broke on 8 August, Cox renewed the offensive towards Hill Q and Hill 971 but again control collapsed amidst the difficult terrain and Cemil's defenders shot the advance to a halt. However, Johnson's New Zealanders caught the tired survivors of the 1st Battalion, 14th Regiment, who had been in constant combat since the initial attack on the evening of 6 August, asleep in their trenches and they punched through reaching and seizing the summit of Chunuk Bair. Most of the battered survivors of 1st Battalion, 14th Regiment, had been pushed uphill to the south-western shoulder of Chunuk Bair directly in the path of the Wellington Battalion. By 4.40am, Johnson's men held the forward and rear crests of Chunuk Bair but the adjacent attack by the 39th Brigade foundered as it ran into the fresh men of the 25th Infantry Regiment. This fight was bitterly contested and marked by hand-to-hand combat. About this time, Ahmet Fevzi arrived on Chunuk Bair to direct the battle.[57]

The battle for control of Chunuk Bair raged through the day as the adjacent Ottoman units on the higher ground of Hill 971 and Hill Q laid down heavy fire on the New Zealanders. Ahmet Fevzi reported at 1.00pm that he planned to conduct a counter-attack with the 7th and 12th Infantry Divisions, which were deploying into Dağ Çeşme and Hill Q respectively. A Fifth Army aide-de-camp arrived with a message from Liman von Sanders that German Lieutenant-Colonel Pötih had been appointed to take command of the 9th Division.[58] Meanwhile, the fighting on Chunuk Bair grew to brutal intensity. Colonel Malone was killed along with hundreds of his men and at 5.40pm, Ahmet Fevzi reported that the 64th Regiment had pushed the enemy about 32 yards (30m) down off the crest of Chunuk Bair and that he was personally present at that location. He also reported that he was preparing to counter-attack with his divisions, which were just now coming into their assembly areas. Moreover, two regiments of reinforcements from the Southern Group were scheduled to arrive at Chunuk Bair at 10.30pm that evening.

Liman von Sanders relieved Colonel Ahmet Fevzi, the commander of the Anafarta Group, on the night of 8/9 August 1915.[59] In his memoirs Liman von Sanders noted with great disapproval that Ahmet Fevzi had not carried out his explicit orders to launch a counter-attack on the night of 8 August 1915 and for this reason replaced him.[60] However, the evolving Ottoman reorganization on Chunuk Bair as well as Ahmet Fevzi's positive report indicates a clear sense of situational awareness by the Fifth Army. And it is a fact that until late in the day on 8 August, Ahmet Fevzi's XVI Corps divisions had not reached their assembly positions.[61] In any case, at 7.00pm Liman von Sanders telephoned Esat Pasha expressing his concern about the situation.[62] Liman von Sanders then telephoned Mustafa Kemal, who was then directing his forces from a position on Battleship Hill, to ask him what he thought about the situation. Kemal thought that because of the nature and quantity of the enemy forces that had landed, it was necessary to ensure command and control by uniting the entire effort under a single commander.[63] Liman von Sanders agreed and immediately ordered Kemal to take command of the Anafarta Group effective at 9.45pm, 8 August. Kemal's 19th Division was at the same time placed in the capable hands of the veteran 27th Infantry Regiment commander, Lieutenant-Colonel Şefik.

In actuality, the decision to relieve Ahmet Fevzi and replace him with Mustafa Kemal likely rested on more pragmatic grounds. First, Kemal was intimately familiar with the ground and the units involved in the fight for Sari Bair. He had been in action on the ANZAC perimeter since 25 April and since early May had commanded the northern shoulder of Esat's Northern Group. As such, the Sari Bair Ridge line fell in Kemal's 'tactical backyard'. Second, there is evidence that Kemal expressed concern to Esat over the vulnerability of Sazlıdere to the north of the Ari Burnu sector in what Turkish historians call the 'Sazlıdere Discussion'. It began as a result of a lengthy correspondence between Kemal and the Northern Group staff over this issue, which irritated Esat so much that he personally came to the 19th Division headquarters with his chief of staff Colonel Fahrettin in mid-June.[64] From there they proceeded to Battleship Hill where Kemal pointed out to Esat the vulnerability of the unguarded territory to the north of Hill 971. According to an Ottoman officer who was present, Fahrettin said 'only a gang of guerrillas could advance there!' Whereupon Kemal then indicated where and how the enemy might successfully advance.[65] Esat remained unconvinced, patting Kemal on his shoulder and telling him not to worry. Another critical factor was Kemal's experience on the peninsula itself in the Balkan Wars of 1912–13 during which he had served as the chief operations officer of the Gallipoli Army. Taking these facts altogether, the unfortunate Ahmet Fevzi was a poor choice to command an ad hoc grouping of forces on unfamiliar ground compared to the experienced Mustafa Kemal, who was intimately familiar with the key terrain of Anafarta.

Suvla Bay, 6–8 August 1915[66]

Hammersley's 11th Division came ashore at Suvla Bay at 9.30pm, 6 August as the 32nd and 33rd Brigades landed on undefended B Beach. The four battalions in the first wave began to move towards their first objectives – the bluffs known as Hill 10 and Lala Baba Tepe. These overlooked the beaches and were held by posts from the Bursa Jandarma Battalion. Lala Baba was taken quickly but at a cost that halted the brigade. Shortly thereafter the 34th Brigade entered Suvla Bay itself and began landing on A Beach. But like the Anzac landings of 25 April, units came ashore in the wrong places, which delayed the assembly for movement. Moreover, the shallow bay contained unmarked shoals making rapid boat movement to the shore impossible. Hill 10 continued to hold out, delaying the landing of Brigadier-General Sitwell and the remaining two battalions of the 34th Brigade. Although the brigade commanders actively attempted to move on Hill 10 the darkness thwarted their actions as subordinate commanders became lost and misoriented.

Hammersley and the divisional staff landed at 12.45am, 7 August on B Beach and established a field headquarters but few reports filtered in to them. Stopford remained on HMS *Jonquil* with Rear Admiral Christian and could only observe an occasional shell bursting on shore. Although the MEF, IX Corps and the 11th Division had prepared redundant communications in anticipation of the friction of war, reports were few and inaccurate. Towards dawn, Hamilton was aware that the landings had been made good but that was all. On the naval side, reports filtered in to Stopford from Commander Unwin indicating that A Beach was unsuitable because of the problems with unmarked shoals. This caused Stopford to reconsider his plan to land six battalions of the incoming 10th Division on A Beach.[67] In turn, Stopford decided to land them at C Beach and ordered Brigadier-General F. F. Hill, who was in executive command, to land at C Beach and place himself under Hammersley's command.[68] Concerned about securing his base area, Stopford told Hill that if Hammersley could not be found Hill was to support the 11th Division near Hill 10 and complete the capture of Kiretch Ridge. Meanwhile, Lieutenant-General Mahon arrived from Mudros with three 10th Division battalions.

As Hill landed he found Hammersley, who ordered him to the extreme right to take Chocolate Hill. About 7.30am, Stopford sent Mahon orders to land two battalions of Brigadier-General L. L. Nicol's 30th Brigade on the northern arm of Suvla Bay and press on to Ejelmer Bay. This split Mahon's division into parts going in different directions. About 8.00am Hill's battalic   ʒan to land with orders to capture Chocolate Hill. Unfortunately for ʳ'   he jandarma commander on Hill 10 continually sent Willmₘ   ₛ, which enabled him to deploy two jandarma compaₜ   2nd Battalion, 31st Infantry Regiment to blockiᵣ   69 At the same time he sent two jandarma cₑ Kiretch Ridge. Each group was well supₚ   of artillery pieces. His situation report to Lₙ   ᵣning accurately reflected the situation with confidencₑ   ₑquesting reinforcements. At this point Willmer had abₑ   ₑn holding approximately 27,000 British and Irish troops.

Hammersley issued orders at about 8.00am for his 32nd and 34th Brigades to push vigorously on Chocolate Hill but tied them to the arrival of Hill's 31st Brigade, which was just landing. Several confusing orders from Hammersley, who was somewhat shaken by a bursting shell that killed and wounded several of his staff, followed when Hill arrived at about 8.45am. By this time the ANZAC had connected the 11th Division by telephone wire to Birdwood's headquarters in the Anzac perimeter. Hammersley now had to decide how to sort out Hill's new instructions from Stopford, fresh intelligence from Birdwood and his original instructions.[70] It was ironic that Hammersley had communications with the ANZAC commander but not with his own corps commander, which led to a muddled morning of chaotic orders and counter-orders. Compounding this abysmal situation was the fact that battalions of the 11th Division brigades were intermixed. Hammersley ordered and then suspended several attacks and, at 2.40pm, ordered a 5.30pm attack under Brigadier-General Sitwell, who would command the 31st, 32nd and 34th

Brigades.[71] There was much confusion as the brigadiers tried to bring their units into assault positions and the attack was delayed. Moreover, the torrid sun and water shortages rapidly drained the strength of the British officers and men, most of whom had no clear idea about what they were supposed to accomplish. In spite of these problems, five battalions managed to push forward with artillery support and as darkness fell Chocolate Hill and Green Hill were in British hands.

On IX Corps' left flank, Brigadier-General Nicol's two battalions landed around noon and moved off the beach at 2.30pm. Darkness fell as these battalions attempted to relieve 11th Battalion, The Manchester Regiment, on the Kiretch Ridge and the advance came to a halt. No further progress was made on the ridge. Thus at the end of 7 August, Stopford's IX Corps held only a small perimeter around the landing beaches and was nowhere close to the Tekke Tepe Ridge nor able to support Birdwood's assaults.

Aspinall-Oglander rightly asserted that the 24 hours lost on 7 August were critical because during that time Liman von Sanders ordered Ahmet Fevzi's XVI Corps south from Saros Bay.[72] Not only did this enable XVI Corps to arrive in time to influence decisively the battle but the additional time allowed Willmer's accurate reports to flow through Fifth Army to Ahmet Fevzi.[73] His first orders as Anafarta Group commander, issued en route from Saros Bay to his divisions, outlined with great clarity the front-line trace as well as identifying the exact locations of his divisional assembly areas near Küçük and Büyük Anafarta.[74] It is clear that the Ottoman reporting system was, once again, creating an enhanced situational awareness for the Turks in comparison to the chaotic reporting of the British.

At dawn on 8 August, Hammersley set off to visit his brigadiers and at 6.30am signalled to IX Corps that all was quiet and Mahon reported the same thing from Kiretch Ridge. Stopford's reaction was to congratulate everyone and consolidate the beachhead by endeavouring to land stores and supplies. An anxious Hamilton grew increasingly concerned about the absence of news from Stopford and, as his assigned destroyer had boiler trouble, dispatched Aspinall-Oglander and Maurice Hankey, who was visiting the Dardanelles, by trawler at 9.30am to Suvla.[75] Aspinall-Oglander and Hankey arrived on the *Jonquil* about noon and talked to Stopford before going ashore to visit Hammersley. Once ashore they were filled with dismay when they found men bathing and relaxing, and after Hammersley informed them that he could not possibly advance on 8 August, returned to the *Jonquil* at 3.00pm.[76] Aspinall-Oglander tried to persuade Stopford to push on to the hills as quickly as possible but Stopford said the men ashore needed rest and more artillery. Aspinall-Oglander returned to the flagship and sent a wireless to the MEF GHQ expressing despair that 'golden opportunities were being lost and look upon the situation as serious'.[77]

While Aspinall-Oglander and Hankey were visiting Stopford, a frustrated Hamilton boarded the *Triad* at 4.30pm. In the meantime, an energized Stopford finally went ashore at 4.00pm to the 11th Division headquarters, but Hammersley was visiting his brigades and Stopford told his staff that an advance was imperative. He returned to the *Jonquil* at 5.30pm to find a message from Hamilton informing him that two brigades of the 53rd Division were due in to Suvla that night and ordering him to advance with his two divisions.[78] Hamilton ordered the 10th and 11th Divisions to advance to the ridge, with Hammersley informing Mahon of the timing. Hamilton further ordered that the incoming brigade reinforce Hammersley. Hamilton apparently did not know that Mahon was only in command of three battalions and that Hammersley was already overburdened. Hamilton arrived at Suvla on the *Jonquil* at 6.00pm to find out that nothing had happened all day. He told Stopford that he wanted an immediate attack that night, to which Stopford explained that that would be impossible.[79] Hamilton then went ashore and talked to Hammersley, who told him the soonest he could attack would be at 8.00am the next day (9 August). Following a vigorous discussion, Hamilton verbally ordered Hammersley to launch the 32nd Brigade against the ridge that night.[80] Hamilton then returned to the *Triad* and remained in Suvla Bay overnight. The confused 32nd Brigade commander tried to execute the night attack, but units became lost and mixed up and were halted by the Ottomans.

Decisions on 9 August 1915

On the night of 8/9 August most of Major-General J. E. Lindley's 53rd Division came ashore and Lindley bivouacked alongside Hammersley's headquarters.[81] Stopford put all troops of the 53rd Division under Hammersley as they became available but told him that they needed to be reassembled by evening under Lindley as the corps reserve. That night Stopford and his corps staff came ashore and established telephonic communications with both the 10th and 11th Divisions. As daylight approached, Stopford had Mahon commanding his own 30th Brigade and two attached battalions from Sitwell's 34th Brigade on Kiretch Ridge and the remainder of Sitwell's brigade lay on Hill 10, the 32nd and 33rd Brigades were to the south-west of the dry salt lake, Brigadier-General Hill with five 10th Division battalions, two of which were temporarily attached to the 33rd Brigade, was on Chocolate Hill. Over the course of the evening and night of 8/9 August, Hammersley had issued three separate orders to his brigades to attack and sent a warning order to Mahon.[82] For reasons that are unclear, Hamilton ordered Hammersley rather than Stopford to coordinate the timing. In any event, the 32nd Brigade moved towards Tekke Tepe about 4.30am, the 33rd Brigade began to move towards Scimitar Hill, which was thought to be held by British troops but which had been abandoned, while Mahon only sent a warning order to Hill to be prepared to advance.

The Ottomans now occupied a continuous front from Kiretch Ridge on the Aegean Sea to Chunuk Bair. The newly appointed commander, Mustafa Kemal, was determined to launch a coordinated counter-attack early on the morning of 9 August. The 12th Division, commanded by Lieutenant-Colonel Selahattin Adil, occupied hilltop assembly areas running on a north–south line from Kidney Hill to Tekke Tepe. Adil had three full-strength infantry regiments as well as an artillery battalion (10,471 men). Willmer's group remained steadfast just beyond the Chocolate Hill supported by part of the 9th Artillery Regiment and Colonel Halil's 7th Division now occupied the ground between Willmer and Cemil's 4th Division on the Abdul Rahman Spur. Halil had only two regiments and the support of an artillery battalion.

At 4.00am, 9 August, the Ottoman 12th Division began to advance in what may be characterized as a movement to contact – its mission was simply to gain and maintain contact as far forward as possible. However, the 35th Infantry Regiment quickly ran into the British 32nd Brigade, which was itself advancing on Tekke Tepe. An engagement ensued in which the experienced Turks – coming downhill and well supported by artillery – crushed the inexperienced British, causing a disorderly retreat.[83] The 34th Regiment's advance ran into the British 33rd Brigade, which was attempting to seize the northern shoulder of Chocolate Hill, in the area of Scimitar Hill, and a desperate meeting engagement ensued. Hammersley sent two battalions of the 160th Brigade, which were committed to the fight by Brigadier-General Maxwell. Fighting was heavy, Turkish and British losses were high and, adding to the confusion, the artillery fire set the scrub on fire which was fanned by brisk winds. In the end the 35th Regiment pushed the British back to their start lines.

The adjacent Ottoman 7th Division's attacks began at 4.30am, under the cover of heavy artillery and machine-gun fire. The division's objective was to seize the enemy positions on Damakjelik Bair. Unlike the 12th Division's movement to contact, the 7th Division faced positions strongly held by the 4th Australian Brigade and the 40th Brigade. The adjacent 4th Division artillery attempted to assist the attack by firing on the enemy. The attack was difficult, with the Ottomans going downhill from Bomba Tepe into the ravine of Kayaçık Dere and then assaulting uphill. Fighting was hard with severe losses and a

British counter-attack at 10.00am pushed the two regiments back down into the Kayaçık Dere. The regimental commanders were badly wounded and both died two days later.[84] Most of the officers in the battalions were killed or wounded as well. The Turks know these battles involving the XVI Corps' divisions as First Anafarta.[85]

On the Kiretch Ridge, Mahon ordered Nicol to advance at 7.30am, supported initially by impressive naval gunfire support. The attacks faltered, despite the small numbers of enemy jandarma holding the trenches, and Nicol did not press the attack. By nightfall, Nicol's men were back in their own trenches. Mahon had watched the attacks and was dissatisfied with the meagre results. Having spent the night on ship at Suvla, Hamilton came ashore at 8.30am on 9 August and found Stopford 'supervising the building of some splinter-proof headquarters huts for himself and staff'.[86] For unknown reasons, Hamilton then decided to visit Mahon on Kiretch Ridge and returned to meet Braithwaite at the IX Corps headquarters. It is unclear why Hamilton chose to visit Mahon rather than Hammersley, who was conducting the main attacks, but Mahon was physically closer to Stopford's headquarters. About noon, Hamilton departed Suvla Bay in a motorboat to visit Birdwood.

The ANZAC situation on Sari Bair was tenuous. By midday on 8 August, it was clear to Godley that 'on no part of the front had success been gained' and, at a corps conference, Birdwood and Godley decided to conduct a dawn attack on 9 August.[87] Moreover, several other decisions were taken. First, because the 4th Australian Brigade had taken heavy casualties, the assault on Hill 971 was called off. Godley's objective was restated as the summit of Chunuk Bair and the ridge to, and including, Hill Q. The main effort would be made by five fresh battalions of Brigadier-General A. H. Baldwin's 38th Brigade assisted by Cox's Indians, who were below Hill Q. Godley ordered Baldwin to assemble his brigade on Rhododendron Spur, followed by an artillery bombardment at 4.30am. Baldwin's infantry would attack at 5.15am passing through the forward lines held by the battered battalions of Johnson's assault column. Because neither Godley nor Baldwin had been up the hill to look at the terrain, they followed Johnson's advice to move along the Aghyl Dere by way of the Farm plateau. Trouble began almost immediately as Baldwin's men going uphill had difficulty trying to get past the large number of wounded men choking the defiles.

The final British attack on the Chunuk Bair ridge began at about 5.15pm against Hill Q after a heavy bombardment. The attack went wrong from the start as Baldwin's battalions had not reached their assembly areas and failed to attack as scheduled. However, on the extreme left, the 1st Battalion, 6th Gurkha Rifles and the 6th Battalion, The South Lancashire Regiment made it to the summit and punched through the lines of the newly arrived Ottoman 24th Infantry Regiment, which had taken over the 64th Regiment's lines on the night of 8/9 August, to occupy Hill Q. Local Ottoman counter-attacks failed to retake the hill.[88] The newly arrived Ottoman 8th Infantry Division commander appealed to the Northern Group, which released a regiment and a battalion from the reserves at Kemalyeri. These reserves proved unnecessary as the division was able to push the Gurkhas off Hill Q within several hours using local reserves. Baldwin's brigade finally advanced on the Farm at 6.00am and there ran into heavy machine-gun fire. He decided to terminate the advance and began to dig in.

By 9.00am the next day (9 August), it was clear to Birdwood and Godley that the third attack on Sari Bair had failed and half an hour later Birdwood issued orders for Godley's forces to stand fast. Godley understood that Johnson's troops were near breaking point after being continuously in action for three days. As a result, he decided to withdraw the tired troops and replace them in the line. Furthermore, Godley decided that the extended line was too much for one divisional staff to manage and he decided to turn over the front at Rhododendron Spur, the Farm and the inner defences at Destroyer Hill, Table Top and Bauchop's Hill to Major-General F. C. Shaw and the 13th Division staff.[89] Johnson was placed under Shaw but remained in executive command of the troops holding a line below the Sari Bair ridgeline, until such time as they could be replaced by New Army troops. This scheme placed Johnson (the New Zealand Brigade commander) under Shaw, who he did not know and who was new to the ANZAC perimeter. Shaw, himself a division commander, remained under Godley, who was also a division commander. Most importantly these decisions placed the MEF main effort directly into the hands of the inexperienced Shaw.

Hamilton arrived at the ANZAC perimeter at midday and climbed up to No. 2 Post where he ate lunch with Birdwood, Godley and Shaw. Hamilton described this as an impromptu council of war.[90] Hamilton offered Birdwood his last reserve, the incoming 54th Division, which Birdwood refused saying that he could not undertake to supply them with water. Hamilton left there very confident that the ANZAC generals would renew the assault on Sari Bair within 24 hours and carry forward to the Narrows. How this could be done successfully following three failed attempts was unclear. Furthermore, Hamilton decided to reinforce IX Corps with the incoming 54th Division as previously planned.

At 5.00pm, Braithwaite sent a letter to Stopford urging him to capture the Anafarta Spur and the W Hills using six to eight battalions under a single commander. Stopford took this to be an order from Hamilton to attack the next morning and, that evening, he decided to attack the central portion of the

Anafarta Spur with nine battalions of Lindley's 53rd Division. He ordered Mahon and Hammersley to stand fast and continue their reorganization. About midnight 9/10 August, Hamilton sent Stopford a letter expressing concern over IX Corps' failures and courteously, but explicitly, asking what was wrong with the commanders and their units.[91] He continued by ordering Stopford to attack the Anafarta Spur and W Hills with vigour. Stopford's reply, which was delivered at daylight, laid the blame on the lack of water, inadequate training, and inadequate artillery support.[92]

Lindley had been told that his 159th Brigade was 'somewhere near Sulajik' and should take Scimitar Hill, which he ordered. He ordered the 158th Brigade, near Lala Baba, to seize the Anafarta Spur thus reducing his assault force from nine battalions to eight. Zero hour was fixed at 6.00am, 10 August, with such artillery and naval gunfire support that could be arranged overnight. Lindley and his brigadiers had precious few maps and were completely unfamiliar with the ground. Two battalions of the 159th Brigade could not be found in the darkness. The brigadier and his staff spent a sleepless night in a vain search for them. This brought the assault force down to six battalions.

On the Ottoman side there were also high levels of confusion as Mustafa Kemal attempted to take control of his new command. Now aware of these problems, Liman von Sanders issued orders at 3.14pm attaching the 8th Division to the Anafatra Group.[93] At 7.00pm, Liman von Sanders sent his first situation report to Enver Pasha stating that, as of 3.00pm, the British attacks were very uncoordinated and unsuccessful. His second report to Enver was more favourable and followed at 11.45pm, 9 August stating that the enemy attacks on Anafarta and Sari Bair had ended and that he felt that his forces could deal with any renewed attacks.[94]

Meanwhile, the newly appointed Anafarta Group commander, Mustafa Kemal, travelled to the headquarters of the 8th Division at Chunuk Bair with his aide-de-camp and went forward to conduct a personal reconnaissance and to survey the condition of the men in the forward positions. He determined that conditions for a multi-divisional counter-attack were favourable due to the presence of relatively fresh Ottoman troops. Kemal was especially pleased with the fact that the enemy trenches were a mere 21–27 yards (20–25m) over the crest of the ridge from his own lines and he believed that his men might even recapture the lost ground on Rhododendron Spur. He began to make preparations for an attack. Kemal ordered the 8th Division to make the main effort in an attack that would begin at 4.30am, 10 August.[95] These orders also contained instructions to conduct a vigorous pursuit after breaking through the enemy lines with a bayonet assault and the 9th Division was ordered to conduct a supporting attack. The tireless Kemal worked through the night to coordinate the counter-attack and ordered the 7th and 12th Divisions to support with an advance as well.

Thus as the day of 9 August ended a number of critical decisions had been made. Hamilton ordered IX Corps to take the Anafarta Spur and the W Hills but failed to ensure that Stopford assembled a sufficient mass to accomplish the mission. At No. 2 Post, Hamilton decided that Birdwood, on his own initiative and with the forces he had in hand, would somehow seize Sari Bair Ridge. Instead Birdwood allowed Godley to go over to the defensive. Hamilton also decided to listen to Birdwood and sent his last reserve division to Suvla Bay. In effect Hamilton had an opportunity to strengthen the MEF's main effort and did not. Stopford ordered Lindley, after dark, to assemble most of his then-scattered division in unfamiliar ground. Birdwood refused reinforcements and allowed Godley to hand off the ANZAC main effort to Shaw, who was unfamiliar with the battlefield. On the Ottoman side, Liman von Sanders, the operational commander, created a single tactical commander and fed him reinforcements. In turn, the Ottoman tactical commander, Mustafa Kemal, decided to wrest the initiative from the Allies by launching a major counter-attack.

Overlapping attacks, 10 August

Lindley's attack began with the 158th Brigade crossing the dry lake from Lala Baba at 5.00am, 10 August. At 6.00am both brigades advanced – the four battalions of the 158th Brigade on the north and the two battalions of the 159th Brigade to the south. The attack quickly became a shambles when the Ottomans checked the advance and sent British battalions fleeing back in disorder. Hammersley tried to support the attack with parts of his 32nd Brigade, but to no avail. Stopford, who had gone to Lala Baba to observe the assault, reported to Hamilton at 1.30pm that the attack had failed. Stopford signalled he would renew the attack at 5.00pm but Hamilton had no faith in a follow-on attack and called it off.

On the Sari Bair Ridge Johnson was attempting to relieve his exhausted men with fresh forces.[96] Two New Army battalions were supposed to relieve the New Zealanders at the Pinnacle and on the slopes of Chunuk Bair. Going up the defiles in the dark they became lost and half of the companies failed to arrive. Moreover, the reinforcing second line did not arrive. By daybreak the head of Rhododendron Spur and the Pinnacle were held by half the number of men required to defend them and most of them were asleep. The forces to the north of the spur were an incredibly mixed-up mass of battalions from four brigades from three different divisions, but supposedly in the hands of Brigadier-General Baldwin's 38th Brigade. On the Farm plateau behind the lines lay the headquarters of 38th Brigade and Brigadier-General Cooper's 29th Brigade headquarters. To the north, the area between the Farm plateau and the 4th Australian Brigade was even more jumbled as companies of the 29th Indian and 39th Brigades were badly intermixed. Not only was Godley's force unready for offensive operations, it was 'in no fit state to meet a determined attack'.[97]

Opposite this disorganized jumble of units, group commander Mustafa Kemal crept forward at 4.30am with his scouting screen in order to give the order to attack when a brief artillery bombardment ended. Kemal hugged the ground while the Ottoman artillery and machine guns raked the enemy positions over his head and then, at the exact moment that the firing ceased, he raised himself up and pointed to the enemy line with his riding crop.[98] Launched downhill from Hill Q, Kemal's main effort – three 8th Division regiments – swept forward. In support, on the 8th Division's right flank, a reinforced 9th Division regiment attacked simultaneously. The Allied histories speak of a six-battalion attack and, while against the Pinnacle area this was true, Kemal actually employed about 16 battalions altogether. It was a massive blow and the Turks achieved almost complete surprise with what amounted to a human wave attack.[99] Aspinall-Oglander wrote that 'dense waves of Turks came pouring over the skyline'.[100] The Ottoman infantry hardly fired their rifles and relied on the shock power of the bayonet to sweep into the British and New Zealand lines.

One Ottoman battalion was able to sweep down from the heights into the small table-like area called the Farm plateau where a brigade headquarters was located and a large number of men were resting. The surprised British died in large numbers and some units were entirely eliminated – perhaps as many as 1,000 British and Irish soldiers were killed in a matter of minutes.[101] Brigadier Baldwin and his brigade-major died in the front lines, Brigadier Cooper was severely wounded and every officer in the 29th Brigade headquarters was killed or wounded. The Turks, for their part, suffered greatly and were too spent to exploit their success. Kemal's attack frittered into stasis by midday but, nevertheless, the Ottomans managed to push the New Zealand Brigade and the 38th Brigade back about 550 yards (500m). The 39th Brigade withdrew 1,100 yards (1,000m) and the 29th Indian Brigade pulled back almost 1,600 yards (1,500m), thus ending the threat to Sari Bair Ridge. The Turks refer to these battles for Sari Bair Ridge as the Conkbayırı battles.

Neither Hamilton's memoirs nor the MEF War Diary reflect a sense of what had happened on 10 August. Birdwood's ANZAC had used up all of its reserves and was incapable of further offensive action. Hamilton seemed unaware that his main effort was in shambles and, as he had told Stopford earlier, the 54th Division began to land at Suvla Bay that night. Hamilton ordered Stopford not to employ it piecemeal as it was the only remaining MEF reserve and, further, ordered that Stopford was not to use it in combat without GHQ approval. Stopford deployed the new division to the right of the 10th Division. By 10.00pm, six battalions from three 54th Division brigades were ashore and trying to find their way through the darkness to front-line positions. There was much marching and counter-marching before they settled in. Overall, operations on Sari Bair and at Suvla had been very costly for both sides with the British losing about 25,000 men and the Turks losing about 20,000 men during the period of 6–10 August.

The day of 11 August passed uneventfully as both sides paused to recover their cohesion. The offensive operations on Sari Bair on 10 August had exhausted Kemal's Anafarta Group. The British, however, planned to continue offensive operations on the next day and Hamilton ordered Stopford to attack. Hamilton knew that Stopford's divisions were incapable of immediate offensive action and 'would have preferred ... a general offensive by the whole of IX Corps' but he ordered the newly arrived 54th Division, under the command of Major-General F. S. Inglefield, to seize the Tekke Tepe Ridge at dawn on 12 August.[102] He also ordered Stopford to get as much artillery as possible ashore to support the assault. Stopford replied with a long letter that condemned the 53rd Division's failures on poor training. Hamilton then 'hastened to Suvla to infuse the corps commander with some of his own resolution'.[103] The meeting was contentious with Stopford characterizing his Territorial divisions as 'sucked oranges'. Hamilton was adamant but, as Stopford had made no preparations or plans for an attack, Hamilton authorized a 24-hour delay for the 54th Division attack. Stopford raised several more objections but when Hamilton left it was definitely settled that the division should assault the ridge at dawn on the 13th.

On the morning of 12 August Stopford held a commanders' conference to arrange the details of the attack. He wanted the 53rd Division to push forward to the foothills and gain contact but the commander demurred. Inglefield volunteered to carry out this task to which Stopford agreed. Inglefield then ordered Brigadier-General C. M. Brunker's 163rd Brigade to push forward that afternoon. Stopford then sent Hamilton a message explaining this but asserting that if Inglefield's troops became disorganized he would ask for another 24-hour delay (until 14 August). A worried Hamilton sent Braithwaite over to Suvla to discuss his concerns with Stopford, who persuaded Braithwaite that he was correct in his assessments. Stopford launched the 54th Infantry Division's 163rd Brigade, supported by a half-brigade of the 11th Division, at 4.00pm in an attempt to push the front forward and gain contact with the enemy on the foothills of the Tekke Tepe hill mass. The attack was poorly planned with no reconnaissance or rehearsals. Moreover, the maps were inaccurate, the officers had no idea of exactly where the enemy positions were or in what strength they were held, and the supporting artillery was employed ineffectively. The inexperienced British Territorials rushed forward into well-laid defensive fire and were mown down. The Ottoman battalions conducted immediate counter-attacks that pushed the survivors back. About 6.30pm, the Ottomans unleashed a slashing bayonet pursuit of 1/5th Battalion, The Norfolk Regiment, part of which was the Sandringham Company, which seemed to disappear entirely in the fighting; the story was made famous in the film *All the King's Men*.[104] That night Hamilton, unaware of IX Corps' problems, continued to plan for offensive operations. To its credit, IX Corps managed to bring Mahon's five battalions, which had been under Hammersley, over to consolidate the 10th Division on Kiretch Ridge.

On the morning of 13 August, Stopford sent several alarming telegrams to Hamilton. The first, at 8.45am, said he doubted that the 54th Division could be ready for an attack before 15 August. The second reported his doubts that the 53rd Division could hold the line under the enemy shelling. Once again Hamilton set off for Suvla and conducted a 'momentous interview' with Stopford that afternoon.[105] Once again Stopford argued that his divisions were unready and needed time to reorganize. Hamilton returned to his headquarters having made no decision, but at midnight he cabled Stopford that he had decided IX Corps should not attack and that Stopford should use the time to reorganize.

With the 10th Division now consolidated, Stopford ordered another attack to be launched on Kiretch Ridge on 15 August by Mahon. Like the attack of 12 August, this attack was badly managed. The British expected to attack the jandarma, which had held the ridge since the landings and they expected to break through and drive on to occupy Kidney Hill. In their favour they held a wonderful flanking position on the hill and a near-perfect opportunity to use naval gunfire support to suppress the Turks. However, the Ottomans had brought up significant reinforcements in the week prior to replace the jandarma. In the ongoing Ottoman tactical reorganization the 5th Division, in Northern Group reserve, saw its organic infantry regiments reassigned to the Lone Pine and Sari Bair fights. As a result the division headquarters element was sent to join Major Willmer, who formed and took command of an ad hoc 5th Division and also had five additional infantry battalions assigned to him in addition to the Gelibolu Jandarma Battalion and the two companies of the 127th Infantry Regiment already in defensive positions on Kiretch Ridge.[106]

General Mahon wanted to begin his attack at 8.40am, 15 August, by launching a multi-directional attack from the west and north simultaneously. Because the orders were late in passing, the attack did not begin until 2.15pm. The attacks gained some ground in the 30th Brigade sector against moderate Ottoman resistance but, as darkness fell, the British were unable to consolidate their gains and were left in a vulnerable position. In the meantime Willmer came to Kiretch Ridge about 8.30pm to examine personally the situation. He was very encouraged and organized a counter-attack using three battalions.[107] At 4.00am, 16 August, Willmer's attack tore into the 30th Brigade's left flank causing heavy casualties and Willmer launched a counter-attack at about 8.00am with hand grenades. At midday Mustafa Kemal diverted incoming reinforcement battalions to Willmer. Unusually, the normally reliable Willmer became personally involved in the fighting and was unable to render timely reports as he had done so effectively on 6/7 August. In any case, Mahon decided to recall his battered brigades about 7.00pm that evening and the Irish pulled back to their start lines ending the battle. On 17 August, Willmer's men reoccupied all of their original positions and restored their outposts.[108]

The supersession of Stopford[109]

Hamilton had had enough by the night of 13/14 August. He had earlier, on 9 August, sent a message to Kitchener that the combination of 'new troops and old generals was proving unsuitable' and again on 14 August, he complained to Kitchener that he was 'bitterly disappointed' with Stopford and his divisional commanders.[110] Hamilton's complaints resonated with Kitchener, who the following day then took the initiative and cabled Hamilton telling him, if necessary, he could replace Stopford, Mahon and Hammersley. At the same time, he cabled Sir John French in France and told him to be prepared to supply a corps commander and two division commanders to the MEF. On 15 August, Hamilton relieved Stopford and replaced him as IX Corps commander with Major-General de Lisle, who was commanding the 29th Division. Because de Lisle was a major-general, Hamilton asked Mahon, who was a lieutenant-general whether he was willing to serve under de Lisle. Mahon refused and asked for relief, to which Hamilton agreed and placed Brigadier Hill temporarily in command of the 10th Division on 16 August. Brigadier-General Marshall temporarily took the 29th Division from de Lisle.

The reliefs did not stop there. At brigade level, because of a bad report from Hammersley, Brigadier Sitwell of the 34th Brigade was relieved on 18 August by Colonel C. C. Hannay. Lindley voluntarily resigned command of the 53rd

Division on 17 August and was succeeded by Major-General H. A. Lawrence. On 23 August Hamilton relieved Hammersley of command of the 11th Division and replaced him with Major-General E. A. Fanshaw. Egerton in the 52nd Division lasted until 17 August when he was replaced by H. A. Lawrence. These changes did not have much of an effect as Aspinall-Oglander later observed: 'These changes, however, were too late. By the 16th August the battle was already lost.'[111]

Relieving commanders in the MEF was something that, very obviously, Sir Ian Hamilton was extremely reluctant to do. Rather than ask Kitchener directly, he complained about his poor performers, until Kitchener himself suggested and authorized him to relieve officers. During the campaign Hamilton's behaviour, in this regard, was reminiscent of his cables to Kitchener in May and June about whether he needed reinforcements. Hamilton could never quite bring himself to admit that the situation required more forces. In the end, Kitchener made the decisions that Hamilton needed reinforcements and he sent them. In contrast, Liman von Sanders operated under no such parameters and was courageous and decisive in his relief of commanders he found wanting. Liman von Sanders relieved both German and Ottoman commanders, including 9th Division commander Halil Sami, 5th Division commander von Sodenstern, Southern Group commander Weber and his chief of staff von Thauvenay, and Anafarta Group commander Ahmet Fevzi. In part this might be explained by the fact that in the small British Army, Hamilton knew personally the commanders under his command while Liman von Sanders did not. In any event, the reliefs in the MEF came too late to affect the situation in a decisive way.

Ottoman reinforcements and reorganization

As the Ottoman VI Corps arrived at Saros Bay with the 24th and 26th Infantry Divisions, Liman von Sanders was able to bring the 6th Infantry Division south to the Anafarta front.[112] Two infantry regiments, cavalry and artillery arrived at an assembly area behind Tekke Tepe at 6.00am, 17 August 1915. As active operations on Sari Bair seemed to subside, Mustafa Kemal pulled most of the 9th Division out of the line into reserve. Thus by 20 August, Kemal's Anafarta Group had the following divisions in contact running from Kiretch Ridge in the north to Battleship Hill in the south: 5th, 12th, 7th, 4th, 28th Regiment (from 9th Division), and 8th Division. Lying just behind the Tekke Tepe Ridge, Kemal had the 9th Division (-) and the 6th Division. The bulk of the Anafarta Group's artillery lay in the W Hills and

Mustafa Kemal's group headquarters was positioned behind the centre on Camlı Tekke, which was the southern hill of the Anafarta Saddle.

As the 6th Division left Saros Bay the lead elements of the 24th Division began to arrive on 16 August followed by the 26th Division two days later. The VI Corps headquarters, with German Colonel Ulrich Back as its chief of staff, moved to houses in the town of Gallipoli, where it merged with the headquarters of General Faik. Previously, on 14 August, Lieutenant-Colonel Freze, a Fifth Army staff officer, had gone to Istanbul to discuss revisions in the operational control of the upper peninsula.[113] The outcome of the discussions was that von der Goltz's First Army would extend its area of responsibility south to cover Saros Bay and the isthmus of Bulair. This reorganization relieved the Fifth Army of responsibility for the amphibious threat to the north.[114] Altogether on 21 August 1915, the Ottoman Army now had 17 infantry divisions, one infantry detachment of brigade strength and an independent cavalry brigade (counting all First and Fifth Army assets) committed to the campaign.

Scimitar Hill and Hill 60 (Second Anafarta), 21–28 August 1915

Uprooted from command of his own division on Cape Helles, de Lisle found himself on unfamiliar ground on 15 August with only a memorandum of instruction from GHQ to guide him.[115] The memorandum stated that the ANZAC offensive was partially successful and that time was needed to reorganize for further attacks. Therefore, it was the task of IX Corps, although badly disorganized, to capture the W Hills and the Anafarta Spur, with the objective of preparing to envelop the enemy via the Anafarta gap. Hamilton promised de Lisle the 5,000 dismounted men of the 2nd Mounted Division, composed of English yeomanry regiments, which was due to arrive at Suvla before 18 August. Neither Hamilton nor de Lisle knew on 15 August that the Kiretch Ridge attacks had failed and that the three brigades involved were now *hors de combat*. De Lisle's initial evaluation to Hamilton on 16 August stressed the depleted and demoralized state of IX Corps. It was a mixed report but de Lisle felt that with the incoming yeomanry division he could mass 10,000 men to take and hold the W Hills.

The crushing weight of failure, relief and the bleak situation finally weakened Hamilton's unbridled optimism. He cabled Kitchener on 17 August explaining that the Ottomans had more men, a commanding position and that the MEF had lost the element of surprise.[116] He asked for 45,000 reinforcements and new formations amounting to 50,000 men. He finished by stating that the enemy was fighting bravely and was well commanded. In view of de Lisle's assessments, Hamilton then decided to reinforce him and ordered a brigade of the 29th Division to Suvla, which landed that evening. De Lisle attached two battalions from the 53rd Division to the brigade and felt more confident about taking the offensive. Also the same day, Commodore Roger Keyes revived the proposal to force the straits using the new minesweepers and monitors. Although supported by Wemyss, de Robeck thought the operation remained infeasible.

On 18 August the yeomanry division began to land. De Lisle gave its commander, Major-General W. E. Peyton, command of the 10th Division and attached the understrength yeomanry division to it as a brigade. Brigadier-General P. Kenna VC then took command of the yeomanry. Hamilton visited IX Corps to discuss the next attack and was pleased to see that de Lisle had consolidated and straightened the corps' front lines. At the planning conference all agreed that IX Corps would take the offensive on 21 August. Hamilton came away from Suvla convinced that IX Corps faced a larger task than he had thought and he ordered the remaining two brigades of the 29th Division to Suvla. The next day de Lisle sent an overly ambitious plan for a general advance combining the seizure of the W Hills, Tekke Tepe and Kiretch Ridge, to GHQ, which troubled Hamilton. On 20 August, he sent Braithwaite to Suvla to tone down de Lisle's plan. The outcome of this visit was that the scope of the IX Corps objective was reduced to the southern end of the Anafarta Spur and Scimitar Hill. Hamilton ordered Birdwood to support de Lisle by seizing Hill 60 and establishing a firm link-up between IX Corps and the ANZAC. De Lisle issued his attack order at 3.00pm on 20 August for an infantry assault the next day at 3.00pm.

It should be noted that there were further fresh troops available to reinforce the ANZAC. The newly raised 2nd Australian Division, commanded by the peninsula-experienced Major-General J. G. Legge, had arrived in Egypt and was conducting training. On 19 August two battalions of the 5th Australian Infantry Brigade landed and were assigned to Godley's division. Godley recognized their inexperience and put them into reserve until they could be blooded and the brigade consolidated. As more battalions arrived, Godley rotated them into the posts along the ridges to give them combat experience. Hamilton asked for the 6th Australian Brigade to be sent to the peninsula on 22 August and two days later asked for the 7th Australian Brigade and division headquarters. The submarine menace caused delays and it was not until September 6 that the brigades and Legge and his staff were ashore.

The British attack on 21 August was a limited offensive – Hamilton hoped simply to get a better position on the W Hills from which IX Corps might then assault the Anafarta Spur.[117] With artillery ammunition as scarce as usual,

IX Corps planned a two-phase attack preceded by a half-hour bombardment with an 11th Division brigade advancing at 3.00pm. At the same time, the ANZAC would launch General Cox, who commanded a 3,000-man provisional brigade of Australian, British, Gurkha and New Zealand units against Hill 60. Half an hour later the remainder of the 11th Division and the 29th Division would advance simultaneously on the W Hills and Scimitar Hill respectively. As the initial objectives were taken, De Lisle assigned General Peyton, commanding the corps reserve, to send the 2nd Mounted Division forward across the open plain between Lala Baba and Chocolate Hill for the final advance.[118]

Shells began to rain on Scimitar Hill and the W Hills from 2.30pm, 21 August, which started to set alight the scrub. The British artillery preparation in this battle was particularly ineffective and scarcely touched the Turkish trenches, causing almost no damage and few casualties. The Ottoman artillery began to fire in return on well-registered and easily observed targets causing many casualties in the 29th Division and in the follow-on yeomanry. The 11th Division kicked off the attack at 3.00pm against a single Ottoman battalion on the southern slopes of the W Hills, which was stopped almost immediately. At 3.30pm the 86th and 87th Brigades attacked towards Scimitar Hill attempting to cross no man's land in front of trenches manned by an alert and unshaken enemy. The seasoned 29th Division was the most effective British division on the peninsula but its brigades fared no better than those of the 11th Division. Because of a change in the plan Cox's force also attacked at 3.30pm with similar results. The British and ANZAC attacks continued fitfully until about 6.00pm, by which time vigorous Ottoman bayonet counter-attacks had restored the entire line. When the British attack began Mustafa Kemal reacted by immediately ordering his reserves into action.[119] He reinforced Scimitar Hill and positioned substantial reserves just behind the lines for immediate use if needed.

Under direct observation by the Ottoman gunners the 2nd Mounted Division began to move at 3.00pm across the plain towards Chocolate Hill, which resulted in heavy artillery fire being brought to bear on the yeomanry. At Chocolate Hill a hurried commanders' conference resulted in Lord Longford's brigade going around the north of the hill while two brigades passed around the south, and one brigade remained in reserve. About 6.00pm the dismounted squadrons passed the British front lines and attempted to advance on Hill 112. The yeomanry commanders, division and brigade, possessed almost no situational or spatial awareness and they simply went forward through the lines of the defeated 29th Division. Fire and smoke from the burning brush obscured the yeomanry advance and gave the dug-in Ottomans an advantage with their pre-ranged rifles and machine guns. By 9.00pm this famously futile attack had destroyed the division and with it the lives of a number of well-known British officers, including Colonel Sir Johnnie Milbanke VC, Lord Longford, and Brigadier-General Kenna VC.

Cox's men would continue the fight for Hill 60 for another two days but, at the end, held only a small salient. Cox advocated renewing the attacks on Hill 60 as it continued to dominate his hard-won ground. After consultations with Birdwood it was approved to attack again with a force of about 1,000 men on 27 August. In the meantime the Ottomans reinforced the strongly held Hill 60 with an infantry battalion. Cox attacked at 4.00pm on the 27th with heavy artillery fire support and his men made some progress capturing several lines of Ottoman trenches.[120] Fighting raged throughout the night and the Ottomans launched a powerful counter-attack, which recaptured all but several sections of the forward trenches. Although these attacks failed, they caused Liman von Sanders to send the 26th Division south on the night of 27/28 August and the division closed on assembly areas in the vicinity of Tursuhn Keui on 28–30 August.

The fight for Scimitar Hill and Hill 60 proved to be the last major battles of the Gallipoli campaign. British losses were extremely heavy. The British IX Corps lost over 6,000 men and Cox's force lost around 1,300 men for almost no gain at all.[121] Ottoman losses are recorded as 2,597 men in the 7th and 12th Divisions.[122] On the evening of 22 August, Mustafa Kemal pulled the 12th Division back from Scimitar Hill and the W Hills and replaced it with the fresh 9th Division.

Strategic, operational and tactical conclusions

At the strategic level, the August offensive at the Dardanelles represented sound thinking about where Britain's available resources might be applied to the greatest effect. The government and general staff continued to recognize that the main theatre of operations was in France but it accepted a limited diversion of the empire's main strategic focus in the hopes of breaking the Ottomans. Kitchener sent the MEF a reinforced army corps but it must be said that the corps and its divisions were poorly led and inexperienced. This was certainly a quantitative commitment but it was never a qualitative commitment to the campaign against the Ottoman Empire. Once again an Anglo-centric sense of superiority asserted itself in British war planning. For the Ottomans, with the destruction and occupation of Serbia looming, the hope of German and Austro-Hungarian support became a real possibility. Strategically, this simplified the Ottoman situation by creating conditions for the Ottoman high command to simply prolong the campaign and hold the Allies to their beachheads.

At the operational level, Birdwood persuaded Hamilton that an ANZAC breakout was possible; however, there was not enough operational space in Birdwood's beachhead. This led to the concept that the incoming IX Corps was best employed in opening up the Suvla Bay area in support of Birdwood. The plan also altered the primary tactical objectives from Achi Baba at Cape Helles to the Sari Bair Ridge and Mal Tepe. Once again, Hamilton approved a plan that failed to mass decisive strength against the principal objective. This resulted in an under-resourced offensive against objectives that were certainly harder than Achi Baba. Moreover, the plan failed to provide Hamilton with a meaningful opportunity to influence the battles by employing his reserve forces. As the attacks progressed Hamilton was never able to encourage Stopford to act aggressively nor was he able to engage Birdwood effectively when his breakout began to disintegrate. In effect, Hamilton was never able to mass his forces effectively in time and space.

The Ottomans on the other hand, continued to maintain large reserves and the operational level within a day's hard march of any point that Hamilton could hit. An effective reporting system again allowed Liman von Sanders to intervene with reserves to effectively influence the battles. This enabled the Fifth Army to shift reserves and mass its forces effectively in time to halt the British attacks. As a result, the Fifth Army was able to take the initiative away from Hamilton in a matter of days, thus ending his offensive design.

Tactically, the Ottoman Army continued its superb performance in battle and it may be maintained that the Fifth Army made very few tactical mistakes during this phase of the campaign. Its forces in contact successfully delayed the British long enough for tactical and operational reserve forces to occupy key terrain features and it was able to launch counter-attacks that disabled further British advances. In truth, Hamilton's August offensive never came close to succeeding and the Ottoman defenders always had more reserves coming up behind them.

Once again, the British failed disastrously at the tactical level by repeating most of their mistakes from previous battles. The ANZAC attempted to execute elaborate and complex plans that were unrehearsed over un-scouted mountainous terrain. Command and control were routinely mired in the cross-attaching of brigades and battalions unknown to one another. Division command was devolved deliberately and division commanders either over-loaded or underutilized. Incredibly inefficient reporting systems left British operational and senior tactical commanders without the situational awareness necessary to fight battles. As usual, much of the failure was blamed on inadequate artillery support and operations conducted in haste. Finally, the corps commanders routinely placed critical operations in the hands of men who were new to modern combat and new to the peninsula.

Chapter Eight

THE ENDING OF THE CAMPAIGN, 29 AUGUST 1915–8 JANUARY 1916

When it became obvious that the Anzac breakout had failed, the decision-makers in London and Paris began to doubt the direction that the campaign had taken. Support for limiting or terminating the campaign gathered in the Dardanelles Committee in London, while in Paris, the French government considered sending large army-level reinforcements. Thus the commitment to the campaign was polarized. This situation cleared rapidly, however, when the collapsing position of Serbia demanded intervention and a bridgehead at Salonika emerged as a competing strategic priority. Compounding this was a distinct weariness in London with a campaign that all had thought would end decisively, rapidly and cheaply. In the end, and gradually over the autumn, London and Paris withdrew support from the Dardanelles expedition.

Kitchener himself finally went out to the peninsula to see for himself what was happening and came away with the opinion that the situation was unsalvageable. There were two evacuations, first of Suvla and Anzac in December 1915, and then of Cape Helles in January 1916. Defying all predictions the Allies got off all of their men and much of their equipment. The divisions that fought there, both Allied and Ottoman were transferred to other active fighting fronts after a period of refitting. Thus the campaign died, 'not with a bang but a whimper'.[1]

Allied strategic indecision and tactical reorganization

Hamilton's cable of 17 August led to gathering doubt in London about the viability of the campaign. Even Kitchener began to vacillate in his strategic thinking and, in spite of his doubts about the viability of another Western Front offensive, he promised Joffre that the BEF would co-operate in an autumn offensive in France. On 20 August, Kitchener explained to the Dardanelles Committee that, although he did not want to undertake another offensive in France, for political reasons Britain must support Joffre. The committee then agreed to support the effort in France as Britain's main strategic effort. This left Hamilton – who had requested some 95,000 additional men – out in the cold. More to the point, Kitchener privately and frankly admitted that he would be thankful if Britain abandoned the Dardanelles enterprise. However, there was agreement that Hamilton, at the end of his tether, needed reinforcement and it was decided to provide Hamilton with about a quarter of his requests. Also, on this day there was renewed interest in the Admiralty to attempt a naval operation to force the Dardanelles. But when the Admiralty staff queried de Robeck about it, he once again sent back his usual reply that it would be a grave error.

Hamilton's report of the failure at Scimitar Hill reached London on 23 August at the same time that rumours and anxieties about Bulgaria joining the Central Powers were beginning to surface. With the collapse of Serbia, an actively hostile Bulgaria would open a floodgate of German assistance to the beleaguered Ottomans. Especially worrisome in this regard would be the arrival of large quantities of artillery munitions for the Ottoman Fifth Army. In the meantime, on 23 August, Lieutenant-General Sir Julian Byng and Major-Generals E. A. Fanshawe and F. S. Maude arrived at the Dardanelles from France. Byng took over IX Corps and de Lisle returned to the 29th Division. Marshall reassumed command of the 53rd Division. Maude went to the 13th Division replacing Shaw, who was invalided home and Fanshawe replaced Hammersley in the 11th Division. Maude's 13th Division was brought to Suvla, joining IX Corps, and the 54th Division took its place at Anzac. Arguably, Hamilton now had a first-class command team for a greatly weakened and poorly equipped second-class army.

London queried Hamilton about the possibilities of renewing the offensive, to which he responded with a very gloomy reply on 23 August. On 30 August, Kitchener sent him a rather surprising cable explaining that the French were contemplating landing six divisions on the Asian side of the Dardanelles. MEF enthusiasm increased when Kitchener sent another message suggesting that he might send the 27th and 28th Divisions from France to replace the two French divisions on Cape Helles, which would redeploy to the Asian side.[2] Although this was a surprise to Hamilton, there had been much wrangling in Paris over the previous three months, notably involving Joffre's desire to replace General Sarrail and move him to an inconsequential command. French politics now combined with Brailloud's troubling 26 August reporting of the definite failure of Hamilton's August offensive.[3] Surprisingly, the French government drew increased resolution from failure and decided to prop up the faltering Dardanelles enterprise. On 11 September at a meeting in Calais, Kitchener, French, Joffre and Sarrail agreed to send two British and four French divisions from France to the Dardanelles.[4] Almost immediately, however, the French backed away from committing a large force to a landing in Asia as the Balkan situation collapsed. Bulgaria mobilized in mid-September causing Greece and Serbia to request that the Allies put 150,000 ashore at Salonika. The French were also put off by Kitchener himself, who thought an Asian landing was full of danger.[5] This decisively changed the strategic landscape by creating a third Mediterranean front in addition to the Dardanelles and Egypt.

On 25 September, Kitchener cabled Hamilton to inform him that he should expect to send two British and one French division to Salonika.[6] Moreover, Kitchener suggested that Hamilton consider abandoning Suvla Bay. Although Kitchener pointed out that there was no intention of abandoning the Dardanelles, this telegram marked the beginning of the end of the campaign. For a short time the Salonika enterprise dangled in a strategic windstorm as decision-makers tried to deal with the king of Greece, who insisted on a charade of maintaining his country's neutrality. Hamilton continued to receive contradictory messages about which forces he would lose. On 7 October in France, the Franco-British Loos–Champagne offensive, which Kitchener had advocated for instead of reinforcing the Dardanelles, failed disastrously. British casualties exceeded 50,000 men – double the losses of Hamilton's August offensive. Strategic dilemmas then beset the decision-makers as resource limits demanded that choices be made between competing priorities. Admiral Sir Henry Jackson advocated for reinforcing the Dardanelles over Salonika while Joffre insisted on another major offensive in France. No definite decisions could be reached and Kitchener asked Hamilton on 11 October what losses an evacuation from the peninsula might number.[7]

In the middle of this strategic quandary, Stopford, who had returned to London, wrote a report for the War Office that questioned Hamilton's leadership. Kitchener felt the pressure and appointed a committee of four senior generals to examine Stopford's claims about the Suvla operation. The generals finally concluded that Hamilton's actions were 'open to criticism'.[8] This happened at the same time that an uncensored and highly inflammatory private letter written by Australian correspondent Keith Murdoch heavily criticizing Hamilton reached Lloyd George and Asquith. These matters, as well as others, were discussed at a contentious Dardanelles Committee meeting on 11 October, which resulted in Sir Edward Carson resigning from the Cabinet over the government's refusal to aid Serbia. Regarding the Dardanelles, the committee resolved to send a senior officer, either Kitchener himself or Haig, out to assess the situation. On 14 October, Hamilton's estimate of losses to be expected in an evacuation – half the force – reached London. This was the final straw for Kitchener, who sent Hamilton a 'secret and personal' on 16 October 1915 ordering him to personally decipher the next message himself.[9] The next message contained compliments for a job well done but also stated that a change was needed and that he would be succeeded by Sir Charles Monro, who would bring out his own chief of staff to replace Braithwaite.[10] But, because Monro could not arrive at Imbros until 28 October, Hamilton turned over command of the MEF to Birdwood and sailed for England on 17 October. Two days later Kitchener queried Birdwood on whether he thought further progress was feasible. Birdwood replied that progress was possible on the northern flank of Suvla provided that units were brought up to strength and two fresh divisions were brought out from Britain.[11] On 23 October Kitchener again queried Birdwood on his views about holding the peninsula positions with the forces at hand. Birdwood's reply was ambiguous – asserting that the positions were only defensible if the MEF could drive the enemy inland in order to create operational depth for the beachheads. This was a roundabout way of saying no because the drive inland would require replacements and reinforcements.

In September and early October, three mounted brigades and five infantry battalions, including the Newfoundland Battalion, arrived on the peninsula which Hamilton distributed to the 29th Division and the 2nd Mounted Division. Set against this, two brigades of the 10th Division left Suvla for Salonika by 2 October with the remainder of the division following. As October ended several more mounted brigades and two more infantry battalions arrived, which were distributed to the Royal Naval Division and the 52nd Division. These forces, along with the arrival of the full-strength 2nd Australian Division, enabled Hamilton to begin a rotational arrangement bringing units to Imbros and Mudros for rest and recuperation. However, these reinforcements barely kept up with attrition and the MEF continued to weaken.

On 25 September, Bailloud notified Hamilton that he had received instructions from Paris to prepare one of his divisions for service elsewhere.[12] Moreover, Bailloud was to organize the new division into two brigades of Metropolitan (white) infantry, fully outfitted with artillery. He finished the message that the forces remaining on the peninsula would fall under the command of General Jean-Marie Brulard. An enraged Hamilton insisted that the French could not hold their front if they sent more than a brigade away. Relations between Hamilton and Bailloud, never very good at their best, broke down almost completely on 30 September when Kitchener asked Hamilton to corroborate Bailloud's claim that one division would suffice to hold the French sector.[13] Moreover, Kitchener then noted that if the French could hold their sector with a single division could not Hamilton 'spare the 53rd Division' as well? Hamilton replied explaining that the French troops (all four white European regiments) who were departing were the only ones he could rely on making it impossible to part with the 53rd Division.[14] Nevertheless, despite Hamilton's opposition, the French began to withdraw forces at the beginning of October. By the end of the month both white regiments and the two regiments composed of Zouaves and Foreign Legionnaires had been withdrawn. This left Brulard 12 battalions of Senegalese and Colonials with which to hold the French front.

Ottoman operational reorganization

On the night of 28/29 August, Mustafa Kemal pulled the exhausted 7th Division out of the line and replaced it with the fresh 6th Division. The 7th Division then moved back into a reserve area just east of Büyük Anafarta for rest and reconstitution. The equally tired 12th Division remained in the line but it shifted to the north, compressing the length of its sector and allowing the 9th Division to move forward into the Scimitar Hill area. To the south, Esat Pasha's Northern Group took advantage of the lull in fighting to rearrange its command arrangements. Esat divided his front in half. He established a right wing sector, which controlled the reinforced 19th Division and two regiments. Esat also established a left wing sector composed of the 11th and 16th Divisions.

Recognizing that Mustafa Kemal might experience difficulty with command and control of an operational group containing over seven infantry divisions, Enver Pasha and Liman von Sanders decided to revise the command architecture.[15] On 29 August, Lieutenant-Colonel Nicolai re-formed the II Corps headquarters and took command of the 5th, 9th, and 12th Divisions and Colonel Ali Rıza was ordered to re-form the XV Corps headquarters and take command of the 4th, 6th and 8th Divisions.[16] The refitting 7th Division would remain as the Anafarta Group reserve along with the 26th Division and the battalions from the 3rd Division. This arrangement gave Kemal a group of two corps rather than a group of seven divisions. Brigadier-General Fevzi was also assigned as Kemal's chief of staff. Additional reinforcements were also arriving in the combat area. On 17 August Enver Pasha ordered XVII Corps, composed of the 15th and 25th Infantry Divisions, to move to the peninsula and both arrived by the end of August. The Ottoman Army now had over

19 infantry divisions committed to the Gallipoli campaign or about 40 per cent of its 48 organized infantry divisions on strength as of 1 September 1915.[17]

On 4 September Enver advised the Fifth Army that he had intelligence that over 77,000 Italian soldiers were poised at Brindisi, Naples and Rhodes to invade the Gallipoli peninsula. This set off another round of movements in which the 2nd Division was moved to Erenköy and the 20th Infantry Division from Smyrna ordered north to reinforce XVII Corps at Saros Bay. Two cavalry brigades and three independent cavalry regiments were deployed to the area from the capital as well. The imminent collapse of Serbia offered the prospect of opening the rail lines between Germany and the Ottoman Empire. In anticipation of this event enabling artillery and ammunition to be sent to the hard-pressed Ottomans, the German general staff sent Colonel Gressman, an artillery specialist from the Western Front, to the Fifth Army to advise Liman von Sanders on the most current artillery tactics.[18] Overall Ottoman strength committed to the campaign in September 1915 stood at 5,282 officers and 255,728 men.[19]

No invasion materialized and, moreover, rumours began circulate that the British intended to evacuate the peninsula or draw down their forces there. Thus, as winter approached, Enver Pasha decided to pull significant forces back into Thrace where they could be more easily sustained. On 6 October he notified the Fifth Army that he intended to reconstitute the Second Army in Constantinople and assign three infantry corps to it.[20] Vehip was ordered to return to the capital with part of his Southern Group staff to begin the process of reconstitution. The infantry corps would be removed from the peninsula in three groups and sent north. The first group included the I Corps headquarters and the 3rd and 2nd Divisions, which departed for Uzunköprü on 8 and 11 October respectively. The II Corps headquarters departed on 16 October with the 4th Division for Keşan and the 13th Division followed on 21 October. The V Corps headquarters with the 5th and 10th Divisions left the following week. Enver remained concerned about the possibility of an Allied offensive and he sent more fresh forces to the area, alerting the 42nd Infantry Division in Smyrna and the 136th Infantry Regiment in Constantinople for service on the peninsula.

At Cape Helles on 9 October, Vehip Pasha departed and was replaced by XIV Corps commander, Brigadier-General Cevat, as the Southern Group commander. On 21 October the 15th Division went into the line at Cape Helles to relieve the 13th Division, which went to Keşan for rest and reconstitution. Because of tactical disasters occurring in faraway Mesopotamia, the Ottoman general staff asked Field Marshal von der Goltz to take over that theatre. As he departed, Enver Pasha appointed Northern Group commander, Esat Pasha, as the new First Army commander. Replacing Esat in the Northern

Group was XV Corps commander, Colonel Ali Rıza from the Anafarta Group. The incoming 42nd Division arrived on 22 October. Replacing II Corps in the Anafarta Group, Colonel Kannengiesser returned and re-formed the XVI Corps headquarters on 27 October. Finally, the 11th Division was re-formed to take the place in line of the departing 5th Division. A provisional division was activated and assigned to the Northern Group's area near Gaba Tepe.[21] Combat in October remained stable and light and was characterized by bombing raids and sniping. As a possible way to break the deadlock, the Ottoman general staff organized the 254th Tunnelling Company and sent it to the peninsula.[22] Ottoman strength committed to the campaign peaked in October 1915 at 5,500 officers and 310,000 men.[23]

Strategic indecision and abandonment

After Hamilton's relief and the exchanges with the French, both at Kitchener's strategic level and operational level with Hamilton and Birdwood, it is hard to imagine a different outcome than the Allied decision to abandon the campaign. General Sir Charles Monro and his chief of staff, Major-General A. L. Lynden-Bell, landed at Imbros on the morning of 28 October taking over command of the MEF from Birdwood. Kitchener had explicitly told Monro that he needed his appreciation of the situation as soon as possible. Upon arrival Monro received a prepared memorandum from the MEF staff suggesting that ten fresh divisions and 250,000 men were required to complete the campaign by opening up an advance on the Asian side. The MEF staff also argued for more artillery and ammunition. Monro sent a message to Kitchener that afternoon but failed to answer the question directly. Monro had not been at his post 24 hours when Kitchener impatiently telegraphed back and directly asked whether the MEF should stay or leave. Monro replied to Kitchener on 31 October in a message outlining the strengths of the enemy and the problems and deficiencies of the MEF, and stating that such forces that could be evacuated would be more favourably placed in Egypt.[24] This was a back-handed way of recommending an evacuation.

Kitchener was stunned by Monro's recommendations because he had read Keyes's scheme for a naval attack and had been informed by Maxwell in Egypt that an evacuation would be disastrous. Kitchener immediately demanded to know if the MEF corps commanders felt the same way. Davies in VIII Corps and Byng in IX Corps agreed with Monro while Birdwood was against evacuation.[25] Monro sent these opinions to Kitchener and estimated that MEF losses in an evacuation would total some 30 to 40 per cent of the force.

The newly restructured War Committee met on 3 November to consider the problem and, as no decision could be reached, concluded that Kitchener himself should go to the Dardanelles and form an appreciation. Kitchener sent a secret and personal telegram to Birdwood expressing his support for Keyes's naval program and telling Birdwood that he intended to employ the ANZAC in support of the attack.[26] Kitchener left for the Mediterranean on 4 November and found, while stopping in Paris, that the French were against evacuation. In the meantime Keyes tried to rally support for a naval assault but failed. In Egypt, Monro learned that his advice had ended in his own supersession when Birdwood was appointed to command the MEF and he was ordered to Salonika. Monro, Maxwell and Mahon then left Egypt for the Dardanelles and, on the way, Monro persuaded them to support the idea of an amphibious landing at Ayas Bay, in the Bay of Alexandretta, an idea that had always appealed to Kitchener.

Kitchener arrived at Mudros on the evening of 9 November and spent the next 12 days visiting the beachheads and in commanders' conferences. By 15 November he remained reluctant to recommend a definitive course of action. Kitchener then sailed to visit Mahon at Salonika to assess the situation there in relation to the Dardanelles question. Then Kitchener went to Athens and secured a pledge of neutrality from the Greek king. On 21 November Kitchener returned to Mudros where he was bombarded by contradictory opinions about staying or leaving. On the morning of 22 November, Kitchener cabled London his long-awaited report.[27] His appreciation cut the question both ways, by recommending that Suvla and Anzac be evacuated but that Cape Helles should continue to be held for the present. Asquith cabled back the following day stating that the War Committee was in favour of total evacuation and would refer the matter for a Cabinet decision.

Recognizing the obvious, Kitchener put Monro in command of British forces in the Mediterranean outside of Egypt, with the MEF headquarters at Mudros as his staff. Kitchener then placed Birdwood in command of a new Dardanelles Army at Gallipoli and charged him with carrying out the evacuation. The next day, 24 November, Kitchener sailed for England. Operationally the Gallipoli campaign was now abandoned but the Cabinet, in very political and contentious discussions, could not decide the issue at the strategic level. Lord Curzon, in particular, stood adamantly against evacuation.

The Cabinet had still not reached a formal decision on 1 December when severe winter storms and freezing temperatures hit the peninsula. On 4 December Asquith, Balfour, Kitchener, and Sir Archibald Murray went over to Calais to confer with the French prime minister and his chiefs. Several days passed without a decision. Finally – 37 days after General Monro had made his first report – the Cabinet decided to evacuate Suvla and Anzac but to hold on to Helles in order to try and salvage something from the campaign.[28] The decision was telegraphed to Monro with orders to act on the decision without delay.

While the British were trying to reach a decision, no such hesitation gripped the Ottoman high command, which increased its forces on the peninsula. Important reinforcements for the Ottoman Fifth Army arrived from northern Europe on 9 and 10 November. These were a motorized battery of Austrian 240mm mortars and a battery of 150m howitzers. The heavy mortars went to the Anafarta Group while the howitzers went to the Southern Group.[29] They were in action around 20 November and were used to pound Chocolate Hill. The long-expected arrival of heavy artillery from Germany and Austria immediately caused Allied morale to plummet. By the end of the month two additional 210mm heavy mortar batteries and six heavy howitzer batteries arrived from Germany.[30] This gave the Ottoman Fifth Army a total of 20 heavy artillery batteries on the peninsula and, equally important, large quantities of ammunition began to arrive as well. The results were immediate and powerful as Colonel Gressman and the German artillery specialists began to organize Ottoman gunners using the latest gunnery techniques from the Western Front. The Germans also sent down several staff officers as technical advisors to advise the Fifth Army about the employment of the latest combat methods in use on the Western Front as well.

Factors accelerating the British evacuation included the arrival of the German heavy artillery and the abysmal tactical position but also the severe Mediterranean storms in November that destroyed many of the landing piers, and an unseasonably severe snow blizzard that caused hundreds of cases of frostbite and hypothermia. In spite of these obstacles Birdwood's evacuation of the remaining IX Corps and ANZAC elements was exceptionally well planned and completed on the night of 19/20 December. The Turks were surprised by the evacuation and were in no condition to exploit the situation. The first news of it reached the Fifth Army headquarters at 4.00am, 20 December when the headquarters received a call from the Northern Group's staff duty officer.[31] The staff woke up Liman von Sanders, who immediately authorized an advance to the beaches. One individual who was not on hand to witness the victory was the tireless Colonel Mustafa Kemal, who had become exhausted and sick and had been evacuated to hospital in Constantinople on 10 December (he was replaced as Anafarta Group commander by V Corps commander, Colonel Fevzi Pasha). It is very possible that had Kemal remained active in his position the evacuation might have been discovered and exploited.[32]

On 23 December, General Sir William Robertson replaced General Murray as Chief of the Imperial General Staff and he notified Monro the next day to begin preparations for the evacuation of Cape Helles, but not to do anything in case the government decided to retain the peninsula. On Christmas day 1915, Birdwood visited Cape Helles and conferred with Davies and Brulard about how the evacuation might work. The well-conceived and successful evacuation plan that had worked so well at Suvla and Anzac was tailored and reworked for conditions at Cape Helles. Part of the scheme involved pulling the 42nd Division off the peninsula and replacing it with the 13th Division, which was on Mudros, while the Royal Naval Division took over the French lines. On 27 December Davies was ordered to draw his garrison down to 15,000 and, on 28 December, Robertson sent a message that the government had decided to evacuate Cape Helles as soon as practicable.

Now alert to what the Allies might try Liman von Sanders instructed his staff to begin work on an attack plan to wipe out the evacuation as it began to unfold. The plan involved an attack employing four to eight divisions using the latest tactical methods from the Western Front.[33] German officers were sent down from the Second Army headquarters in Thrace to assist the Fifth Army planners. Liman von Sanders briefed Enver Pasha on the plan as it evolved and received approval to carry it out. The Ottoman staffs worked hard to quickly bring the plan together and brought the 12th Division from Anafarta to the Cape Helles front where it began intensive assault training. On 7 January 1916, the Southern Group launched the 12th Division, now lavishly supported by artillery, against the British 13th Division on Gully Spur. Two mines were exploded under the British trenches immediately followed by a violent artillery bombardment starting at 4.00pm that shook the British, who handily repulsed the Ottoman advance.[34] The stalwart British defence served to convince the Southern Group that the enemy was still actively defending the Cape Helles lines. As a result they almost missed the second evacuation, which took place the very next night on 8/9 January 1916. In places the Ottomans pushed forward when their fire was not returned and there were some minor skirmishes as the British conducted an evacuation partly under fire. Nevertheless, the last man got off successfully at 3.45am completing the evacuation. The campaign was over.

The withdrawal of the Ottoman Fifth Army
Liman von Sanders notified Enver Pasha by telegraph at 8.45am, 9 January, that the British had withdrawn entirely from the peninsula.[35] The Fifth Army commander immediately followed this with a congratulatory order to his troops

lauding their achievements and promising to get them off the peninsula as soon as possible.[36] The three-division III Corps departed 13–15 January, while the following two-division corps left as follows; XVI Corps 9–16 January, XV Corps 19–20 January, and the XVII Corps 17–18 January. Two infantry divisions assigned to army corps headquarters left on 11 and 12 January as well.[37]

Most of these divisions were sent up into Thrace to such pre-war garrison towns as Adrianople, Çorlu, and Pinarhısar where they could be easily resupplied and refitted. Liman von Sanders himself and his chief of staff, Lieutenant-Colonel Kazım, left their headquarters at Yalova at 9.30pm, 15 January 1916, by road to Uzunköprü to catch the train to Constantinople. The Fifth Army headquarters and staff moved to Akbaş Pier where they took a steamer named the *Akdeniz* to Constantinople at 8.00pm, 18 January 1916. Remaining behind to garrison the peninsula was a truncated army named the Gallipoli Group Command commanded by Brigadier-General Cevat Pasha. The new command was composed of VI Corps (24th and 26th Divisions) and XIV Corps (25th and 42nd Divisions) as well as a cavalry regiment, an independent infantry regiment, four jandarma battalions, and two independent artillery battalions. The heavy artillery was left in place and then moved out later to active theatres of war.

On the British side, the MEF headquarters was dissolved, the VIII and IX Corps headquarters went to France by way of Egypt. The regulars, the 29th Division and the Royal Naval Division as later did the Territorial 42nd Division, went to France as did the New Army 11th Division. The ANZAC expanded to become two corps headquarters in France and absorbed both the 1st and 2nd Australian Divisions. The Australian and New Zealand Division disbanded and an entirely new New Zealand Division emerged from it, while the 2nd Mounted Division disbanded forever.

A number of the Gallipoli divisions would meet the Ottomans again in Egypt and Palestine. These were the Territorial 52nd, 53rd and 54th Divisions. The New Army 10th Division went to Salonika and then joined them in Palestine later. Finally, the New Army 13th Division was dispatched to faraway Mesopotamia. The peninsula was never attacked again.

Performance at the strategic level

British decision-makers in the War Council were determined to conduct a campaign against the Ottoman Empire on the cheap and refused to send first-line forces to the Mediterranean. This was compounded by a lack of strategic clarity that was brought about by ambiguity of how to go about balancing ends, ways and means. This failure to apply overwhelming force became the main reason for campaign failure. There were three separate campaign designs, none of which were completely supported by all members of the War Council, and none of which were supported by adequate forces. This was a result of a disastrous underestimation of the Ottoman Army's capability and capacity.

The Gallipoli campaign was a peripheral campaign until June 1915 when it became Britain's main strategic effort. At this point, the War Council once again failed to resource the campaign by failing to send first-class commanders and first-class units necessary to ensure success, preferring to continue to send inexperienced units and elderly commanders.

The Ottoman Army's strategic strength in the straits region was an accidental outcome of an obsolete mobilization and concentration plan. However, this enabled Enver to deploy divisions to the Gallipoli peninsula throughout the campaign. Enver and the Ottoman general staff maintained strategic clarity by committing resources adequate to hold the British to their tiny beachheads. However, there were never enough Ottoman divisions to push the British back into the sea. This was a result of inadequate strategic intelligence, which led the Ottomans to believe the Russians would assault the Bosporus, in turn, causing Enver to withhold major forces near Constantinople when they were needed by the Fifth Army.

Performance at the operational level

British execution of the Gallipoli campaign was notably unsuccessful at the operational level of war. Sir Ian Hamilton was unable to use the principles of war effectively during the planning and execution of the campaign. In particular, he was unable to mass forces at decisive points in the campaign and, often, he disregarded unity of command. These problems were the result of the absence of higher-level doctrines within the British Army and from an institutionally devolved system of command. Hamilton's plans were overly complex, a violation of the principle of simplicity. Hamilton's decision-making was hampered by an absence of information which led to an inability to control his operations effectively. The MEF was crippled by an inability to manoeuvre caused primarily by an failure to plan for and control the use of reserves. The principal outcome of this was the MEF's failure to gain adequate operational depth and space, which negatively affected its ability to position artillery and forces. The MEF's performance at the operational level can be characterized by a lack of capability rather than a lack of capacity.

The Ottoman Fifth Army successfully orchestrated the defence of the Gallipoli peninsula over a nine-month period to win the campaign. Liman von

Sanders was always in possession of timely and accurate information, which enabled him to make decisions effectively. The Ottomans were able to release operational reserves rapidly and mass forces at decisive points. Reciprocally, he was able to maximize massing forces by economy of force measures elsewhere. This incurred risk, but effective situational awareness enabled him to achieve massing forces effectively. Fifth Army operational commanders frequently exercised individual initiative within the framework of commonly understood doctrines. The Fifth Army's performance at the operational level can be characterized by the employment of effective capabilities that were backed up by adequate capacity.

Performance at the tactical level

At corps and below, British commanders frequently placed subordinates in executive command. This proved ineffective and directly led to frequent failures to control tactical operations. This particularly manifested itself in an inability to use reserves effectively. British commanders and staff were also unable to mass forces decisively at the appropriate place and time at the tactical level. British reporting systems and the location of commanders created bewildering conditions often leading to a nearly total absence of situational awareness. Institutionally, the British were unable to tailor their forces and cross-attach brigades and battalions between divisions. Moreover, commanders were prone to overloading subordinates with too many units. During the entire campaign, British commanders misunderstood why they were unsuccessful, most frequently by pinpointing the absence of artillery and shells as the primary cause of tactical failure. The MEF's performance at the tactical level can be characterized by both a lack of capability and a lack of capacity.

Ottoman commanders frequently made rapid and effective decisions on their own initiative to take control of the tactical battle. They were able to operate effectively by understanding their higher commander's intent and were able to make independent decisions. This was a function of effective doctrines and training that stressed the concentration of forces and the integration of combined arms. The Ottoman Army's unique triangular organizational architecture accommodated the tailoring and cross-attaching of units to achieve optimal force ratios to the available battlespace. This capability enabled commanders at all levels to create groups and ad hoc task force-like command arrangements. Ottoman and German commanders maintained control on a continuous basis and effectively influenced the outcomes of battles. This was also a function of doctrines and training but also reflected a high degree of interoperability between Germans and Ottomans. The Ottoman Army's performance at the tactical level can also be characterized by the employment of effective capabilities that were backed up by adequate capacity.

APPENDIX

Dardanelles Commission Report: Conclusions (1917), CAB 19/1

GENERAL CONCLUSIONS

1. We think that, when it was decided to undertake an important military expedition to the Gallipoli Peninsula, sufficient consideration was not given to the measures necessary to carry out such an expedition with success. We have already pointed out in paragraph 15 that it had been apparent in February, 1915, that serious military operations might be necessary. Under these circumstances we think that the conditions of a military attack on the Peninsula should have been studied and a general plan prepared by the Chief of the Imperial General Staff, Sir James Wolfe-Murray, special attention being paid to the probable effect of naval gun fire in support of the troops; and that it was the duty of the Secretary of State for War to ensure that this was done.

2. We think that the difficulties of the operations were much underestimated. At the outset all decisions were taken and all provisions based on the assumption that, if a landing were effected, the resistance would be slight and the advance rapid. We can see no sufficient ground for this assumption. The short naval bombardment in November, 1914, had given the Turks warning of a possible attack, and the naval operations in February and March of 1915 led naturally to a great strengthening of the Turkish defences. The Turks were known to be led by German officers, and there was no reason to think that they would not fight well, especially in defensive positions. These facts had been reported by Admiral de Robeck and Sir Ian Hamilton.

3. We think that the position, which in fact, existed after the first attacks in April and the early days of May should have been regarded from the outset as possible and the requisite means of meeting it considered. This would have made it necessary to examine and decide whether the demands of such

233

extended operations could be met consistently with our obligations in other theatres of war. In fact those obligations made it impossible in May, June and July to supply the forces with the necessary drafts, gun ammunition, high explosives and other modern appliances of war.

4.   We are of the opinion that, with the resources then available, success in the Dardanelles, if possible, was only possible upon condition that the Government concentrated their efforts upon the enterprise and limited their expenditure of men and material in the Western theatre of war. This condition was never fulfilled.

5.   After the failure of the attacks which followed the first landing there was undue delay deciding upon the course to be pursued in the future. Sir Ian Hamilton's appreciation was forwarded on May 17th, 1915. It was not considered by the War Council or the Cabinet until June 7th. The reconstruction of the Government which took place at this most critical period was the main cause of the delay. As a consequence the despatch of the reinforcements asked for by Sir Ian Hamilton in his appreciation was postponed for six weeks.

6.   We think that the plan of attack from Anzac and Suvla in the beginning of August was open to criticism. The country over which the attack had to be made was very difficult, especially at Anzac. In order to obtain if possible the element of surprise, the main advance of the Anzac force up the north-western spurs of Sari Bahr [Sari Bair] was undertaken at night, the risk of misdirection and failure being much increased thereby. The plan, however, was decided upon after a consideration of other plans, and with the concurrence of the commander of the Anzac Corps, who had been in command since the first landing.

7.   The operations at Suvla were a severe trial for the force consisting of troops who had never been under fire, but we think that after taking into consideration and making every allowance for the difficulties of the attack and the inexperience of the troops, the attack was not pressed as it should have been at Suvla on the 7th and 8th August, and we attribute this in a great measure to a want of determination and competence in the Divisional Commander and one of his Brigadiers. The leading of the 11th Division and the attached battalions of the 10th Division, which constituted the main body of the attack, was not satisfactory. As explained in paragraphs 108 and 109, the orders given by General Hammersley were confused and the work of his staff defective. Major-General Hammersley's health had in the past been such that it was dangerous to select him for a divisional command in the field, although he seemed to have recovered. We think that the defects that we have mentioned

in his leading probably arose from this cause. General Sitwell, the senior Brigade Commander, did not, in our opinion, show sufficient energy and decision.

8. Sir Frederick Stopford was hampered by the want of effective leading above referred to, and the inexperience of his troops, but we do not think he took sufficient means to inform himself of the progress of operations. On August 7th, when he became aware that the troops had not advanced as rapidly as had been intended, we think that he should have asked for some explanation from General Hammersley. In that case he would have been informed of the difference which had arisen between General Sitwell and General Hill, and of General Sitwell's lack of vigour and energy in leading. We think that at this point his intervention was needed. We think that he and his staff were partly responsible for the failure to supply the troops with water on August 7th and 8th. Our detailed conclusions on the water supply will be found below.

    We cannot endorse Sir Ian Hamilton's condemnation of the orders given by Sir Frederick Stopford on the morning of August 8th, 1915, whether the account of them given in Sir Ian Hamilton's despatch or that in Sir Frederick Stopford's report to him be accepted. According to the evidence of Sir Bryan Mahon and General Hammersley they were not deterred from advancing by those orders.

    On the evening of August 8th we think that Sir Frederick Stopford's difficulties were increased by the intervention of Sir Ian Hamilton. Sir Ian Hamilton seems to have considered Sir Frederick Stopford lacking in energy in the operations between August 9th and August 15th. As this opinion is based more upon general conduct than upon any specific acts or omissions, we are not in a position to pronounce upon it. We realise, however, that importance attaches to the impressions of a Commander-in-Chief on such a subject.

9. As regards Sir Ian Hamilton it is inevitable that the capabilities of a commander in war should be judged by the results he achieves, even though, if these results are disappointing, his failure may be due to causes for which he is only partially responsible.

    In April, 1915, Sir Ian Hamilton succeeded in landing his troops at the places which he had chosen: but the operations that were intended immediately to follow the landing were abruptly checked owing to a miscalculation of the strength of the Turkish defences and the fighting qualities of the Turkish troops. This rebuff should have convinced Sir Ian Hamilton that the Turkish entrenchments were skilfully disposed and well armed, and that naval gun fire was ineffective against trenches and entanglements of the modern type. We doubt, however, whether the failure of the operations sufficiently impressed Sir Ian Hamilton and the military authorities at home with the serious nature of the opposition likely to be encountered.

During May, June, and July severe fighting took place, but its results were not commensurate with the efforts made and the losses incurred.

During July a plan of combined operations was elaborated, which was carried into effect early in August. Sir Ian Hamilton was confident of success, but was again baffled by the obstinacy of the Turkish resistance. Moreover, the failure of night advances in a difficult and unexplored country, which formed part of the plan, led to heavy casualties and temporarily disorganised the forces employed.

Sir Ian Hamilton was relieved of his command on October 15th.

We recognise Sir Ian Hamilton's personal gallantry and energy, his sanguine disposition, and his determination to win at all costs. We recognise also that the task entrusted to him was one of extreme difficulty, the more so as the authorities at home at first misconceived the nature and duration of the operations, and afterwards were slow to realise that to drive the Turks out of their entrenchments and occupy the heights commanding the Straits was a formidable and hazardous enterprise which demanded a concentration of force and effort. It must further be borne in mind that Lord Kitchener, whom Sir Ian Hamilton appears to have regarded as a Commander-in-Chief rather than as a Secretary of State, pressed upon him the paramount importance, if it were by any means possible, of carrying out the task assigned to him.

Though from time to time Sir Ian Hamilton represented the need of drafts, reinforcements, guns and munitions, which the Government found it impossible to supply, he was nevertheless always ready to renew the struggle with the resources at his disposal, and to the last was confident of success. For this it would be hard to blame him; but viewing the Expedition in the light of events it would, in our opinion, have been well had he examined the situation as disclosed by the first landings in a more critical spirit, impartially weighed the probabilities of success and failure, having regard to the resources in men and material which could be placed at his disposal, and submitted to the Secretary of State for War a comprehensive statement of the arguments for and against a continuance of the operations.

10. The failure at Anzac was due mainly to the difficulties of the country and the strength of the enemy. The failure at Suvla also prevented any pressure being put upon the Turkish force in that direction, and success at Suvla might have lessened the resistance at Anzac

11. We think that after the attacks ending on August 9th had failed, the operations contemplated could not have been successfully carried out without large reinforcements. The fighting after General de Lisle replaced Sir Frederick Stopford was really of a defensive character.

12. We think that after the advice of Sir Charles Monro had been confirmed by Lord Kitchener the decision to evacuate should have been taken at once. We recognise, however, that the question of evacuation was connected with other questions of high policy which do not appear to us to come within the scope of our enquiry.

13. We think that the decision to evacuate when taken was right.

14. We think that the operations were hampered throughout by the failure to supply sufficient artillery and munitions, and to keep the original formations up to strength by the provision of adequate drafts as well as reinforcements. In our opinion this was not owing to any neglect on the part of the Heads of Departments charged with such provision, but to the demands proving much larger than was expected when the operations were undertaken and to demands which had to be met in other theatres of war.

    On the other hand, a considerable amount of artillery was available in Egypt and at Mudros for the Suvla operations, but it was not utilized.

15. Many minor frontal attacks were made without adequate artillery preparation, which produced little or no material advantage. Evidence was given that these attacks entailed an unnecessary loss of life. Without a more intimate knowledge of the locality and conditions than it is possible to obtain, we cannot express an opinion as to whether it was right to undertake such attacks. We think that the evidence disproves the allegation made before us that useless attacks were made because of the neglect on the part of superior Commanders and Staff Officers to visit and inspect the trenches and positions.

16. There was full co-operation between the Navy and Army and the two services worked well and harmoniously together.

ENDNOTES

INTRODUCTION
1. Full citations for the books mentioned in this introduction can be found in the Select Bibliography.
2. See Nigel Hamilton, *Master of the Battlefield, Monty's War Years 1942–1944* (New York: McGraw Hill, 1984), for an excellent discussion of the term 'grip' at the operational and tactical levels of war.

CHAPTER ONE
1. Maurice Hankey, *The Supreme Command, 1914–1918, Volume One* (London: George Allen and Unwin Limited, 1961), 222.
2. A full narrative of the council and its dilemmas and actions is outside the scope of this work. For further reading, see Hankey, *The Supreme Command, Vol I*, 244–295 and Winston S. Churchill, *The World Crisis, Vol II* (New York: Charles Scribner's Sons, 1929), 84–117.
3. Hankey, *The Supreme Command*, 244–250.
4. Ibid., 250.
5. Ibid., 251.
6. Graham T. Clews, *Churchill's Dilemma, The Real Story Behind the Origins of the 1915 Dardanelles Campaign* (Santa Barbara, CA: Praeger, 2010), 62.
7. Ibid., 93.
8. Ibid.
9. Ibid., 94.
10. Ibid., 107.
11. Hankey, *The Supreme Command*, 267.
12. Clews, *Churchill's Dilemma*, 118.
13. Edward J. Erickson, *Defeat in Detail, The Ottoman Army in the Balkans, 1912–1913* (Westport, CT: Praeger, 2003), 246–248.
14. M. Naim Turfan, *Rise of the Young Turks: Politics, the Military and Ottoman Collapse* (London: I. B. Tauris, 2000), 327–330.
15. Shaw, *History of the Ottoman Empire and Modern Turkey, Vol II*, 306.
16. Ibid.

17. Uyar and Erickson, *A Military History of the Ottomans,* 237–238.
18. Karatamu, *Türk Silahlı Kuvvetleri Tarihi (1908–1920),* 242–243.
19. Ibid., 52. The totals of officers who were forcibly retired were astonishing: two field marshals, three lieutenant-generals, 30 major-generals, 95 brigadier-generals, 184 colonels, 236 lieutenant-colonels and majors and some 800 captains and lieutenants.
20. Raymond H. Kévorkian, *The Armenian Genocide, A Complete History* (London: I. B. Tauris, 2011), 168.
21. Turfan, *Rise of the Young Turks,* 293.
22. Cemal Akbay, *Birinci Dünya Harbinde Türk Harbi, 1nci Cilt, Osmanli Imparatorlugu'nun Siyası ve Askeri Hazırlıkları ve Harbe Girisi* (Ankara: Genelkurmay Basımevi, 1970), 157. Hereafter, Akbay, *Military Mobilisation and Entry into the War.*
23. Fahri Belen, *Birinci Cihan Harbinde Türk Harbi 1914, 1915 Yılı Hareketleri* (Ankara: Genelkurmay Basımevi, 1964), 55–57.
24. Akbay, *Military Mobilization and Entry into the War,* 157–162.
25. Sir G. Barclay to Sir Edward Grey, 4 August 1914, G. P. Gooch and Harold Temperley (eds.), *British Documents on the Origins of the War 1898–1914, Vol. XI* (London, HMSO, 1926), 306.
26. See Edward J. Erickson, *Ordered to Die, A History of the Ottoman Army in the First World War* (Westport, CT: Greenwood Press, 2001), 25–28 for a summary of the specific clauses and the time lines. See Mustafa Aksakal, *The Ottoman Road to War in 1914: The Ottoman Empire and the First World War* (Cambridge: Cambridge University Press, 2008) for the definitive comprehensive treatment of this subject.
27. Ulrich Trumpener, *Germany and the Ottoman Empire* (Princeton: Princeton University Press, 1968), 54.
28. Ibid.
29. Bernd Langensiepen and Ahmet Guleryuz, *The Ottoman Steam Navy* (Annapolis: Naval Institute Press, 1995), 44.
30. Akbay, *Military Mobilization and Entry into the War,* 162–176.
31. Fevzi Çakmak, *Birinci Dünya Savaşı'nda Doğu Cephesi* (Ankara: Genelkurmay Basımevi, 2005), 10–15.

CHAPTER TWO
1. Churchill, *The World Crisis, Vol II,* 186–189.
2. George H. Cassar, *Kitchener's War, British Strategy from 1914–1916* (Washington, DC: Brassey's Inc., 2004), 137. See also C. F. Aspinall-Oglander, *History of the Great War, based on Official Documents: Military Operations Gallipoli, Vol I* (London: HMSO, 1924), 71. Hereafter Aspinall-Oglander, *Military Operations, Gallipoli, Vol I.*
3. Clews, *Churchill's Dilemma,* 202.
4. Ibid., 199–207.
5. Hankey, *The Supreme Command, Vol I,* 258–262.
6. Clews, *Churchill's Dilemma,* 199–207.
7. A total of 60,000 men was generally thought to be sufficient for such a campaign and had its origins in pre-war negotiations with the Greek government, which occurred in mid-August 1914, with the object of using the Greek army and Royal Navy to force the Dardanelles. See Graham T. Clews, *Churchill's Dilemma* (Santa Barbara, CA: Praeger, 2010) 43-48 for the best discussion of these events

8. Paul G. Halpern, *The Naval War in the Mediterranean 1914–1918* (Annapolis: Naval Institute Press, 1987), 47–83.
9. Robert K. Massie, *Castles of Steel* (New York: Random House, 2003), 428–430.
10. Robin Prior, *Gallipoli, The End of the Myth* (New Haven: Yale University Press, 2009), 36.
11. Ibid., 98. See also Clews, *Churchill's Dilemma*, 70–75.
12. Churchill, *The World Crisis, Vol II*, 190–192.
13. Prior, *Gallipoli, The End of the Myth*, 41.
14. The material for this paragraph comes from Edward J. Erickson, 'Strength Against Weakness, Gallipoli 1915', *Journal of Military History* 65 (October 2001), 981–1012.
15. Muhterem Saral, Alpaslan Orhon and Şükrü Erkal, *Birinci Dünya Harbinde Türk Harbi Vncü Cilt, Çanakkale Cephesi Harekati Inci Kitap (Haziran 1914–Nisan 1915)* ['First World War, Turkish War, Gallipoli Front Operations, June 1914–April 1915'] (Ankara: Genelkurmay Basımevi, 1993), 80–91. Hereafter, Saral et al, *Gallipoli Front Operations, June 1914–April 1915*.
16. T. C. Genelkurmay Başkanlığı, *Şark Ordusu, Ikinci Çatalca Muharebesi ve Şarkoy Çikmarmasi*, 66–67. See also Edward J. Erickson, 'Strength Against Weakness: Ottoman Military Effectiveness at Gallipoli, 1915', *The Journal of Military History*, 65 (October 2001), 981–1012 for a description and comparative maps of the 1912, February 1915, and April 1915 defences.
17. The Ottomans used the name of the largest town in the region – Çanakkale – as a military term for its headquarters and for the campaign itself. The Turks identify the Gallipoli campaign as *Çanakkale Harekâtı*.
18. Genelkurmay Başkanlığı, *Şark Ordusu, Ikinci Çatalca Muharebesi ve Şarköy Cikarmasi*, 66–67.
19. Ibid., Kroki (Map) 79.
20. The Australians would later discover what they called 'the Balkan Pits' in their sector in 1915, which were the remnants of these defensive preparations. The late modern-day Gallipoli enthusiast Jul Snelders (from Belgium) uncovered these pits in 1998.
21. Genelkurmay Başkanlığı, *Şark Ordusu, Ikinci Çatalca Muharebesi ve Şarköy Cikarmasi*, Kroki (Map) 19.
22. Genelkurmay Başkanlığı, *Şark Ordusu, Ikinci Çatalca Muharebesi ve Şarköy Cikarmasi*, 251, 262. It is sometimes forgotten that Mustafa Kemal served in a combat role during the Balkan Wars and generally unknown that he served as a corps-level operations officer on the Gallipoli peninsula in 1913.
23. See Erickson, *Defeat in Detail*, 153–156, 252–259, and 325–328 for details of these operations.
24. Richard Hall, *The Balkan Wars 1912–1913: Prelude to the First World War* (London: Routledge, 2000), 81.
25. The material for this paragraph comes from Erickson, 'Strength Against Weakness', 981–1012.
26. Saral et al, *Gallipoli Front Operations, June 1914–April 1915*, 83–84.
27. Ibid., 51–52.
28. Ibid., 49–51.
29. Ibid., 49–51.
30. Ibid., 79.
31. ATASE Archive 121, Record 573, File 10-3, Enver Pasha to Çanakkale fortress commander, 12 August 1914 reproduced in T. C. Genelkurmay Başkanlığı, *Askeri*

Tarih Belgeleri Dergisi, Yıl 38, Sayı 88, Augustos 1989 (Ankara: Genelkurmay
Basımevi, 1989), 7–8.
32. Saral et al, *Gallipoli Front Operations, June 1914–April 1915,* 52.
33. Ibid., 61–62.
34. Ibid., 54.
35. III Corps report to First Army, 22 November 1914, ATASE Archive 4669, Record
H-3, File 1-107, quoted in Saral et al, *Gallipoli Front Operations, June 1914–April
1915,* 103.
36. 19ncu Tümen Tarihçesi, 1970, 9, unpublished staff study (Mekki Erertem),
Genelkurmay Askeri Tarih ve Stratejik Etut, ATASE Library, Record 26-834.
37. Ibid., 38–40.
38. Ibid., Kroki (Map) 4.
39. Ibid., 85–88.
40. Ibid., 89.
41. Ibid., 85–86.
42. Ibid., 44–45.
43. Ibid., 45.
44. Ibid., Chart 9.
45. Saral et al, *Gallipoli Front Operations, June 1914–April 1915,* 97–99, 106–107, 217.

CHAPTER THREE

1. Change of command directives, 6 January 1914, Prime Minister Archives, Archive
Number 6, reprinted in T. C. Genelkurmay Başkanlığı, *Turk Silahli Kuvvetleri Tarihi
(1908–1920),* 195–6.
2. Liman von Sanders, *Five Years in Turkey* (London: Bailliere, Tindall & Cox, 1928), 78–9.
3. Remzi Yiğitgüden, Muhterem Saral and Reşat Hallı. *Birinci Dünya Harbinde Türk Harbi
Vnci Cilt, Çanakkale Cephesi Harekati (Amfibi Harekat)* ['First World War, Turkish War,
Gallipoli Front Operations, Amphibious Operations'] (Ankara: Genelkurmay Basımevi,
1979), 61–2. Hereafter Yiğitgüden et al, *Gallipoli Front Amphibious Operations.*
4. Saral et al, *Gallipoli Front Operations, June 1914–April 1915,* 96–101.
5. III Corps Orders, 8 November 1914, ATASE Archive 3964, Record H-5, File 1-10/11.
6. 26nci Piyade Alay Tarihçesi, 7, ATASE Archive, Cabinet 91, Record 29, Shelf 2, File 169.
7. 9th Division Orders, 19 August 1914, ATASE Archive 5025, Record 27, File 1/86–88, Ek-1.
8. 26nci Piyade Alay Tarihçesi, 8, ATASE Archive, Cabinet 91, Record 29, Shelf 2, File 169.
9. 27ncu Piyade Alay Tarihçesi, 7, ATASE Archive, Cabinet 91, Record 29, Shelf 2, File 170.
10. Ibid., 8.
11. 27th Infantry Regiment Order No. 5, 10 September 1914, reprinted in Binbaşı Halis
Bey (Ataksor), *Çanakkale Raporu* (Istanbul: Arma Yayınları, nd [reprint of 1975
edition]), 42–43.
12. 27ncu Piyade Alay Tarihçesi, 7, ATASE Archive 91/2.
13. Detachment Orders No. 8, 10, and 18, 1914, reprinted in Halis Bey (Ataksor),
Çanakkale Raporu, 46–58.
14. 27ncu Piyade Alay Tarihçesi, 7, ATASE Archive 91/2.
15. 25nci Piyade Alay Tarihçesi, unpublished staff study (Lütfi Doğanci) 1977, 7, ATASE
Library, Record 26-485.
16. 9ncu Topçu Alay Tarihçesi, unpublished staff study (Mete Şefik) 1970, ATASE Library,
Record 26-346.

17. Interview with General Askir Arkayan, undated, Liddle Collection (LC), Box Gall 216/1.
18. Interview with Lieutenant-Colonel Abil Savasman, July 1972, LC, Box TU 01, item 4, tape 49.
19. Robin Prior, *Gallipoli, The End of the Myth* (New Haven: Yale University Press, 2009), 45.
20. Churchill, *The World Crisis, Vol II*, 187–189.
21. Prior, *Gallipoli, The End of the Myth*, 43–50.
22. Churchill, *The World Crisis, Vol II*, 215.
23. Ibid., 215–17.
24. Clews, *Churchill's Dilemma*, 219.
25. Cassar, *Kitchener's War*, 142.
26. Aspinall-Oglander, *Military Operations, Gallipoli, Vol I*, 84–85.
27. Ibid., 87–88
28. Kitchener's instructions to Sir Ian Hamilton, 13 March 1915, reproduced in Aspinall-Oglander, *Military Operations, Vol I, Maps and Appendices*, 1–4.
29. Aspinall-Oglander, *Military Operations, Gallipoli, Vol I*, 90.
30. Sir Ian Hamilton, *Gallipoli Diary, Volume I* (New York: George H. Doran Company, 1920), 16.
31. Churchill, *The World Crisis, Vol II*, 220–222.
32. Ibid., 221–222.
33. Ibid., 222–223.
34. Ibid., 223–224.
35. Ibid., 223.
36. Hamilton, *Gallipoli Diary, Vol I*, 21–23.
37. Ibid., 224.
38. Saral et al, *Gallipoli Front Operations, June 1914–April 1915*, 113.
39. See Prior, *Gallipoli, The End of the Myth*, 44–59. Professor Robin Prior's Chapter 4 is particularly valuable in understanding the difficulties in and probabilities of hitting targets from the battleships available at the Dardanelles.
40. Ibid., 277.
41. Ibid., 242.
42. Commander, 9th Division to Commander, Çanakkale Fortress, 5 March 1915, ATASE Archive 4618, Record 43, File 57, reproduced in T. C. Genelkurmay Başkanlığı, *Askeri Tarih Belgeleri Dergisi 38/88*, 11–14.
43. Ibid., 6–140.
44. Ibid., 148–165.
45. Ibid., 148–154.
46. Saral et al, *Gallipoli Front Operations, June 1914–April 1915*, 316.
47. Ibid., 211.
48. Orders No. 129, Çanakkale Fortress Command, 19 March 1915, ATASE Archive 4701, Record H-1, File 1-181, cited in Saral et al, *Gallipoli Front Operations, June 1914–April 1915*, 279. The Silver Combat Medal of Distinction was awarded to Colonel Talat (commander, 2nd Heavy Artillery Regiment), Colonel Şükrü (Engineer Corps), Lieutenant-Colonel Wossidlo (German advisor) and Major Nuri (Signal Corps). The Silver Combat Medal of Merit was awarded to Lieutenant Ali (fortress command headquarters), Captain Hilmi (commander, Rumeli Mecidiye Fort), Lieutenant Nazmi (Rumeli Hamidiye Fort), Captain Herschel (German commander, Anadolu Hamidiye Fort) and Platoon Commander Remzi (Dardanos Fort).
49. Expending their heavy shells at the same rate of the 18 March engagement, the

Ottomans had enough shells for five more days of battle without even firing their 20/22 calibre heavy guns.

50. Saral et al, *Gallipoli Front Operations, June 1914–April 1915*, 211–212.
51. Arthur J. Marder, 'The Dardanelles: Post-Mortem', in *From The Dreadnought to Scapa Flow* (London: Oxford University Press, 1965), vol. 2.
52. Ibid., 263. Professor Marder's account of the conception, planning, execution, and post-mortem of the naval attack is the finest in print and has stood the test of time.
53. Sir Julian S. Corbett, *History of the Great War based on Official Documents, Naval Operations, vol. 2.* (London: Longmans, Green and Co, 1921), 224.
54. Saral et al, *Gallipoli Front Operations, June 1914–April 1915*, Map 1. Some western histories show the numerical serials erroneously numbered from north to south, an example is Corbett, *Naval Operations, vol. 2*, map facing 230.
55. Ibid., 38–40.
56. Marder, *From The Dreadnought to Scapa Flow*, 248–250; 254–255. Professor Marder noted that reinforcements were dispatched immediately to replace losses. His analysis of the reorganized minesweeping arrangements using faster ships and better techniques planned for a subsequent assault is noteworthy and indicates the intellectual energy the navy was expending to solve the tactical problems involving the enemy defences.

CHAPTER FOUR

1. Martin Samuels, *Command or Control? Command, Training and Tactics in the British and German Armies, 1888–1918* (London: Frank Cass, 1995), 47.
2. A. F. Becke, *Order of Battle of Divisions, Part 4* (reprint of 1944 edition by Uckfield, UK: The Naval & Military Press Ltd, 2007), 179–183, 185–191.
3. Martin Middlebrook, *Your Country Needs You, Expansion of British Army Infantry Divisions 1914–1918* (Barnsley, UK: Leo Cooper, 2000), 21–112.
4. *Field Service Regulations (1909) Part 1 (Operations)* (FSR I), accessed at https://archive.org/details/pt1fieldservicer00greauoft
5. Christopher Pugsley, 'We have Been Here Before: the Evolution of the Doctrine of Decentalised Command in the British Army 1905–1989', *Sandhurst Occasional Papers No 9* (2011), 12.
6. See the work of Tim Travers, *The Killing Ground, the British Army, the Western Front & the Emergence of Modern War 1900–1918* (London: Allen & Unwin, 1987).
7. See the work of Nikolas Gardner, *Trial by Fire, Command and the British Expeditionary Force in 1914* (Westport, CT: Praeger, 2003).
8. Martin Samuels, *Command or Control? Command, Training and Tactics in the British and German Armies, 1888–1918* (London: Frank Cass, 1995), 5.
9. Ibid.
10. T. C. Genelkurmay Başkanlığı, *Birinci Dünya Harbinde Türk Harbi Kafkas Cephesi 3ncu Ordu Harekati, Cilt I* (Ankara: Genelkurmay Basımevi, 1993), 52 and, in English, Erickson, *Defeat in Detail*, 336–340.
11. General Orders (*Ordu Emirnamesi*), No. 1, reprinted in T. C. Genelkurmay Başkanlığı, *Türk Silahlı Kuvvetleri Tarihi (1908–1920)*, 405–411.
12. Ibid., 405 and, in English, Erickson, *Defeat in Detail*, 336.
13. General Orders No. 9, 24 May 1914, reprinted in T. C. Genelkurmay Başkanlığı, *Türk Silahlı Kuvvetleri Tarihi (1908–1920)*, 327–328.
14. The modern Turkish General Staff Archives in Ankara contain thousands of sequential

war diaries from regiment through army group level, attesting to the thoroughness and integrity of the Ottoman Army's war diary system.

15. Genelkurmay Başkanlığı, *Türk Silahlı Kuvvetleri Tarihi (1908–1920)*, 329–330.

16. The material for the following biographical information on Esat was assembled from İsmet Görgülü, *Türk Harp Tarıhı Derslerinde Adı Geçen Komutanlar* (Istanbul: Harp Akademileri Yayını, 1983), 298–300.

17. For a detailed discussion of Esat's defence of Yanya, see T. C. Genelkurmay Başkanlığı, *Türk Silahli Kuvvetleri Tarihi, Balkan Harbi (1912–1913), IIIncü Cilt, 2nci Kisim, Garp Ordusu Vardar Ordusu, Yunan Cephesi Harekati* (Ankara: Genelkurmay Basımevi, 1993), 518–672 and Erickson, *Defeat in Detail*, 293–316.

18. Change of command directives, 6 January 1914, Prime Minister Archives, Archive Number 6, reprinted in Genelkurmay Başkanlığı, *Türk Silahli Kuvvetleri Tarihi (1908–1920)*, 195–196.

19. T. C. Genelkurmay Başkanlığı, *Türk Istiklal Harbi'ne Kalilan Tümen ve Daha Ust Kademelerdeki Komutanların Biyografileri* (Ankara: Genelkurmay Basımevi, 1989), 124–126. The biographical material for Lieutenant-Colonel Kazım comes from this source.

20. Paul-Marie de la Gorce, *The French Army, A Military-Political History* (London: Weidenfeld and Nicolson, 1963), 50–59.

21. Colonel Henry Wilson, British Army DMO (October 1913).

22. NARA, General Information on the Gallipoli peninsula, Captain Williams to Chief of Staff, War College Division, 6 Nov 1915, M 1271, File 8544-1, Dispatch 446. Williams had numerous detailed discussions with Turkish officers on the peninsula throughout the campaign.

23. Ibid.

CHAPTER FIVE

1. Vice-Admiral de Robeck to Admiralty, 18 March 1915, reproduced in Churchill, *The World Crisis, Vol II*, 233–234.

2. Vice-Admiral de Robeck to Admiralty, 18 March 1915, reproduced in Churchill, *The World Crisis, Vol II*, 234.

3. Hamilton, *Gallipoli Diary*, 41.

4. Robert Rhodes James, *Gallipoli* (New York: Macmillan, 1965), 67.

5. Vice-Admiral de Robeck to Admiralty, 23 March 1915, reproduced in Churchill, *The World Crisis, Vol II*, 236–237.

6. Hankey, *The Supreme Command*, 292–293.

7. Ibid., 293–294.

8. Ibid., 294.

9. Hamilton, *Gallipoli Diary*, 57–60.

10. Kitchener to Hamilton, 3 April 1915, attachment to MEF War Diary, AWM RCD/G1002281.

11. MEF GHQ, MEF War Diary, 12.20pm, 4 April, AWM RCD/G1002280.

12. MEF GHQ, MEF War Diary, 5.00pm, 8 April, AWM, AWM RCD/G1002280.

13. Hamilton to Kitchener, 8.00pm, 10 April 1915, attachment to MEF War Diary, AWM RCD/G1002281.

14. MEF GHQ, Force Order No. 1, 13 April 1915, attachment to MEF War Diary, AWM RCD/G1002281.

15. Hamilton, *Gallipoli Diary*, 96.

16. Ibid., 97.
17. Ibid., 98. This clarifies Hamilton's thinking about how long it would take to seize the initial objectives.
18. Instructions for GOC A&NZ Army Corps, MEF GHQ, 13 April 1915, attachment to MEF War Diary, AWM RCD/G1002281.
19. Instructions for the Helles Covering Force, MEF GHQ, 19 April 1915, attachment to MEF War Diary, AWM RCD/G1002281.
20. Aspinall-Oglander, *Military Operations, Gallipoli, Vol I*, 127.
21. GOC MEF to d'Amade, GHQ MEF, 18 April 1915, attachment to MEF War Diary, AWM RCD/G1002281.
22. Kitchener to Hamilton, 12.15pm, 19 April 1915, attachment to MEF War Diary, AWM RCD/G1002281.
23. Instructions to GOC Corps Expéditionnaire Francois D'Orient, 21 April 1915, GHQ MEF, attachment to MEF War Diary, AWM RCD/G1002281.
24. Suggested action in the event of the 29th Division, or the Australians failing to establish themselves ashore, MEF GHQ, 24 April 1915, attachment to MEF War Diary, AWM RCD/G1002281.
25. Ottoman General Hqs Orders, 9 March 1915, ATASE Archives 4669, Record H-12, File 1-85, cited in Saral et al, *Gallipoli Front Operations, June 1914–April 1915*, 171.
26. Saral et al, *Gallipoli Front Operations, June 1914–April 1915*, 212.
27. General Hqs message, 22 March 1915, ATASE Archive 4669, Record H-13, File 1-19, and General Hqs message, 23 March 1915, ATASE Archive 4669, Record H-13, File 1-2, cited in Saral et al, *Gallipoli Front Operations, June 1914–April 1915*, 213–214.
28. Ottoman Army headquarters Number 2793 to Ottoman general staff, 7.45am, 25 March 1915, ATASE Archive 180, Record 774, File 1-5, reproduced in T. C. Genelkurmay Başkanlığı, *Askeri Tarih Belgeleri Dergisi 38/88*, 18-20.
29. Orders (top secret), 26 March 1915, ATASE Archive 180, Record 774, File 1-6, cited in Saral et al, *Gallipoli Front Operations, June 1914–April 1915*, 218.
30. Carl Mühlmann, *Der Kampf un die Dardanellen 1915* (Berlin: Drud und Berlag von Gerhard Gtalling, 1927), 82–83 and Liman von Sanders, *Five Years in Turkey*, 59–60.
31. Provisional Corps Orders, 1 April 1915, ATASE Archive 3474, Folder H-1, File 1-21, cited in Saral et al, *Gallipoli Front Operations, June 1914–April 1915*, 226.
32. Provisional Corps Orders, 5 April 1915, ATASE Archive 3474, Folder H-3, File 2-5 & 2-6, cited in Saral et al, *Gallipoli Front Operations, June 1914–April 1915*, 227.
33. Fifth Army Orders, 19 April 1915, ATASE Archive 3474, Folder H-3, File 2-14, cited in Saral et al, *Gallipoli Front Operations, June 1914–April 1915*, 234–234.
34. Fifth Army Orders, 7 April 1915, ATASE Archive 3474, Folder H-4, File 2-19, reproduced in Saral et al, *Gallipoli Front Operations, June 1914–April 1915*, 228–230.
35. Yiğitgüden et al, *Gallipoli Front Amphibious Operations*, 8–10.
36. Liman von Sanders, *Five Years in Turkey*, 61. This myth was perpetuated by all subsequent western writers, for example Churchill, *The World Crisis*, 412; Alan Moorehead, *Gallipoli*, New York: Harper & Row, 1956, 104; and James, *Gallipoli*, 71. For a more recent example see Travers, *Gallipoli 1915* (Stroud, UK: Tempus, 2001), 38–39. Travers stated that the Ottoman defensive structure scattered the troops too widely for an effective defence.
37. Ibid.
38. Saral et al, *Gallipoli Front Operations, June 1914–April 1915*, Kroki (Overlay) 14.
39. Ibid., Kroki (Overlay) 15.

40. The details of the Cape Helles landings may be found in Aspinall-Oglander, *Military Operations, Gallipoli, Vol I*, 201–251.
41. Aspinall-Oglander, *Military Operations, Gallipoli, Vol I*, 201–215.
42. Hamilton, *Gallipoli Diary, Vol I*, 126–128.
43. GHQ MEF, MEF War Diary, Entries between 4.00am and 7.30pm, 25 April 1915, AWM RCD/G1002280.
44. Ibid.
45. Tim Travers, *Gallipoli 1915*, 61.
46. C. E. W. Bean, *The Story of ANZAC. From the outbreak of the war to the end of the first phase of the Gallipoli Campaign, May 4, 1915, Vol I* (reprint of 1921 edition, St Lucia, Queensland, 1981), 245–303.
47. See Edward J. Erickson, *Ottoman Army Effectiveness in World War I, A Comparative Study* (Abingdon, UK: Routledge, 2007), 36. See also for the best commentary on Sinclair-MacLagan's actions, Chris Roberts, *The Landing at Anzac 1915* (Canberra: Army History Unit, 2013), 84–94.
48. Roberts, *The Landing at Anzac 1915*, 124–130.
49. Hamilton, *Gallipoli Diary, Vol I*, 142–144.
50. 9th Division Orders, 5.55am, 25 April 1915, ATASE Archive, Record H-10, File 1-73.
51. Yiğitgüden et al, *Gallipoli Front Amphibious Operations,* 30.
52. Ibid., 32.
53. Liman von Sanders, *Five Years in Turkey*, 64.
54. III Corps Orders, 10.10am, 25 April 1915, full text copy reprinted in Yiğitgüden et al, *Gallipoli Front Amphibious Operations*, 32.
55. Fifth Army Orders to XV Corps, 12.00pm, 25 April 1915, ATASE Archive 3474, Record H-3, File 3-32, reproduced in Yiğitgüden et al, *Gallipoli Front Amphibious Operations*, 65.
56. Fifth Army report, 5.00pm, 25 April 1915, ATASE Archive 3474, Record H-3, File 3-32, reproduced in Yiğitgüden et al, *Gallipoli Front Amphibious Operations*, 65.
57. See for example Message Number 3486, Fifth Army headquarters to Enver Pasha, 26 April 1915, ATASE Archive 180, Record 776, File 4/4-1, reproduced in Genelkurmay Başkanlığı, *Askeri Tarih Belgeleri Dergisi 38/88*, 32–34. This message, concerning the army's actions during the afternoon of 25 April was sent at 1.50am, acknowledgement was received at 3.35am and it was passed to the duty officer at 4.50am.
58. See for example Intelligence Directorate, Ottoman general staff to commander, Fifth Army, 26 April 1915, ATASE Archive 180, Record 777, File 7-23, reproduced in Genelkurmay Başkanlığı, *Askeri Tarih Belgeleri Dergisi 38/88*, 34–36.
59. Ibid., 32–33.
60. 9th Division Orders, 5.55am, 25 April 1915, ATASE Archive 4836, Record H-10, File 1-73.
61. 9th Division Orders, 25 April 1915, ATASE Archive 4836, Record H-11, File 1-19.
62. Haluk Oral, *Gallipoli Through Turkish Eyes 1915* (translated by Amy Spangler) (Istanbul: Türkiye İş Bankası Kültür Yayınları, 2007), 58 and ATASE Archive 5026, Record 28, File 1-12, Combat Report, 27th Infantry Regiment.
63. T. C. Genelkurmay Başkanlığı, *Birinci Dunya Harbinde Türk Harbi Vncu, Çanakkale Cephesi Harekati, 1nci, 2nci, 3ncu Kitaplarin Özetlenmiş Tarihi* (Ankara: Genelkurmay Basımevi, 2002) 69.
64. Yiğitgüden et al, *Gallipoli Front Amphibious Operations*, 265.
65. 25nci Piyade Alay Tarihçesi, unpublished staff study (Doğanci), 12, ATASE Library, Record 26-485.
66. MEF GHQ, MEF War Diary, 4.32pm, 28 April 1915, AWM RCD/G1002280.

67. MEF GHQ, MEF War Diary, 6.25am, 26 April 1915, AWM RCD/G1002280.
68. ANZAC GHQ, ANZAC War Diary, 26 April 1915, AWM RCD/G1009980.
69. Fifth Army message to Ministry of War, 1.50am, 26 April 1915, ATASE Archive 180, Record 776, File 4/4-1.
70. Yiğitgüden et al, *Gallipoli Front Amphibious Operations*, 127.
71. Combat Orders, 9th Division, 28 April 1915, ATASE Archive 4836, Record H-11, File 1-27.
72. Aspinall-Oglander, *Military Operations, Gallipoli, Vol I*, 282.
73. MEF GHQ, MEF War Diary, 5.30pm, 28 April 1915, AWM RCD/G1002280.
74. Cassar, *The French and the Dardanelles*, 120–121.
75. Ibid., 121.
76. Ibid., 122–123.
77. Hamilton, *Gallipoli Diary, Vol I*, 183.
78. MEF GHQ, MEF War Diary, 11.53am, 29 April 1915, AWM RCD/G1002281.
79. MEF GHQ, MEF War Diary, 9.15am, 29 April 1915, AWM RCD/G1002281.

CHAPTER SIX

1. Fifth Army Orders to III Corps, 28/29 April 1915, ATASE Archive 4836, Record H-10, File 1-86, cited in Yiğitgüden et al, *Gallipoli Front Amphibious Operations*, 327.
2. Yiğitgüden et al, *Gallipoli Front Amphibious Operations*, 328.
3. Ibid., 333–334.
4. Yiğitgüden et al, *Gallipoli Front Amphibious Operations*, 346.
5. Ibid., 348–349.
6. Ibid., 353.
7. Ibid.
8. Ibid., 360.
9. Ibid., 393–365.
10. Ibid., 368–369.
11. Attack Order, Southern Group, 3 May 1915, quoted from Remzi Yiğitgüden, *Çanakkale Cephesi* (Ankara: ATASE Dossier 51, nd) 2336–2337, and reproduced in Yiğitgüden et al, *Gallipoli Front Amphibious Operations*, 366.
12. Ibid.
13. Yiğitgüden et al, *Gallipoli Front Amphibious Operations*, 382–383.
14. Ibid., 389.
15. Ibid., 394–395.
16. Fifth Army strength reports 25 April 1915, Çizelge 1 (Table 1), reproduced in Yiğitgüden et al, *Gallipoli Front Amphibious Operations*, 442.
17. Ottoman General Staff to Fifth Army, 4 May 1915, ATASE Archive 3964, Record H-171, File 1-14, quoted in Yiğitgüden et al, *Gallipoli Front Amphibious Operations*, 395.
18. Ibid., 396.
19. Aspinall-Oglander, *Military Operations, Gallipoli, Vol I*, 316–317.
20. Kitchener to Hamilton, 11.30am, 4 May 1915, attachment to MEF War Diary, AWM RCD/G1004174.
21. MEF GHQ, Force Order No. 5, 4 May 1915, attachment to MEF War Diary, AWM RCD/G1004174.
22. MEF GHQ, MEF War Diary, 4 May 1915, AWM RCD/G1004172.
23. MEF GHQ, MEF War Diary, 6 May 1915, AWM RCD/G1004172.

24. Aspinall-Oglander, *Military Operations, Gallipoli, Vol I*, 320–328.
25. Aspinall-Oglander, *Military Operations, Gallipoli, Vol I*, 328–332.
26. MEF GHQ, Force Order No. 6, 7 May 1915, attachment MEF War Diary, AWM RCD/G1004174.
27. Ismet Görgülü, *On Yıllık Harbin Kadrosu 1912–1922* (Ankara: Türk Tarih Kurum Basımevi, 1993), 70–71.
28. MEF GHQ, Force Order No. 8, 11 May 1915, attachment to MEF War Diary, AWM RCD/G1004174.
29. MEF GHQ, MEF War Diary entries from 14–20 May 1915, AWM RCD/G1004172.
30. Aspinall-Oglander, *Military Operations, Gallipoli, Vol I*, 360–365.
31. Churchill, *The World Crisis, Vol II*, 364–371 and Hankey, *The Supreme Command, Vol I*, 335–337.
32. Birdwood to Hamilton, GHQ ANZAC, 13 May 1915, attachment to MEF War Diary, AWM RCD/G1004174.
33. See Hamilton's marginalia on Birdwood to Hamilton, GHQ ANZAC, 13 May 1915, attachment to MEF War Diary, AWM RCD/G1004174.
34. Birdwood to Hamilton, GHQ ANZAC, 16 May 1915, attachment to MEF War Diary, AWM RCD/G1004175.
35. ATASE Archive 3474, Record H-5, File 2-30, General Headquarters to Commander, Fifth Army, 13 May 1915, reproduced in T. C. Genelkurmay Başkanlığı, *Çanakkale Cephesi Harekati (Amfibi Harekati)*, 180–181.
36. Colonel Süleyman Askeri was a well-known guerrilla commander of the Ottoman Teşkilat-ı Mahsusa, who led irregular forces in western Thrace after the Balkan Wars and who was then commanding in Mesopotamia against the British. He was also a member of the inner circle of the CUP (Young Turk) party. Badly wounded in action against the British, Süleyman Askeri committed suicide in mid-April 1915.
37. 'Operations', Headquarters Northern Group to Fifth Army, 14 May 1915, ATASE Archive 3474, Record H-6, File 3-16, reproduced in Yiğitgüden et al, *Gallipoli Front Amphibious Operations*, 185–187.
38. Fifth Army Orders, 11.15am, 17 May 1915, ATASE Archive 3474, Record H-6, File 3-24, reproduced in Yiğitgüden et al, *Gallipoli Front Amphibious Operations*, 184.
39. Report from Commander 19th Division to Northern Group, 17 May 1915, ATASE Archive 3474, Record H-6, File 3-15, reproduced in Yiğitgüden et al, *Gallipoli Front Amphibious Operations*, 187–188.
40. Fifth Army Orders to Northern Group, 1.50pm, 17 May 1915, ATASE Archive 3474, Record H-6, File 3-30, reproduced in Yiğitgüden et al, *Gallipoli Front Amphibious Operations*, 191–192.
41. Corps Order No. 15, Northern Group, 8.00pm, 18 May 1915, ATASE Archive 3964, Record H-22, File 1-12, reproduced in Yiğitgüden et al, *Gallipoli Front Amphibious Operations*, 193–194. Esat's Northern group retained the numbered corps orders system of his III Corps headquarters.
42. Yiğitgüden et al, *Gallipoli Front Amphibious Operations*, 195.
43. Ibid., 198.
44. Combat Report from 2 Div to Northern Group, 05.10am, 18 May 1915, ATASE Archive 3964, Record H-2, File 1-7 reproduced in Yiğitgüden et al, *Gallipoli Front Amphibious Operations*, 201.
45. Yiğitgüden et al, *Gallipoli Front Amphibious Operations*, see 205–209 for a complete discussion of these events.

46. Report from Northern Group to Fifth Army, 11.20am, 19 May 1915, ATASE Archive 3964, Record H-23, File 1-11, reproduced in Yiğitgüden et al, *Gallipoli Front Amphibious Operations*, 210–211.
47. Fifth Army Report Divisional Losses, 19 May 1915, ATASE Archive 3474, Record H-14, File 5-38, reproduced in Yiğitgüden et al, *Gallipoli Front Amphibious Operations*, 211.
48. See Aspinall-Oglander, *Military Operations; Gallipoli, Vol II*, 20–22 for a complete version of how the ceasefire came into being. The Turkish official history treats the incident with a single paragraph but notes that the ceasefire was welcomed because the constant sight of such a large number of Ottoman dead in front of their own trenches caused a severe morale problem for the Northern Group.
49. MEF GHQ, MEF War Diary, 17 May 1915, AWM RCD/G1004173.
50. Cassar, *The French and the Dardanelles*, 122–123.
51. MEF GHQ, Force Order No. 16, 24 May 1915, attachment to MEF War Diary AWM RCD/G1004173.
52. MEF GHQ, MEF War Diary, 29 May 1915, AWM RCD/G1004173.
53. Army Corps Order No. 1, 1 June 1915, attachment to MEF War Diary AWM RCD/G1004177.
54. MEF GHQ, Instructions to General Officers Commanding Corps, 2 June 1915, attachment to MEF War Diary AWM RCD/G1004177.
55. Army Corps Order No. 3, 3 June 1915, attachment to MEF War Diary AWM RCD/G1004177.
56. Special Orders, 9th Division, 28 May 1915, ATASE Archive 4836, Record H-17, File 1-4, reproduced in İrfan Tekşüt and Necati Ökse, *Türk Silahi Kuvvetleri Tarihi Osmanli Devri Birinci Dünya Harbinde Türk Harbi Vnci Cilt 3ncu Kitap, Çanakkale Cephesi Harekati (Haziran 1915–Ocak 1916)* ['Turkish Armed Forces History, Ottoman State in the First World War, Turkish War, Gallipoli Front Operations, June 1915–January 1916'] (Ankara: Genelkurmay Basımevi, 1980), 31–32. Hereafter Tekşüt and Ökse, *Gallipoli Front, June 1915–January 1916*.
57. Aspinall-Oglander, *Military Operations; Gallipoli, Vol II*, 41–55.
58. Ibid., 22.
59. Aspinall-Oglander, *Military Operations; Gallipoli, Vol II*, 49–53. Aspinall-Oglander's assertion is based on comments by German Colonel Hans Kannengiesser, who was a 'trustworthy eye witness'. It is unclear what position Kannengiesser served in as he was neither a staff officer in the XV Corps headquarters nor did he command any tactical units at this time.
60. Southern Group combat reports, 5 June 1915, ATASE Archive 3474, Record H-8, File 1-4 and Record H-9, File 6, reproduced in Tekşüt and Ökse, *Gallipoli Front, June 1915–January 1916*, 60–61.
61. 12th Division Order No. 8, 6.30pm 5 June 1915, ATASE Archive 4865, Record H-8, File 1-4 and Record H-6, File 1-5, reproduced in Tekşüt and Ökse, *Gallipoli Front, June 1915–January 1916*, 66.
62. After-action report from Colonel Weber to Fifth Army, 10 June 1915, ATASE Archive 3474, Record H-9, File 6-24, reproduced in Tekşüt and Ökse, *Gallipoli Front, June 1915–January 1916* as Ek 7 (Document 7), 583–585. The discrepancy in reported Ottoman losses for Third Krithia is highlighted in the Turkish official history, which estimated about 9,000 total casualties in three days of combat.
63. For a more complete understanding of how and why Ottoman divisions were able to

maintain combat effectiveness readers may wish to refer to Edward J. Erickson, *Ottoman Combat Effectiveness in World War I: A Comparative Study* (Routledge, 2007).

64. Army Order No. 40, Headquarters Fifth Army, 7 June 1915, ATASE Archive 3474, Record H-9, File 6-7, reproduced in Tekşüt and Ökse, *Gallipoli Front, June 1915–January 1916*, 82.
65. Tekşüt and Ökse, *Gallipoli Front, June 1915–January 1916*, 83–84.
66. Weber to division commanders, 7.30pm, 8 June 1915, ATASE Archive 4857, Record H-8, File 1-15, cited in Tekşüt and Ökse, *Gallipoli Front, June 1915–January 1916*, 88.
67. Liman von Sanders to Enver, 17 June 1915, ATASE Archive 3474, Record H-10, File 1-9, reproduced in Tekşüt and Ökse, *Gallipoli Front, June 1915–January 1916*, 587.
68. Enver to Liman von Sanders, 17 June 1915, ATASE Archive 3474, Record H-10, File 1-5, reproduced in Tekşüt and Ökse, *Gallipoli Front, June 1915–January 1916*, 589.
69. Hankey, *The Supreme Command, Vol I*, 339–341.
70. Ibid.
71. Aspinall-Oglander, *Military Operations, Gallipoli, Vol II*, 67–68
72. VIII Army Corps to GHQ, 23 June 1915, attachment to MEF War Diary AWM RCD/G1004178.
73. See for example, Kitchener to Hamilton, 23 June 1915, attachment to MEF War Diary AWM RCD/G1004178.
74. Aspinall-Oglander, *Military Operations, Gallipoli, Vol II*, 72.
75. Secret cipher Southern Group to Fifth Army, 20 June 1915, ATASE Archive 3474, Record H-10, File 1-47, reproduced in Tekşüt and Ökse, *Gallipoli Front, June 1915–January 1916* as Ek (Document) 10, 591–593.
76. Tekşüt and Ökse, *Gallipoli Front, June 1915–January 1916*, 122–124.
77. Situation report, 2nd Division, 7.15pm, 21 June 1915, ATASE Archive 4761, Record H-6, File 1-11, reproduced in Tekşüt and Ökse, *Gallipoli Front, June 1915–January 1916*, 130–131.
78. 34th Regiment Situation Report to 2nd Division, 3.40pm, 22 June 1915, ATASE Archive 4761, Record H-6, File 1-13, reproduced in Tekşüt and Ökse, *Gallipoli Front, June 1915–January 1916*, 134–135.
79. Tekşüt and Ökse, *Gallipoli Front, June 1915–January 1916*, 152.
80. Süleyman Şakir, *Cepheden Hatıralar, Altıncı Fırka Çanakkale Harbi'nde* (Ankara: Vadi Yayınları, 2006), translated by Servet Avşar and Hasan Babacan from *Donanma Mecmuası, No. 158–159* (18 March 1918), 32–33.
81. Southern Group orders 12.00pm, 28 June 1915, ATASE Archive 4857, Record H-12, File 1, quoted in Tekşüt and Ökse, *Gallipoli Front, June 1915–January 1916*, 154.
82. Lüftü to commander 11th Division, 4.25pm, 28 June 1915, ATASE Archive 4857, Record H-12, File 1-4, quoted in Tekşüt and Ökse, *Gallipoli Front, June 1915–January 1916*, 155.
83. Weber to Faik, 8.30am, 29 June 1915, ATASE Archive 4857, Record H-12, File 1-11, quoted in Tekşüt and Ökse, *Gallipoli Front, June 1915–January 1916*, 161.
84. II Corps orders, attack order for 29 June, 143 Rakımlı Tepe, 6.00pm, 29 June 1915, ATASE Archive 4857, Record H-12, File 1-13, reproduced in Tekşüt and Ökse, *Gallipoli Front, June 1915–January 1916*, 165–167.
85. Tekşüt and Ökse, *Gallipoli Front, June 1915–January 1916*, 168.
86. After-action report from Major Reşat, 21 August 1915, ATASE Archive 4763, Record H-7, File 1-52, reproduced in Tekşüt and Ökse, *Gallipoli Front, June 1915–January 1916*, 181.
87. Ibid., 193–194.

ENDNOTES

88. See Erickson, *Defeat in Detail*, 131–136 for a thorough description of the artillery command arrangements and dispositions during the Çatalca battles in 1912/13.
89. Tekşüt and Ökse, *Gallipoli Front, June 1915–January 1916*, 195.
90. Ibid., 195–196.
91. Situation report from Lieutenant-Colonel Ismail Hakkı, 5.25am, 5 July 1915, ATASE Archive 4775, Record H-4, File 1-18, reproduced in Tekşüt and Ökse, *Gallipoli Front, June 1915–January 1916*, 196.
92. 5th Division strength returns, 5 July 1915, and 5th Division casualty reports, 6 July 1915, ATASE Archive 3849, Record H-22, Files 1-37, 1–40, reproduced in Tekşüt and Ökse, *Gallipoli Front, June 1915–January 1916*, 206.
93. Report from Staff Captain Nihat to Çanakkale Group Commander, 20 March 1918 (no archival citation), reproduced in Tekşüt and Ökse, *Gallipoli Front, June 1915–January 1916*, 209–210.
94. Ciphered report from Commander, Fifth Army to Enver Pasha, 4.00am, 22 June 1915, ATASE Archive 181, Record H-779, File 4, reproduced in Genelkurmay Başkanlığı, *Askeri Tarih Belgeleri Dergisi 38/88*, 72–73.
95. Ciphered report from Commander, Fifth Army to Enver Pasha, 5.10am, 25 June 1915, ATASE Archive 181, Record H-779, File 4-1, reproduced in Genelkurmay Başkanlığı, *Askeri Tarih Belgeleri Dergisi 38/88*, 79–80.
96. Ciphered report from Commander, Fifth Army to Ottoman general staff, 22 June 1915, ATASE Archive 181, Record H-778, File 105-1, reproduced in Genelkurmay Başkanlığı, *Askeri Tarih Belgeleri Dergisi 38/88*, 76–77.
97. Enver Pasha to Commander, Fifth Army, 6 July 1915, ATASE Archive 3474, Record H-12, File 8-25, reproduced in Tekşüt and Ökse, *Gallipoli Front, June 1915–January 1916*, 211.
98. Ciphered telegram from Ahmet Fevzi, Saros Group to Enver, 2 July 1915, ATASE Archive 181, Record H-779, File 31, reproduced in Genelkurmay Başkanlığı, *Askeri Tarih Belgeleri Dergisi 38/88*, 87.
99. Liman von Sanders to Commander, Northern Group, 7.50pm, 6 July 1915, ATASE Archive 3474, Record H-12, File 8-24, reproduced in Tekşüt and Ökse, *Gallipoli Front, June 1915–January 1916*, 219.
100. Liman von Sanders, *Five Years in Turkey*, 79–82.
101. Southern Group Orders, 11 July 1915, ATASE Archive 4763, Record H-7, File 1-104, reproduced in Tekşüt and Ökse, *Gallipoli Front, June 1915–January 1916*, 228–229.
102. MEF GHQ, MEF War Diary, 2 July 1915, AWM RCD/G1004179.
103. MEF GHQ, Hamilton to Horse Guards, London, 9 July 1915, attachment to MEF War Diary, AWM RCD/G1004181.
104. See GHQ MEF, GHQ to GOC, VIII Corps, 10 July 1915, attachment to MEF War Diary, AWM RCD/G1004181 for an example of this thinking.
105. Aspinall-Oglander, *Military Operations, Gallipoli, Vol II*, 98–103.
106. Ibid.
107. Ibid.
108. MEF GHQ, MEF War Diary, 13 July 1915, AWM RCD/G1004179.
109. Aspinall-Oglander, *Military Operations, Gallipoli, Vol II*, 110–111.
110. MEF GHQ, MEF War Diary, 14 July 1915, AWM RCD/G1004179.
111. Mehmet Vehip to commander, 6th Division, 9.15am, 12 July 1915, ATASE Archive 4821, Record H-22, File 1-29, reproduced in Tekşüt and Ökse, *Gallipoli Front, June 1915–January 1916*, 245.

112. Southern Group Orders, 10.00pm, 12 July 1915, reproduced in Şakir, *Cepheden Hatıralar*, 82–83.
113. Tekşüt and Ökse, *Gallipoli Front, June 1915–January 1916*, 249.
114. Copy of 6th Division Orders sent to commander, Southern Group, 8.00pm, 13 July 1915, reproduced in Şakir, *Cepheden Hatıralar*, 83–84. Şakir's memoirs for the period 12–14 July 1915 contain dozens of group, area, division and regimental orders and messages, making the period one of the most fully documented wartime episodes available in secondary sources.
115. Ibid., 263.
116. Enver Pasha to commander, Fifth Army, 17 July 1915, ATASE Archive 3474, Record H-13, File 9-45, reproduced in Tekşüt and Ökse, *Gallipoli Front, June 1915–January 1916*, 264.
117. Liman von Sanders to Straits Fortress Command, 26 July 1915, ATASE Archive 3474, Record H-14, File 10-7, reproduced in Tekşüt and Ökse, *Gallipoli Front, June 1915–January* 1916267.
118. Tekşüt and Ökse, *Gallipoli Front, June 1915–January 1916*, 269.

CHAPTER SEVEN

1. GOC ANZAC to GOC MEF, 21 July 1915, attachment to MEF War Diary, AWM RCD/G1004181.
2. Aspinall-Oglander, *Military Operations, Gallipoli, Vol II*, 127–129
3. Ibid., 131–137.
4. Ibid., 133.
5. Bean, *The Story of ANZAC, Vol II*, 453–460.
6. Ibid., 461–463
7. Aspinall-Oglander, *Military Operations, Gallipoli, Vol II*, 182–186.
8. Ibid., 186.
9. Hamilton, *Gallipoli Diary, Vol II*, 2.
10. Hamilton to Kitchener, 11.50am, 22 July 1915, attachment to MEF War Diary, AWM RCD/G1004181.
11. MEF GHQ, MEF War Diary, 17 July 1915, AWM RCD/G1004179.
12. Hamilton, *Gallipoli Diary, Vol II*, 22.
13. MEF GHQ, MEF War Diary, 17 July 1915, AWM RCD/G1004180.
14. MEF GHQ, Instructions to IX Corps for Suvla Operations, 22 July 1915, attachment to MEF War Diary AWM RCD/G1004180.
15. Ibid.
16. MEF GHQ, Instructions to IX Corps for Suvla Operations, 29 July 1915, attachment to MEF War Diary AWM RCD/G1004180.
17. Aspinall-Oglander, *Military Operations, Gallipoli, Vol II*, 151.
18. Operations Order No. 1, GHQ IX Corps, 3 August 1915, reproduced in Aspinall-Oglander, *Military Operations, Gallipoli, Volume II Appendices*, 26–33.
19. Aspinall-Oglander, *Military Operations, Gallipoli, Vol II*, 148–158.
20. MEF GHQ, Instructions to IX Corps for Suvla Operations, 29 July 1915, attachment to MEF War Diary AWM RCD/G1004180.
21. Aspinall-Oglander, *Military Operations, Gallipoli, Vol II*, 169.
22. Ibid., 168.
23. Andrew Mango, *Atatürk, The Biography of the Founder of Modern Turkey* (Woodstock &

NY: The Overlook Press, 1999), 151. Other than his assertion to this effect there is little evidence to support Mustafa Kemal's claim. See also Mustafa Kemal, *Anafarta Hatıraları* (Ankara, 1962), reprinted in *Esat Paşa, Çanakkale Savaşı Hatıraları* (Istanbul: Orgun Yayınevi, 2003), 507–508.

24. See Aspinall-Oglander, *Military Operations, Gallipoli, Vol II*, 168–177.
25. Mehmet Vehip to Fifth Army, 4.30pm, 6 August 1915, ATASE Archive 4846, Record H-8, File 4-32, reproduced in Tekşüt and Ökse, *Gallipoli Front, June 1915–January 1916*, 314–315.
26. Mehmet Vehip to Fifth Army, 6.55pm, 7 August 1915, ATASE Archive 4350, Record H-5, File 4-38, reproduced in Tekşüt and Ökse, *Gallipoli Front, June 1915–January 1916*, 321–322.
27. Fifth Army to Southern Group, 11.30 am, 7 August 1915, ATASE Archive 4350, Record H-5, File 4-35, quoted in Tekşüt and Ökse, *Gallipoli Front, June 1915–January 1916*, 323.
28. Liman von Sanders to Southern Group, 2.25pm, 7 August 1915, ATASE Archive 4350, Record H-5, File 4-36, reproduced in Tekşüt and Ökse, *Gallipoli Front, June 1915– January 1916*, 324.
29. Esat Pasha, *Çanakkale Şavası Hatıraları*, 187–189.
30. See Bean, *The Story of ANZAC, Vol II*, 497–566.
31. See Aspinall-Oglander, *Military Operations, Gallipoli*, Vol II, 178–181.
32. Fifth Army to von Usedom, 26 July 1915, ATASE Archive 3474, Record H-14, File 1-17 quoted in Tekşüt and Ökse, *Gallipoli Front, June 1915–January 1916*, 330.
33. Görgülü, *On Yıllık Harbin Kadrosu*, 88.
34. Tekşüt and Ökse, *Gallipoli Front, June 1915–January 1916*, 335–337.
35. Ibid., 337. This conflicts with what Major Zeki told C. E. W. Bean in 1919, which was that Tevfik's death occurred 'on the second night of fighting or third morning'. See C. E. W. Bean, *Gallipoli Mission*, (Canberra: Australian War Memorial, 1952), 191.
36. Report by Colonel Rüştü forwarded by Commander Northern Group to Commander Fifth Army, 7 August 1915, ATASE Archive 3402, Record H-72, File 10-25, reproduced in TCGB, *Askeri Tarih Belgeleri Dergisi 38/88*, 100–101.
37. Liman von Sanders to Enver, 7 August 1915, ATASE Archive 3474, Record H-15, File 11-1, quoted in Tekşüt and Ökse, *Gallipoli Front, June 1915–January 1916*, 337–338.
38. Commander 16th Division to Northern Group, 6.00am, 7 August 1915, ATASE Archive 4883, Record H-8, File 1-7, quoted in Tekşüt and Ökse, *Gallipoli Front, June 1915–January 1916*, 338.
39. See also H. B. Danışman, *Gallipoli 1915, Bloody Ridge (Lone Pine) Diary of Lt. Mehmed Fasih*, (Istanbul: Denizler Kitabevi, 2003) for information on and photographs of Lone Pine during the period 11 October to 19 December 1915.
40. Aspinall-Oglander, *Military Operations, Gallipoli, Vol II*, 182–195.
41. Bean, *The Story of ANZAC, Vol II*, 608–623.
42. Aspinall-Oglander, *Military Operations, Gallipoli, Vol II*, 195–200.
43. Combat report from Commander, 1st Battalion, 72nd Regiment, 1.30am, 7 August 1915, ATASE Archive 4936, Record H-25, File 1-3, quoted in Tekşüt and Ökse, *Gallipoli Front, June 1915–January 1916*, 346.
44. Tekşüt and Ökse, *Gallipoli Front, June 1915–January 1916*, Kroki (Map) 39.
45. Commander 19th Division to Commander Northern Group, 5.05am, 7 August 1915,

ATASE Archive 4936, Record H-25, File 1-3, reproduced in Tekşüt and Ökse, *Gallipoli Front, June 1915–January 1916*, 348.
46. Tekşüt and Ökse, *Gallipoli Front, June 1915–January 1916*, 350.
47. Aspinall-Oglander, *Military Operations, Gallipoli, Vol II*, 201–208.
48. Tekşüt and Ökse, *Gallipoli Front, June 1915–January 1916*, 350.
49. See Esat Pasha to Commander Fifth Army, 9.50am, 7 August 1915, ATASE Archive 3402, Record H-72, File 10-17, reproduced in Genelkurmay Başkanlığı, *Askeri Tarih Belgeleri Dergisi 38/88*, 98–99, in which Esat explicitly outlines the enemy attacks on Chunuk Bair and Hill 971 as well his response with the 9th and 19th Divisions.
50. Cemil Conk Paşa, *Çanakkale Hatıraları*, 199.
51. Northern Group orders, Kemalyeri, 11.10am, 7 August 1915, reproduced in Cemil Conk Paşa, *Çanakkale Hatıraları*, 200–201.
52. Commander 4th Division to Commander Northern Group, 3.30pm, 7 August 1915, ATASE Archive 4798, Record H-4, File 1-137, quoted in Tekşüt and Ökse, *Gallipoli Front, June 1915–January 1916*, 353.
53. Tekşüt and Ökse, *Gallipoli Front, June 1915–January 1916*, 354.
54. Aspinall-Oglander, *Military Operations, Gallipoli, Vol II*, 210–212.
55. Tekşüt and Ökse, *Gallipoli Front, June 1915–January 1916*, 355.
56. Commander Fifth Army to Commander Northern Group, 10.10pm, 7 August 1915, ATASE Archive 4798, Record H-2, File 1-103, quoted in Tekşüt and Ökse, *Gallipoli Front, June 1915–January 1916*, 356.
57. Although Liman von Sanders had issued this order at 10.10pm the previous evening copies did not make it through to Cemil until 9.00am, 8 August 1915.
58. Tekşüt and Ökse, *Gallipoli Front, June 1915–January 1916*, 360.
59. Travers, *Gallipoli 1915*, 166–167.
60. Liman von Sanders, *Five Years in Turkey*, 84–85.
61. Professor Travers asserted that the 7th and 12th Divisions 'certainly arrived late on 7 August'. See Travers, *Gallipoli 1915*, 199. However, Ahmet Fevzi's orders of 3.40am, 8 August, place the lead elements of the 12th Division arriving just west of Turşunköyü and the 7th Division just east of Kücük Anafarta. Moreover, Ahmet Fevzi ordered them to send a battalion forward to secure their assembly areas. It is clear from these orders that the main bodies of the divisions could not have closed on their assembly areas until midday 8 August. See Group Orders, Anafarta Group, 3.40am, 8 August 1915, ATASE Archive 4863, Record H-12, File 1-15, reproduced in Tekşüt and Ökse, *Gallipoli Front, June 1915–January 1916*, 403–404.
62. Record of telephone conversation (secret) between Liman von Sanders and the Northern Group, 7.00pm, 8 August 1915, ATASE Archive 4936, Record H-34, File 1-3, reproduced in Tekşüt and Ökse, *Gallipoli Front, June 1915–January 1916*, 361.
63. Oral, *Gallipoli 1915*, 338–339.
64. Ibid., 327.
65. Izzettin Çalışlar, *On Yıllık Savaşın Günlüğü*, edited by Dr Ismet Görgülü (Ankara: KYK, 1999), 104 cited in Oral, *Gallipoli 1915*, 327.
66. Aspinall-Oglander, *Military Operations, Gallipoli, Vol II*, 235–247.
67. Ibid., 245–247.
68. Ibid., 248.
69. Tekşüt and Ökse, *Gallipoli Front, June 1915–January 1916*, 391.
70. Ibid., 251.
71. Ibid., 255–257.

72. Ibid., 282–283.
73. See Aspinall-Oglander, *Gallipoli, Vol II*, 266 for Willmer's report to Fifth Army, 7.00pm, 7 August 1915.
74. Group Orders, Anafarta Group, 3.40am, 8 August 1915, ATASE Archive 4863, Record H-12, File 1-15, reproduced in Tekşüt and Ökse, *Gallipoli Front, June 1915–January 1916*, 403–404.
75. Hankey, *The Supreme Command*, 390–405.
76. Ibid., 399–400.
77. Aspinall-Oglander, *Military Operations, Gallipoli, Vol II*, 277.
78. Ibid., 278.
79. Hamilton, *Gallipoli Diary, Vol II*, 62–64.
80. Aspinall-Oglander, *Military Operations*, Gallipoli, *Vol II*, 280.
81. Ibid., 286.
82. Ibid., 287.
83. Tekşüt and Ökse, *Gallipoli Front, June 1915–January 1916*, 413.
84. These two officers were buried side by side and are remembered with a fine memorial monument in the Büyük Anafarta cemetery. See Gürsel Göncü and Şahin Aldoğan, *Çanakkale Muharebe Alanları Gezi Rehberi (Gallipoli Battlefield Guide)* (Istanbul: MB Yayınevi, 2004), 129.
85. Tekşüt and Ökse, *Gallipoli Front, June 1915–January 1916*, 416.
86. Hamilton, *Gallipoli Diary, Vol II*, 72.
87. Aspinall-Oglander, *Military Operations, Gallipoli, Vol II*, 251–216.
88. Tekşüt and Ökse, *Gallipoli Front, June 1915–January 1916*, 366.
89. Aspinall-Oglander, *Military Operations, Gallipoli, Vol II*, 215–216.
90. Hamilton, *Gallipoli Diary, Vol II*, 79–80.
91. Hamilton to Stopford, 11.25pm, 9 August 1915, reproduced in Aspinall-Oglander, *Military Operations, Gallipoli, Vol II*, 298.
92. Stopford to Hamilton, 10 August 1915, reproduced in Aspinall-Oglander, *Military Operations, Gallipoli, Vol II*, 299–300.
93. Telephonic orders from Fifth Army to Northern Group commander, 3.14pm, 9 August 1915, ATASE Archive 4835, Record H-9, File 1-195, reproduced in Tekşüt and Ökse, *Gallipoli Front, June 1915–January 1916*, 369.
94. Tekşüt and Ökse, *Gallipoli Front, June 1915–January 1916*, 416–417.
95. Orders to 8th Division commander from Anafarta Group commander, 10.20pm, 9 August 1915, ATASE Archive 4835, Record H-9, File 1-195, reproduced in Tekşüt and Ökse, *Gallipoli Front, June 1915–January 1916*, 374.
96. Aspinall-Oglander, *Military Operations, Gallipoli, Vol II*, 303–304.
97. Ibid., 305.
98. Mango, *Atatürk*, 152.
99. Tekşüt and Ökse, *Gallipoli Front, June 1915–January 1916*, 374.
100. Aspinall-Oglander, *Gallipoli, Vol II*, 307.
101. James, *Gallipoli*, 299–300. James asserted that over a 1,000 men died at the Pinnacle and another 1,000 died in the debacle at the Farm within a matter of minutes.
102. MEF GHQ, Hamilton to Stopford, 11 August 1915, attachment to MEF War Diary, AWM RCD/G1017513.
103. Aspinall-Oglander, *Gallipoli, Vol II*, 314.
104. Tekşüt and Ökse, *Gallipoli Front, June 1915–January 1916*, 422.
105. Aspinall-Oglander, *Gallipoli, Vol II*, 320.

106. Ibid., 426–427.
107. Ibid., 428.
108. Ibid., 432.
109. Aspinall-Oglander, *Gallipoli, Vol II*, 325–329.
110. Hamilton to Kitchener, 9 August 1915 and 14 August 1915, quoted in Aspinall-Oglander, *Gallipoli, Vol II*, 325.
111. Aspinall-Oglander, *Gallipoli, Vol II*, 327.
112. ATASE Archive 3474, Record H-16, File 2-23, Telegraph message from Liman von Sanders to Enver Pasha, 16 August 1915 quoted in Tekşüt and Ökse, *Gallipoli Front, June 1915–January 1916*, 437.
113. Tekşüt and Ökse, *Gallipoli Front, June 1915–January 1916*, 438.
114. Saros Group orders, 7.40pm, 17 August 1915, ATASE Archive 3474, Record H-16, File 2-25, quoted in Tekşüt and Ökse, *Gallipoli Front, June 1915–January 1916*, 439.
115. MEF GHQ, Instructions to Major General de Lisle, 15 August 1915, attachment to MEF War Diary, AWM RCD/G1017513.
116. Hamilton to Kitchener, 17 August 1915, quoted in Aspinall-Oglander, *Military Operations, Gallipoli, Vol II*, 336.
117. Aspinall-Oglander, *Military Operations, Gallipoli, Vol II*, 341–342.
118. Tekşüt and Ökse, *Gallipoli Front, June 1915–January 1916*, 450.
119. Ibid., 452.
120. Ibid., 457.
121. Ibid., 453.
122. Ibid., 454.

CHAPTER EIGHT

1. T. S. Eliot, 'The Hollow Men' (1925).
2. Aspinall-Oglander, *Military Operations, Gallipoli, Vol II*, 369.
3. Ibid., 372.
4. Cassar, *The French and the Dardanelles*, 189–190.
5. Ibid., 195.
6. Aspinall-Oglander, *Military Operations, Gallipoli, Vol II*, 376.
7. Ibid., 383.
8. Report to Kitchener, 11 October 1915, quoted in Aspinall-Oglander, *Military Operations, Gallipoli, Vol II*, 384.
9. Hamilton, *Gallipoli Diary, Vol II*, 271–272.
10. Aspinall-Oglander, *Military Operations, Gallipoli, Vol II*, 386.
11. Ibid., 388.
12. Cassar, *The French and the Dardanelles*, 201.
13. Ibid., 202–203.
14. Hamilton to Kitchener, 30 September 1915, reproduced in Hamilton, *Gallipoli Diary, Vol II*, 226.
15. Liman von Sanders to Commander, Anafarta Group, 29 August 1915, ATASE Archive 3474, Record H-17, File 3-25, reproduced in Tekşüt and Ökse, *Gallipoli Front, June 1915–January 1916*, as Ek 15, 612–613.
16. Ibid.
17. Fahri Belen, *Birinci Cihan Harbinde Türk Harbi, 1918 Yılı Hareketleri, Vnci Cilt* (Ankara: Genelkurmay Basımevi, 1967), Ek 1 after 250. This table contains a complete

list of all 62 Ottoman infantry divisions (as well as the five Caucasian infantry divisions) mobilized during the First World War. Belen's table also contains activation and deactivation dates as well as the location of activation or home garrison.

18. Tekşüt and Ökse, *Gallipoli Front, June 1915–January 1916*, 467.

19. Ibid., 472.

20. Ibid., 471.

21. Ibid., 473.

22. Ibid., 474.

23. Ibid., 472.

24. Monro to Kitchener, 31 October 1915, reproduced in Aspinall-Oglander, *Military Operations, Gallipoli, Vol II*, 402–404.

25. Statements by Davies, Byng and Birdwood, 2 November 1915, reproduced in Aspinall-Oglander, *Military Operations, Gallipoli, Vol II*, 405–407.

26. Aspinall-Oglander, *Military Operations, Gallipoli, Vol II*, 409–411.

27. Kitchener to War Committee, 22 November 1915, quoted in Aspinall-Oglander, *Military Operations, Gallipoli, Vol II*, 421–422.

28. Aspinall-Oglander, *Military Operations, Gallipoli, Vol II*, 438–439.

29. Ibid., 475.

30. Ibid., 477.

31. Ibid., 494.

32. The Turkish official history makes the point that had Mustafa Kemal been healthy enough to lead, his active command style would have made the British and ANZAC evacuation much more problematic. See Tekşüt and Ökse, *Gallipoli Front, June 1915–January 1916*, 493–494 for commentary.

33. Tekşüt and Ökse, *Gallipoli Front, June 1915–January 1916*, 494.

34. Aspinall-Oglander, *Gallipoli, Vol. II*, 472–473.

35. Liman von Sanders to Enver Pasha, 8.45am, 9 January 1916, ATASE Archive 3474, Record H-56, File 1-9, reproduced in Tekşüt and Ökse, *Gallipoli Front, June 1915–January 1916*, 499.

36. Orders No. 107, Fifth Army headquarters, 9 January 1916, ATASE Archive 3474, Record H-17, File 1-7, reproduced in Tekşüt and Ökse, *Gallipoli Front, June 1915–January 1916*, 501.

37. *Çanakkale Cephesi Harekati (Haziran 1915–Ocak 1916)*, 502.

SELECT BIBLIOGRAPHY

Archival sources

Ankara: Askeri Tarihı ve Stratejik Etut Başkanlığı (ATASE) – Turkish General Staff
    TGS Archives – archives
    TGS Archives – unpublished staff studies
Ankara: Askeri Tarihı ve Stratejik Etut Başkanlığı Kutuphane (ATASE Library)
    TGS Library Archives – unpublished staff studies
Canberra: Australian War Memorial (AWM)
Kew: United Kingdom National Archives (TNA)
Leeds: Brotherton Library, Liddle Collection (LC)
    Gall 216 – Gallipoli interviews
    TU 01 – Turkish interviews
Washington, DC: National Archives and Records Administration (NARA)
    RG 120, Boxes 5828, 5836 – GHQ, AEF
    RG 353 – US State Department, Internal Affairs, Turkey
    RG 1271, Files 6368, 844, 8759 – War College Division, General Staff
Washington, DC: National Defense University (NDU) Library
    Gallipoli Collection

Printed document collections

Askeri Tarih Belgeleri Dergisi, Auğustos 1989, Yıl 38, Sayı 88. Ankara: Genelkurmay Basımevi, 1989.
Gooch, G. P. and Temperley, Harold (eds.). *British Documents on the Origins of the War 1898–1914, Vol. XI*. London, HMSO, 1926.

Ottoman and German Army training manuals

Hidemati Seferiye Nizamnamesi (Felddienst Ordnung). 1908.
Piyade Talimnamesi (Exerzier-Reglement für die Infanterie). 1906.
Takimin Muharebe Talimi and Bölügün Muharebe Talimi (Beifrage zur Taktischen Ausbildung unser Offiziere). 1904.

Official histories based on official records

Akbay, Cemal. *Birinci Dünya Harbinde Türk Harbi, 1nci Cilt, Osmanli Imparatorlugu'nun Siyası ve Askeri Hazırlıkları ve Harbe Girisi* ['Ottoman Empire Military Mobilisation and Entry into the War']. Ankara: Genelkurmay Basımevi, 1991.

Ari, Kemal. *Birinci Dünya Savası Kronolojisi* ['First World War Chronology']. Ankara: Genelkurmay Basımevi, 1997.

Aspinall-Oglander, C. F. *History of the Great War, based on Official Documents: Military Operations Gallipoli, vol.1 and 2.* London: HMSO, 1924–1930.

Bean, C. E. W. *Official History of Australia in the War of 1914–1918: The Story of ANZAC, vol. 1–2.* Queensland: University of Queensland Press, 1981 (reprint of 1942 edition).

Belen, Fahri. *Birinci Cihan Harbinde Türk Harbi 1914, 1915 Yili Hareketleri, I–V Cilt* ['The Turkish Front in the First World War, Years 1914–1915']. Ankara: Genelkurmay Basımevi, 1965–67 (five volume series).

Çakin, Naci and Orhon, Nafız. *Türk Silahli Kuvvetleri Tarihi, IIIncü Cilt 5nci Kısım (1793–1908)1nci Kitap* ['Turkish Armed Forces History, 1793–1908']. Ankara: Genelkurmay Basımevi, 1978.

Corbett, Sir Julian S. *History of the Great War based on Official Documents, Naval Operations, vol. 2.* London: Longmans, Green and Co, 1921.

Erkal, Şükrü. *Birinci Dünya Harbinde Türk Harbi Vncü, Çanakkale Cephesi Harekati,1nci, 2nci, 3ncü Kitapların Özetlenmiş Tarihi* ['First World War, Turkish War, Gallipoli Front Operations, Condensed History of vol. 1–3']. Ankara: Genelkurmay Basımevi, 2002.

Göyman, İhsan. *Birinci Dünya Harbi IXncü Cilt, Türk Hava Harekatı* ['First World War, Turkish Air Operations']. Ankara: Genelkurrmay Basımevi, 1969.

Iskora, Muharrem Mazlum. *Harp Akademileri Tarihçesi, 1846—1965, Cilt I (2nci Baskı)* ['History of the Staff College, 1846–1965'] Ankara: Genelkurmay Basımevi, 1966.

Karamatu, Selâhattin. *Türk Silahli Kuvvetleri Tarihi, IIIncu Cilt 6ncu Kisim (1908–1920) 1nci Kitap.* ['Turkish Armed Forces History, 1908–1920']. Ankara: Genelkurmay Basımevi, 1971.

Koral, N., Önal, R., Atakan, R., Baycan, N. and Kızılırmak, S. *Türk Silahli Kuvvetleri Tarihi Osmanli Devri Birinci Dünya Harbi Idari Faaliyetler ve Lojistik, Xncu Cilt* ['Turkish Armed Forces History, Ottoman State in the First World War, Administration and Logistics']. Ankara: Genelkurmay Basımevi, 1985.

Ökse, N., Baycan, N. and Sakaryalı, S. *Türk Istiklal Harbi'ne Kalilan Tümen ve Daha Ust Kademelerdeki Komutanların Biyografileri* ['Turkish War of Independence, Biographies of Divisional-level Commanders and Above']. Ankara: Genelkurmay Basımevi, 1989.

Saral, M., Orhon, A. and Erkal, Ş. *Birinci Dünya Harbinde Türk Harbi Vncü Cilt, Çanakkale Cephesi Harekati Inci Kitap (Haziran 1914–Nisan 1915)* ['First World War, Turkish War, Gallipoli Front Operations, June 1914–April 1915']. Ankara: Genelkurmay Basımevi, 1993.

Süer, Hikmet. *Türk Silahli Kuvvetleri Tarihi, Balkan Harbi (1912–1913), II Cilt, 2nci Kısım, 1nci Kitap, Şark Ordusu, Ikinci Çatalca Muharebesi ve Şarkoy Çikmarması* ['Turkish Armed Forces History, Balkan War, Battle of Second Catalca and the Sarkoy Amphibious Invasion']. Ankara: Genelkurmay Basımevi, 1993.

Sükan, Şadi. *Türk Silahli Kuvvetleri Tarihi, Balkan Harbi (1912–1913), II Cilt, Edirne Kalesi Etrafindaki Muhareber* ['Turkish Armed Forces History, Balkan War, Battles around the Edirne Fortress']. Ankara: Genelkurmay Basımevi, 1993.

Tekşüt, İrfan and Ökse, Necati. *Türk Silahi Kuvvetleri Tarihi Osmanli Devri Birinci Dünya Harbinde Türk Harbi Vnci Cilt 3ncu Kitap, Çanakkale Cephesi Harekati (Haziran 1915–*

Ocak 1916) ['Turkish Armed Forces History, Ottoman State in the First World War, Turkish War, Gallipoli Front Operations, June 1915–January 1916']. Ankara: Genelkurmay Basımevi, 1980.

Thomazi, Albay A. *Canakkale Deniz Savası* ['Gallipoli Naval Campaign']. Ankara: Genelkurmay Basımevi, 1997.

Yasar, Raif and Kabasakal, Hüseyin. *Türk Silahli Kuvvetleri Tarihi, Balkan Harbi (1912– 1913), IIIncü Cilt, 2nci Kisim, Garp Ordusu Vardar Ordusu, Yunan Cephesi Harekati* ['Turkish Armed Forces History, Balkan War, Western Army, Vardar Army and Greek Front Operations']. Ankara: Genelkurmay Basimevi, 1993.

Yiğitgüden, R., Saral, M. and Hallı, R. *Birinci Dünya Harbinde Türk Harbi Vnci Cilt, Çanakkale Cephesi Harekati (Amfibi Harekat)* ['First World War, Turkish War, Gallipoli Front Operations, Amphibious Operations']. Ankara: Genelkurmay Basımevi, 1979.

Memoirs and primary sources

Adil, Selhattin. *Çanakkale Hatiraları (1982)* in *Çanakkale Hatiraları, 1. Cilt*. Istanbul: Arma Yayınları, 2001.

Ahmad Izzet Pascha. *Denkwurdigkeiten Des Marschalls Izzet Pascha*. Leipzig: Verlag von K. F. Koehler, 1927.

Aker, Şefik. *Çanakkale-Arıburnu Savaşları ve 27. Alay (1935)* in *Çanakkale Hatiraları, 1. Cilt*. Istanbul: Arma Yayınları, 2001.

Altay, Fahrettın. *Çanakkale Hatıraları (nd)* in *Çanakkale Hatiraları, 2. Cilt*. Istanbul: Arma Yayınları, 2002.

Atatürk, Mustafa Kemal. *Anafartaları Hatıraları (1955)* in *Çanakkale Hatiraları, 1. Cilt*. Istanbul: Arma Yayınları, 2001.

British General Staff. *Armies of the Balkan States, 1914–1916*. Nashville, Tennessee: Battery Press, 1997 (reprint).

Çakmak, Fevzi. *Birinci Dünya Savaşı'nda Doğu Cephesi*, Ankara: Genelkurmay Basımevi, 2005.

Conk, Cemil. *Çanakkale Hatıraları ve Conkbayırı Savaşları (1955)* in *Çanakkale Hatiraları, 2. Cilt*. Istanbul: Arma Yayınları, 2002.

Danişman, H. B. (ed.). *Gallipoli 1915, Bloody Ridge Diary of Lt. Mehmed Fasih*. Istanbul: Denizler Kitabevi, 2003.

Eşref, Ruşen. *Anafartalar Kumandanı Mustafa Kemal ile Mülakak (1930)* in *Çanakkale Hatiraları, 3. Cilt*. Istanbul: Arma Yayınları, 2003.

Gücüyener, Şükrğ Fuad. *Çanakkale'de Kumkale Muharebesi Çanakkale'de Intepe Topçuları (1932)* (Binbaşı Şevki Bey, Taşköprülü Aloş, Bursalı Mehmet Onbası, Çerkeşli Ömer, Aydınlı Ethem Çavuş) in *Çanakkale Hatiraları, 3. Cilt*. Istanbul: Arma Yayınları, 2003.

Güralp, Şerif. *Çanakkale Cephesinden Filistin'e*. Istanbul: Güncel Yayıncılık, 2003.

Halis Bey (Ataksor), Binbaşı . *Çanakkale Raporu*. Istanbul: Arma Yayınları, nd (reprint of 1975 edition).

Hamilton, Sir Ian., *Gallipoli Diary, Volume I and II*. New York: George H. Doran Company, 1920.

Ilgar, İhsan and Uğurlu, Nurer (eds.). *Esat Paşa'nın Çanakkale Savaşı Hatıraları*. Istanbul: Örgün Yayinevi, 2003 (reprint of 1975 edition).

İncescu, Sokrat. *Birinci Dünya Savaşinda, Çanakkale-Arıburnu Hatıralarım* in *Çanakkale Hatiraları, 1. Cilt*. Istanbul: Arma Yayınları, 2001.

Intelligence Section, Cairo, British Army. *Handbook of the Turkish Army, 8th Provisional ed.,*

February 1916. Nashville: Battery Press, 1996 (reprint).Kannengiesser, Hans. *The Campaign in Gallipoli*. London: Hutchinson & Co, undated.

Kemalyeri, Mucip. *Çanakkale Ruhu Nasıl Doğu? (1972)* in *Çanakkale Hatiraları, 3.Cilt*. Istanbul: Arma Yayınları, 2003.

Liman von Sanders, General of Cavalry. *Five Years in Turkey*. London: Bailliere, Tindall & Cox, 1928.

Mühlmann, Carl. *Der Kampf um die Dardanellen 1915*. Berlin: Drud und Berlag von Gerhard Stalling, 1927.

Münim, Mustafa. *Cepheden Cepheye, Çanakkale ve Kanal Seferi Hatıraları*. Istanbul: Arma Yayınları, 1998 (reprint of 1940 edition).

Sabri, Mahmut. *Seddülbahir Muharebeleri ve 26. Alay 3. Tabur Harekatı (1933)* in *Çanakkale Hatiraları, 3. Cilt*. Istanbul: Arma Yayınları, 2003.

Şakir, Süleyman. *Cepheden Hatıralar, Altıncı Fırka Çanakkale Harbi'nde*. Ankara: Vadi Yayınları, 2006.

Sunata, İ. Hakkı. *Gelibolu'dan Kafkaslara, Birinci Dünya Şavası Anılarım*. Istanbul: Kültür Yayınları, 2003.

Tunççapa, M. Şakir. *Çanakkale Muharebeleri Hatıralarım (1958)* in *Çanakkale Hatiraları, 3. Cilt*. Istanbul: Arma Yayınları, 2003.

Secondary sources

Abadan, Yavuz. *Mustafa Kemal ve Ceteçilik*. Istanbul: Varlık Kitabevi, 1972.

Aksakal, Mustafa. *The Ottoman Road to War in 1914: The Ottoman Empire and the First World War*. Cambridge: Cambridge University Press, 2008.

Atatürk, Mustafa Kemal. *Zabit ve Kumandan ile Hasbihal*. Ankara: Türk Tarih Kurumu Basimevi, 1956.

Bean, C. E. W. *Gallipoli Mission*. Australian War Memorial, 1952.

Bond, Brian (ed.). *The First World War and British Military History*. Oxford: Clarendon Press, 1991.

Broadbent, Harvey. *Gallipoli, The Fatal Shore*. Camberwell, Australia: Penguin, 2005.

Carlyon, Les. *Gallipoli*. Sydney: Macmillan, 2001.

Carver, Field Marshal Lord. *The Turkish Front 1914–1918*. London: Sidgwick & Jackson, 2003.

Cassar, George H. *Kitchener's War, British Strategy from 1914 to 1916*. Washington, DC: Brassey's Inc., 2004.

Cebesoy, Ali Fuat. *Sınıf Arkadasım Atatürk*. Istanbul: Kanaat, 1996.

Cecil, Hugh and Liddle, Peter (eds.). *Facing Armageddon, The First World War Experienced*. London: Leo Cooper, 1996.

Chaussaud, Peter and Doyle, Peter. *Grasping Gallipoli: Terrain, Maps and the Failure at the Dardanelles 1915*. Staplehurst: Spellmont, 2005.Churchill, Winston S. *The World Crisis*. New York: Charles Scribner's Sons, 1931.

Clews, Graham T. *Churchill's Dilemma, The Real Story Behind the Origins of the 1915 Dardanelles Campaign*. Santa Barbara, CA: Praeger, 2010.

Cohen, Eliot A. and Gooch, John. *Military Misfortunes, The Anatomy of Failure in War*. New York: The Free Press, 1990.

Cron, Herman. *The Imperial German Army, 1914–1918: Organisation, Structure, Orders-of-Battle*. Solihull: 2002.

Crutwell, C.R.M.F. *A History of the Great War*. Chicago: Chicago review Press, 2001 (reprint of 1936 edition).

Çulcu, Murat. *Ikdam, Gazetesi'nde Çanakkale Cephesi, 3 Kasım 1914 – 3 Şubat 1916 (Cilt 1 & 2)*. Istanbul: Denizler Kitabevi, 2004.

Danışman, H. B. *Gallipoli 1915, Day One Plus...27th Ottoman Inf. Regt. Vs. ANZACS*. Istanbul: Denizler Kitabevi, 2007.

Dolan, Hugh. *36 Days, The Untold Story of the Gallipoli Landings*. Melbourne: Macmillan, 2010.

Doughty, Robert A. *Pyrrhic Victory, French Strategy and Operations in the Great War*. Cambridge, MA: The Belknap Press, 2005.

Erickson, Edward J. *Ordered To Die, A History of the Ottoman Army in the First World War*. Westport, Connecticut: Greenwood Press, 2000.

Erickson, Edward J. *Defeat in Detail, The Ottoman Army in the Balkans 1912–1913*. Westport, Connecticut: Praeger, 2003.Erickson, Edward J. *Ottoman Army Effectiveness in WW1: A Comparative Study* (London: Routledge, 2007).

Erickson, Edward J. *Gallipoli, The Ottoman Campaign*. Barnsley, UK: Pen and Sword, 2010.

Falls, Cyril. *The Great War*. New York: G. P. Putnam's Sons, 1959.

Falls, Cyril. *Armageddon: 1918*. Philadelphia: J. B. Lippincott Company, 1964.

Ferguson, Niall. *The Pity of War*. New York: Basic Books, 1999.

Fewster, K., Başarın, V. and Başarın, H. *Gallipoli, The Turkish Story*. Crows nest, Aust: Allen and Unwin, 1985.

Fosten, D. S. V. and Marrion, R. J. *The British Army 1914–18*. London: Osprey Publishing, Ltd., 1978.

Gardner, Nikolas. *Trial by Fire, Command and the British Expeditionary Force in 1914*. Westport, CT: Praeger, 2003.

Gillon, Captain Stair. *The Story of the 29th Division, A Record of Gallant Deeds*. London: Thomas Nelson and Sons, Ltd., 1925.

Godwin-Austin, A. R. *The Staff and the Staff College*. London: Constable and Company, Ltd., 1927.

Göncü, Gürsel and Aldoğan, Şahin. *Çanakkale Muharebe Alanları Gezi Rehberi (Gallipoli Battlefield Guide)*. Istanbul: MB Yayınevi, 2004.

Gooch, John. *The Plans of War, The General Staff and British Military Strategy c.1900–1916*. New York: John Wiley & Sons, 1974.

Gorce, Paul-Marie de la. *The French Army, A Military-Political History*. London: Weidenfeld and Nicolson, 1963.

Görgülü, İsmet, *Türk Harp Tarihi Derslerinde Adı Geçen Komutanlar*. Istanbul: Harp Akademileri Yayını, 1983.

Görgülü, Ismet. *On Yillik Harbin Kadrosu 1912—1913, Balkan—Birinci Dünya ve Istiklal Harbi*. Ankara: Türk Tarih Kurum Basimevi, 1993.Gudmundsson, Bruce I. *On Artillery*. Westport, Connecticut: Praeger, 1993.

Hall, Richard C. *The Balkan Wars 1912—1913, Prelude to the First World War*. London: Routledge, 2000.

Halpern, Paul G. *The Naval War in the Mediterranean 1914–1918*. Annapolis, MD: Naval Institute Press, 1987.

Hamilton, Nigel. *Master of the Battlefield, Monty's War Years 1942–1944*. New York: McGraw Hill, 1984.

Hankey, Maurice. *The Supreme Command, 1914–1918, Volume One*. London: George Allen and Unwin Limited, 1961.

Hart, Peter. *Gallipoli*. London: Profile Books, 2011.

Haythornthwaite, Phillip J. *Gallipoli 1915*. London: Osprey Press, n.d.

Heller, Joseph. *British Policy Towards The Ottoman Empire*. London: Frank Cass and Company, 1983.

Herrmann, David G. *The Arming of Europe and the Making of the First World War*. Princeton: Princeton University Press, 1996.

Hickey, Michael. *Gallipoli*. London: John Murray, 1995.

Hickey. Michael. *The First World War, The Mediterranean Front 1914–1923*. Oxford: Osprey Publishing, 2002.

Holt, Tonie and Valmai. *Major and Mrs Holt's Battlefield Guide Gallipoli*. Barnsley, South Yorkshire: Leo Cooper, 2000.

Hughes, Daniel J. (ed.). *Moltke on the Art of War, Selected Writings*. New York: Presidio Press, 1993.

James, Robert Rhodes. *Gallipoli*. New York: Macmillan, 1965.

Johnstone, Tom. *Orange, Green and Khaki, The Story of the Irish Regiments in the Great War, 1914–18*. Dublin: Gill and Macmillan Ltd, 1992.

Kannengiesser, Hans. *The Campaign in Gallipoli* in 1928. London: Hutchinson, 1928.

Keegan, John. *The First World War*. New York: Alfred A. Knopf, 1999.

Kent, Marian (ed.). *The Great Powers and the End of the Ottoman Empire*. London: George Allen & Unwin, 1984.

Kévorkian, Raymond H. *The Armenian Genocide, A Complete History*. London: I. B. Tauris, 2011.

Laffin, John. *Damn the Dardanelles!*. South Melbourne: Sun Papermac, 1980. *British Butchers and Bunglers of World War One*. Melbourne: Macmillan, 1988.

Langensiepen, Bernd and Ahmet Güleryuz. *The Ottoman Steam Navy*. Annapolis Md.: Naval Institute Press, 1995.

Larcher, Commandant M. *La Guerre Turque Dans La Guerre Mondiale*. Paris: Chiron&Berger-Levrault, 1926.

Latter, Major-General J. C. *The History of the Lancashire Fusiliers 1914–1918*. Aldershot: Gale & Polden Limited, 1949.

Lee, John. *A Soldier's Life, General Sir Ian Hamilton 1853–1947*. London: Macmillan, 2000. Liddle, Peter. *Men of Gallipoli, The Dardanelles and Gallipoli Experience August 1914 to January 1916*. London: Allen Lane 1976.

Liddle, Peter. *Men of Gallipoli: The Dardanelles and the Gallipoli Experience*. London: Allen Lane, 1976.

Mackenzie, Compton. *Gallipoli Memories*. London: Cassell, 1929.

Macleod, Jenny. *Gallipoli, Making history*. London: Frank Cass, 2004.

Macleod, Jenny. *Reconsidering Gallipoli*. Manchester: Manchester University Press, 2004.

Mango, Andrew. *Atatürk, The Biography of the Founder of Modern Turkey*. Woodstock, New York: Overlook Press, 1999.

Marder, Arthur, J. *From The Dreadnought to Scapa Flow, Vol. 2*. London: Oxford University Press, 1965.

Middlebrook, Martin. *Your Country Needs You, From Six to Sixty-five Divisions*. Barnsley, South Yorkshire: Leo Cooper, 2000.

Miller, Geoffrey. *Straits: British policy towards the Ottoman Empire and the origins of the Dardanelles Campaign*. Hull: University of Hull Press, 1997.

Millett, Allan R. and Murray, Williamson (eds.). *Military Effectiveness, Volume I: The First World War*. Boston: Unwin Hyman, 1988.

Moorehead, Alan. *Gallipoli*. New York: Harper & Row, 1956.

Moorhouse, Geoffrey. *Hell's Foundations, A Town, Its Myths & Gallipoli*. Sevenoaks, Kent: Hodder and Staughton Ltd., 1992.

Mortlock, Michael J. *The Landings at Suvla Bay, 1915*. Jefferson, NC: McFarland & Company, Inc, 2007.

Mühlmann, Carl. *Das Deutsch-Türkische Waffenbundnis im Weltkriege*. Leipzig: Verlag Koehler & Amelang, 1940.

Newman, Steve. *Gallipoli Then and Now*. London: Battle of Britain International Ltd. 2000.

Nicolle, David. *The Ottoman Army 1914–1918*. London: Reed International Books, 1996.

Oral, Haluk. *Gallipoli Through Turkish Eyes 1915* (translated by Amy Spangler). Istanbul: Türkiye İş Bankası Kültür Yayınları, 2007.

Örses, Tunca and Özçelik, Necmettin. *I. Dünya Savaşı'nda, Türk Askeri Kıyafetleri*. Istanbul: Denizler Kitabevi, nd.

Özdemir, Hikmet. *The Ottoman Army 1914–1918, Disease and Death on the Battlefield*. Salt Lake City: University of Utah Press, 2008.

Pakenham, Thomas. *The Boer War*. New York: Random House, 1979.

Prior, Robin. *Churchill's 'World Crisis' as History*. London: Croom Helm, 1983.

Prior, Robin. *Gallipoli, The End of the Myth*. New Haven: Yale University Press, 2009.

Pugsley, Christopher. *Gallipoli: The New Zealand Story*. Auckland: Hodder and Stoughton, 1984.

Roberts, Chris. *The Landing at Anzac 1915*. Canberra: Army History Unit, 2013.

Robertson, John. *Anzac and Empire, The Tragedy & Glory of Gallipoli*. London: Leo Cooper, 1990.

Samuels, Martin. *Command or Control? Command, Training and Tactics in the British and German Armies, 1888–1918*. London: Frank Cass, 1995.

Schulte, Bernd F. *Vor dem Kriegsausbruch 1914, Deutschland, die Türkei und der Balkan*. Düsseldorf: Drost Verlag, 1980.

Shaw, Stanford J. and Shaw, Ezel Kural. *History of the Ottoman Empire, Volume 2: Reform, Revolution, and Republic: The Rise of Modern Turkey, 1808–1975*. Cambridge: Cambridge University Press, 1977.

Shaw, Stanford. *The Ottoman Empire in World War I, Volumes 1 and 2*. Ankara: Türk Tarih Kurumu, 2007.

Sixsmith, E. K. G. *British Generalship in the Twentieth Century*. London: Arms and Armour Press, 1970.

Steel, Nigel and Hart, Peter. *Defeat at Gallipoli*. London: Macmillan, 1994.

Stevenson, David. *Armaments and the Coming of War: Europe, 1904–1914*. Oxford: Clarendon Press, 1996.

Strachan, Hew. *The First World War, Volume I, To Arms*. Oxford, Oxford University Press, 2001.

Taylor, Phil and Cupper, Pam. *Gallipoli A Battlefield Guide*. Kenthurst: Kangaroo Press, 1989.

Toker, Feza and Örnek, Tolga. *Çanakkale Savaşı Gerçeği, Gelibolu*. Istanbul: Ekip Film Yayınları, n.d.

Travers, Tim. *The Killing Ground*. London: Allen & Unwin, 1987.

Travers, Tim. *Gallipoli 1915*. Charleston, SC: Tempus Publishing Inc., 2001.

Trumpener, Ulrich. *Germany and the Ottoman Empire*. Princeton, NJ: Princeton University Press, 1968.

Tuncoku, Mete. *Çanakkale 1915 Buzdağının Altı*. Ankara: Türk Tarih Kurumu, 2007.

Turfan, M. Naim. *Rise of the Young Turks: Politics, the Military and Ottoman Collapse*. London: I. B. Tauris & Co Ltd., 2000.

Van Creveld, Martin. *Command in War*. Cambridge: Harvard University Press, 1985.

Wallach, Jehuda L. *Anatomie Einer Militärhilfe, Die preussisch-deutschen Militärmissionen in der Türkei 1835–1919*. Düsseldorf: Droste Verlag, 1976.

Weber, Frank G. *Eagles on the Crescent: Germany Austria, and the Diplomacy of the Turkish Alliance, 1914–1918*. Ithaca, NY: Cornell University Press, 1970.

Woodward, David. *Armies of the World 1854–1914*. New York: G. P. Putnam's Sons, 1978.

Yalman, Ahmed Emin. *Turkey in the World War*. New Haven, CT: Yale University Press, 1930.

Yilmaz, Veli. *Birinci Dünya Harbinde Türk-Alman Ittifaki ve Askeri Yardımları*. Istanbul: Gem Offset, 1993.

Articles, chapters and papers

Cain, Frank. 'A Colonial Army in Ottoman Fields: Australia's Involvement in the Gallipoli Debacle' in Sheffy, Yigal and Shai, Saul, *The First World War: Middle Eastern Perspectives*. Tel Aviv: Tel Aviv University, 2000.

Doyle, Peter and Bennett, Matthew R. 'Military Geography: the influence of terrain in the outcome of the Gallipoli Campaign 1915', *The Geographical Journal*, 165 (1) (March 1999), 12–36.

Erickson, Edward J. 'One More Push: Forcing the Dardanelles in March 1915', *The Journal of Strategic Studies*, 24 (3) (September 2001), 158–176.

Erickson, Edward J. 'Strength Against Weakness: Ottoman Military Effectiveness at Gallipoli, 1915', *The Journal of Military History*, 65 (October 2001), 981–1012.

Erickson, Edward J. 'The Turkish Official Military Histories of the First World War, A Bibliographic Essay', *Middle Eastern Studies*. 39 (3) (July 2003), 190–198.

Erickson, Edward J. 'Ottoman Encirclement Operations, 1912–1922', *Middle Eastern Studies*, 40 (1) (January 2004), 45–64.

Pugsley, Christopher. 'We have Been Here Before: the Evolution of the Doctrine of Decentalised Command in the British Army 1905–1989', *Sandhurst Occasional Papers*, No 9 (2011).

Roberts, Christopher. 'Gallipoli: A flawed strategy' in Dennis, Peter, (ed.). *Armies and Maritime Strategy*. Canberra: Big Sky Publishing, 2014.

Travers, T. H. E. 'Command and Leadership Styles in the British Army: The 1915 Gallipoli Model', *Journal of Contemporary History*, 29 (July 1994), 403–442.

Travers, Timothy H. E. 'When Technology and Tactics Fail: Gallipoli 1915' in Chiabotti, Stephen D. (ed.). *Tooling for War, Military Transformation in the Industrial Age*. Chicago: Imprint Publications, 1996.

Travers, Tim. 'The Other Side of the Hill', *Military History Quarterly*, 12 (3) (Spring 2000), 2–20.

Trumpener, Ulrich. 'Suez, Baku, Gallipoli: The Military Dimensions of the German-Ottoman Coalition, 1914–1918' in Kiraly, Bela K. and Dreisziger, Nandor F. (eds.). *East Central European Society in World War I*. New York: Columbia University Press, 1985.

Yanıkdağ, Yücel. 'Educating the Peasants: The Ottoman Army and Enlisted Men in Uniform', *Middle Eastern Studies*, 40 (6) (November 2004), 92–108.

Yasamee, F. A. K. 'Abdülhamid II and the Ottoman Defence Problem', *Diplomacy & Statecraft*, 4 (1) (March 1993), 20–36.

Yasamee, F. A. K. 'Some Military Problems faced by the Ottoman Empire at the beginning of the 20th Century', *KÖK Sosyal ve Stratejik Araştırmalar, Osmanlı Özel Sayısı* (2000), 71–79.

Zürcher, Erik-Jan. 'The Ottoman Conscription System In Theory And Practice, 1844–1918', *International Review of Social History*, 43 (3) (1988), 437–449.

INDEX

Page numbers in **bold** refer to maps.

INDEX